Ingredients
for Women's Employment Policy

SUNY Series in Women and Work
Joan Smith, Editor

Christine Bose and Glenna Spitze, *Editors*

INGREDIENTS FOR WOMEN'S EMPLOYMENT POLICY

State University of New York Press

The authors gratefully acknowledge permission from Harcourt Brace Jovanovich, Inc. to reprint Figure 4.1 from *Black Metropolis* by St. Clair Drake and Horace R. Cayton, copyright 1946 by St. Clair Drake and Horace R. Cayton; renewed 1973 by St. Clair Drake and Susan C. Woodson.

Published by
State University of New York Press, Albany

For information, address State University of New York
Press, State University Plaza, Albany, N.Y., 12246

Library of Congress Cataloging in Publication Data

Ingredients for women's employment policy.

(Women and work series)
Papers presented at the conference held on Apr. 19–20,
1985 at the State University of New York at Albany.
Bibliography: p.
Includes index.
1. Women—Employment—United States—Congresses.
2. Women—Government policy—United States—Congresses.
3. Sex discrimination in employment—United States—
Congresses. 4. Equal pay for equal work—United States—
Congresses. I. Bose, Christine E. II. Spitze, Glenna D.
III. Series.
HD6095.I54   1987   331.4'0973   86-14550
ISBN 0-88706-420-5
ISBN 0-88706-421-3 (pbk.)

10 9 8 7 6 5 4 3 2 1

To our mothers
Ellen June Christensen Bose
and
Hazel Taylor Spitze

Contents

Preface

The papers and commentary in this volume are drawn from a conference of the same name, "Ingredients for Women's Employment Policy," held on April 19 and 20, 1985 at the State University of New York at Albany. The conference brought together, both in its presenters and in its registrants, a diverse group of leading scholars who study women's employment from theoretical, empirical, and policy-oriented viewpoints. This group of policy analysts and scholars represented the several sociological subareas of demography, organizations, and stratification, including input from economists, historians, and political scientists. The conference provided a forum in which to synthesize knowledge on how the processes of inequality have worked in the past, the kinds of change now in progress in the occupational structure, and the effectiveness of a variety of policies and strategies in achieving their intended improvements in women's relative employment position. The original conference presentations have been revised and reorganized for this volume into three major sections: structural and historical trends, policy and change strategies, and commentary.

Several organizations and individuals contributed to the original conference by giving us their generous financial assistance, and we would like to thank them for their support. The American Sociological Association provided a "Problems of the Discipline" grant. We were also able to draw on the combined resources of several units at SUNY/Albany including: the Affirmative Action Office and its Director, Gloria DeSole; the Center for Social and Demographic Analysis and its Director, Richard Alba; Judith Ramaley, Vice President for Academic Affairs; John Shumaker, then Vice President for Research and Educational Development; the Sociology

Department and its Chair, Richard Hall; John Webb, Dean of the College of Social and Behavioral Sciences; and the Women's Studies Program and its Director, Bonnie Spanier.

Several individuals invested a great deal of time and effort in the development of the conference, and we would like to thank them as well. Foremost among these is Gail Gates, upon whose conference planning expertise we had the pleasure of relying. Next is Ronnie Steinberg, an original conference co-organizer whose busy schedule prevented her from continuing in that role, but whose ideas on major decisions were always useful and welcome. Edna Acosta-Belén, Chair of Puerto Rican, Latin American and Caribbean Studies, provided a model for graciousness, efficiency, and flair in conference organizing. Richard Hall, Chair of the Sociology Department, encouraged our efforts in planning the conference, and even helped in naming it. Bob Franklin provided support in a variety of ways before, during, and since the conference. Within the Sociology Department our appreciation is also extended to Joan Cipperley, Eileen Pellegrino, Debbie Neuls, and the graduate students of Alpha Kappa Delta.

Many others who served as conference participants—session chairs or discussants—are not included in the volume, but their work made the conference more stimulating. Among these are Iris Berger (SUNY/Albany), Elia Hidalgo Christensen (New York State Department of Civil Service), Alice Cook (Cornell University School of Labor and Industrial Relations, Emeritus), Joan Huber (Ohio State University), Myra Marx Ferree (University of Connecticut), Jacqueline Kane (New York State, Higher Education Opportunity Program), and Ruth Milkman (Queens College of CUNY). We would also like to thank Joan Smith for selecting this volume for her book series, Myra Marx Ferree and Carole Turbin for their constructive comments and Mary Feeley for an excellent job of index construction. We enjoyed working with Michele Martin, Peggy Gifford, and Elizabeth Moore at SUNY Press. Finally, we would like to thank each other for co-organizing and contributing equally to a project neither of us would have taken on alone, and for being excellent colleagues with complementary interests.

Chris Bose and Glenna Spitze
Albany, May 1986

Introduction

CHRISTINE BOSE AND GLENNA SPITZE

There is a pressing need for a coherent and effective employment policy for women and families in the United States. Although the rate of women's employment has increased rapidly since the 1950s, there have been few changes in gender stratification. The second wave of the women's movement which began in the 1960s fostered considerable research on women's status, but studies over the last 20 years confirm the continued existence of occupational segregation, with only modest declines during the 1970s; a fairly constant wage gap of about 40 percent between women and men; and an unequal division of household labor, the latter modified only slightly when women seek employment and thus have less time available for housework. While women have achieved a stronger numerical foothold in the realm of paid employment, other gains appear illusory. Women have been employed increasingly, but in service sector jobs which are often called *deskilled* and are characterized by low pay, limited training, and lack of advancement opportunity or job security. Further, female labor force participation rates present a misleading picture of women's actual place in the labor market, because only 45 percent of all employed women are working full-time and year-round.

Such problems point to the need for new strategies to improve women's collective economic position and for a more coherent set of employment policies for women. Overall family policies, which recognize the links between women's paid and unpaid work, already exist in many other countries.

What would be the ingredients necessary to develop a women's employment policy useful for the United States? There are several, each addressed by authors in this volume. First, a knowledge of the historical trends which are the background for our contemporary situation is essential. This information helps us to understand which economic patterns are part of long-term trends, and which are a product of recent demographic, occupational, industrial, or political changes. Several articles herein address these issues. Tienda and Ortiz describe how changes within industries during the 1970s have affected the wage gap. Sokoloff and Higginbotham each illustrate how the changing nature of the professions has influenced the employment of black and white women within these jobs, while Reskin and Roos examine the impact of women's entry into other male-dominated jobs. Taking a longer historical view, Glenn illustrates the impact of immigration on women's occupational options.

A second ingredient for effective employment policy is a multilevel analysis which looks both at the structure of underlying market mechanisms and at how an individual becomes placed within that larger structure. Most of the articles in this volume assume a structural perspective—one the average individual does not perceive on a day-to-day basis. However, Berryman and Waite also provide insight into young women's own perception of and plans for their occupational goals.

The third policy ingredient is an understanding of the interrelationship between women's market work and housework. Policy to aid women's employment situation must also consider women's unpaid family work. There are many facets to this home/work interface. Roby illustrates how women's occupational roles often require flexibility on the part of their families. In contrast, Pearce shows how women's home responsibilities often lead to underemployment or unemployment. From yet another perspective, Glenn's analysis of Japanese immigrant women shows that women's paid work in the homes of others makes accomplishing their own housework difficult, at the same time that wage work provides a form of liberation.

The fourth, and perhaps most obvious, ingredient in developing women's employment policy is an evaluation of previous policies and strategies including unionization, affirmative action, and unemployment policies, as well as the more recent alternative: comparable worth. Section two of this volume assesses each of these approaches with an eye to improvements, additions, or alternatives which would create the most comprehensive employment policy.

The fifth and final ingredient is political action. In their commentary, both Chertos and Feldberg remind us that research may uncover the needs of women, and policy may address them, but without political action there is no reason to expect those policies to be implemented. In fact, the development of a research and policy agenda to meet women's employment-related needs is a political act in and of itself.

Each of these basic ingredients for women's employment policy—historical background, a combined individual and structural level approach, an examination of the intertwining of home and market work, a reassessment of current policy, and plans to implement new policies—are combined in the chapters of this volume. Further, the authors represent a necessary interdisciplinary approach, utilizing sociological and economic perspectives, as well as qualitative and quantitative analyses. Finally, the diversity among women is recognized, as various chapters focus on young and older women, professional and poor women, and black, Japanese, and white women. Not all groups are represented: there is little data in the volume on Hispanic or Native American women, or on the employment situation of other groups such as disabled or lesbian women. Any final employment policy must address the full range of women's needs. The intent here, as we begin with ingredients for such a policy, is to present state-of-the-art analyses of the trends in women's employment so that we can best judge the needs of a variety of women (Part I) and to assess the effectiveness of the policies intended to improve their position in the labor market (Part II).

The first section examines both historical and recent trends in the structure of the U.S. labor force, using aggregate data, individual-level survey data, and case studies of occupations and ethnic groups. The first four papers address in a variety of ways the following general question: Are seeming recent improvements in indicators of gender and racial inequality in the labor force real or illusory?

It is generally agreed that occupational sex segregation is a major reason for the persistent wage gap, and that levels of segregation have been fairly steady during this century with a slight recent downturn (Beller, 1984). Barbara Reskin and Patricia Roos question the consequences of the recent entry of women into certain male-dominated occupations. They view occupational sex segregation within a conceptual framework of gender hierarchies, whereby gender stratification is maintained through physical segregation, functional differentiation, and social distance.

They predict that the entry of women into male-dominated occupations may be accompanied by other changes, such as more detailed segregation by specific occupation or firm, declines in the occupation's status, or male exit. Social distance mechanisms may arise, including feminization of women's dress and more stringent etiquette rules. While the issue of causal ordering will be addressed in a later statistical analysis, results of case studies of four occupations completed thus far support their expectations. Within the occupations of pharmacist, insurance adjustor, systems analyst, and banker, they find numerous examples of internal segregation, deskilling, and resegregation.

Given these findings and the continued functional differentiation of gender roles in the family, they question the salience of recent gains in indexes of occupational sex segregation. The goal of their future research will be to search for those social processes that facilitate truly meaningful occupational integration.

Despite dramatic increases in female labor force participation, female education, and the expansion of high status occupations, the gender earnings gap remains stagnant. Marta Tienda and Vilma Ortiz question how the industrial restructuring process (in particular the shift toward service employment) during the 1970s, and the changing gender composition of jobs, influenced this gender gap. In other words, did the rate at which jobs became feminized during the 1970s enhance or diminish earnings disparities between men and women, net of changes in relative growth or decline of specific jobs? Their analysis, highly technical in contrast to the preceding one, makes for difficult but rewarding reading.

For 335 occupation by industry job cells, constructed from 1970 and 1980 census data, they compute the extent to which the labor force in that cell grew faster or slower than the total labor force. This difference is then decomposed into an industry shift effect, or changes due to industrial transformation, and occupational mix effect, or occupational changes within industries, and an interaction between the two. Changes within major occupational groups for men and women are reviewed and evaluated for possible contributions to a decreased earnings gap. For example, overall upgrading toward professional, semiprofessional, and managerial occupations for both sexes arose from different processes: for women, due to occupational restructuring within industries; for men, due to industrial shifts.

An analysis of the impact of these structural changes on earnings suggests differential effects by gender. They conclude with tempered optimism about the possibility of narrowing the income gap through industrial restructuring or increased feminization of jobs, since the earnings enhancing effects of industrial restructuring were offset and contingent upon the level of feminization.

The preceding analysis points to an overall occupational upgrading of professional and managerial jobs. Natalie Sokoloff, citing this trend for both black and white women and the extensive news coverage it has generated, questions whether it represents a real improvement in the lives of working women. Although only about one-sixth of employed women are in professional jobs, she argues that processes affecting professional and nonprofessional women may be similar, such that their examination can promote alliances across groups.

Numerical increases in female professionals are real, particularly since 1970, and have occurred for both female 'semiprofessions' and male-dominated professions. Increases are particularly striking for black women. These increases are explained in popular theorizing with reference to the women's movement, and to Affirmative Action policies, which are supposed to have helped black women in particular since they possess two salient traits.

In questioning the meaningfulness of these trends, Sokoloff suggests attention to several issues. First, aggregate data can be abused and cited to substantiate a variety of points. In particular, percentage increases can look dramatic when they are calculated from a very low base, such as the number of black women lawyers several decades ago. Such aggregate data also do not reveal the extent of intraorganizational sex segregation, as pointed out by Reskin and Roos. Second, the meaning of 'professions' must be analyzed. The category 'professional and technical' has added proportionately more new technical than professional job titles in the past decade. Women have made greater advances in the female-dominated semiprofessions than in the male-dominated ones, while the latter jobs continue to maintain certain female specialties. Third, she points to the process of deskilling (such as the creation of legal clinics), documented in other occupations by Reskin and Roos. Finally, she suggests further attention to the extent to which race still operates as a barrier for professional black women.

This question is addressed fully by Elizabeth Higginbotham, who presents a longer-range view of professional black women's situation during this century. At the beginning of the century, black women were typically employed after marriage, unlike whites, and were found predominantly in private household work and laundering. During the early decades of the century, white women moved into factory work and teaching, and later into clerical and sales work, while black women experienced little occupational movement. The few blacks who could afford higher education were limited to a few institutions of learning, and to professional employment serving black clienteles. In the public sector, their employment opportunities were greater in the South than the North since Jim Crow policies in the South dictated that segregated blacks be served by black professionals, such as teachers. Black women faced double barriers, and were paid less than either black men or white women.

Since World War II we have seen the slow steady growth of the black middle class, due to both the expansion of the welfare state and the civil rights movement. Black professionals are highly dependent on public sector employment, and thus on political relationships and the fiscal health of governmental units. Black professional women are more concentrated than whites in female-dominated professions, and within those professions, in the public sector. Data from the 15 standard metropolitan statistical areas with the largest black populations show that the majority of black women professionals are in the public sector, while the majority of white women professionals are in the private sector. Higginbotham cautions that we should avoid the "great women" view of black professional women, and should continue to examine those inequities that keep them segregated sectorally and occupationally.

The last two papers in this section use a different perspective to analyze the structure of the labor force: the analysis of individual-level data, both qualitative and quantitative. The paper by Evelyn Nakano Glenn presents an historical perspective on the paid and unpaid labor of Japanese-American women migrants before World War II, including interview data from elderly women who recall that period. Like the paper by Higginbotham, it shows women in an ethnic/racial group being channelled into a particular occupation, domestic service, which was being exited by nonim-migrant majority women. In contrast, the paper by Sue Berryman and Linda Waite uses quantitative analysis of data on the labor market experiences of contemporary young women.

Glenn argues for the importance of an historical perspective on the experience of labor migrants, and for looking at the entire picture, including both family and work experiences of men and women. Her case study of pre-World War II Japanese women immigrants (*issei*), uses retrospective qualitative interview data to reconstruct their experiences of paid and unpaid work. Most of these women arrived between 1908 and 1924, in response to the demand from earlier Japanese male migrants for wives. This demand was in large part economic: those men who were having trouble saving enough money to return home quickly needed a wife's labor in the fields or the shop, or her income from other economic activities. According to the accounts, although only a minority of these women were enumerated by the census as employed, almost all were involved in some income-producing activity. Those with jobs outside the home were often involved in laundry or domestic work, or in manufacturing. The 'family wage economy' made it necessary for all workers to pool incomes in order to support the household.

There were similarities and differences from the family economy they had experienced in Japan. In both systems, family members worked together to support the household, but in the U.S., many women had an independent income, giving them in some cases more interpersonal influence. Also, they were not under the control of a mother-in-law as they had been in Japan. However, they missed the kin support and seasonality of work in Japan—in the U.S., work was never-ending. Most husbands contributed little to household labor or child care, although a few older retired husbands (or aging fathers) assumed a housekeeping role. The problem of child care, which did not exist when all work occurred at home, led to a variety of solutions, including sending children to relatives in Japan temporarily.

Glenn stresses the importance of viewing migrants in their family context, and points out that even solo male migrants are usually part of a family strategy, which may include sending money back to relatives and eventually returning or sending for the rest of the family. She draws parallels between these Japanese-American women and more recent migrants to the U.S., showing how both have needs not only for services normally sought by working women, but for additional ones necessitated by their language and immigrant status.

The Berryman and Waite paper looks at labor market structure from the supply side, or the individual choices of young women. They attempt to model the determinants of the female typicality of future occupational choice for teenage women, and of the probability of choosing a male-dominated occupation. They focus on how a young woman's plans for home versus market work and her family background influence those occupational choices.

They find that those women who would prefer to be full-time homemakers at age 35, those who prefer early marriage, and those with traditional sex-role attitudes choose more typically female occupations. Verbal and quantitative ability increase the choice of male occupations, as do high educational expectations. Living in a female-headed household increases male occupational choice for both Hispanic and non-Hispanic whites, but not for black women, perhaps because such households are more common among blacks and their effects more diffuse. Several findings are anomalous and the authors suggest the need for further research on these topics, including the effects of mother's occupation and of dropping out of high school.

The authors suggest a number of policy implications of their research. The effects of a continued likely increase in female headed households may have implications for the future distribution of young women's occupational outcomes, while their results on the home/work choice suggest that policies attempting to influence young women toward more high-paying male occupational choices should address plans for continuity of labor force participation as well.

The second part of this volume addresses a variety of policy strategies which are being used (or could be used) to decrease gender inequality in the labor force. Separate papers address the involvement of women in union leadership, comparable worth implementation, policies which affect unemployed and underemployed women, and the more general issue of how various policy strategies can be combined in an integrated approach.

Pamela Roby argues that the role of the union steward is influential in determining the everyday experiences of workers, since they are involved in the handling of grievances, enforcement of contracts and laws, and representing workers to management. These positions can also be a step to higher level leadership in unions. Women workers are still less unionized than men, although unions are beginning to pay more attention to women workers as the economy moves toward more service and less manufacturing, the traditional source of union growth. Women are also underrepresented as union leaders. Roby's in-depth interviews with 26 women and 9 men stewards revealed how women attain those positions and how their experience differs from that of their male counterparts. She argues that female participation as union stewards is one important strategy for improving the conditions of women's employment. In general, her study revealed women as agents, taking charge of their own lives, rather than passive victims.

Most stewards in her sample received encouragement from family members, who were themselves active, to become union leaders. Their parents were also active in other organizations. Many had supervisory experience on the job before becoming stewards. For many, the women's movement had "made a difference."

In their experience as stewards, women were responsible for twice as many members as the men, reflecting the different organizational structures of their unions, and the women put in more hours in their work as stewards. They had a variety of mentors, both from work and family ties.

Union work is added to the employed woman's normal double burden, creating a triple set of responsibilities. The attitude of the female stewards' spouses or mates was clearly important, and in some cases union work had led to conflict and divorce. Of course others, not in this sample, may well become nonactive union members in order to avoid such conflicts. These suggestive findings provide interesting points of departure for Roby's ongoing research as well as that of others.

The next two papers discuss the most controversial issue in women's employment policy today, comparable worth. Both assume a knowledge of its philosophical rationale, and given that many resources are being allocated to implementation studies right now, they move on to discuss the methodological issues involved. The paper by Ronnie Steinberg and Lois Haignere reviews the entire process of job evaluation and salary setting so as to identify and correct potential sex bias throughout the process. They take as their operational definition of comparable worth "correcting the practice of paying women and minorities less than white men for work that requires equivalent skills, responsibilities, stresses, personal contacts, and working conditions."

The job evaluation process involves three major steps: job description (through observation, interviews, questionnaires); evaluation (assigning points to job characteristics and ranking jobs through an *a priori* system; or analyzing the manner in which characteristics relate to current salaries, the policy-capturing approach); and salary setting, using both internal criteria, based on the evaluation, and external ones, comparing key jobs within a firm to similar ones in the outside labor market.

Steinberg and Haignere discuss each of these three steps in detail and identify ways in which (sometimes subtle) sex or race bias may creep in. For example, compensable characteristics of typically female jobs may be ignored in evaluation systems, on the assumption that they are part of women's nature (*e.g.*, the ability to take care of children). Male workers tend to overdescribe their job relative to females, and evaluation systems may repeat male job requirements under ostensibly different scales.

The authors' prescriptions, based on extensive experience in two state studies, should help others attempting to carry out these policies to do so more effectively. As the authors argue, much has been written about comparable worth at the ideological level; it is time now to move on to the methodological.

The paper by Joan Acker complements the previous one nicely by continuing the focus on methodological issues in comparable worth but moving to a specific case which illustrates some of their points. Based on her experience as a member of the Oregon State Task Force on Compensation and Classification Equity, the paper documents the process of attempting to minimize sex bias in an *a priori* job evaluation system.

In negotiations with the consulting firm hired to provide an evaluation system, the task force attempted to modify a scale measuring human relations skills, which they were convinced was leading to an underevaluation of certain skills in typically female jobs such as clerical work. The consultants viewed human relations skills narrowly in terms of supervising and managing, while the task force wanted to expand this view to include relations with coworkers, supervisors, the public, and dealing with irate clients and disturbed patients. They suggested expanding the scale to five rather than three levels. A compromise was reached with a four-level scale, but in later job descriptions one level was ignored, thus negating the task force's entire purpose. While this was not the only change made as a result of their work, this outcome does illustrate the complex and difficult process involved in attempting to implement the suggestions of Steinberg and Haignere in an environment which will always have a large political component.

Acker concludes that most adjustments made as a result of comparable worth implementation will involve working class men and women, and questions how working class men will respond to the process. She discusses the issue as one embodying the intersection of class and gender, with potential conflict between subgroups resulting.

Shifting focus, Diana Pearce argues that those interested in policies for employed women should not lose sight of the large component of unemployed and underemployed women. She provides documentation that a majority of employed women are marginal, in the sense of not working full-time, year-round according to the 'regular worker' model. Such workers not only have low incomes (often from minimum wage work) but also are not covered by fringe benefits such as health insurance, disability, and sick leave. In particular, a number of women who work at home (in day care, computer work, or assembly on a piecework basis) are not only marginal but isolated from other workers.

In addition to those women who are employed marginally, women are more likely to be unemployed or 'discouraged workers,' and less likely to receive unemployment insurance than men. This is in part because they are more likely to be entering the labor force, or to be leaving a job due to 'voluntary' reasons connected with sexual harassment or conflicts between work and domestic responsibilities.

Pearce reviews current policies in five areas, all of which are defined or implemented in ways that disadvantage women workers. She suggests that alternative policies should be based on the assumption that employment must provide the minimum resources needed to maintain a family (including income, fringe benefits, and unemployment insurance), should not be based on the regular worker model, and should value homemaking (just as current policies value other service such as the military). Specific suggestions include changes in the minimum wage, tax credit and income support programs, unemployment coverage, and job training.

The final paper, by William Bielby and James Baron, provides an overview of the implications of their extensive research findings for women's employment policy. They argue that sociologists are more reluctant than economists to draw policy conclusions, and thus the dominant human capital model informs the majority of policymaking today. They review evidence, based on both qualitative and quantitative studies they have conducted, to support four major conclusions. 1) Job segregation is the immediate cause of sex differences in earnings and career prospects. 2) Human capital theory does not account for this pattern. 3) Sex segregation is imbedded in organizational policies and sustained by organizational inertia. 4) Sex segregation is sustained by behavior as well as structure. This assertion is bolstered by a review of social psychological research on expectations and belief systems.

Bielby and Baron argue convincingly that comparable worth and job integration are not alternative policy strategies, nor even complementary ones, but rather must both form part of a single unified approach within specific organizations. They suggest ways in which managers can become motivated toward a commitment to change, in particular by making progress toward gender integration a significant part of performance evaluations. Policies must be kept flexible in such a way that adjustments in one system of goals can be used to help achieve other goals.

The final section in this volume contains commentary on papers in the first two sections. These comments were selected from among a larger number at the conference, because they not only made salient points about the other papers but also made original substantive contributions.

Joan Smith discusses a variety of issues arising from the Bielby and Baron paper. She praises it highly for providing the first empirical refutation of human capital theory, accomplished by showing that the theory's explanation of segregation at the *occupational* level is inconsistent with the firm-specific job segregation which actually takes place. Further, they document those specific organizational practices which create occupational segregation, and question the usefulness of research which uses occupational-level data.

However, she takes their analysis further, showing how it must be extended to remain useful. Given increasing gender segregation by industrial sector, and women's concentration in those sectors with little chance for mobility, she questions the usefulness of comparable worth in female-dominated settings where it would yield little gain for women. She suggests that the organizational practices Bielby and Baron identify are becoming outmoded, that women are decreasingly employed in settings with centralized personnel procedures, and that we must continue to identify those *changing* organizational mechanisms affecting them. Finally, she points out that their analysis, by rejecting totally the focus on women's nonwaged labor offered by neoclassical economics, is unable to explain why job segregation is based on gender rather than some other distinction.

Francine Blau discusses the papers by Reskin and Roos, and Tienda and Ortiz, which she sees as complementary. After briefly reviewing recent trends in occupational segregation and the earnings gap (modest gains in both), she reviews Reskin and Roos's framework for examining desegregation qualitatively. She suggests that the processes they document—internal segregation, deskilling, and resegregation—are not new and that unless these processes have increased in recent years, at least some of the apparent desegregation may represent real progress for women. Further, she cites other evidence that the economic payoff for women to being in a male job increased for women during the 1970s, although it increased even more for men. In many ways, Blau's dialogue with Reskin and Roos reveals the contradictory changes which Sokoloff discussed earlier.

Blau's comments also highlight salient points from the Tienda and Ortiz paper. She views their simultaneous analysis of industrial and occupational shifts as groundbreaking, and looks forward to a followup at a less aggregated level.

Roslyn Feldberg draws on the evidence presented by Acker and by Steinberg and Haignere regarding methodological issues in comparable worth to discuss the "politics of method." She points out, first, that there is a political dimension of knowledge, that the researcher or expert involved in job evaluation has power which may be exercised on behalf of a variety of interests. Since those experts are usually hired by management, they may be reluctant to challenge the assumptions of management about job worth. In particular, as both papers show, the usual political context makes it difficult to develop job description and evaluation systems that do not automatically lead to higher points and wages for management. However, despite these major limitations, she feels that comparable worth can be used to remedy inequities between nonmanagerial white males and other workers.

Her second major point is that there is a gap between knowledge and implementation. The process of job evaluation provides the evidence for a struggle over wages, but that struggle must take place, whether through strikes, court battles, or other methods. Everyone concerned about wage inequity must get involved in the process of job evaluation, and those who are more knowledgeable must be willing to help educate other workers, concerning both the operation of the job evaluation systems and the unrecognized dimensions of worth in their own jobs.

Heidi Hartmann discusses the chapters by Joan Acker, and by Ronnie Steinberg and Lois Haignere. While both focus on methodological issues to some degree, Hartmann finds the Steinberg-Haignere chapter discusses methodology more comprehensively in a manner useful to practitioners, while the Acker chapter uses a methodological issue to explore the political debate underlying comparable worth. Hartmann argues that comparable worth implementation would not be highly costly for employers, requiring less than 12.5 percent of the current wage bill. Nevertheless, it would have revolutionary implications by enabling women to become economically independent from men, able to support themselves and their children through their own earnings. She points out other positive consequences of comparable worth as well, such as encouraging collective struggle and openness about the bases of remunerating work. However, since comparable worth, by increasing women's wages, could lead to decreased demand in those jobs, it must be coupled with Affirmative Action policies and political pressure for full employment.

Cynthia Chertos reviews the entire conference, and thus the papers in this volume, ending on an upbeat note. First, she reminds us of the 1975 conference on occupational segregation, organized by Martha Blaxall and Barbara Reagan, which in many ways was an inspiration for our conference and this volume on employment policy. Although much was known about segregation even then, we have learned a great deal in the intervening ten years, and in particular the concept of pay equity has entered our vocabulary as a strategy to deal with the problems caused by such segregation. Chertos discusses Kenneth Boulding's comments at that conference, in which he contrasted positive science and normative science, or the study of "what is" and the study of "what should be". While positive science constrains normative science, telling us what is possible, normative science may prompt us to figure out how to make possible what we want.

Chertos points out that the traditional positivist model for ending a research paper, a listing of ideas for future research, is followed by few of the papers in this volume. Rather, they generally conclude with policy implications, taking a cue from normative science. She urges us to continue to make not only *broad* policy recommendations, but also very *specific* prescriptions, based on our unique knowledge of the processes we study.

We have already outlined some of these broad areas for employment policy recommendations. First, as long as women retain prime responsibility for the home, attention needs to be paid to policies which will alleviate this burden, such as the availability of parental leaves and reasonably priced quality child care. Of course, better still would be a policy to relieve women of an inequitable share of the household labor. Second, policies need to be developed which avoid the problems of women's unemployment or underemployment, such as those suggested by Pearce. Since so many women work part-time, part-year, or both, policies which provide better benefits for such workers are crucial. Third, new strategies are needed to deal with the wage gap between women and men and as Bielby and Baron suggest, some combination of strategies might be best here. Fourth, new ideas for challenging occupational segregation are in order, as women continue to be concentrated in the growing service sector with its low-mobility occupations. Fifth, even before women enter the labor force, policy might focus on ensuring that women obtain important educational content such as sufficient mathematics training, accurate knowledge of the labor market, and a multitude of role models. Finally, specific policies within each of these broad areas should be sensitive to the different needs of various groups of employed women: young and old; white, black, Hispanic, Asian, and Native American; single, divorced, and married; with children or not. These categories are suggestive of the many areas where we might advance policy issues. We invite you to read the papers and look for issues of concern to you; then, for further reading, turn to the extensive reference list at the end of the volume.

Part One

STRUCTURAL AND HISTORICAL TRENDS

CHAPTER 1

Status Hierarchies and Sex Segregation*

BARBARA F. RESKIN AND PATRICIA A. ROOS

We gratefully acknowledge the contributions of our graduate assistants Polly A. Phipps and Barbara Kritt of the University of Michigan, and Katharine Donato of the State University of New York at Stony Brook whose preliminary case studies of several occupations are described in this paper. We also wish to thank Fran Blau, Joan Huber, and Mary Jackman for helpful comments on earlier versions of this paper, but we take full responsibility for any failings that remain. This research was funded in part by a University of Michigan Rackham Faculty Fellowship to the first author.

INTRODUCTION

The segregation of the sexes into different occupations, industries, and establishments is one of the most enduring features of the workplace. Its stability between 1890 and 1960 (Williams, 1979; Blau and Hendricks, 1979) is especially noteworthy in view of the revolutionary transformations of the occupational structure and labor force during this period.[1] Though sex segregation declined slightly during World War II when women were hired for factory jobs, the 1950s showed no additional decline (Treiman and Terrell, 1975), and the slight drop during the 1960s stemmed from men's movement into female-dominated semiprofessions such as nurse, librarian, and social worker (Blau and Hendricks, 1979).

There are several reasons to expect that women's representation in traditionally male occupations would increase during the 1970s. In the

*For comments on this chapter see Blau (pp 239-243) in this volume.

3

wake of the Civil Rights and women's liberation movements, equal employment opportunity became a national priority. Women questioned the
traditional sexual division of labor, the mass media showed women in sex-
atypical jobs, new laws and regulations barred sex discrimination in employment, and the courts restricted employers' rights to prefer either sex.
Congress also prohibited sex discrimination in publicly-funded education
and mandated sex equity in vocational education and federally funded job
training programs (for details, see Reskin and Hartmann, 1985).

Women's representation in the labor force increased by 4.6 percentage
points between 1970 and 1980, and 1980 census data suggest that women's
occupational opportunities expanded (Bianchi and Rytina, 1984). In about
60 of the 503 detailed occupations—including some heavily male occupations—women's proportional gains exceeded that in the labor force as
a whole (U.S. Bureau of the Census, 1983a). However, women's gains were
not evenly distributed across occupations, and increases of more than nine
percentage points were rare. In a few male-dominated occupations (*e.g.*,
heavy equipment mechanics, lathe and turning-machine operators, production testers) women actually lost ground, but in others (typesetter and compositor, insurance adjuster and examiner), they replaced men as the dominant sex (U.S. Bureau of the Census, 1984).[2] Table 1.1 lists several
traditionally male occupations in which women's representation increased
by at least twice their increased representation in the labor force as a whole,
as well as two female-dominated occupations in which women's representation declined during the decade.

This variability in women's progress across occupations raises several
questions. First, what rendered a few male occupations more hospitable to
women than most others? Second, do these statistical gains mean that sex
barriers have really been breached? Third, has the nature of work changed
with changes in occupations' sex composition? Fourth, has women's integration been accompanied by declining occupational rewards? Finally,
are these changes just one stage in a process whereby some male-dominated
occupations are ultimately resegregated as predominantly female? Traditional approaches to sex segregation that focus on the preferences of labor
market participants cannot answer these questions, and we contend that to
do so requires considering segregation in the broader context of status
hierarchies.

STATUS HIERARCHIES

We propose a theoretical approach to investigating occupational sex
segregation that builds on the conceptual framework of status hierarchies.
Status hierarchies are systems of stratification based on status group membership, such as race, ethnicity, sex, and age. In such hierarchies members
of the dominant status group enjoy a variety of privileges at the expense of

Table 1.1: Percent Female in Selected Occupations, 1970 and 1980[a]

Selected male-dominated occupations in which women's representation increased disproportionately[a]

Occupation	1970	1980	Change
Pharmacists	12.1	24.0	11.9
Accountants and auditors	24.6	38.1	13.5
Operations and systems researchers/analysts	11.1	27.7	16.6
Personnel and labor relations workers	33.4	47.0	13.6
Public relations specialists	26.6	48.8	22.2
Financial managers	19.4	31.4	12.0
Managers, marketing*	7.9	17.6	9.7
Buyers	27.8	44.5	16.7
Administrators, education and related fields	27.8	38.1	10.3
Insurance adjusters, examiners	29.6	60.2	30.6
Supervisors, sales*	17.0	28.2	11.2
Insurance agents	12.9	25.4	12.5
Real estate salespersons	31.2	45.2	14.0
Expediters	35.4	54.1	18.7
Dispatchers	14.6	31.5	16.9
Shipping and receiving clerks	13.4	23.6	10.2
Production coordinators	20.2	44.4	24.2
Bakers	25.4	40.7	15.3
Compositors and typesetters	16.8	55.7	38.9
Guards, excluding public*	4.0	13.5	9.5
Bus drivers	28.3	45.8	17.5
Bartenders	21.2	44.3	23.1
Janitors and cleaners	13.1	23.4	10.3

Selected female-dominated occupations in which men's representation increased disproportionately

Kitchen workers	91.8	78.2	−13.6
Cooks	67.2	57.2	−10.0
Labor force as a whole	38.0	42.6	4.6

[a]We define a disproportionate increase as 9.2 percentage points which is at least twice women's increased representation in the labor force as a whole.

Sources: U.S. Bureau of the Census (1984). Occupations denoted by an asterisk come from Rytina and Bianchi (1984).

subordinate group members. Such hierarchies are prescribed in a supporting ideology and maintained by mechanisms that physically or symbolically set apart members of dominant and subordinate status groups. These include mechanisms that segregate persons from different status groups, differentiate their behavior, and require or emphasize the social distance between them. All are supported by coercion. The most enduring status hierarchies, such as the centuries-old Indian caste system, employ all of these mechanisms. In this paper we examine the role each plays in producing and maintaining gender hierarchies in general, and occupational sex segregation in particular.

Segregation

Segregation maintains status hierarchies by literally "setting apart" members of different status groups, as exemplified by *purdah* in Moslem societies or the all-black "homelands" under South African apartheid. Physical segregation both reinforces the dominant ideology that group differences require differential treatment and facilitates treating groups unequally, as Lieberson (1980) has shown with respect to the sharp inequities between black and white public schools in the South. It also can discourage the emergence of collective protests by masking unequal treatment.

Physical segregation is socially costly if societal norms require duplication of facilities for subordinate groups or if the dominant group depends on the proximity of the subordinate group for various services. Solutions to the duplication problem may involve providing cheaper facilities for the subordinate group or permitting subordinate group members to share facilities with the dominants under restricted conditions. For example, prior to the 1964 Civil Rights Act that barred race discrimination in public accommodations, public recreational facilities in some Southern cities were available to blacks only a few hours a week. Contemporary examples include restricting children's access to university swimming pools to a few hours a week, or closing certain parts of campuses to student automobile traffic except at nights and weekends.

A solution to the problem of interdependence consistent with the status order involves requiring members of the low-status group to bear the costs of their separation—as witnessed, for example, by the long bus rides that black and Hispanic cleaning women take from their neighborhoods to those where they work. Alternatively, persons outside the status system—status-group neutrals—may be employed as intermediaries. For example, a study of working women in Egypt found that female clerical workers were confined to an all-female building and that very old men were used as go-betweens to male coworkers in another building (Ibrahim, 1980). Thus, a "genderless" group, analogous to the eunuchs who guarded harems, was used. When ideology forbids cross-status-group contact, expense and inefficiency are tolerated.[3]

Functional Differentiation

Status groups are also set apart through functional differentiation, in which tasks are assigned based on status-group membership. In view of the prevailing ideology that social and economic rewards should be commensurate with what one does, functional differentiation can ensure that lower-status groups are assigned less prestigious and poorly rewarded tasks.[4] These in turn symbolize their lower status, maintain their economic inferiority, and ensure that menial tasks are carried out.

The degree of interdependence of functionally differentiated status groups determines whether or not they are physically segregated. It is important to recognize that physical integration produced by the functional interdependence of status groups does not denote the absence of hierarchy. Consider the legally mandated racial segregation of railroad cars in the last century. The law was not enforced for black women who were caring for white children because they were present in their capacity as subordinates (Van den Berghe, 1960). As a rule, the physical integration that results when status inferiors perform subordinate functions reinforces rather than undermines the status hierarchy by advertising to all parties the subordinate group's inferior position.

Social Distance

Social practices that create or exaggerate the social distance between status groups by differentiating them in appearance or behavior represent a third way that status groups are set apart. Van den Berghe (1960) has argued that when dominant-subordinate groups are physically integrated, social distance mechanisms are necessary to maintain the status hierarchy, by symbolically denoting the inferiority of the socially subordinate group. As Weber pointed out, status groups are characterized by consciousness of kind and within-status group relations occur between status "equals". Cross-status-group contacts are acceptable when behavioral markers signal to all parties the social distance between the groups. As Van den Berghe pointed out, this is often achieved through *sumptuary* rules or rules of *etiquette*.

Sumptuary rules require certain modes of dress, diet, lifestyle, and so forth for members of subordinate groups as emblems of their inferior status while reserving others for members of the dominant group. For example, peasants were prohibited by law from wearing the curved toe shoes favored by members of medieval courts. Theoretically such rules should be common when status groups are physically integrated. Thus, in fifteenth-century Italy when Jews were highly assimilated, Jewish men were required to wear a circle of yellow cord and Jewish women to wear earrings (Hughes, 1984). Contemporary parallels are the uniforms required of service personnel who mix with the people they are serving to signal that the former are not interacting as equals with their employers or clientele.[5] These are especially likely when social interaction among the dominants is occurring simultaneously, as is true for circulating waiters at private parties or live-in domestic help.

Etiquette rules maintain social distance by requiring ritualized deference behavior by subordinate group members to the dominant group. The traditional signs of respect that children "owe" to adults, employees to bosses, and students to their teachers exemplify etiquette rules. Often such deference is expressed in the dominants' right to define the extent of intimacy (Henley and Freeman, 1984). Kanter's (1977) description of the patrimonial relationship between secretaries and their bosses exemplifies the operation of deference in the corporate world. It is seen even more clearly in the military, where enlisted personnel are required to salute superior officers and stand at attention in their officers' presence. The extreme attention to uniform distinctions and etiquette rules in the military is essential because the physical segregation of officers and enlisted persons typical in peacetime cannot be maintained during combat, when conformity to the hierarchical authority system is most critical (Van den Berghe, 1960).

Note that any form of differentiation—whether it is physical segregation, functional differentiation, or required displays of social distance—helps maintain status hierarchies by implying that status groups differ in socially relevant ways and that such distinctions are appropriate, necessary, and perhaps even natural.

Thus, even minor violations of these distinctions symbolically threaten the hierarchy and may be sanctioned severely. The beatings and lynchings of blacks who violated minor etiquette rules illustrate this point.[6] The use of coercion—whether it is formally sanctioned by the state or simply permitted to occur—underlies all status hierarchies. It is in the dominant group's interest to avoid using coercion, because doing so is costly and inefficient in the long run.[7] Nevertheless, it must be available to enforce required physical segregation, functional differentiation, and insignia and etiquette marking social distance as well as to protect the privileges and power reserved for the upper-status group.[8]

GENDER HIERARCHIES

The gender hierarchy of American society incorporates segregation, functional differentiation, and social distance mechanisms. In this section we briefly illustrate each and review evidence for its prevalence in American society and particularly in the workplace.

Physical Sex Segregation

Physical sex segregation, whose American origin lies in the 19th century doctrine of "separate spheres" (Welter, 1966), was manifest until recently in the relegation of the majority of women to their homes. Although over half of all women now work for wages outside the home, men's virtual absence from their homes during weekdays illustrates the physical segregation of the sexes. Sex segregation is also visible in the public sphere such as supermarkets, sporting events, bars, school playfields and classrooms, private clubs (Schafran, 1981), and voluntary associations (McPherson and Smith-Lovin, 1986).

Although the extent of physical sex segregation in the workplace is substantial, it eludes exact measurement. However, more than 32 million workers are in industries that employ at least 80 percent females or males, and many of these undoubtedly are employed at work sites with no other members of their sex (U.S. Department of Labor, Bureau of Labor Statistics, 1981, Table 30).[9]

Functional Sex Differentiation

Even more pervasive than physical sex segregation is functional differentiation by sex. This sexual division of labor is grounded in stereotypes of innate sex differences in traits and abilities, and maintained by gender-role socialization and various social control mechanisms. Functional differentiation by sex can be seen in the traditional allocation of expressive behavior to women, but not to men (Fishman, 1982), in the sex-based differentiation of market work and nonmarket work, in the well-documented sexual division of domestic work within the home, and in the sex segregation of occupations and jobs.

Estimating the total extent of functional sex differentiation in the workplace is impossible, but the index of occupational sex segregation provides an estimate.[10] The index of segregation, which represents the minimum proportion of workers of one sex who would have to change to an occupation in which the other sex is overrepresented, was .62 in 1981 for 262 detailed occupations (Beller, 1984). This value understates the extent of occupational segregation, since it fails to capture the segregation of the sexes *within* detailed occupations. For example, in 1970 half of all assemblers were female, but within motor vehicle manufacturing—a male-dominated industry—only 17 percent of assemblers were women; in electrical manufacturing—a female-intensive industry—women made up 74 percent of the assemblers (Reskin and Hartmann, 1985). Moreover, women and men in the same occupations often work in different firms (Blau, 1977), and within establishments the sexes rarely hold the same jobs (Bielby and Baron, 1984a).[11]

The interdependence of female and male coworkers in different occupations tends to mask their hierarchical relations. Hospitals offer a familiar example of functional differentiation in the context of physical integration. As outsiders we see female and male employees interacting: joking together in the corridors, working side by side over patients, often similarly clad. Yet nurses, technicians, clerical workers, and food service workers are overwhelmingly female, while doctors, administrators and orderlies are predominantly male. It is their functional differentiation that renders them interdependent and ensures their physical integration. It is worth noting that this workaday integration is preceded by largely sex-segregated training programs that help prepare women and men for un-equal rewards once they are nominally integrated.

Sex-Based Social Distance Mechanisms

Sex-specific sumptuary and etiquette rules, produced and maintained by sex-role socialization and social control mechanisms, are most visible in sex-specific dress codes and adornment fashions that exist in every known society and have been historically prescribed by law, custom and religion.[12] In the workplace they are manifest in dress standards or rules that stipulate "sex-appropriate clothing." Minimally this means dresses or skirts, nylon stockings, and feminine—usually high heeled—shoes. At the extreme it in-volves clothing that displays women's bodies such as abbreviated outfits for barmaids of which the most familiar is the Playboy bunny costume.

Gender-specific etiquette rules shape much of the casual social interac-tion between the sexes. The paternalism of behavior required of some men toward some women ("chivalry") obscures the hierarchical nature of much gender etiquette. In reality, the requirement that women be treated protec-tively has justified their exclusion from certain settings (*e.g.*, men's bars) and occupations. On a day-to-day basis, etiquette rules reinforce the gender hierarchy primarily through occupational segregation, since typically female lower-level employees are expected to display deference toward their often male superiors. The deference predominantly male doctors exact from the largely female nursing and technical staff illustrates this point.

CONCOMITANTS OF WOMEN'S INTEGRATION IN PREDOMINANTLY MALE OCCUPATIONS

We began this paper by noting the decline in occupational sex segregation in the 1970s and women's disproportionate progress in a small number of traditionally male occupations. We argued that changes in occupational sex segregation must be seen in the context of existing gender hierarchies. We should note that the term occupational segregation encompasses both physical and functional segregation. Our theoretical framework views these as parallel processes, both of which maintain the gender hierarchy. But it also recognizes their analytical independence as status-hierarchy maintain-ing mechanisms. Thus, it is necessary to consider both mechanisms when examining the causes and concomitants of the changing sex composition of occupations.

What does our theoretical perspective on status hierarchies imply about the representational gains women made in some male occupations in the 1970s? Can we interpret these changes as evidence that gender hierarchies are giving way? Or do declines in functional differentiation at the occupational level mask within-occupation physical segregation or functional differentiation by sex? Has the nature of work changed in these occupations to render them more hospitable to women? Has women's entry been accompanied by declining occupational rewards? Finally, are we observing one stage in a process of occupational resegregation in which men are abandoning newly integrated occupations to women, so that temporary movement toward more balanced sex compositions does not threaten the gender hierarchy? Examining what has occurred in occupations in which women made numerical gains can help us to determine whether women have begun to breach the gender hierarchy or whether it is simply changing form in response to various pressures.

While we do not deny the possibility of a real reduction in the pervasiveness of the gender hierarchy, the status-hierarchy perspective suggests that one or more of the following processes may be present in male occupations that have become more female. First, occupational-level integration might be largely nominal, concealing segregation within more detailed occupational categories or across employment sectors, industries, or firms. Second, when women enter occupations men have formerly monopolized, other mechanisms for ensuring women's subordination might emerge. In particular, their monetary rewards and prestige might be lower than men's or their jobs might offer less autonomy than those of male incumbents. In addition, sex differentiated etiquette rules or dress styles might be exaggerated. Third, feminizing occupations might decline in status and show corresponding declines in various occupational rewards (*e.g.*, income) relative to less integrated occupations. Fourth, either women's increasing presence or the resulting decline in occupational rewards might prompt men to abandon integrating occupations for those still dominated by their sex.

While it is not possible at this point to pursue fully all the theoretical issues we have raised, we address some of them here. Our discussion is based on preliminary findings from an ongoing investigation of the determinants and consequences of changes in occupations' sex composition between 1970 and 1980 (Reskin and Roos, 1985). Our data come primarily from in-progress case studies of four occupations—pharmacist, insurance adjuster and examiner, systems analyst, and baker—carried out by members of our research team, Polly Phipps and Barbara Kritt of the University of Michigan and Katharine Donato of SUNY Stony Brook. These case studies relied on documentary and published sources, including trade journals and the research of occupational associations, published and unpublished statistical data, and interviews.[13] We also refer to the results of related research.[14]

Our results provide revealing illustrations of the conceptual issues we have raised. They suggest that three interrelated processes—internal segregation, deskilling, and resegregation—are occurring in male occupations that became appreciably more female in the 1970s, although the causal order between these processes and women's entry is not yet clear.

Intraoccupational Segregation

The preliminary case studies clearly suggest that what have been labelled as gains for women reflect the elaboration of a sexual division of labor *within* detailed occupations that were predominantly male in the past. Illustrative are our case studies of pharmacists, bakers, and systems analysts as well as the findings of others. Between 1970 and 1980 women's representation among pharmacists doubled. Yet Phipps (1985) found that female pharmacists are concentrated in different work settings than males. Women work disproportionately in hospitals, a female industry, while men are concentrated in managerial positions, retail pharmacies, and research. In 1970 women were only one-quarter of all bakers; now proportionately represented, they are overrepresented in the largely automated production of cakes and cookies, while men dominate the less automated bread baking (Kritt, 1984). Even in the rapidly expanding occupation of systems analyst women work in female-intensive and lower paying industries such as health care, while men are concentrated in male-intensive industries such as manufacturing (Donato, 1985).[15] Among bus drivers women made dramatic representational gains in the 1970s, but a closer look revealed that they are seldom employed by large metropolitan transit systems, and instead work disproportionately for school systems driving school buses on a part-time basis (Burke, 1983). It is not coincidental that their "clientele" are children over whom women's authority is culturally appropriate. Strober and Best's (1979) study of the feminization of the teaching occupation also illustrates internal segregation. When teaching was "feminized" after the Civil War, it became internally stratified by sex, with administrative positions reserved for men.

Bank and financial managers—an occupation in which women showed considerable gains during the 70s—may represent another instance of nominal rather than real gains. In the 1970s the Office for Federal Contract Compliance targetted the banking and insurance industries for enforcement of the Presidential Executive Order 11246 requiring affirmative action among federal contractors. Although we lack systematic data, it appears that women were moved up into management positions in small branch banks. Such positions involve relatively little responsibility and are physically segregated from main branches where significant decisions are made and important contacts that facilitate career progress nurtured. Wage data are consistent with the interpretation that women's gains in banking and financial management represent nominal promotions or job-title inflation rather than real occupational advancement (Beller, 1982).[16]

Fragmentation and Job Deskilling

The preliminary case studies also suggest that women are hired in male-dominated occupations when work has been fragmented and jobs deskilled. Deskilling occurs when organizational or technological changes cause occupational duties to be modified to routinize work and eliminate worker discretion. Braverman (1974) argued that deskilling often affords employers the opportunity to lower wages. The process might enhance women's access to occupations men had formerly dominated either because employers consciously recruit women when lower wages no longer attract qualified men[17] or because men's stake in monopolizing occupational access declines under such conditions.

The link between deskilling and occupational sex integration is illustrated both in Hacker's (1979) study of the aftermath of the landmark AT&T-EEOC consent decree, and Strober and her colleagues' (Tyack and Strober, 1981; Strober and Arnold, 1984a) analyses of the shifts of teachers and bank tellers from male to female occupations. According to Hacker, after agreeing to integrate various jobs that had been reserved for white men, AT&T moved women into men's jobs that had been scheduled for reduction because of technological change, since women's allegedly higher turnover would necessitate fewer firings. Hacker also reported that AT&T placed women in what had previously been men's jobs that technological change was expected to simplify. For example, they started employing women as installers shortly before installation became a simple matter of plugging standardized parts into standardized outlets. Installers have since all but disappeared.

Women replaced men as teachers after the low-paying jobs became unattractive to men in view of the stricter training requirements, the extended teaching year, and the increasing bureaucratization of teaching that reduced teachers' autonomy (Rotella and Margo, 1981; Tyack and Strober, 1981). A contemporary example is typesetting and compositing, a highly paid and unionized craft monopolized for centuries by men. Automated in the 1970s, newspapers now rely overwhelmingly on electronic methods of compositing and typesetting. Concurrently unions lost membership and power, and wages dropped. As Kalleberg and his colleagues' (1986) data—which we reproduce in the first two rows of the table below—clearly show, it was in the context of these changes that the proportion of female typesetters skyrocketed.

	1970	1980
Hot metal linotype machines	10,290	465
Video display terminals at newspapers	23	27,078
Percent female typesetters/compositors	16.8	55.7

Deskilling in pharmacy has been under way since the 1940s when drug manufacturers began to take over the "compounding" of drugs (Phipps, 1985). The contemporary pharmacist's role is primarily dispensing, answering questions, and record-keeping. Along with the clericalization of pharmacists' duties, chain drugstores and discount department store pharmacies have proliferated, supplanting independently owned pharmacies. The functions of pharmacists in the former settings, in which women appear to be concentrated, increasingly resemble those of retail sales clerks, a low-status, traditionally female occupation. In a similar fashion, our preliminary observations suggest that the proliferation of in-store bakeries in supermarkets may have contributed to women's numerical gains in baking. There too deskilling may be taking place: baking may simply involve inserting already prepared pans of breads, rolls and cookies in ovens so the duties of in-store bakers largely involve retail selling (Kritt, 1984). For both these occupations, wage comparisons, which must await income data for comparable 1970 and 1980 occupational categories, will be instructive.

Phipps' (1986) case study of insurance adjusters and examiners provides a detailed illustration of both deskilling and intraoccupational segregation. Women's representation in this occupation increased dramatically during the 1970s, second only to the progress they made among typesetters and compositors. As the title indicates, the occupation is composed of two different specialties. Adjusters, who were predominantly male in 1970, determine whether the policy covers the claim and the amount of the loss and deal primarily with property and liability claims. They include outside adjusters, who go to accident sites to assess the damage, and lower paid inside adjusters, who work by phone. As claim processing is computerized and work is increasingly done by telephone, less judgment is required. Industry representatives and trade magazines now depict the ideal adjuster as one who projects "empathy, sincerity and integrity over the phone," and one industry spokesperson noted that "this is why a growing number of companies are hiring women" (Phipps, 1986). Another industry representative described the adjuster as an "ideal job for women with a college background." Our case study suggests that it was job deskilling that gained women's access to the occupation adjuster and that men continue to monopolize the better-paying outside adjuster jobs. Property and liability adjusting seems to be in an early stage of deskilling; Phipps predicts this subspecialty will be resegregated as a female occupation by 1990.

The occupation examiner in health and life appears to be in a late stage of deskilling. This position, which is responsible for reviewing claims and authorizing payment, was about half female-represented in 1970, and is now overwhelmingly female. Increasing reliance on electronic data processing has deskilled work. At Prudential Insurance Company's health division, for example, examiners use terminals to view the file history, determine coverage, adjudicate the claim, calculate benefits and generate the necessary correspondence in an average of 30 separate screen displays of less than two seconds each (Braden, 1979). The feminization of these jobs has given employers access to less skilled and traditionally cheaper workers. Blue Cross-Blue Shield now leases terminals to women who process health claims at home at piece rates and without benefits (*New York Times,* May 20,

1984) and U.S. companies are soliciting women in Barbados to process data via satellite (*Business Week*, March 15, 1982).

Many observers of the computer industry claim that programming occupations have undergone deskilling (for a review, see Donato, 1985). Whereas programmers once controlled the process and pace of their work, programming is now divided into systems analysts and systems programmers who perform the more conceptual tasks involved in systems design, and lower-paid software programmers and programmer/analysts who perform the more mechanical tasks of writing, applying, and maintaining programs (Kraft, 1979; Strober and Arnold, 1984b).

Kraft and Dubnoff (1983) provide evidence that women are concentrated in the most routine and lowest paid of these software jobs, such as business programming, documentation, and maintenance, as well as in the lowest paid industries (financial/real estate and communications). Even women in the higher-paid systems analyst positions tend to work in the lowest-paying industries (Donato, 1985). This evidence suggests that the division of labor by sex is replicated in the high-growth computer software field (Kraft, 1984; Strober and Arnold, 1984b).[18]

Occupational Decline

Our preliminary case studies offer little direct evidence for the hypothesis that occupational rewards decline with or precede women's entry. This tendency was first described in a paper by Carter and Carter (1981) on women's recent progress in the professions aptly subtitled, "Women get a ticket to ride after the gravy train has left the station." Carter and Carter argued that women's opportunities in the professions were concentrated in those already undergoing declines in status and autonomy, such as college and university teaching.[19]

To test the hypothesis of declining rewards, income data for comparable occupational categories for 1970 and 1980 are necessary. Of course, the well-known negative relationship between wage levels of both men and women in an occupation and the proportion of females in that occupation (Treiman and Hartmann, 1981; Roos, 1981) is consistent with employers paying workers less because an occupation is highly female, but other causal orderings are possible. Evidence for the 1940s and 1950s indicate a weak tendency for occupations in which men were poorly paid to become more female a decade later (Treiman and Terrell, 1975). Other findings are consistent with this hypothesis, though the causal order is often in doubt. For example, the work of computer specialists was reorganized during the same period that the occupation became more female and earnings growth tapered off (Greenbaum, 1976). There is some evidence that insurance adjusters' incomes declined between 1970 and 1980 (Cornfield *et al.*, 1986), the decade in which the occupation's sex composition shifted sharply.

Resegregation

The resegregation hypothesis originated in the pattern in which members of a lower status group began moving into a neighborhood previously
restricted to a higher status group, but after some "tipping point" was
reached, members of the higher status group fled, leaving the resegregated
neighborhood to the lower status group. Applied to occupational segregation, the resegregation hypothesis raises the possibility that sex integration
may also be short lived. Evidence for occupational resegregation is found in
the historical shifts in the predominant sex of teachers, librarians, secretaries, and bank tellers (Davies, 1982; Tyack and Strober, 1981; Strober
and Arnold, 1984a). In each instance the sex shift was followed by a decline
in earnings and/or career possibilities. Between 1960 and 1980 the dominant sex of insurance adjusters, bill collectors, window dressers, compositors, and peddlers and hucksters has shifted. Men probably abandon or
fail to enter some traditionally male occupations in response to their perceptions of declining opportunities before women begin to enter in large
numbers and this may create openings for women. For example, given the
declining number of owner-operated pharmacies, being a pharmacist presents a less attractive career for people with entrepreneurial aspirations,
and this factor as well as deskilling within the occupation may contribute to
men's willingness to abandon the occupation to women. In this case,
women's enrollment began to climb only after slots in pharmacy schools
went unfilled in the 1960s (Phipps, 1985). Our discussion of compositors
and typesetters and insurance adjusters suggests that redefining work led to
both women's entry and men's departure, though the former may have has-
tened the latter. Our planned statistical analyses of census data will permit
firmer conclusions about the causal order and relationships between
women's entry; deskilling; declining occupational status, income, career
prospects and autonomy; and men's departure.

Women's Integration and Social Distance Mechanisms

Our preliminary case studies do not address whether women's occupational integration gave rise to changes in social distance mechanisms in
the form of sumptuary and etiquette rules that emphasize women's subordinate status, but casual observation suggests that both may be heightened
in some male-dominated occupations in which both physical and functional
sex segregation have declined.

Sumptuary rules. Women's challenges to traditional sex-specific dress codes
accompanied their demand for access to the full range of occupations, and
the 1970s saw increasing numbers of women in white-collar jobs win the
right to wear trousers to work though some establishments required pants-
suits. But as increasing numbers of women entered management and the
professions, there appears to be renewed pressure for them to dress in

traditionally female styles. The pantssuit is rare in most workplaces, and the arbiters of successful dress for business and professional women now look askance at the severely tailored, pin-striped skirt suit of the 1970s. Instead, popular magazine articles, advertisements and best selling books encourage women on the fast-track to express their "femininity" by wearing ruffled blouses with softer business suits, and some advisers favor colorful, "feminine" dresses. A perusal of fashion magazines reveals a little-girl look—anklets, dresses with attached tie-belts, blouses that button up the back—which symbolize women's subordinate status. This emphasis on sex differentiation in appearance may well be a response to women's challenge to the gender hierarchy and their increasing presence in roles formerly reserved for men.

Etiquette rules. This decade of nominal gains for women at work has also witnessed close scrutiny on cross-sex relations among coworkers. The extreme care with which Geraldine Ferraro conducted herself with her running mate reflect the pressure on women in male settings to monitor how their dealings with male colleagues may look to others. Flirtatious or sexual relationships between male dominants and female subordinates (boss and secretary; producer and starlet; professor and graduate assistant) did not threaten the existing gender hierarchy. In fact, in some settings symbolic or actual sexual access to female underlings was seen as a male-status perquisite that is reflected in part in the high incidence of sexual harassment. Gender etiquette only began to merit corporate concern with the decline of functional differentiation by sex. Hence, Bendix Corporation's strong response to the alleged relationship between Mary Cunningham and her boss was not anomalous, and with women's growing involvement in managerial roles, attention continues to focus on relationships between women and men who occupy equal-status positions. Not only do magazine columns advise businesswomen on how to handle relationships,[20] but prestigious establishment publications like the *Harvard Business Review* (Collins, 1983) have tackled the issue of how women managers should relate to male coworkers.

CONCLUSIONS

We contend that both women's position and progress in the labor market can be best understood in the context of the gender hierarchy characterizing contemporary American society. This perspective views the two processes that comprise occupational segregation—the physical separation of the sexes into different work settings and their functional differentiation into different occupations and tasks—as mechanisms contributing to the maintenance of men's global social and economic advantages. It recognizes that a system of social control which includes both the social-distance

mechanisms we discussed and coercion reinforces functional differentiation. This perspective directs us to ask what social processes underlay or accompanied women's disproportionate gains in the 1970s in several traditionally male ocupations. Case studies of those occupations and others
suggest that women's integration often masks intraoccupational segregation, that it is often accompanied by deskilling, and that men may be abandoning occupations to women. This does not preclude the possibility that
women's challenges to sex stratification have been partly effective.

Often illegal, physical segregation is hard to defend in the face of legal
challenges and is the barrier most readily breached. Thus, women have
gained access to occupational settings previously considered off limits, such
as navy and merchant marine ships, coal mines, and the locker rooms of
professional sports teams. But when physical segregation declines our
perspective suggests that, insofar as dominants have the power to do so,
they will foster increased functional differentiation and heightened emphasis on sex differentiated etiquette and sumptuary rules.

Functional differentiation is a more subtle barrier, produced by a combination of complex forces, including deep-seated beliefs in innate sex differences. Nevertheless, women have challenged functional differentiation
both in the home and in the form of occupational segregation, and these
challenges constitute a significant threat to the underlying ideology that
supports gender hierarchies. The occupations we have examined closely
suggest that simply gaining greater numerical access to traditionally male
occupations has not brought the social and economic gains the statistics
alone imply. Preliminary evidence of within-occupation functional differentiation, changing work content, declining rewards, and resegregation
lead us to question the value of these statistical gains for women.

We do not deny that some women made considerable progress in the
1970s, and that as a group, women have improved their representation in
almost all customarily male occupations and have narrowed the wage gap
by a few cents. Young women now aspire to a much wider range of professional and managerial occupations than their mothers did and routinely
plan continuous employment. Even token representation of women in male
occupations transmits a different message to new generations of workers
than the traditional message of men only. It would be a mistake to ignore
these forms of progress. But we believe that observers would be equally
mistaken to overestimate women's gains or underestimate the pervasiveness of the barriers women still face. Beneficiaries of hierarchical status systems rarely yield willingly when their privileges are challenged (Goode,
1982), and gender hierarchies are deeply rooted, buttressed by the biologi-
cal interdependence of the sexes and the institutionalization of heterosexuality (Rich, 1980), and firmly entrenched in the sexual division of domestic
labor. The latter is of particular importance in view of the relationship between the family and work, and the failure for significant declines in
functional differentiation in the family makes major declines in sex

stratification in the workplace unlikely in the near future. Nevertheless, some social processes undoubtedly facilitate women's occupational integration, and we hope in our current study to identify them. We believe that understanding the concomitants of women's integration in male occupations and the conditions under which gender hierarchies in the workplace are changing offers promise for achieving real change in the future.

NOTES

1. Technological changes eliminated some occupations and fostered the emergence of others. The extractive industries, farming, and occupations requiring sheer muscle power declined in importance, while at the same time the bureaucratization of work and the growth of the service sector created new occupations. The composition of the labor force was dramatically transformed with the abolition of child labor, women's increasing involvement in wage work, and an increasingly educated workforce. The nature of labor markets changed as the strength of organized labor varied and with federal intervention prompted by the Great Depression and World War II.

2. These estimates of percentage female are based on a preliminary attempt by the Census Bureau to establish comparability between the 1970 and 1980 occupational classifications using a subsample of 1970 respondents who were coded with both sets of codes.

3. Economic theories of discrimination which predict that the cost of discriminating will lead to its disappearance fail to take this into account. As Stolzenberg (1982) pointed out, large employers may see a segregated workforce as an noneconomic "amenity" that advances some other goal.

4. To the extent that members of the dominant group monopolize positions involving the most effort and responsibility, setting wages in terms of "comparable worth" will not substantially undermine any wage gap between dominant and subordinate status-group members.

5. When, as in the police or military, members of both superordinate and subordinate groups wear uniforms, design or insignia clearly mark the wearer's position in the hierarchy.

6. This explains why status hierarchies are threatened when members of unequal status groups come together as equals (Pettigrew, 1969). Researchers continue to consider whether equal-status contacts lead us to declines in racial intolerance (Ford, 1984; Jackman and Crane, 1985).

7. Jackman and Muha (1984) discuss the responses by dominants to challenges by subordinate status groups.

8. Using similar logic, Goode (1971) pointed out that male dominance in the family could not survive if men did not have the threat of violence as a resource.

9. Males made up at least 90 percent of the workers in metal and coal mining, fisheries, horticultural services, logging, construction, and railroads in 1980 (U.S. Department of Labor, Bureau of Labor Statistics, 1981, Table 30).

10. In 1980 one-quarter of all employed women were concentrated in 22 occupations that were over 90 percent female, whereas three-eighths of the male labor force were distributed across 165 occupations that were at least 90 percent male.

11. The job titles in 202 of the 393 establishments Bielby and Baron (1984a)

studied were completely sex segregated, fewer than one-fifth of the firms had indexes below .90, and only one worker in ten shared the same job title with any coworker of the other sex.

12. For example, the Old Testament enjoins that "women shall not wear that which pertain unto a man, neither shall a man put on a woman's garment: for all that do so are an abomination unto the Lord thy God" (Deuteronomy, 22:5).

13. Since we wrote this paper, we have embarked on additional case studies of other male-dominated occupations in which women made appreciable gains in the 1970s (typesetter and compositor, real estate broker, insurance sales agent, editor and reporter, bus driver, baker, and public relations specialist), and we plan studies of otherwise similar occupations in which women made little progress or even lost ground, and studies of a few female-dominated occupations that became more male. We will supplement these findings with the results of quantitative analyses of the 1970–80 changes in the sex compositions of the 503 detailed occupations in the 1980 census. The statistical analyses, which we will begin in 1986 when the comparable 1970 and 1980 occupational data are available, will identify the factors associated with changes in the occupations' sex composition for all 503 detailed (3-digit) occupations. We will explore the effects of a variety of occupational characteristics, including changes in incumbents' median educational level, median earnings, and opportunity for part-time and part-year employment; changing employment opportunities; labor market and economic sectors; female-intensiveness of industry; working conditions including physical demands of the job, heavy, outdoor, or dirty work, access to authority, complexity of tasks, and so forth. For further details on study design, see Reskin and Roos, 1985.

14. Myra Strober and her colleagues (Strober and Best, 1979; Tyack and Strober, 1981; Strober and Arnold, 1984a) are studying resegregation between 1870 and 1980 in three occupations that switched from male- to female-dominated—teaching, bank tellers and secretaries.

15. In their survey of software workers, Kraft and Dubnoff (1983) observed that women often worked in jobs that were routine or required attention to detail.

16. Indirect evidence for the claim that women's progress in financial management is largely nominal is the fact that in 1979 35 percent of all female managers earned less than $10,400, and that in 1980 female managers in the finance and insurance industries earned less than half of what males earned (Nussbaum, personal communication, 1982).

17. Strober and Arnold's (1984a) analysis of the feminization of bank tellers concludes that the evidence regarding deskilling is inconclusive, but suggests that it occurred earlier than the 1940s which is the decade when women began to enter the occupation in large numbers. They do hypothesize, however, that teaching became predominantly female because men with the necessary education sought better paying jobs.

18. This replication of the traditional sexual division of labor must be viewed in the historical context of the development of the occupation of programming. The ENIAC, the first operational computer built during World War II, spawned the occupation of programming. Because programming was thought to be a clerical task, ENIAC's project leaders initially selected only women. When it became clear that programming required knowledge of abstract logic, math, electrical circuits, and machines, programming became men's work (Kraft, 1979). While women maintained a constant presence in the programming field (about 20 percent; Kraft, 1984),

only recently has women's representation increased as they moved into the now-fragmented programming occupations (Donato, 1985).

19. Previous research is consistent with prestige and power loss. For example, Touhey (1974) found that the higher the proportion of female workers in an occupation, the lower the prestige respondents accorded it. A study of female managers in two large retail companies revealed that when work groups' sex composition shifted from all female to integrated, the supervisors' power and credibility declined (Harlan and Weiss, 1981).

20. Women are warned, however, not to show up in the same business suit two days in a row, lest it be thought they spent the previous night away from home. Implicitly, men may take this risk without worrying about its consequences.

CHAPTER 2

Intraindustry Occupational Recomposition and Gender Inequality in Earnings*

Marta Tienda and Vilma Ortiz

This research was supported by the College of Agricultural and Life Sciences, the University of Wisconsin-Madison, Hatch Project No. 2886. Computational work was supported by a grant to the Center for Demography and Ecology, University of Wisconsin-Madison, from the Center of Population, the National Institute of Child Health and Human Development (HD-05876). We gratefully acknowledge technical assistance from Susan Robinson, Gary Heisserer, Ron Miller, and Diane Deusterhoeff and appreciate thoughtful comments from Shelley A. Smith and Jennifer Glass.

INTRODUCTION

The last 20 years have witnessed remarkable changes in the labor force activity of women. Female labor force participation rose from 38 to 53 percent over a period of 20 years, and the 1970s witnessed an increase in the share of the female labor force who worked full-time on a year-round basis. By 1980 over half of all working women were less than 35 years old compared with approximately 38 percent in 1960. Also, the share of married women who worked outside the home rose sharply, increasing from 31 percent in 1960 to 51 percent in 1980 (Norwood, 1982). In 1960, 19 percent of married women with children under age 6 were economically active, com-

*For comments on this chapter see Blau (pp 239-243) in this volume.

23

pared to 39 percent of those with children aged 6—17, but by 1980 the comparable figures were 45 and 62 percent, respectively.

Changes in both the supply of women workers and the demand factors which draw them into the labor market have been responsible for the sharp rise in female employment over the past two decades (Oppenheimer, 1970). On the supply side, increases in women's educational levels qualify them to enter a broader range of jobs, particularly those requiring post-secondary training. Between 1970 and 1980, the proportion of working women with college degrees rose from 11 to 17 percent for white females and from 7 to 12 percent for black females (Tienda, Ortiz and Smith, 1985). The increase of college-educated Hispanic origin working women was more modest, rising from 6 to 8 percent during the 1970s. Educational upgrading contributed to the increased representation of women in higher status jobs over the past two decades. However, changed social norms about the acceptability of mothers working outside the home coupled with financial exigencies associated with the sharp increases in the incidence of female-headed households also propelled many women into the labor market (Tienda and Glass, 1985).

Although most discussions of women's employment emphasize supply considerations, on the demand side of the labor market equation, changes in the industrial composition of employment also have facilitated increases in women's labor force participation (Norwood, 1982). Declines in the relative prevalence of agricultural and manufacturing jobs have been particularly conducive to rising levels of female employment. That three-fourths of the increase in the number of women working in nonagricultural jobs between 1970 and 1980 involved employment in service industries (Norwood, 1982) attests to the profound importance of the industrial transformation of employment for future trends in women's market activity.

The problem, simply stated, is that there has been very little change in the gender gap in earnings over the past two decades, despite the sharp rise in female labor force participation, the relative expansion of high status occupations (Singelmann and Tienda, 1985), and the increased educational credentials of women workers. The shift from goods to service production potentially could help close the gender gap in earnings, provided that the shrinking job opportunities in male-dominated industries resulted in the growth of high paying jobs that were more accessible to women compared to those jobs which declined.

An alternative scenario would predict the opposite. If the industrial restructuring processes toward service employment result in the growth of low-wage jobs which are disproportionately held by women, and/or if women are channeled to lower status and low wage jobs at a rate higher than men, then it is conceivable that the massive changes in the nature and organization of work brought on by the industrial transformation of employment will leave intact the gender gap in earnings. That the gender gap in earnings narrowed very slightly during the last intercensal decade (see

England and McLaughlin, 1979), despite the sharp rise in female labor force participation rates and women's increased representation in high status occupations (Smith and Tienda, forthcoming; Tienda, Jensen and Bach, 1984), lends support for the second scenario.

In brief, the challenge facing earnings analysts is to explain why the relative expansion of high status jobs seems to have had little impact in closing the gender gap in earnings. Accordingly, we investigate how the industrial restructuring process and the changing gender composition of jobs influenced the aggregate gender gap in earnings during the 1970s. Our main objective is to ascertain whether men and women benefited equally from the industrial transformation of the U.S. employment structure, both in terms of their representation in rapidly growing jobs and in the pecuniary rewards associated with them. Rephrased as a question, we ask: did the entry of women into jobs that became more (or less) prevalent in the employment structure enhance or diminish their earnings levels relative to those of men? Since past research has documented the salience of occupational segregation in maintaining gender-linked earnings inequities (Oppenheimer, 1968; England and McLaughlin, 1979), we consider whether the gender composition of jobs has changed over time, and we analyze whether this feature of the employment structure contributed to maintaining the male/female disparity in earnings, net of monetary gains resulting from greater job opportunities.

Following a selective review of theoretical issues on the determinants of men's and women's earnings, we introduce our concern with the industrial transformation of employment and formulate working propositions about the significance of industrial and occupational restructuring processes for sex differences in earnings. In developing our arguments, we emphasize the importance of the gender composition of jobs as a salient factor in maintaining sex-linked earnings differences. We support our arguments through an analysis of the gender composition of occupations and associated earnings ratios between men and women.

To document how the changing employment structure altered the occupational allocation of men and women between 1970 and 1980, we compute a shift-share analysis which decomposes the observed intercensal change into its structural components. Not only is this aggregate analysis of interest in its own right, but it also generates for each of 335 job cells two indexes of structural change which we subsequently use to predict average earnings for men and women and the job-specific male/female earnings ratio for these jobs. These details are considered at some length in the methodology section.

Our findings highlight the existence of sex-based discrimination which maintains intact the earnings disparities between men and women. Based on these results we argue that structural changes in the economy mask the persistence of gender inequities by giving the appearance of improvements in the labor market position of women relative to men.

GENDER INEQUITIES IN EARNINGS: THEORETICAL CONSIDERATIONS

Several bodies of literature have sought to explain why women earn less than men, on average. One explanation, which draws from the human capital perspective of earnings determination (Mincer and Polachek, 1974; 1978; Polachek, 1975; 1979), explains differences in men's and women's earnings as a function of variation in the productive characteristics of workers. In general, these approaches to wage differentials explain less than 20 percent of the gender gap in earnings, even after controlling for a variety of personal characteristics and achieved statuses such as race, marital and family status, and market conditions (Shack-Marquez, 1984). A notable exception is the study by Corcoran and Duncan (1979) which utilized longitudinal work history data and accounted for almost half of the earnings disparity between men and women.

That even the most ambitious studies using individual characteristics left at least half of the gender gap in earnings unexplained prompted a search for structural explanations of these disparities. Much of this discussion has focused on occupational segregation (Oppenheimer, 1968; 1970; England and McLaughlin, 1979; England, 1981; 1982; Rosenfeld, 1983) and the relationship between job characteristics and earnings levels. While instructive, information on how patterns of occupational segregation by gender translate into persisting wage differences between men and women begs the question as to why such segregation patterns arise in the first place, and why they persist in the face of profound changes in the nature and organization of work.

Sex Segregation of Occupations

Besides reaffirming the pervasiveness of occupational segregation by gender and its persistence over time, research which examined the linkage between segregation and earnings disparities has established three basic issues worthy of brief summary. First is the importance of distinguishing between the *distributional* aspects of earnings differences (*i.e.,* those arising strictly from the uneven allocation of men and women in the employment structure) and *intrajob* earnings differences (*i.e.,* those arising from paying men and women differently for similar work).[1] A second point is that the measured extent of job segregation increases with the detail used to specify job categories. Finally, while recognizing that most of the observed earnings disparity between men and women arises from the concentration of women in lower-paying jobs, England and McLaughlin (see also Shack-Marquez, 1984) suggested that some jobs may actually pay less *because* women are concentrated in them.[2] This third point—that the gender composition of jobs is a structural attribute which itself defines earnings levels—is crucial for understanding the persistence of the gender gap in earnings because of infinite possibilities for redefining sex-typed jobs under changing industrial regimes.

Our analysis does not probe directly into the causes of labor market and premarket discrimination which channels men and women into different job paths. Instead, we propose a structural approach to discrimination which takes the pervasiveness of sex-based discrimination as a given, and which posits that discrimination adapts to changed industrial regimes through new patterns of occupational segregation and sex-labeling of jobs. This view is consistent with the persistence of extensive occupational segregation in the face of major transformations in the nature of work. Like England and McLaughlin (1979), we believe that a redefinition of sex labels for jobs is possible largely because occupational segregation renders discrimination somewhat invisible to the individuals involved—at least when compared to different pay for like work—and because the sex-labeling of occupations recreates and reinforces gender boundaries in the employment structure (Rosenfeld, 1983).

We examine the possibility that sex-labeling of occupations serves to maintain or redefine gender boundaries in the employment structure by exploring whether the rate at which jobs became feminized during the 1970s enhanced or diminished the earnings disparity between men and women, net of the changes in the relative growth or decline of specific jobs during the 1970s. We also consider whether changes in the gender composition of jobs, which reflects the uneven allocation of men and women among positions, influenced men's and women's average earnings levels, and whether these influences depended upon the changing prevalence of jobs. Such a finding would lend support to our proposition that the redefinition of job boundaries for men and women prevents the industrial restructuring processes from narrowing the earnings gap between men and women.

Industrial Transformation and Gender Segregation

One of the most remarkable trends during the post-World War II period has been the shift toward service employment. Just under half of all workers were engaged in service industries in 1940; in 1970 that share had increased to 62 percent, and by 1980 two of every three workers were so employed. Accompanying the transformation of the production structure were pervasive changes in the occupational structure, many stemming from modifications in the technical division of labor and the increasing specialization of occupational roles. As a result of these macrosocial trends, the 1960s and 1970s witnessed the proliferation of a vast array of entirely new jobs, especially in the broad grouping of technical and semiprofessional occupations.

Unfortunately, with few exceptions (Browning and Singelmann, 1978; Singelmann and Browning, 1980; Singelmann and Tienda, 1985), labor force analysts interested in occupational configurations have not directly examined the implications of transformations in industry structures for changes in the relative prevalence of specific occupations. Of the efforts already undertaken to explore both theoretically and empirically the dimensions of change in the employment structure simultaneously using industry and occupation distributions, the work of Browning and Singelmann (1975; 1978) is most comprehensive. Their landmark study documented the emergence of a service society in the United States from the early years of this century through 1970, and concluded with a detailed analysis of the components of change in the occupational structure between 1960 and 1970 (Singelmann and Browning, 1980). Although they speculated about the sociological implications of a service society for various groups, including women and part-time workers, they stopped short of analyzing whether men and women have benefited uniformly from the expanded job opportunities in services. Nonetheless, their work established a benchmark for other researchers to pursue similar lines of inquiry.

A more recent analysis by Singelmann and Tienda (1985) extended to 1980 the work of Browning and Singelmann which ended in 1970. Their analyses showed that during the early 1970s the pace of industrial transformation from a goods to a service economy had begun slowing due largely to the negligible reduction of agricultural employment after 1970. Since the decline in agricultural employment largely had been responsible for the rapid growth of the service industries during the 1950s and 1960s, and since by 1970 agricultural employment had fallen to very low levels (just under 4 percent of total employment), further reductions of jobs in agricultural industries could modify the occupational structure only slightly.

That the rate of occupational change during the 1970s had not slowed as much as Browning and Singelmann (1975; 1978) predicted resulted from important changes in the technical division of labor *within* industries. Singelmann and Tienda (1985) showed that during the 1970s, the intra-industry occupational restructuring process in the United States produced further occupational upgrading,[3] despite the slower pace of industrial transformation. What is sociologically significant about this upgrading trend is its implied demand for more highly skilled labor. If continued, the greater relative importance of intraindustry occupational recomposition portends further possibilities for occupational mobility, even after the industrial transformation toward a service economy—which was the central force of past occupational upgrading—has been completed.

While informative about the aggregate dynamics of occupational change, the existing studies made no reference as to whether men and women experienced similar levels of occupational upgrading over the past two decades, nor did they examine how these changes in the structure of opportunities were linked to earnings levels and differentials between men and women. We address the first question by decomposing changes in the occupational structure between 1970 and 1980 into three components (using the shift-share technique) separately for men and women, and the second question by using the structural measures generated from this analysis to predict men's and women's earnings in 1980. Like Singelmann and his associates, we decompose occupational change into components representing the relative importance of industrial shifts and intraindustry occupational shifts in altering the relative prevalence of major occupation groups.

To recapitulate, we wish to emphasize the theoretical importance of linking shifts in the relative size of jobs to earnings. Labor demand theory would predict a positive influence of rapidly growing jobs on earnings, but would leave unexplained gender differences in these influences. However, a sharp increase in the supply of women willing and able to enter the labor market, coupled with the rapidly expanding jobs deemed appropriate for women, could exert downward pressure on wage payments for both men and women. Such downward pressure on women's wages could be exacerbated if the increased rates of female labor force participation reinforced existing patterns of occupational segregation either by furthering concentration of women in sex-typed jobs, or by redefining gender-based patterns of occupational segregation as the employment structure is itself transformed, or both. Hence, while the proliferation of a vast array of new jobs as a result of industrial restructuring holds potential to degender occupational roles, whether this did in fact occur is an empirical question we address for the 1970–80 intercensal period.

DATA AND METHODS

Our analyses are based on the Public Use Microdata Sample files from the 1970 and 1980 censuses. For examining the changes in the employment structure between 1970 and 1980, we included all individuals aged 16 or over who were in the labor force in the respective year and for whom nonmissing industry and occupation data were available. We did not differentiate between full-time, year-round workers and those who worked on a part-time or part-year basis for the shift-share analysis because both are integral to the definition of an employment structure. However, we based comparisons of men's and women's earnings on the subset of full-time, year-round workers to control for well documented differences in their labor supply. This restriction ensured that the sample of working men and women were roughly comparable in terms of labor force effort, and rendered the measured earnings gap more conservative.

Our analysis involved extensive file construction and data manipulation which we can summarize briefly. First we generated industry-by-occupation matrices for both men and women for both periods. We used the 37-industry scheme initially developed by Browning and Singelmann (1978) and a broad 11 category occupation classification scheme. Matrices used to compute the shift-share analyses involved 407 job cells. However, because two occupational categories—farmers and farm laborers—are only found in the agricultural industry, 72 of the 407 cells were structurally impossible and contained no observations. Our analyses which use jobs as analytic units, consequently, are based on the 335 cells created by the industry by occupation matrix.

Shift-Share Technique

The shift-share technique used here was adapted from Singelmann and Browning (1980). This technique, which is a form of standardization, permits us to decompose changes in the occupation structure into three components. The *industry shift effect* represents the net change in the occupational structure between two points in time which is attributable to the transformation of the industry structure, net of the effects of intercensal growth, changes in the intraindustry occupational mix, and the interaction of industry and occupational mix effects. The *occupational mix effect* results from changes in the technical division of labor within industries (intraindustry occupational composition), net of the effects of other components. Finally, the third component is an *interaction effect*, which reflects the changes in the occupational structure arising from the joint influence of industry shifts and occupational mix effects.[4]

The sum of the industry shifts, occupational mix shifts, and interaction shifts, denoted as the *net shift effect* in our tables, indicates the extent to which the labor force (male or female) in a given occupation grew or declined faster than the growth of the total labor force. Thus, the net shifts and their constituent parts are crucial for addressing whether the growth of specific jobs (and the mechanisms underlying that growth) contributed to the closing or widening of the gender gap in earnings.

Structural Change Measures

For each of the 335 job cells, we generated several structural measures based on their incumbents' social and demographic characteristics, and changes in these characteristics over time. Variables of central interest for the questions addressed below include mean earnings, gender composition (percent female), mean education, mean age, percent Hispanic, and percent black. Since these characteristics were computed for both men and women and for both years, our file of jobs permits us to compute measures of change in these characteristics during the intercensal period. Our primary concern was in computing a change measure of the sex composition of jobs.

We also appended to the file of job cells, two measures of structural change gauging the relative importance of industry shifts and changing intraindustry occupational mix in accounting for the relative prevalence of a given job cell in the 1980 employment structure. These shift measures, denoted the *industry shift* and *occupation mix* were generated as by-products from the shift-share analysis, and are also gender specific. The two structural change measures are expressed as follows, in algebraic terms:

Industry Shift

$$s_{ijk_{2-1}} = \frac{n_{ijkt_2} - \hat{n}_{ijkt_2}}{n_{ijkt_1}}$$

Occupational Mix

$$o_{ijkt_{2-1}} = \frac{n_{ijkt_2} - \hat{\hat{n}}_{ijkt_2}}{n_{ijkt_1}}$$

where, i = detailed industry $(1 \ldots 37)$
I = industry marginal
j = broad occupation $(1 \ldots 11)$
J = occupational category marginal
k = gender
N = size of labor force
t_1 = 1970
t_2 = 1980

$$\hat{n} = \frac{n_{ijkt_1}}{n_{Ikt_1}} \left(n_{ikt_2} \right)$$

$$\hat{\hat{n}} = \left(\frac{n_{ijkt_2}}{n_{Ikt_2}} \right) \left[\frac{(n_{Ikt_1}) \, (n_{IJkt_2})}{N_{IJkt_1}} \right]$$

Expressed algebraically, these measures appear more complex than they are computationally. The formulation of both involves subtraction of an expected 1980 cell size, say $\hat{n}_{ijkt_2}$ from the observed cell size n_{ijkt_2}, under differing assumptions about how labor force growth and structural reallocation manifested themselves in the employment structure. The expected cell size holds the key to interpreting these changes. In the industrial shift measure, we hold constant the occupational composition by assuming that the 1970 intraindustry occupational structure did not change over the period. Allowing for observed employment changes among industries between 1970 and 1980, we derive the actual industry shift by subtracting the expected count under the assumption of no occupational restructuring within industries. Likewise, the occupation mix effect is computed by subtracting from the 1980 actual cell counts an expected cell count, $\hat{\hat{n}}_{ijkt_2}$, which is derived assuming a constant industry structure. Thus, reversing the standard (*i.e.,* holding constant the industry structure rather than the intraindustry occupational mix) enables us to isolate the effect of occupational restructuring within industries on the overall occupational structure.[5]

Empirical Analyses

We begin our empirical analysis by presenting descriptive data about women's mean earnings, the gender gap in earnings, and the sex composition of broad occupation groups. Subsequently, we describe differences in the process of occupational change between men and women during the most recent intercensal decade. These results show the relative importance of industrial transformation and intraindustry occupational reorganization in altering the aggregate occupational structures of men and women.

The remainder of our analysis links the process of occupational change for men and women with the average earnings they received in 1979, depending on the job they held at the time. In this endeavor, we analyze the average earnings associated with 335 jobs in 1979. By performing separate analyses of average male and female earnings in these jobs, we hold sex constant while estimating the effects of our two structural shift measures and changing gender composition on the average earnings of men and women in a specific job.

RESULTS

The argument that an increasing feminization of the labor force is associated with greater earnings disparities between men and women finds little support in our tabulations for the 1970—80 intercensal period. Data presented in Table 2.1 show that the aggregate gender gap in annual earnings decreased slightly (from .58 to .60) as the total labor force became more feminized. However, this relationship varied among the broad occupational groups.

A cursory examination of the changes in the gender composition of occupations and their accompanying female/male earnings disparities reveals the complexity of the aggregate association. For several occupational groups, the female/male earnings ratio remained fairly stable over the period despite substantial to modest increases in the share of women they employed. This pattern characterized not only the high status professional and semiprofessional categories, but also the semiskilled blue collar craft and operative occupations and the female-dominated clerical occupations.

Only in service occupations did the representation of women workers decline between 1970 and 1980, but the decrease was slight—about 1.5 percentage points. This decline in women's presence was accompanied by a smaller earnings gap between men and women. Only in the farmer occupation was the increased presence of women accompanied by a sharp increase in the earnings gap—roughly 32 percentage points. In all of the remaining occupational categories, the average earnings gap between men and women decreased over the decade anywhere from 4–5 percentage points (managers; service workers; laborers) to over 10 percentage points (farm laborers; sales workers). Moreover, all but one of these occupational

Table 2.1. Changes in Mean Earnings and Gender Composition of Broad Occupation Groups, 1970–1980 (Full-Time, Year-Round Workers)

	1970			1980		
	Women's Mean Annual Earnings[a]	F/M Earnings Ratio	Percent Female	Women's Mean Annual Earnings[a]	F/M Earnings Ratio	Percent Female
Professional	$7,119	.64	24.9	$13,837	.63	35.2
Semiprofessional	$6,224	.66	22.2	$11,764	.65	36.4
Farmer	$1,057	.84	3.8	$1,713	.52	7.2
Manager	$5,800	.51	13.4	$12,621	.55	22.7
Clerical	$5,218	.63	67.1	$10,391	.62	73.2
Sales	$3,890	.41	22.7	$10,170	.54	26.8
Craft	$5,377	.65	4.1	$11,196	.67	6.1
Operative	$4,411	.61	23.4	$9,355	.61	26.7
Service	$3,317	.52	45.4	$7,449	.57	44.0
Laborer	$3,970	.65	7.1	$8,928	.70	11.2
Farm Laborer	$1,698	.43	9.9	$4,757	.53	15.9
Overall Averages	$4,958	.58	27.4	$10,664	.60	33.8

Source: U.S. Bureau of the Census, 1970 and 1980 Public Use Microdata Samples.
[a]Rounded to nearest dollar; annual earnings correspond to 1969 and 1979, respectively.

categories (service workers) became more feminized during the 1970s, with the greatest increase corresponding to the traditionally male-dominated managerial category.

On balance, the increased representation of women among (all but one) broad occupational categories did not change the sex-stereotyping patterns in any significant way. Occupations that were highly male-dominated at the beginning of the period remained so at its close. Not surprisingly, clerical employment became more female-dominated, as the share of women workers in this occupation rose from 67 to 73 percent over the 10 year period. For the total labor force the descriptive evidence suggests a weak association between the level of feminization of an occupation and its average economic rewards (see last row, Table 2.1).

Gender and the Process of Occupational Change, 1970–80

Previous research (Norwood, 1980) claimed that the transformation of the employment structure from a goods to a service economy facilitated the entry of women into the labor force. To the extent that this process increased in relative terms the jobs in which women concentrate, and in the absence of forces to reduce the sex-typing of jobs, we would expect an increase in the proportion of the total labor force comprised of women, as occurred during the period under consideration. Results from the shift-share analysis reported in Table 2.2 provide further information about how macrostructural processes responsible for the industrial transformation of employment altered occupational opportunities for men and women during the 1970s.

Recall that the *absolute net shift* indicates whether and by how much a particular occupational category expanded relative to the growth of the labor force. In our analyses these shifts are gender specific. For example, a positive absolute net shift, as occurred for professional men (see first entry in Table 2.3), indicates that the allocation of men into this occupation outpaced the growth of the male labor force during the 1970s. However, the absolute value of the net shifts does not represent *actual* persons. Because some net changes are quite small in magnitude, a larger contribution to net change by either shift component would affect an occupational category less than a smaller share of large net shifts. These scale effects are reflected in the percentage changes. Therefore, to clarify the meaning of these calculations, we expressed the absolute net shifts relative to the size of the occupational category at the beginning of the period, and denoted these relative net shifts.

That the transformation of the employment structure rendered different job opportunities for men and women was most dramatically illustrated by the finding that women experienced positive net shifts in the two lowest status job categories—laborers and farm laborers—while men did not. During the 1970s, the pattern of net shifts for women points to a process of occupational bifurcation whereby women increased their representation among both the high status and low status occupations. This pattern did not occur for men except to the extent that the positive net shift in service occupations may have involved deskilling or routinization of their jobs. We could not address this possibility with our data, however.

The overall picture of occupational change shown in Table 2.2 does contain some encouraging news. Positive net shifts in the three highest status occupations for both men and women indicate substantial upgrading of the occupational structure. In fact, the rate at which women entered these occupations, as reflected by the relative net shifts, was greater than that experienced by men. These results are consistent with those reported in Table 2.1 which showed increasing feminization of the higher-status occupations during the 1970s.

The positive effects of the industrial transformation and the intraindustry occupational mix on the relative expansion of the higher-status occupations are especially important because of what they portend for occupational mobility in the future. However, optimism generated by the finding of occupational upgrading must be tempered by acknowledging results of other studies which show that within the high status occupational groups, women tend to occupy the lower paying jobs, and those which are highly gender typed, such as nursing, teaching and social work professions (see Norwood, 1982). The differing relative importance of industrial shifts and intraindustry occupational mixes on occupational changes between men and women is important because this holds one of the keys to unlocking the mechanisms of occupational segregation and differential economic rewards. We provide supporting evidence in the final part of this section.

Our results provide clues about the mechanisms that produce occupational segregation. While both men and women benefited from the employment changes which increased professional, semiprofessional, and managerial job opportunities, the relative importance of industrial and occupational mix components differed by sex. Yet, in some ways the mechanisms producing the observed occupational upgrading were similar for men and women. For example, the expansion of industries utilizing professional, semiprofessional, and managerial occupations contributed relatively less than the reorganization of industries toward a greater reliance on highly skilled occupations (as reflected in the industry and occupation net shifts expressed in percentages). Male professional employment stands as a notable exception. Changing occupation mixes of industries accounted for virtually all of the increase in managerial employment over the decade for both men and women, yet the transformation of the industrial structure reinforced the relative expansion of management positions.[6]

For women, it was the intraindustry occupational restructuring process which largely accounted for their increased representation in professional and semiprofessional jobs. Between half and three-fourths of the growth of professional and semiprofessional jobs due to occupational recomposition of industries can be traced to social service (medical services, hospitals, and public administration) and retail trade industries. The reinforcing (albeit modest) industrial shifts resulting in the growth of professional and semiprofessional positions for women involved medical and hospital industries.

In contrast to women, the growth of industries requiring professionals accounted for most of the increase in male professional employment during the 1970s, with most of this expansion occurring in the legal and miscellaneous producer services, in medical services, and in the education industry. The industry shift and occupation mix effects which increased semiprofessional employment for men during the 1970s were of roughly equal magnitude and mutually reinforcing. Expansion of engineering firms, miscellaneous producer services, and hospitals accounted for most of the positive industry shift effect, while approximately half of the occupation recomposition effect involved hospitals and miscellaneous manufacturing enterprises.

The farmer occupation exhibits a peculiar pattern of change resulting in a net increase for women and a net decrease for men. For the latter, the negative shift continues a long-term trend of shrinking employment opportunities in the agricultural industry owing to extensive mechanization and

Table 2.2. Components of Occupational Change by Gender, 1970–1980

Occupation	Absolute Net Shift	Relative Net Shift	Components of Net Shift (Absolute Changes)			Components of Net Shift (In Percent)		
			Industry Shift Effect	Occupation Shift Effect	Interaction Shift Effect	Industry Shift Effect	Occupation Shift Effect	Interaction Shift Effect
				Men				
Professionals	7453.0	.132	5297.8	1922.1	233.1	71.1	25.8	3.1
Semiprofessionals	2663.4	.248	1241.7	1477.9	−56.2	46.6	55.5	−2.1
Farmers	−4149.6	−.311	−3026.9	−1391.9	269.3	72.9	33.5	−6.5
Managers	15920.3	.302	1487.0	14917.5	−484.3	9.3	93.7	−3.0
Clericals	−948.8	−.026	−514.2	−384.9	−49.6	54.2	40.6	5.2
Sales	−3706.6	−.109	−647.6	−3513.2	454.2	17.5	94.8	−12.3
Crafts	−7128.2	−.072	−740.7	−5534.5	−852.9	10.4	77.6	12.0
Operatives	−10486.4	−.113	−5684.1	−5328.8	521.4	54.2	50.8	−5.0
Service Workers	4738.2	.120	6178.1	−1300.7	−139.2	130.4	−27.5	−2.9
Laborers	−2154.8	−.068	−1828.1	−317.4	−9.4	84.8	14.7	0.4
Farm Laborers	−2200.6	−.283	−1763.0	−551.0	113.4	80.1	25.0	−5.2
Total	0.0		0.0	0.1	−0.2			

	Women							
Professionals	9683.9	.235	2030.3	6712.9	940.7	21.0	69.3	9.7
Semiprofessionals	5400.2	1.180	768.8	4258.8	372.6	14.2	78.9	6.9
Farmers	210.6	.291	241.4	-25.0	-5.8	114.6	-11.9	-2.8
Managers	13224.9	1.249	990.2	12002.7	232.1	7.5	90.8	1.8
Clericals	919.1	.009	10035.8	-5956.6	-3160.1	1092.0	-648.1	-343.8
Sales	-3478.1	-.162	-1486.2	-2924.6	932.7	42.7	84.1	-26.8
Crafts	584.9	.110	-556.6	1579.2	-437.7	-95.1	270.0	-74.8
Operatives	-14204.4	-.342	-9214.1	-5663.3	673.0	64.9	39.9	-4.7
Service Workers	-13854.1	-.232	-2986.7	-11496.4	629.0	21.6	83.0	-4.5
Laborers	1361.5	.461	-271.1	1744.7	-112.2	-19.9	128.1	-8.2
Farm Laborers	151.5	.113	448.3	-232.3	-64.5	295.9	-153.3	-42.6
Total	0.0		0.1	0.0	-0.1			

Source: U.S. Bureau of the Census, 1970 and 1980 Public Use Microdata Samples.

increases in the scale of farming operations. These structural changes in U.S. agriculture have greatly reduced the number of farmers since World War II, and are captured by the negative and reinforcing industry and intra-industry occupational shifts on the prevalence of farming occupations for men. For women, a rather unexpected positive shift effect emerged, representing a 30 percent increase over the decade. We suspect that this reflects the tendency for women to inherit farms from their spouses or parents because the number of farmers has declined steadily over the past two decades, although somewhat more slowly during the 1970s (Singelmann and Tienda, 1985).

Among lower level nonmanual occupations (sales and clerical occupations), the process of occupational change also differed between men and women. Male employment in these categories decreased owing to mutually reinforcing negative industry shift and occupational mix effects, but the pattern for women was more complex. While women's employment in sales occupations failed to keep pace with the growth of the female labor force as a consequence of the reorganization of retail establishments, their presence in clerical jobs expanded through the 1970s. That women's involvement in clerical work experienced a large and positive absolute shift, but only a modest *relative* net shift, reflects the high concentration of women in this occupation at the beginning of the period. The continued expansion of clerical occupations resulted exclusively from the expansion of industries that utilize clerical workers, particularly banking, miscellaneous producer services, and public administration. The vigorous growth of these industries offset the declines in clerical employment resulting from the intraindustry occupational reorganization away from clerical jobs.

Of the manual occupations, only in operatives did men and women undergo similar patterns of change during the decade. The decrease of operative employment during the 1970s, which continued a long-term secular trend (Singelmann and Browning, 1980), resulted from mutually reinforcing negative effects of the industrial transformation and the intraindustry occupational restructuring processes. For women, the industrial transformation was the more dominant factor in this change, accounting for over half of the decrease of operative workers between 1970 and 1980, while for men both mechanisms contributed roughly equally to this decline. Similarly, both the industrial transformation and the intraindustry occupational restructuring process contributed to the decline of craft jobs for men, with the latter dominating the net decrease. Women, on the other hand, experienced net gains in this occupation owing largely to the reorganization of textile, machine, and miscellaneous manufacturing firms. The restructuring processes affecting women crafts workers most likely involve an increased reliance on off-site piece work, deskilling of job tasks, and in electronics industries, the use of equipment requiring dexterity and patience.

Overall, our results on occupational transformation generate optimism and pessimism about the prospects for reducing gender differences in occupational placement. On the positive side is the evidence of occupational upgrading enjoyed by both men and women. This optimism must be tempered by noting that women increased their presence in the lowest status jobs during the decade, while men did not. Nevertheless, if the changes in the employment structure signaling an increased representation of women in professional, semiprofessional, and managerial occupations have improved the labor market position of women relative to men, we would expect positive correlations between the structural measures gauging the influence of both the industrial shifts and changed intraindustry occupational mix on the average earnings of men and women, and negative correlations with the gender gap in earnings. Such evidence would establish links between the processes which transform the employment structure and gender inequality in earnings. Moreover, it would indicate whether the transformation of the economy toward services and high tech industries—those presumably requiring less physical stamina—holds promise for achieving earnings parity between men and women.

To the extent that the process of job segregation was itself advanced by the structural transformation of the economy from goods to service production, improvements in women's labor market position which manifest themselves as a greater representation in high status jobs could be offset by an increased concentration in jobs which are highly gender typed. Thus, if the transformation of the employment structure was accompanied by continued intraoccupational segregation such that the changing prevalence of specific jobs merely resulted in new sex-typed boundaries for jobs, it is conceivable that the improvements in women's occupational allocation made possible by the structural transformation of the economy would be offset in whole or in part by the persistence and redefinition of job segregation.

Based on past research which shows a negative correlation between the percent of a job comprised by women and its associated average earnings (Norwood, 1982), we expect a negative correlation between the level of feminization of jobs and their average earnings. Furthermore, we expect that the level and rate of feminization of a job would condition the influence on earnings of the industrial restructuring process. The following section evaluates these propositions.

Industrial Transformation, Job Feminization,
and Gender Disparities in Earnings

Table 2.3 summarizes the influence of structural change on the 1979 average earnings of women and men using the 335 job cells as units of observation. Model (1) regressed average earnings[7] for each sex on the like-sex measures of industrial transformation and intraindustry occupational recomposition, and a set of controls which covary with earnings (mean education, mean age, and race/ethnic composition of jobs). Models (2) and (4) each introduced an additional structural attribute of jobs, respectively the 1980 gender composition (percent female) and the interdecade difference in gender composition (1980 percent female minus 1970 percent female). The cross-sectional measure shows whether, net of interdecade structural shifts which altered the relative preponderance of positions, and in accordance with other findings (England and McLaughlin, 1979; Bridges, 1980), there persisted a negative correlation between the gender composition of jobs and their average earnings levels. Likewise, the interdecade difference measure indicates whether the changed representation of women among jobs influenced the relative valuation of the work performed, and, consequently, the average economic rewards received. Models (3) and (5) add the interactions between the structural industry and occupation shift measures and each of the gender composition measures. The upper and lower panels of Table 2.3 report the results for women and men, respectively.

Model (1) shows that the intraindustry occupational restructuring process was associated with higher earnings for both men and women in 1979, while the influence of industrial shifts was statistically trivial for both. Although it appears that men benefited more than women from the changing occupational mix of industries, the observed differences in the metric coefficients are not statistically different from each other. Our previous analysis suggests that the net positive influence on earnings of intraindustry restructuring was a direct outcome of occupational upgrading during the decade (See Table 2.2). Since the structural change variables are measured in very small increments, the metric coefficients, expressed in dollars, are quite large. However the standardized coefficients (in parentheses), while not comparable between men and women, show in relative terms the magnitudes of the effects of occupational restructuring versus industrial change on the average wages of men and women.

Models (2) and (4), which introduce the effects of gender composition on average earnings, concur with the findings of others (England and McLaughlin, 1979; Bridges, 1980) in showing that incumbents of female-typed jobs received lower average earnings compared to those engaged in male-typed jobs. Both men and women were penalized for incumbency in female-dominated jobs, but this penalty was statistically greater for men (T-test between coefficients = 2.28). Note also that the introduction of the gender composition term altered the influence of the structural change terms for men and women in different ways. For women, this resulted in a slight attenuation of the influence of occupational restructuring, while increasing the influence (and statistical significance) of the industrial transformation term. Just the opposite occurred for men. That is, after adjusting for the effects of gender composition on earnings, the positive influence of occupational recomposition on men's average earnings was enhanced, rather than attenuated, and the influence of industrial restructuring rendered even more trivial.

A comparison of the magnitudes of the standardized coefficients within gender models provides further evidence about the relative importance and potentially offsetting influences of these sources of change. Whereas for men the stronger negative effect of holding a highly female-typed job swamped the (weak) positive earnings benefits stemming from intraindustry occupational recomposition by a factor of 2.4, for women only half of the earnings bonus associated with occupational recomposition was offset by higher levels of job femininity in 1980. Stated differently, women's 1979 average earnings reflected a strong negative effect of incumbency in female-typed jobs which was only partly compensated by the positive influence of occupational restructuring. For men the pattern was roughly similar, but the relative magnitudes of these effects were quite different.

Model (4) produced additional evidence of different effects of gender composition on men's and women's earnings. At first glance, these results appear inconsistent with those based on the model with the additive measure of gender composition, but upon careful inspection they actually reinforce the contention that structural change in the organization of work affords men and women different rewards. Note that for women an increase in the female composition of jobs between 1970 and 1980 was of no consequence for their average annual earnings. In contrast, men received a strong positive earnings bonus for incumbency in jobs where the representation of women increased over the decade. Moreover, after adjusting for the interdecade change in the gender composition of jobs, the effects on men's earnings of intraindustry occupational recomposition or industrial restructuring became insignificant.

That the gender composition of jobs not only rendered unequal rewards to men and women, but also altered the influence of the structural change measures in different ways, depending on sex, suggests the existence of a complex interaction between the processes of industrial and occupational restructuring and the redefinition of gender boundaries in the employment structure. We examine this possibility in models (3) and (5) which introduce terms representing the interactions among the two structural change measures (*i.e.*, industrial shift and occupational mix) and the alternative measures of gender composition. A comparison of the goodness of fit statistic (R^2) indicates that model (3) is the most parsimonious for both men and women. Accordingly, we focus our discussion on this set of results.

Taking into account the possibility that patterns of occupational segregation by sex condition the influence of changing employment opportunities, produces a different picture of the structural determinants of men's and women's earnings. One important difference is that the influence of the industrial restructuring process rather than the intraindustry occupational recomposition process emerges as the salient determinant of earnings for both men and women, but in markedly different ways. Note that the main effects of industrial shifts differ in sign between men and women, as do the

Table 2.3. Effects[a] of Industry Shift, Occupational Mix and Gender Composition on Average 1979 Earnings for 335 Jobs (Beta Coefficients in Parentheses)

Independent Variables	Models				
			Women		
	(1)	(2)	(3)	(4)	(5)
Female Occupational Mix	679**	591**	865	566*	703**
	(.165)	(.144)	(.210)	(.138)	(.171)
Female Industrial Shift	323	340†	−2586*	275	143
	(.069)	(.073)	(−.556)	(.059)	(.031)
Percent Female, 1980	—	−2770**	−2966**	—	—
		(−.229)	(−.246)		
Percent Female 1980 X Female Occupational Mix	—	—	−336	—	—
			(−.055)		
Percent Female 1980 X Female Industrial Shift	—	—	4034**	—	—
			(.647)		
Change in Percent Female, 1970 to 1980	—	—	—	3537	4214
				(.073)	(.087)
Change in Percent Female X Female Occupational Mix	—	—	—	—	−4327
					(−.086)
Change in Percent Female X Female Industrial Shift	—	—	—	—	6112
					(.061)
Constant	−13013	−9942	−9713	−12559	−11851
R^2	.467	.516	.533	.471	.478

<table>
			Men		
Male Occupational Mix[b]	1617*	1884*	1781*	1436	1886*
	(.084)	(.098)	(.093)	(.075)	(.098)
Male Industrial Shift[b]	368	51	3763*	697	514
	(.019)	(.003)	(.193)	(.036)	(.026)
Percent Female, 1980	—	−5431**	−4696**	—	—
		(−.237)	(−.205)		
Percent Female 1980 X Male Occupational Mix	—	—	2696	—	—
			(.029)		
Percent Female 1980 X Male Industrial Shift	—	—	−9152*	—	—
			(−.219)		
Change in Percent Female, 1970 to 1980	—	—	—	9380*	10281*
				(.095)	(.105)
Change in Percent Female X Male Occupational Mix	—	—	—	—	−14960
					(−.038)
Change in Percent Female X Male Industrial Shift	—	—	—	—	5784
					(.015)
Constant	−11396	−13311	−13453	−10428	−9888
R^2	.516	.552	.561	.523	.524
</table>

Source: U.S. Bureau of the Census, 1970 and 1980 Public Use Microdata Samples.

[a]Net of the effects of mean education, mean age, and race/ethnic composition of job cells.

[b]Defined in text.

*$p < .05$
**$p < .001$
†$p < .10$
note: dash denotes coefficient omitted from equation.

interaction effects conditioned by occupational segregation. Also, model (3) shows that the earning-enhancing effects of occupational recomposition remain statistically significant for men, but not for women.

Figure 2.1 depicts this relationship graphically for easier visual appreciation of the complex statistical interaction between changed job opportunities and patterns of gender segregation among them. For the effects of occupational recomposition, the curves are considerably flatter for women than for men, and there are large intercept differences between men and women. In the absence of a statistically significant interaction term between percent female and the male occupational mix coefficients, the incipient tendency toward convergence of the male curves is not substantively meaningful. The essential message derived from the left panel is that men benefited economically more than women from the intraindustry occupational recomposition toward the greater prevalence of higher paying jobs during the 1970s, and that their average gains were lower in those jobs where women were more highly represented. Although the flat curves for women show a trivial main effect of the changing occupational mix of industries on their average earnings in 1979, the statistically significant negative effect of percent female on earnings reinforces the common feature of all comparisons showing that female-dominated jobs paid less in 1979 compared to male-dominated jobs.

In contrast to the occupational mix effects, the influence of industrial restructuring on men's and women's earnings depended on their gender mix. That men stand to benefit from the persistence of gender-based job segregation is illustrated by the two upper curves of Figure 2.2. Substantively, these curves indicate that men's rewards from industrial shifts toward higher-paying jobs were greater among those occupations where women were underrepresented (relative to the average share of women in the labor force), but that such rewards were not forthcoming if the job was female-typed. For women, a more complex relationship obtained whereby the influence on earnings of gender composition depended on the magnitude of industrial restructuring, or more concretely, on the ways in which the rise and decline of specific industries altered the preponderance of occupations which women entered during the decade. Our shift-share analysis indicated which occupations and industries were involved; the present analysis establishes how these processes differentiated the economic rewards received by men and women.

What is disturbing about these results is not only the evidence that the industrial restructuring processes rendered different monetary rewards to economically active men and women, but, based on the opposed effects, the indication that the aggregate wage gap between men and women could have increased as a result of the persistence of gender segregation, were it not counterbalanced by the net tendency toward occupational upgrading. We address this concern in Table 2.4, which replicates the previous analysis with an alternative dependent variable, that is, the 1979 male/female earn-

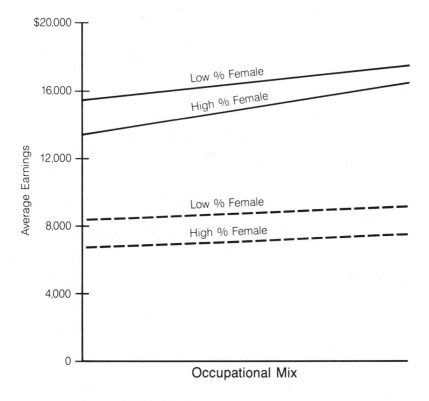

Source: Model 3, Table 3.

Note: High and Low % Female was defined as one standard deviation above and below the mean, respectively.

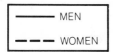

Figure 2.1

ings ratio for each job cell. In an effort to strengthen our conclusion that the industrial restructuring processes and their earnings consequences differed between men and women, we regressed the male/female earnings ratio on both the female and male occupational mix and industrial shift indexes. These results are reported in the upper and lower panels, respectively, of Table 2.4.

That the industrial restructuring processes portend different outcomes for men and women is most starkly illustrated by evidence that changes in women's employment opportunities did not affect the 1979 male/female earnings ratio, while changes in men's employment opportunities sig-

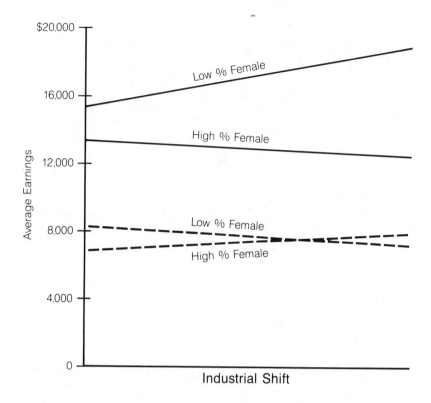

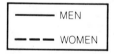

Figure 2.2

nificantly reduced the gender gap in earnings (see column (1), upper and lower panels, respectively). Substantively, these results suggest that if the changing job and income opportunities enjoyed by men during the 1970s were equally extended to women, the aggregate male/female earnings differntial could have been reduced by roughly one-quarter standard deviation ($-.13 + -.11 = -.24$). Recall that men earned 1.7 times what women did in 1979 on an average annual basis. Thus, by allowing women to enter the higher paying jobs which expanded during the 1970s at the same rate that men did, their average pay differential would have been compressed. Under this scenario of employment restructuring (lower panel), changes in the sex ratio of jobs would neither widen nor reduce the average earnings differences between men and women.

Under an alternative scenario where the pattern of changing employment opportunities was defined by the female restructuring process (top panel), the basic strategy for reducing the gender gap in earnings would involve increasing women's presence among all jobs, particularly those where they are relatively underrepresented. This interpretation follows from the strong and statistically significant negative effect of the gender composition term on the male/female earnings ratio, which would be reduced by roughly one-quarter standard deviation for every percentage increase in the gender composition of jobholders.

Use of the percent female difference terms to predict variation in the gender gap in earnings, as in model (4), requires some qualification of these interpretations, although the less precise fit of the model renders the alternative evidence less compelling. The positively signed coefficient for the gender segregation term suggests a widening of the gender gap in earnings as jobs became more feminized. Although seemingly inconsistent with the results based on model (2), a more careful consideration of the meaning of the percent female difference variable makes this result more plausible and consistent with that produced by model (2). That is, since this term does not differentiate among jobs that were highly male- or female-typed at the start of the period, larger absolute percentage changes, which usually signal the continued concentration of women in sex-typed jobs, most likely increase the gender gap in earnings because of the negative correlation between percent female and the average wages of a job. By contrast, smaller increases in the female composition of a job, which often reflect women's entry into male-dominated positions, most likely would decrease the gender gap in earnings.

On balance, results in Table 2.4 call for tempered optimism about the possibility of narrowing the gender gap in earnings either through the industrial restructuring processes, or through an increased feminization of jobs, unless the latter strived for uniformity in women's presence among the array of new and old jobs. To the extent that the industrial restructuring processes opened *different* job opportunities for men and women, it is unlikely that these macrolevel social forces will have much effect in reducing the earnings inequality between the sexes. Moreover, if the patterns of gender segregation are modified as the industrial restructuring processes unfold such that women's entry into male-dominated jobs leads to further job segregation, then it is even less likely that earnings disparities between men and women will be reduced through aggregate occupational upgrading and/ or the increased presence of women in high status professional, technical, and managerial positions.

Table 2.4. Effects[a] of Industry Shift, Occupational Mix and Gender Composition on 1979 Male/Female Earnings Ratio for 335 Jobs (Beta Coefficients in Parentheses)

Independent Variables	Models				
	(1)	(2)	(3)	(4)	(5)

Female Weights

Independent Variables	(1)	(2)	(3)	(4)	(5)
Female Occupational Mix[b]	−.024 (−.042)	−.051† (−.090)	−.156† (−.274)	−.061† (−.107)	−.072† (−.127)
Female Industrial Shift[b]	−.050 (−.071)	−.027 (−.038)	−.096 (−.137)	−.061 (−.086)	−.075 (−.107)
Percent Female, 1980	—	−.329** (−.279)	−.346** (−.294)	—	—
Percent Female, 1980 X Female Occupational Mix	—	—	.183 (.194)	—	—
Percent Female, 1980 X Female Industrial Shift	—	—	.112 (.112)	—	—
Change in Percent Female, 1970 to 1980	—	—	—	.892* (.148)	.737† (.122)
Change in Percent Female X Female Occupational Mix	—	—	—	—	.258 (.042)
Change in Percent Female X Female Industrial Shift	—	—	—	—	.493 (.038)
Constant	1.356	1.359	1.316	1.439	1.503
R^2	.096	.168	.173	.112	.113

Male Weights

Independent Variables	(1)	(2)	(3)	(4)	(5)
Male Occupational Mix	−.193* (−.134)	−.191* (−.132)	−.140 (−.097)	−.191* (−.132)	−.239* (−.166)
Male Industrial Shift	−.126* (−.108)	−.128* (−.109)	−.074 (−.063)	−.131* (−.112)	−.124† (−.106)
Percent Female, 1980	—	−.029 (−.024)	−.021 (−.018)	—	—
Percent Female 1980 X Male Occupational Mix	—	—	−.249 (−.055)	—	—
Percent Female 1980 X Male Industrial Shift	—	—	−.118 (−.053)	—	—
Change in Percent Female, 1970 to 1980	—	—	—	−.176 (−.029)	−.297 (−.049)
Change in Percent Female X Male Occupational Mix	—	—	—	—	1.699 (.065)
Change in Percent Female X Male Industrial Shift	—	—	—	—	−.250 (−.009)
Constant	1.198	1.197	1.225	1.181	1.155
R^2	.222	.222	.224	.223	.225

Source: U.S. Bureau of the Census, 1970 and 1980 Public Use Microdata Samples.
[a]Net of the effects of mean education, mean age, and race/ethnic composition of job cells.
[b]Defined in text.
*$p < .05$
**$p < .001$
†$p < .10$
note: dash denotes coefficient omitted from equation.

DISCUSSION

Our primary objectives were to analyze how the industrial restructuring processes which resulted in the contraction and expansion of specific jobs maintained the average differences in earnings between men and women during the 1970s, and to determine whether the extent of job segregation by sex reinforced or reduced gender-linked earnings differences in 1979. Our story provides a basis for optimism and pessimism about the prospects for narrowing the gender gap in earnings through changes in the nature and organization of work. On the positive side, we observed extensive occupational upgrading for both men and women during the 1970s, and an increase in the share of women engaged in professional, semiprofessional, and managerial jobs. Furthermore, we documented positive earnings effects of industrial shifts and intraindustry occupational recomposition on women's average annual earnings. However, since men also benefited from occupational upgrading and the industrial restructuring of employment, these macrosocial processes have been less effective in narrowing the gender gap in earnings than one might have expected.

We believe that the main reason why the employment restructuring processes were less effective in narrowing the gender gap in earnings is that sex boundaries of jobs were also redefined in such a manner that new patterns of occupational segregation effectively keep men apart from women in the work place. Our results showed that not only did the level of feminization of jobs in 1980 strongly and negatively influence the earnings of both men and women, but the earnings-enhancing effects of industrial restructuring were actually offset and contingent upon the level of feminization of jobs. Since men faced greater income penalties for holding 'female' occupations, they have stronger economic incentives to avoid these jobs. Lamentably, this situation has not changed much despite the massive changes in the nature and organization of work during the past several decades, and the proliferation of legislation designed to reduce discrimination on the basis of sex.

Although the descriptive tabulations reported in Table 2.1 indicated no major changes in the levels of gender typing of occupations during the decade, with such a broad occupational classification it is easy to overlook the ways in which intraindustry occupational segregation results in the devaluation of women's work. The significant interactions between the gender composition of jobs and their changing importance in the overall employment structure, however, lends support to our argument that the benefits of industrial restructuring, which theoretically could provide the conditions for eliminating gender boundaries in the world of work, are mitigated by new patterns of gender-typing. That the aggregate earnings gap did not widen during the 1970s, but actually narrowed slightly—closing from .58 to .60 between 1970 and 1980—reflects the counterbalancing influence of the structural transformation of employment opportunities on men's and women's earnings, coupled with increases in the supply of highly skilled workers.

While providing new insights into the question of the gender gap in earnings, our results are more suggestive than they are conclusive about the underlying mechanisms. They do invite further research which considers in different and innovative ways questions concerning the impact of technological change on employment, and gender differences in occupational roles and economic rewards. Our analysis also raises theoretical questions deserving of further thought and deliberation. The most important is: why should the influence of industrial shifts and intraindustry occupational restructuring render different economic rewards to men and women? Are these the key mechanisms for redefining societal-level boundaries for sextyped occupational roles? Alternatively, do they also hold promise for degendering occupational roles?

Answers to these questions are crucial in order to understand the prospects for closing the gender gap in earnings by the end of the century. Currently there is much discussion about the possible impact of comparable worth policy strategies for narrowing male-female wage differentials. But it is unclear whether this and similar approaches will have any impact in closing the wage gap between men and women as long as the mechanisms of occupational allocation continue to segregate men and women into different positions. These "invisible" sources of wage discrimination could be left essentially unaltered by comparable worth strategies because of their ever-changing nature. Even more discouraging is the possibility that the motors fueling the structural transformation of employment may advance or maintain intact the level of occupational segregation between men and women, even under job configurations adapted to a high-technology economy.

We encourage further research to explore these issues, and to experiment with more fine-grained occupational typologies than we have in this exercise. Additional work should also consider in greater detail than was possible in this analysis the implications of the changed occupational classification scheme for the extent of upgrading the occupational structure. And, future elaborations of this line of work should seek to establish whether members of various racial and ethnic groups benefited uniformly from the structural transformation of employment, and in what ways. Given the high-tech orientation of rapidly growing job categories, it is conceivable that more educated groups may benefit from a growing demand for their skills more than was true in the past.

NOTES

1. For detailed discussion of this point, see England and McLaughlin, 1979.
2. Their empirical results, as well as our own, are consistent with this premise.

3. Upgrading refers to the increased prevalence of professional, semiprofessional, and managerial occupations as a share of all occupations.

4. For further discussion of the details of the computational procedure, see Singelmann and Browning, 1980.

5. By virtue of computing sex-specific standardization exercises, the structural change indexes are weighted by the relative distribution of men and women among job cells.

6. The shifts in managerial employment are complicated by the change in the occupational classification scheme adopted by the Bureau of the Census in 1980. Specifically, in 1980 the Bureau reclassified several jobs as managers which in 1970 were classified as professional and semiprofessional jobs. Since perfect comparability of the 1980 and 1970 occupational classifications is not possible, the magnitude of the increase in managerial employment for both men and women must be interpreted with caution.

7. We did not log the dependent variable because the distribution of cell means did not warrant such transformation. Moreover, semi-log functions often distort significance tests for complex interaction terms, such as those we compute.

CHAPTER 3

The Increase of Black and White Women in the Professions: A Contradictory Process

Natalie J. Sokoloff*

In an attempt to explore both real and illusory progress of women in the world of paid work, I will examine professional jobs. A significantly larger number of women, both black and white, have entered the professions and male-dominated professions in particular, since 1960—most particularly since 1970. Yet, this impressive increase does not necessarily represent a genuine betterment in the lives of all groups of professional women in our society. Further, while it is true that black women have increased numeri-cally in the professions, we need to challenge the claims that black women have allegedly gained on white women (and men) in the professions as the major beneficiaries of Civil Rights and women's movements. In short, this paper addresses the question of whether there is a decrease in the sex segregation of professional occupations, as many have suggested, for women in general and black women in particular, and what this might mean for professional women.[1] I develop the theory that this change process has contradictory aspects.

Recent newspaper headlines have proclaimed all kinds of gains for women and racial/ethnic minorities in the professions: "Census Shows

The author would like to thank the faculty and students at the Women's Seminar of Johns Hopkins University, where the ideas in this article were first presented in February 1984, as well as the members of the Women and Work Study Group, and especially Chris Bose, for helpful and encouraging comments. Also, my gratitude to Rachel Bernstein for her insightful editorial comments on an earlier version of this material. This article was presented, in its revised version, at the American Sociological Association Meetings, Washington, D.C., August 1985.

Gains in Jobs by Women and Blacks in 70s" (Herbers, 1983), "More Women Work at Traditional Male Jobs" (Prial, 1982), "Women Far Surpass Men in Gains in Employment Over the Recession" (Peterson, 1983), "Women Now the Majority in Professions" (Greer, 1986). These articles erroneously lead us to believe women are doing well in general and particularly in the most prestigious and rewarding occupations in our society: the professions. However, while it is absolutely true that there is a real and significant numerical increase of women entering elite male professions today, such an increase does *not* mean: (1) that women are equal to men in the professions, (2) that women are doing very well, or (3) that black women are doing the best. In fact, I will try to show that such conclusions erroneously support the myth of equality between men and women, black and white, in the professions today.

Before I continue to show how women's presence has increased in the professions, I want to address the issue of *why* I have chosen this topic. To begin, I believe it is important to understand that the processes affecting professional women are part of the same processes affecting the vast majority of women in U.S. society. Within this context, it is important to take into account the following issues.

First, one might reasonably argue professional women represent a small percent of all employed women (16.5 percent in 1980) and a more privileged sector of society. How much better it would be to study the problems and needs of the 80 percent employed women who work in low pay, low status, segregated jobs without much if any career mobility or security.

In fact, this argument is of utmost importance and was successfully made in the 1970s. In the 1960s, social science research focused on women in the professions (*e.g.,* see Etzioni, 1969; Theodore, 1971). The 1970s saw a shift to the needs and experiences of nonprofessional or working class women (*e.g.,* Howe, 1977; Feldberg and Glenn, 1977; Walshok, 1981). During this period much was learned about the underlying social, political, economic, and gender-biased processes which led to a huge increase of female employment post-World War II and a concentration of these women in poorly paid, low status, less than year-round/full-time, segmented jobs in clerical, service and factory assembly work (see Sokoloff, 1980). Now it is time to understand how many of these underlying social processes affect more privileged professional women within the context of a changing labor process—and therefore not in isolation from nonprofessional workers.

Second, even though the professions represent a small percent (less than 20 percent in 1980) of all workers, they are seen as the most desirable occupations in our society. These beliefs influence career decisions people make. So long as the professions are seen as prestigious and desirable, it is important to learn the ways in which professions are changing and how these changes are involved in the inclusion of ever greater numbers of women, black and white, especially in the recent past. Thus, in this regard, one might ask: are women who enter the professions today entering the same kind of high status, high paying, powerful jobs men entered in the past or has something dramatic changed? And do black women enter the professions in the same or different ways as white women?

Moreover, with regard to career decisions, people are encouraged to get as much education as possible for professional jobs which are said to require newer and more sophisticated levels of skills. However, large numbers of college graduates cannot find jobs for which they are trained (Sargent, 1982; Rumberger and Levin, 1983); and since the late 1970s, a "glut" of doctors, lawyers, college and noncollege teachers is said to exist in the professional jobs market (Barbanel, 1980; Reinhold, 1980). And while the number of jobs in elite professions *did* increase greatly over the last decade, current data and future employment predictions indicate the largest number of professional jobs will be in the lowest status, poorest paying ones: in fact, the only two professional jobs to be included in the top twenty of all jobs in the labor market with the greatest numerical gain potential between 1978–1990 were nurses and elementary school teachers (Leon, 1982; Rumberger and Levin, 1983).

Third, it has been most common for researchers and policymakers to focus on the *differences* between professional and nonprofessional women. It is essential to respect and struggle over real life differences in opportunities, daily living, and rewards experienced by professional vs. nonprofessional women, white vs. racial/ethnic women (see Dill, 1983; Higginbotham, this volume). However, I want to argue it is *also* important to focus on *similarities* of experience among these different groups of women. In this way we may be able to create alliances that encourage different groups of women (and men) to investigate broader social forces underlying many of the occupational changes they experience (both positive and negative) and determine common goals in their work for the betterment of all women (and men)—all the while acknowledging and struggling over differences among women. This may help different groups of people to *not* look so much at each other as "the problem," but to refocus questions toward the broader issues which affect both groups and force them to compete with each other for the same small piece of the pie.

Thus, to be sure, middle class educated women are more confident in job prospects and life chances than less privileged women. However, the bureaucratization and segmentation of professional work (see Larson, 1977) is not unlike the rationalization of work experienced by many groups of nonprofessional women (see Feldberg and Glenn, 1977) and has serious implications not only for professional and nonprofessional women as a group but also for black and white women within each of these areas of work (*e.g.*, see Aldridge, 1975; Higginbotham, this volume).

Next, cuts by the Reagan administration in health, education, and social services mean job losses for women in some of the best paying, highest status jobs for black and white women in traditional and nontraditional jobs, since professional and minority women are more likely to work for government than private industry (Shea, et al., 1970; Higginbotham, this volume). Finally, whatever growth for black and white women that occurred in the professions as they were expanding needs to be questioned during periods of contraction or at least slow expansion today and in the future.

In short, we need to focus on both similarities and differences between diverse groups of women in order to develop strategies for combating systematic sex, race, and class discrimination in the labor force. This can be accomplished, in part, by clarifying those processes that affect the progress and lack thereof of both black and white women in the professions.

THE NUMERICAL INCREASE OF BLACK AND WHITE WOMEN IN THE PROFESSIONS

Although it is erroneous to conclude, as many newspaper accounts do, that women's accomplishments in the professions have lead to far greater equality with men, it is important to recognize the very real numerical increase of women in the professions. This is particularly true in the male-dominated professions, and for black as well as white women. A review of the data between 1960 and 1980 is instructive.

To begin, the index of sex segregation shows a steady and steep decline in sex segregation in the professions since 1950, with a sharp decline during the 1970s explained mainly by the increase of women into male-dominated occupations (see Burris and Wharton, 1982; Jacobs, n.d.; Beller, 1984; Rytina and Bianchi, 1984).[2]

Next, between 1960 and 1980 it is easy to see that an increasing proportion of all employed women are in the "professional/technical/kindred" occupational category: from 12 percent in 1960 to 16.5 percent in 1980 (USDL, BLS, 1980; USDL, BLS, *Employment and Earnings,* 1983). For black women, the gain is even more dramatic with almost a doubling of black women in professional/technical occupations: from less than 8 percent in 1960 to about 14 percent in 1980.

Some of the most impressive gains have occurred in the upper tier of predominantly male-dominated professions. Between 1970 and 1980 alone, all women at least doubled their representation in most of the high status male-dominated professions (see Table 3.1).

Take the legal profession as an example. Between 1910 and 1960, the percentage of women lawyers grew from 1.1 percent to only 3.3 percent of all lawyers. By 1970, these numbers almost doubled (from 7,543 in 1960 to 13,000 in 1970) to reach 4.7 percent of all lawyers. But between 1970 and 1980 alone, the numbers jumped dramatically to 62,000 and represented 12 percent of all lawyers. More women entered the legal profession in the past decade than during the rest of the entire century (Epstein, 1983). In terms of law school, the figures are even more impressive. Here, women moved from 3.8 percent of law students in 1963 to 8.5 percent in 1970, but to a full

Table 3.1 Percent of Women in Male-Dominated Professions, 1970, 1980

	1970	1980
Physician	7%	13%
Dentist	3	7
Lawyer & Judge	5	14
Clergy	3	6
Engineer	2	5
College Faculty	19	37

Sources: 1970 data: USDL, BLS, 1980;
    1980 data: USDC, BC, 1983a.

one-third (33.5 percent) in 1980. Not only was there a tremendous rate of increase, but the numbers are likewise impressive. There are almost the same number of women in law school today (42,045 in 1980) as there were *all* students (49,552 women and men in 1963) 20 years ago (Epstein, 1983).

If the gains for the white female majority are large—and they are, the gains for black women in male-dominated professions are outstanding. For example, black women showed an almost ten-fold increase between 1970 and 1980 in such male-dominated professions as law (from 446 to 4,272), medicine (from less than 265 to 3,245), and psychology (from 401 to 4,551) (Herbers, 1983). In addition the rate of increase for black women in the professions is also quite high. Between 1966 and 1979, black women increased their representation in all professions 3.5 times (from .6 to 3.2 percent of all professionals)—far greater than any other racial/gender group (Rule, 1982; see also Malveaux, 1981).

If these data are correct, and I believe they are, we must ask if these impressive numerical increases represent genuine progress for women in the professions? We can do this by analyzing a variety of reasons *why* the increases have occurred in the professions (see next paragraph), with particular emphasis on understanding the underlying processes that help explain this increase of women in the professions, especially male-dominated professions.

In the remainder of this paper we will look first at two popular theories that purport to explain women's occupational achievements, followed by two competing theories about the relationship between black and white women's progress in the job market today. After arguing for the inadequacy of these approaches, we will suggest three further areas requiring exploration: (1) an evaluation of the above data which encourages misleading, if not false, conclusions about women's progress in the professions; (2) an evaluation of the meaning and nature of "professions" and how they have changed over time; and (3) an understanding of the changing nature of work in the professions—especially male-dominated ones—and how professional jobs may have changed to include larger numbers of women and racial/ethnic minorities but not in the same way as white males in the past. These explorations lead us to an understanding of black and white women's contradictory progress in the professions.

WOMEN IN THE PROFESSIONS IN GENERAL AND IN MALE-DOMINATED PROFESSIONS IN PARTICULAR: THEORETICAL PERSPECTIVES

Two competing views of women's role in the profession have dominated the empirical and theoretical literature in sociology and economics. The first is known as status attainment, human capital, or individual analysis; the second as occupational sex segregation, dual labor market, or structural theory. (For reviews of this literature, see Sokoloff, 1980, and Fox and Hesse-Biber, 1984.)

The first position argues that women have made dramatic gains in the labor force since the upsurge of the women's movement in the 1960s. As early as 1972, George May Brown, then director of the Census Bureau, said in evaluating the 1970 census data on women: "Women in the seventies are rapidly moving toward full equality" (quoted in Rosenthal, 1972). The reasoning here is that what people bring with them into the labor market— primarily their education, and secondarily their occupational training and experience and sex role training—is said to be the most important determinant of occupational success.

According to this position, if women can get the same education—both qualitatively as well as quantitatively—as men, they should be able to achieve the same occupational status as men in general; and in particular they would be able to make their way into the higher status, more privileged male-dominated professions. What is needed, the argument says, is a resocialization of women to aspire to, educate themselves and train for more prestigious male occupations. They conclude that women's increased participation in the profession is largely due to their getting the needed education and training, and changing their attitudes and behaviors around sex roles, children, and work continuity.

In the 1970s, this position was challenged by those who saw the problems women faced in the labor market not so much as women's own attitudes and qualifications, but the fact that the jobs and labor markets in which women are employed are structurally organized to disadvantage and segregate men and women. Women, they argue, are employed in sectors of the economy characterized by job instability, low capitalization, small profits, low wages, little advancement opportunity or job security, poor worker organization, and high turnover. In short, women are more likely to find employment in low status, low pay, sex segregated occupations such as clerical and service work. This is equally true in the professions in general and within male-dominated professions where women are minimally allowed.

In order to explain women's increased participation in high status male-dominated professions, this competing position looks to broader structural changes—in the economy and in the society. For example, it would look to the importance of broad scale social movements such as Civil Rights, women's movements, Affirmative Action legislation and policies, and occupational expansion, as well as occupational changes such as the increased emphasis on the importance of services in our society.

However, structural theorists have argued, *despite* all these changes on both structural and individual levels, the amount of sex segregation overall and in the professions has remained fairly constant throughout the twentieth century.[3]

Yet, even here, ardent supporters of occupational sex segregation theory are beginning to point out that despite continuing high overall levels of sex segregation throughout the 20th century, women in the more privileged sectors of the job market (professional/managerial) are doing much better than before and better than women in lower status jobs (Burris and Wharton, 1982), or have done much better specifically under Reagan administration policies (Power, 1984).

In short, both popularly prevailing theories argue for the numerical increase of women in the professions but do not adequately explain if this increase means genuine progress for black and white women in the professions. Before we look at several serious problems and omissions in these two types of analyses, let us briefly look at currently popular theories that try to compare the progress of black and white women in the professions today.

BLACK AND WHITE WOMEN IN THE PROFESSIONS

In comparing the progress of black and white women in the professions, two competing views likewise dominate. On the one hand, it has commonly been argued that white women—particularly well-educated, middle class white women—are the major beneficiaries of Affirmative Action and the women's movement (see Rule, 1982) as well as the specific policies of the Reagan administration (see Power, 1984). Thus, white women moved from holding a little more than 1 in 10 professional jobs (13.0 percent) in 1966 to holding almost one-third (31.6 percent) of all such jobs by 1979. In contrast, black women increased from only 0.6 percent of all professionals to a measly 2.2 percent (and black men from 0.7 to 1.9 percent), hardly a challenge to the gains of white women. Moreover, given that 12 percent of the population is black, 4 percent of all professionals being black is a great underrepresentation. While white women are seen as the group with the best chances to move up the occupational, professional, and corporate ladders, neither black men nor black women gain very much, and white males are found to be the major losers: the white male proportion of the total professional labor force dropped from 83.5 percent in 1960 to 58.9 percent in 1979 (Rule, 1982).

In discussing the overall impact of Affirmative Action between 1968 and 1979 (based on unpublished Bureau of the Census data), Malveaux (1981) concludes that despite certain important gains made by black women:

> the gainers of so-called "affirmative action" in the period of 1972 to 1977 have been white women more than anyone else. The rates of change for both black men and black women have declined since 1972, whereas from 1968 to 1972 the major gains were made by black men as opposed to black women. The reasoning is simple. Race was stressed in the 1964 Executive Order; sex was added in 1972. So black men were brought into the workplace in so-called non-black jobs between 1968 and 1972, and the focus switched in a sense to women somewhat thereafter (pp. 44–45).

A second, and more commonly held view in the mass media and some scholarly literature is that not only have women done particularly well over the past 20 years in the professions, but black women are said to have done the best. The advantages experienced by black women are alleged to have led to greater equality between black and white women. Thus, as one journalist reports on a census study comparing 1970 and 1980 occupational data: as women and minorities made remarkable gains during the decade of the 1970s, "black women seem to be the most mobile group of all. Confined mostly to menial jobs in the past, they (black women) made big gains in the professional, service and blue collar work" (Herbers, 1983: 1). To back up such a statement, data are shown that black women lawyers increased from 446 to 1970 to 4,272 in 1980. Likewise, an equally large numerical increase of black women occurred among psychologists, physicians, and computer operators (Herbers, 1983).

As far as the economics of the situation are concerned, the gains of black women in comparison to white women in general are elaborated. Thus, the median income of black women employed full-time, year-round increased from 38 percent of white women workers' incomes in 1939 to nearly 94 percent in 1978. Not only are these data used to show the progress of black women in relation to white women, but they are also used "as evidence that black women have an income advantage over black men because they have closed the gap on white women's earnings at a more rapid pace than black males have closed the gap on white male's earnings" —*i.e.*, black males increased from 45 to only 74 percent of white males incomes during the same time period—(Fox and Hesse-Biber, 1984: 165). Moreover, as the income gap between black and white women in general has closed, among professional, technical, and managerial workers, black women have been found to have somewhat higher earnings, on the average, than white women (Young, 1977).

In addition, the rates of changes made by black women in the professions before and after significant Affirmative Action legislation was implemented are found to be greater than for black men and white women: In one study, black women increased their representation in the professions 3.5 times between 1966-1979, greater than any other racial/gender group (Rule, 1982). In another study, while both black men and women show the greatest rate of change in the professions between 1968-1972, black women alone showed the greatest rate of increase in the professions between 1972-1977. The average annual rate of increase in professional/technical employment in 1968-1972 was 2.7 and in 1972-1977 was 3.9. For black females it was as high as 7.0 in 1968-1972 and 10.6 in 1972-1977 (Malveaux, 1981: 160, Table 3.)

While neither Malveaux nor Rule draw such conclusions, these kinds of data have been used to support the hypothesis that because of their "doubly disadvantaged" status—being black and being female, black women have been able to benefit twice from Affirmative Action thereby outdoing all other disadvantaged groups—including white women and black men. Black men, in particular, are said to be "devastated" psychologically and occupationally (Hare and Hare, 1970: 66) by black women's double oppression which leads to their "unnatural superiority" over black men (Bock, 1971: 128).

This doubly disadvantaged status is sometimes referred to as the "twofer myth" (see Hernandez, 1981: 16; Malveaux, 1981). The "positive effects of the multiple negative" status of black women are argued specifically in the case of black women lawyers and physicians (Epstein, 1973; 1983). Here Epstein argues that black women lawyers and physicians are aided in their pursuits because the combination of the two negative statuses of black and female either cancels each other out or creates a unique position which is not devalued in the labor force. As several authors note, numerous questionable assumptions are embedded in these hypotheses. (*See* Almquist, 1979; Fox and Hesse-Biber, 1984).

Once again, we are left with a rather confused picture about the progress of black women in the professions: one approach argues for the advantages to white women in the professions, the other to the superiority of black women over both white women and black men. Neither, however, use white males, the dominant majority group, as the standard against which to genuinely compare the achievements of black or white professional women in terms of job tasks, power, decision making, prestige, income, etc. Nor do they try to disentangle the impacts of both racial and sexual discrimination simultaneously. (For limited exceptions to this criticism, see Szymanski, 1974; Almquist, 1979. However, neither deal with the question of women's increase in male-dominated professions specifically, 1960-1980.)

In short, the above theories at best only explain the quantitative increase of women in the professions—not the accompanying problem of the highly disadvantaged state these women remain in. Nor do they note that the numerical increase of black women in the professions does not necessarily represent genuine progress for black women today.

Thus, while these theories try to explain women's position in the professions, there are serious problems and omissions in their analyses. Below I would like to suggest several additional or alternative factors that must be explored to understand how the numerical increase is in contradiction to lack of progress on other measures of equality.

The Use and Abuse of Aggregate Data: The Need for a Total Picture

All too often, only the most favorable aspect of aggregate data is stressed. The appearance of progress under these conditions is misleading if not incorrect. For example, between 1970 and 1980, women doubled their participation in several important male-dominated professions: as physicians, dentists, lawyers, clergy, and engineers (see Table 3.1)—a not insignificant finding. In every case, however, the more telling data comparing women's position to men's is underplayed: In 1980, men overwhelmingly dominate the professions to the tune of 85 to 90 percent.

The overstatement of black women's progress in the male-dominated professions demands special consideration. Both numbers and percents are given for the increase of black women in male-dominated professions. That the number of black women increased almost ten-fold in such professions as law and medicine (Herbers, 1983) is of great importance. Yet these data must be interpreted in the context that they make up *less than 1 percent* of all lawyers or doctors in 1980. Such change is hardly a challenge to white males dominating these professions. To say that black women are the major beneficiaries of social movements from the 1950s on—based on these results—is simply wrong.

Furthermore, in addition to the numerical growth, the *rate of growth* of women in the professions can be quite high. Yet this high rate of growth can be grossly overstated since it is often based on a very small number of women being in these jobs in the past. For the professions in general, the proportion of professional jobs held by black women multiplied more than 3.5 times between 1966–1979. For black men and white women it increased only 2.5 times. And for white men, their proportion of professional jobs decreased by 29 percent. However, despite these gains (for all but white males), black women still end up with only 2.2 percent of all professional jobs in 1979. It is obvious that the ten-fold increase of women is so high only because the base numbers at which the count for black women began was so outrageously low.

Finally, studies using aggregate occupational data (*e.g.,* census' 3-digit detailed occupational category most typically used in sex segregation studies) severely underestimate the amount of sex segregation that exists within and between organizations: According to Bielby and Baron's (1984; 1986) very important study of 400 California establishments between 1959 and 1979, the more detailed the occupational categories used, the more segregation that was revealed. In fact, using firm specific job titles leads them to conclude that virtually all jobs are totally segregated. The index of sex segregation under these conditions is .96! That is, 96 percent of all women—or men—would have to change jobs for there to be an equal distribution of men and women in the labor force. Even though the sex segregation literature, as mentioned above, shows a steady and steep decline in sex segregation in the professions post-World War II, Bielby and Baron find that when one uses firm-specific job titles as the unit of measurement, segregation in the professions is almost total: here the index of sex segregation is .94! Thus, they would argue, men and women in the same profession do not typically work in the same organizations; and when they do, they are typically assigned to different job titles, with different occupational opportunities and rewards.

In short, this means that whatever increases black and white women experience in employment in the professional/technical occupations, or male-dominated professions in particular, can be obscured if they are not evaluated in the context of the total set of data reflecting black and white professional women's lives.

The Ambiguity and Expansion of the Concept of the "Professions"

Here let us consider a second important reason why black and white women have increased in the professions, but in far less favorable ways than is indicated by the numerical increases. All too often, when the media announces that more women are in the professions than ever before, people assume that women are moving into better, higher status, more powerful jobs today than in the past. However, the term *professions* as used by the census and social scientists covers a wide variety of occupational categories. A closer look at what jobs women are actually moving into shows many of these jobs do not fulfill the original criteria of the ideal type professions (see Carr-Saunders, as described in Kaufman, 1984).

Professions vs. Technicians. First we need to look at how some of the older, more established prestigious professions are decreasing as a proportion of all professions; and conversely how some of the newer professions are far less attractive and most likely do not fit the criteria of what we expect when we talk about the professions. Thus, Blitz's (1974) study of women in the professions, 1870–1970, shows that in 1890, 5 occupational categories dominated the professions: elementary school teachers, physicians and healers, social workers and clergy, lawyers and judges, musicians and music teachers. While in 1890 these 5 categories constituted almost three-fourths (72 percent) of all professions, almost a century later, in 1970, these same five categories represent only about one-fourth (23 percent) of all professions. By 1980, approximately 80 percent of all occupations included in the professions are *not* part of the old established professions. The obvious

question is: what job categories have newly been included or expanded between 1890 and 1980 for there to be such a drastic decline in the established
professions? How are women affected differently than men by these new
professional job categories? What differences exist for black vs. white
women?

As a prime example of changes within the professional category which influence the total number of women professionals, it would be important to
investigate the *technicians* category (*e.g.*, lab technicians, X-ray technicians,
electronic technicians and technologists, etc.).[4] In the 1950 census, the occupational category previously reserved for the professions ("professions
and semiprofessions,") was expanded to include "professional, technical,
and kindred workers" (Kaplan and Casey, 1958). Thus, the concept of the
professions, a very high status occupational category, requiring high levels
of education and granting financial rewards, power, status, self satisfaction,
etc. was significantly altered with the inclusion of the term "technicians."
Technicians are usually much less educated, have far less prestige, less
power and autonomy at work, and lower pay than members of the
professions.

The exact impact of the inclusion of technicians on the increase of both
black and white women in the professional/technical/kindred (p/t/k)
category is, thus very important; it has never been examined. My preliminary calculations indicate that between 1970 and 1980 alone, the proportion of technicians among p/t/k workers increased from just over one
out of every ten (Almquist, 1979) to almost one out of every five such jobs
(USDC, BC, 1983a). How women vs. men, blacks vs. whites are represented in these important changes requires further elaboration if we are to understand the sources of improvement of women, black and white, in the
professional category.

Male-Dominated Professions vs. Female-Dominated Semiprofessions. In addition
to technicians artificially inflating the professional job category, so too the
inclusion of female-dominated "semiprofessions" changes the meaning of
the most powerful and respected male-dominated professions.[5] This is especially important in evaluating the purported progress of black and white
women in the professions since over half of all women professionals in 1970
were actually in only two female-dominated jobs: nurses and elementary
school teachers (Theodore, 1971). This is likewise the case for black professional women (see Malveaux, 1981).

Thus, Theodore (1971) suggested that a way to look at the degree of sex
segregation in the professions was to compare women in the professions (as
traditionally defined by Carr-Saunders[6]) and women in the semiprofessions.[7] She confines the professions to male-dominated medicine, dentistry,
law, science, engineering and the ministry; semiprofessions to female-dominated nursing, teaching, librarians, and social workers.

When one compares women in the professions and semiprofessions for 1970 and 1980, using Theodore's categories, an interesting problem emerges. In 1970, Theodore found: "At the present time, females comprise approximately two-thirds of all workers in the semi-professions and only one-tenth in the professions, indicating a considerably greater degree of sex typing in the male-dominated professions" (p.4). In comparison, my preliminary calculations for 1980 show that women have *increased* to *75* percent of all semiprofessionals, and *maintained* at *10* percent of the professionals (USDC, BC, 1983a). These findings are in clear contradiction to earlier findings (see Table 1 above) that told us that black and white women doubled and even tripled their representation in some of the highest status male-dominated professions between 1970 and 1980. Clearly, several explanations are possible; further research is needed to clarify which are the most important.

Of course, to the degree these data are accurate, they hardly represent an improvement in women's overall status in the professions, broadly defined, and bring into question the conclusion that sex segregation has decreased significantly during the past decade in the professions—either male-dominated professions or female-dominated semiprofessions. Further, exactly how black women compare with white women in this process has only recently begun to be explored (see Kilson, 1977; Malveaux, 1981; Westcott, 1982).

As Higginbotham (this volume) shows, despite gains of professional black women through recent Civil Rights and women's movements, black women continue to be concentrated in traditional women's professions. In the early and mid-twentieth century, black women entered human service and teaching careers, particularly in segregated or predominantly black settings. Today, black women, like other black professionals, she argues, are colonized in deteriorating public sector jobs, which service predominantly poorer and often racially segregated populations.

In short, even though many more women are moving into the professions, it may not be the case that even a majority are moving into better, more powerful and higher status jobs than in the past. A comparison by race of women's representation in high status male professions with lower status female professions may in fact show little or no change: despite numerical increases in the professions in general and male-dominated professions in particular, professional women appear to continue to be recruited into "secondary" professional positions.

Sex Segregation Within Male-Dominated Professions. Third, while it is of utmost importance to recognize women's abilities to enter male-dominated professions from which they were previously excluded, the gains made by women are often masked by the fact that women are usually allowed to enter only the female specialties. Because the census does not classify occupations by specialization in an adequate way, none of the large scale research investigating sex segregation has been able to get at this type of segregation. Only case studies of a particular profession can do this.

In studies of individual elite male professions (such as medicine, law, and university teaching), women have been found to be more likely to enter mainly in secondary positions—lower status, lower paying, less powerful, female specialties. For example, in medicine, women are found more in pediatrics, psychiatry, public health, anesthesiology, and pathology instead of surgery, gastroenterology, and cardiovascular medicine; in law, they appear in trusts, estates, and domestic relations instead of litigation and corporate work. (For a summary and review of this literature, see Patterson and Engleberg, 1978; Fox and Hesse-Biber, 1984; Kaufman, 1984; and numerous articles in Theodore, 1971). Such studies are only beginning to emerge with 1980 or later data (Reskin and Roos, this volume; Strober and Arnold, 1984a and 1984b). None compare black and white women. However, one question that needs to be explored is: given that some of the elite, established male professions have opened themselves to women, especially during the 1970s, are women's numbers increasing in the female specialties or have they also made real gains in the male specialties? Further, in what ways are black vs. white women's representation in male and female specialties the same and different?[8]

Finally, when looking at male-dominated professions, it is important to remember that not all of them are necessarily high status nor respected and admired in the same way. Thus we need to explore whether women, black and white, are more likely to be employed in high (elite) or low (nonelite) status male-dominated professions: *e.g.*, as physicians and lawyers instead of as accountants, surveyors, or photographers. There simply are no systematic studies here. However, given that the literature finds that women tend to be recruited into the lowest levels of all occupational and job hierarchies (*e.g.*, Deckard, 1979; Fox and Hesse-Biber, 1984), it is important to see whether this exists likewise in terms of elite vs. nonelite sex segregated professions as well.

To conclude, a second important factor to understand in evaluating women's progress in the professions is the *meaning* of whatever numerical increases exist for women in the professions. In each case discussed above, qualitative gains for women in the professions hardly match the quantitative gains. In fact one might argue, that not only has sex segregation *not* diminished in the professions, but that women are even more entrenched in secondary positions in the professions in general and male-dominated professions in particular.

The Changing Nature of Work: Deskilling as an Explanation for Women's Increase in Male-Dominated Professions

The third and final area to be mentioned here that must be explored if we are to understand the inclusion of ever greater numbers of women into the highest status professions is the overall changing nature of work in the professions, particularly male-dominated professions. I am thinking of cases in particular where the job itself changes so much that women may not be found going into the same job as men, either in the past or today, even though the name of the elite male profession itself stays the same. Below I will mention only one instance of these changes which I believe to be important to understanding the contradiction that women's numerical increase in the male-dominated professions does not represent genuine gain for women there: that of deskilling.

I will not focus on this very important aspect because a summary of some of the issues here are presented by Reskin and Roos in this volume. In their analysis of selected case studies of male-dominated occupations, including professions, they include a variety of processes that fall within this rubric. In addition to technological change or work reorganization, usually involving deskilling, they argue that the illusory progress of women in male-dominated occupations also involves: (1) the resegregation of occupations when women enter; (2) the nominal integration of job titles; and (3) internal segregation within occupational categories in addition to technological change and occupational growth.

Below I will briefly mention how the deskilling of male-dominated professions is essential to consider in any discussion of the increase of women, both white and black, in these occupations.

In the previous section we suggested that the progress of women in the male-dominated professions was exaggerated when we did not look also at the type of specialties women worked in. Thus, for example, what is the meaning of progress or equality for women if they continue to be recruited into lower status, lower paid, female specialties? Are women still heavily recruited into these specialties? Are these specialties on the increase? In order to meaningfully evaluate the numerical increase of women in the professions we must be able to answer these questions.

Likewise, could it be that the changes in the organization and structure—*e.g.,* increasing rationalization, bureaucratization, and proletarianization—of the elite male professions during the current period of monopoly capital has led to the development of new and lower status sectors and specialties which have permitted the entrance of greater numbers of women—but in a very different way than their white male predecessors in the past or many counterparts today? In fact, evidence is beginning to emerge that this is precisely what has happened. (Again, see here Reskin and Roos, this volume and Strober and Arnold, 1984a and 1984b.)

Deskilling is a process whereby, in this case, professional work becomes increasingly simplified, segmented, rationalized, and bureaucratized. New forms and relations of work have been created in the professions. According to Carter and Carter (1981), deskilling in the prestigious professions is best seen in the rapidly developing split in work between: (1) prestige jobs with good pay, autonomy, and opportunity for growth and development—which are small in number and limited to men; and (2) a new class of more routinized, less skilled, poorly paid jobs with little autonomy, influence, control over the work process, and unconnected to centers of power, prestige, and high pay within the profession itself. It is these jobs which are growing in size and which, it is hypothesized, are overwhelmingly where women in prestigious male professions (*e.g.*, doctors, lawyers) are increasingly being concentrated.

In this sense, it is misleading to praise women's increasing representation in elite male-dominated professions as genuine progress. More women enter these professions just as they are changing—to be less under the control of the professionals themselves, less powerful, less profitable, and less prestigious. This means that women are not employed in the very same male-dominated professions as men—of either yesterday or today. In some very important ways, conclude Carter and Carter, women are working in male-dominated professions *in name only*. As they suggest in the title of their article about women's progress in elite male professions of law, medicine, and university teaching: "Women Get a Ticket to Ride after the Gravy Train Left the Station."

As an example of deskilling in the legal profession, Carter and Carter look at the legal clinic. It is an institution which results from and results in the routinization of much legal work. Legal clinics emerged in the early 1970s. Originally intended for poor clients, they are increasingly used by middle class people as legal fees have become out of reach of even middle income people.

Legal clinics resemble discount legal department stores. A good example is that of Jacoby and Meyers, begun in 1972 and today with an estimated 75 branches across the country and 200 such legal clinics nationwide. The clinics specialize in routine legal problems facing the average consumer— consumer law and family related problems: probate, divorce, separation, custody, and child support.

Although attorneys establishing the clinics do well and those working in them are probably grateful for the work, considering the "oversupply" of lawyers today:

> Conditions of work and opportunities for advancement within legal clinics are decidedly inferior, however, to conditions that attorneys enjoyed in traditional law firms. Not only do legal clinics specialize in the sort of cases which have little relation to the higher prestige and higher-paying fields of business and corporate law, but their style of work differs markedly from that in the prestige firms (Carter and Carter, 1981: 492).

They continue by giving an example from Linda Cawley of Cawley and Schmidt, a chain of 12 legal clinics employing 30 lawyers. She says that manuals have been developed for issues such as divorce, which the firm does a lot of work in. "There are only so many options on alimony, and the manual lists them all. This cuts the attorney's drafting time by seventy percent." (Carter and Carter, 1981: 492). Limited, rationalized options can be easily computerized. This decreases the costs even more, but at the expense of lawyers continually losing important skills of the profession by not having to learn the basics of searching and thinking involved in the legal decision-making process.

So, not only is much of the traditional work of the legal clinic rationalized, but it also saves time and money for the corporate owners. Moreover, argue Carter and Carter, this kind of experience could actually *"disqualify* an attorney for consideration for a post that demands more varied skills" (p. 492, emphasis mine). In short, there is little transferability of skills learned in legal clinics and even fewer avenues of mobility from legal clinics to prestigious law firms.

Some critics might argue that not all women have entered the lower status, more deskilled areas of the legal profession. In fact, they might argue, more women than ever before have made it into the ranks of the legal establishment: the large office on Wall Street and large corporate firms across the country. However, while many more women have been allowed into the legal establishment and thus have broken the barrier to high level elitist circles, they are *not* let in in the same way as men.

Thus, as Epstein, (1983) shows, while new spaces in the establishment made room for more women overall, discrimination in specialization and tasks assigned to women still persisted. Women making partnerships on Wall Street—a prestigious and permanent position—are few and far between: only 3 percent of all Wall Street partners were women in 1982. Moreover, and most importantly, women are less likely to become partners *in the same way and with the same rights* as men who become partners. Thus, Epstein (1983) finds:

> For women and minority associates, there is a greater chance of becoming a partner, but promotion may be to a partnership bearing less power and influence and a proportionately smaller share of profit at the end of the year. There is some suspicion on the part of older women attorneys that this is the kind of partnership many young women are likely to get when their firms feel pressed to promote them. Although it is a step upward, it does not mean that women have 'made it' in the same way as the men who are rising in the hierarchy (p. 214).

Finally, how the changing nature of work, as well as outright and subtle discrimination are related to women doing certain tasks and types of legal work in the Wall Street firms is not clarified. In order to better understand how and where women are incorporated, even in the most prestigious levels of the most prestigious professions, demands further investigation: are women more likely found in the lower status, more routinized sectors here too?

Just as in all other professional occupational categories, we must likewise study here the differential ways in which black and white women are employed in these highest status professions as they are changing. Are black women not only more likely to be found in the more segmented and de-skilled work of the more prestigious male-dominated professions, but also in levels within that career lower than white females? In short, does the pattern that appears throughout the job hierarchy persist in its highest levels? And how much of women's so-called progress, even here, is threatened by the social and economic policies of today?

No one has studied these questions on racial stratification in the professions for women as well as men in any detail. However, Higginbotham's (this volume) study of black professional women hints at the possibilities of this kind of racial stratification in male-dominated professions *as they are changing* when she argues that the "minority of Black women who enter traditionally male professions, also tend to be ghettoized in the public defenders office, city run hospitals, dental clinics, and minority relations for corporate firms" (p. 75).

SUMMARY

In this chapter I have argued that despite a genuine numerical increase and challenge to important barriers preventing women from entering the most prestigious occupations in our society, both black and white women remain seriously disadvantaged in the professions. In addition to the traditional theories purporting to explain both women's disadvantaged position and their gains in the economy and in the professions in particular, I have suggested a few areas requiring investigation to explain the above contradiction. These include: (1) a more meaningful and totalistic analysis of aggregate data on black and white women in the professions; (2) a break-down of the ambiguous "professional" category to understand the wide variety of occupational categories included in the professions, many of which are heavily disadvantaged and heavily female-dominated; and (3) an analysis of the changing nature of work in contemporary society and particularly on the degradation and deskilling of elite professions.

Finally, and most importantly, we must ask the degree to which black and white women are treated alike in these processes and how racial/ethnic background continues to act as another key barrier for black women.

I would like to end by asking the reader to consider two very important issues that affect all professional women. First, the contradictory processes by which more and more women enter the work world, but (in comparison to men) in lower status, lower paid, and often degraded work is not unique to professional women. Rather, it happened to nonprofessional women earlier and at several points throughout the twentieth century, as part of a long-term trend in U.S. employment patterns. Thus, despite the many differences and privileges accorded to higher educated professional as opposed to lesser educated nonprofessional women, a look at many of the similarities in our histories may be an important issue through which women of different backgrounds and experiences could organize to help themselves and make needed changes in our society. All too often, professional women and white women think they are somehow protected from the forces that hurt nonprofessional and black women. While there certainly are advantages in each case, the larger political and economic forces of society cut into many of these privileges *without people ever being aware of it.* By uniting around common interests and problems, we might be able to not only benefit others, but ourselves as well.

Secondly, we must recognize the dilemma often experienced by people typically relegated to disadvantaged status in our society. For certain individual women who make it into the professions, or male-dominated professions in particular, this movement may represent genuine improvement over other less powerful and less remunerative work they would otherwise have had to do. This is true despite the fact that black and white women and black men have been more likely to enter lower levels even within the elite male-dominated professions. However, at the same time that individual black or white women are experiencing upward mobility, the occupation itself is being downgraded. This occupational downgrading may, in the short and/or long run, have severe consequences for the upwardly mobile black or white woman, even though employment in a degraded profession is not experienced personally as downgrading at all. This happens with regard to both professional and nonprofessional work as well as in terms of black women's employment more generally. The problem is that the newly available job (*e.g.,* clerical work for many black women today or elite professional work for all women today) may be much better than what they had in the past or could have had if this expansion had not occurred; however it is not as good as whites or men had in the past—and will probably get worse in the future unless we work together to reshape its content, form, and goals.

NOTES

1. There are several reasons why I have chosen to compare white women with black, as opposed to all minority, women: (1) Among racial/ethnic people, black women have been the major and explicit target of many anti-Affirmative Action forces in our society. (2) The experiences of blacks in this country are unique. Other racial/ethnic peoples have their own unique experiences which should also be studied. (3) The black population is the largest proportion (85 percent in 1980) of all racial/ethnic minorities in the U.S. (USDC, BC, 1983a).

2. For a summary of occupational sex and race segregation literature in the total labor force and among the professions, see Sokoloff, 1986.

3. Classic studies on sex segregation begin with Gross, 1968; and Oppenheimer 1970. Both look at the amount of sex segregation 1900–1960. Further work includes Council of Economic Advisors, 1973; Stevenson, 1975; Williams, 1975; Blau and Hendricks, 1979; and Dubnoff, 1979; most recent data are covered in Burris and Wharton, 1982; Jacobs, n.d. Specific reference to the professions can be found in

Blitz, 1974; Kilson, 1977; Burris and Wharton, 1982; Fox and Hesse-Biber, 1984; Kaufman, 1984.

4. The 1980 census begins to recognize this, in part, by separating professional specialties from technical workers.

5. There is no universal agreement on the use of the terms professional and semiprofessional. I have used this distinction here because it is useful in making a point: women tend to remain clustered in female-dominated professions (termed semiprofessions by some researchers).

6. The professions are defined as professionalized, established, more prestigious, more self-controlled and autonomous, more exclusionary by men of women.

7. The semiprofessions are defined as occupations that are more bureaucratized, lacking the distinct theoretical base and autonomy to control themselves, with less power, income, and prestige, developed as extensions of traditional female family functions as well as handmaidens to male professionals.

8. Moreover, the opposite side to the question of female recruitment into the lower levels of male-dominated professions is the recruitment of men into the higher levels of female-dominated professions. How much of this has been happening? And has there been any change in this process over the last several decades? This is particularly important since the few studies that document this process find that when men enter women's professions or semiprofessions, they do so much more commonly in the higher ranks of the profession.

CHAPTER 4

Employment for Professional Black Women In The Twentieth Century

ELIZABETH HIGGINBOTHAM

The author wishes to thank Lynn Weber Cannon, Jobe Henry Jr., and Marie Santucci for their assistance on this project. I would also like to thank the editors for their comments.

INTRODUCTION

In a total work force of 5.18 million Black women, 16.1 percent are in managerial positions and professional specialities. Among Black males, only 12.6 percent hold such positions in the labor force. Yet, both Black females and males lag behind whites; 23.3 percent of white females and 25.9 percent of white males have attained those occupational positions (Bureau of Labor Statistics, 1984). While employment patterns have changed over the century, high labor force participation rates and strong representation among the ranks of Black professionals have characterized employment for Black women. Most Black women face unemployment, underemployment, or work in low wage clerical, sales, and service occupations. In light of these realities, the minority of educated, professional Black women stand out in sharp contrast. As a consequence, the successes of these women are frequently exaggerated and rarely placed within a context of racial and sex discrimination.

In their introduction to *But Some of Us Are Brave*, Gloria Hull and Barbara Smith warn:

A descriptive approach to the lives of Black women, a "great Black women" in history or literature approach, or any traditional male-identified approach will not result in intellectually groundbreaking or politically transforming work. We cannot change our lives by teaching solely about "exceptions" to the ravages of white-male oppression. Only through exploring the experiences of supposedly "ordinary" Black women whose "unexceptional" actions enabled us and the race to survive, will we be able to begin to develop an overview and an analytical framework for understanding the lives of Afro-American women (1982: xxi–xxii).

There is no group of Black women, outside the elite of Harriet Tubman, Sojourner Truth, Ida Wells-Barnett, and Mary Bethune, more subject to "exceptionalism" perspectives than Black professional women. They are assumed to have moved through the cracks of racism and sexism to prestigious employment (Epstein, 1973). There are myths about the ease with which Black women achieve success. In the face of misperceptions and the continued growth of the Black middle class, there is a need for theoretical work which places their achievements within a broader context. Such a perspective would explicate how they are restrained by racial and sexual barriers. It would also highlight how oppression differentially affects poor, working class and middle class Black women and professional Black and white women.

This paper begins that effort by drawing upon the class-differentiated colonial perspective developed by Mario Barrera (1979) in his work on Chicanos. Like Barrera's subjects, middle class Blacks[1] enjoy certain occupational benefits and have greater resources than their working class counterparts. Those resources include increased housing options, access to improved educational settings, better medical care, and so forth. Yet, racism is still a major factor in their lives. This is indicated in the ways Blacks form a subordinate segment of the middle class.

Black people have fewer life choices than whites in the same class position. This is especially true for Black females. Blocked access into many traditionally female occupations forced Black women to seek alternatives. The only significant mobility channel for those with the opportunity was higher education. Both in direct and indirect ways, racism spurred the growth of a small group of Black professional women. As Black women completed their educational training, they found that both racism and sexism shaped the nature of professional employment for them. This paper uses historical research and sociological studies of the Black community to detail the segmentation of Black professional women.

Historically, Black professional women have only found significant professional options in two sectors: independent agencies and employers in the Black community, and the public sector. In both cases, they worked as colonized professionals in capacities where the majority of their clients were people of color. Institutionalized discrimination limited employment options for them to inside the internal colony. Until recently, professional employment outside the Black community, which was opened to whites with comparable education and training, was closed to Blacks.

Patterns of racial stratification are evident in the genesis of this segment of employed women, their development throughout the twentieth century, and today. The dependency of Black professional females on these two job sectors has had a profound impact on their growth. Early in the century, limited access to public sector jobs kept the cadre of Black professional women small. The New Deal and Civil Rights movement enabled more Black women to gain access to public sector jobs. This development, heralded as a major breakthrough in employment discrimination, is viewed differently today—when it appears as if Black professional women cannot get out of public sector employment. Data from the 1980 census will be used to illustrate that the majority of Black professional and managerial women continue to serve a predominantly Black clientele in a few occupational positions: teachers, social workers, counselors, librarians, nurses, and other traditionally female professions. The minority of Black women who enter traditionally male professions, also tend to be ghettoized in the public defender's office, city-run hospitals, dental clinics, and minority relations for corporate firms. These patterns illustrate the persistence of racial stratification, even in the development of a Black middle class.

BLACK WOMEN AND EMPLOYMENT DISCRIMINATION

We will begin an exploration of the unexceptional lives of professional Black women with a look at their history. At the turn of the century, white women—both American-born and immigrant—left paid employment when they married (Kessler-Harris, 1982). Yet, Black women found no refuge from the labor market in matrimony. The racism of the day limited their husbands' job options to manual service work. The low wages paid to Black males kept Black females—as daughters and wives—on the job (Kessler-Harris, 1982; Pleck, 1979). While they were forced by economic circumstances to work, only a few occupations were open to women. Racism even further restricted the occupational movement of Black females. Because Black females had fewer occupational choices than white women, they were relegated to the lowest of women's jobs. In the early part of the century many were still on the farm, but as they sought paid employment, the majority could only find jobs as private household workers and laundry workers (Jones, 1985; Katzman, 1978; Kessler-Harris, 1982).

At the beginning of the twentieth century, domestic employment was the most common occupation for all women (Katzman, 1978). But very quickly ethnic and racial patterns emerged. Industrialization created new job opportunities for women. They found employment in light manufacturing, especially the garment and textile industries, canneries, and meat packing houses. Many white immigrant women—especially single daughters—filled these positions (Tentler, 1979). American-born white women moved into newly created clerical and sales jobs, as well as kindergarten and normal school teaching. As American-born white women abandoned domestic work, their positions were filled by immigrant and Black women. Over time, many white immigrant women slowly moved out of private household work and into operative, clerical and sales jobs. Nationwide, Black women remained trapped in domestic work until World War II (Katzman, 1978). Kenneth Kusmer's comments about Cleveland demonstrate the trend which was common to many Northern and some southern cities.

> Prior to World War I, the position of black women was not unique, since a large proportion of immigrant women were also mired in low-paying domestic work. But between 1910 and 1920 foreign-born women began for the first time to obtain white-collar employment in sizable numbers, and at the same time the proportion of immigrant females working as domestics fell from 41 to 25.6 percent (1978:203).

In contrast, 63 percent of employed Black women in Cleveland were domestics in 1920 and this number increased to 69.8 percent in 1930. As both females and members of a racial minority, their limited options reflected multiple barriers.

In their research on Chicago during the depression, St. Clair Drake and Horace Cayton (1970) identified a "job ceiling," which prohibited Blacks from freely competing for positions in the labor market.

> The employment policies of individual firms, trade-union restrictions, and racial discrimination in training and promotion made it exceedingly difficult for them (Blacks) to secure employment in the skilled trades, in clerical and sales work, and as foremen and managers (Drake and Cayton, 1970:112).

The job ceiling was a factor limiting employment options for both males and females. While a tiny number of Blacks in any city would achieve occupational mobility, the majority were unable to translate their education and talents into better jobs and higher wages.

Blanket discrimination in the predominantly white private sector meant that only a few Black women could convert their high school educations into clerical and sales jobs. Drake and Cayton found "most of the colored women in clerical and sales work, prior to the Second World War were employed in the Black Belt (the Black community) and there were less than 1,500 of them" (1970:258).[2] Black establishments could sustain only a few Black women in white collar jobs. Thus, in Chicago, 55.7 percent of employed Black women did domestic work in 1930 and this increased to 64.1 percent by 1940. During World War II many Black women entered new industries and they maintained many of those jobs after the war, especially as "semi-skilled workers in canning factories, paper and pulp mills, cleaning and pressing establishments and in the garment industry" (Drake and Cayton, 1970:262). But they could not make serious inroads into clerical and sales work—even though these are traditional women's jobs. Their plight is vividly captured in Figure 4.1 below, developed by Drake and Cayton (1970:259).

PROFESSIONAL EMPLOYMENT FOR BLACKS

Before the Civil Rights era, a college education was one means of increasing employment options for Blacks. But as Black professionals they were limited to two segments of the market: the private sector in the Black com-

ECONOMIC OPPORTUNITY FOR WOMEN

OF EVERY 10 TEEN-AGE WHITE GIRLS 5 ARE IN HIGH SCHOOL

OF THESE 6 CAN EXPECT WHITE-COLLAR JOBS

OF EVERY 10 TEEN-AGE NEGRO GIRLS 5 ARE IN HIGH SCHOOL

OF THESE ONLY 1 CAN EXPECT A WHITE-COLLAR JOB

Figure 4.1. *The estimate of "economic opportunity for women" in Figure 4.1 is based on an analysis of 1930 and 1940 Census data, and on the assumption that most of the war-time clerical jobs held by Negro women are only temporary. Not more than 3 percent of the Negro women held bona fide clerical and sales jobs in 1940. The saturation point for employment had been reached in Black Belt stores and offices. Yet, the high schools were continuing to turn out girls with "white-collar aspirations."

munity and the public sector. First, they served the Black community as independent entrepreneurs or as employees of Black organizations, churches,
businesses, and schools. This was the case for most physicians, dentists,
ministers, lawyers, and college professors. In fact, the migration of many
Blacks and the development of northern Black ghettos during World War I
did much to promote the growth of this tiny elite (Osofsky, 1971; Spear,
1967). Thus, the majority of Black physicians were located in cities, where
the concentration of Blacks insured a sufficient number of paying patients
to keep their offices open (Myrdal, 1962). Black college professors were frequently employed at private Black colleges and universities, such as Fisk,
Lincoln, Spelman, and so forth. Many ministers held other jobs to supplement their earnings, but the most successful of this group served large con-
gregations in cities. Many Black lawyers worked in their own small firms,
but had difficulty supporting themselves because many Black clients preferred white attorneys who had more clout in the white halls of justice.

Prior to World War II, only a few Black women were educated to be
physicians, lawyers, or college teachers. Thus, few could sustain a living as
independent entrepreneurs. Instead, Black women working in the private
sector of the Black community were typically employed in Black organizations or by Black male entrepreneurs as nurses, social workers, and administrators. And their numbers were frequently small.

The second market for Black professionals was the public sector. This is
the sectoral location for the majority of Black professional women, who
were overwhelmingly employed as primary and secondary school teachers,
nurses, and social workers. In these traditionally female occupations they
were unable to sustain themselves as independent entrepreneurs and were
dependent upon various levels of government (local, state, and federal) for
their livelihoods. Drake and Cayton provide details on Chicago which are
reflective of the status of Black employment patterns in most Northern
cities:

> The number and proportion of Negroes employed in minor supervisory
> capacities by government agencies fluctuates. In 1930, there were 161 col-
> ored policemen, 120 schoolteachers, and some 400 colored social workers
> and their activities were confined largely to the Negro community
> (1970:256).

The development of urban ghettos in the North around World War I,
aided the growth of this segment of the labor market. As Blacks moved
North, clustered in densely populated districts, and voted, they became
powerful constituencies in local urban areas. In the South, public sector
professional employment for Blacks was promoted chiefly by the need to
provide segregated facilities, including schools, public health clinics, and
human service agencies. On the national level, Blacks, as loyal Democrats,
were able to participate, (if only in a limited way) in the expansion of the

federal job sector. Beginning with the New Deal, the proportion of federal jobs occupied by Blacks has consistently increased (Newman, *et al.*, 1978).

Education was the major channel for Blacks, thus it was highly valued in the community (Bullock, 1967; Drake and Cayton, 1970). Yet, there were discriminatory barriers which relegated Blacks to a few institutions, and few families could afford to send their children. In the face of these obstacles, Black parents frequently had to make sacrifices to provide their children with the educational foundation to advance in life (Higginbotham, 1985). E. Wilkins Bock (1971) identified a pattern among rural Black families of sponsoring their daughter's quest for higher education. Males had more employment options without a college education. Educating females afforded the best means to protect females from sexual assaults and abuse because it kept them from working in the homes of white people. Whether one accepts the notion of the farmer's daughter effect[3] or not, there is a long history of coeducation and support for higher education for both sexes in the Black community.

For many years a college education and even a high school diploma were prized achievements in the Black community. The educational attainment of the Black population has been steadily improving, especially since the 1940s. "By 1975, black young men and women born after 1940 had completed high school in about the same proportion as whites, and many had gone to college" (Newman, *et al.*, 1978).

Prior to the Civil Rights movement, the lack of educational opportunities kept the number of Black women in the professions to a minority. In each decade since 1940, the percentage of Black women employed in professional and managerial positions had remained behind white women, (see Table 4.1). But Black women are often singled out for special acknowledgement because they are more concentrated in the professions than Black men. This contrasts with the experiences of white women whose concentration in the professions is less than for white men (Kilson, 1977).

BARRIERS TO PROFESSIONAL EMPLOYMENT FOR BLACK WOMEN

For most of this century, Black women intent upon securing professional training faced serious racial and sex barriers as they challenged their prescribed places in the society. Training and employment were often only assured in all-Black facilities. Yet, Black institutions were only able to accommodate a few Blacks and within them Black females were frequently directed to predominantly female occupations. Upon the completion of their degrees, they found segregation was still a major part of their experiences. In the South, Jim Crow legislation created the parameters for all-Black institutions. Black women taught in segregated schools, nursed in the

Table 4.1. Occupational Status for Women by Race for Various Years

Occupational Category	1910 Black	White	1940 Black	White	1950 Black	White	1960 Black	White	1970 Black	White	1980 Black	White	1984 Black	White
Professional & Technical	1.5	11.6	4.3	14.7	5.3	13.3	7.7	14.1	10.0	15.5	15.3	17.4	14.3	17.5
Managers, Officials & Proprietors, Except Farm	.2	1.5	.7	4.3	1.3	4.7	1.1	4.2	1.4	4.7	4.2	7.3	5.4	8.8
Clerical & Sales	.3	17.5	1.3	32.8	5.4	39.3	9.8	43.2	21.4	43.4	32.6	43.4	33.0	44.0
Craftsmen & Foremen	2.0	8.2	.2	1.1	.7	1.4	.7	1.4	.8	1.1	1.4	2.1	2.8	2.2
Operatives	1.4	21.2	6.2	20.3	15.2	21.5	14.3	17.6	16.8	14.5	14.9	10.0	12.1	7.4
Nonfarm Laborers	.9	1.5	.8	.9	1.6	.7	1.2	.5	.9	.4	1.5	1.3	2.5	1.7
Private Household Workers	38.5	17.2	59.9	10.9	42.0	4.3	38.1	4.4	19.5	3.7	5.8	2.4	6.0	1.6
Service Workers (Except Private Household)	3.2	9.2	11.1	12.7	19.1	11.6	23.0	13.1	28.5	15.1	23.9	16.5	23.5	15.4
Farmers & Farm Managers	4.0	3.1	3.0	1.1	1.7	.6	.6	.5	.2	.3	.1	.5	—	.5
Farm Laborers & Foremen	48.0	9.0	12.9	1.2	7.7	2.3	3.5	1.0	.3	1.3	.5	.6	.4	1.2

Source: Data from 1910 to 1970 from Aldridge (1975). Her sources were: Data for 1910 from U.S. Bureau of the Census, 1940 Census of Population, *Comparative Occupation Statistics for the United States 1870–1940*, Table 15, pp. 166–172. Data for 1940 from U.S. Bureau of the Census, 1940 Census of Population, Vol. 3, *The Labor Force*, Table 52, pp. 87–88. Data for 1950 from U.S. Bureau of the Census, 1950 Census of Population, *Occupational Characteristics*, Table 3 (Washington, D.C., 1963), pp. 11–21. Data for 1970 from U.S. Bureau of the Census, *Social and Economic Characteristics of the Population to Metropolitan Areas: 1970 and 1960 Current Population Reports* (Washington, D.C.: U.S. Government Printing Office, 1971). and U.S. Bureau of the Census, *The Social and Economic Status of the Black Population in the United States, 1972*, Current Population Reports, Series P-23, No. 46 (Washington, D.C.: Government Printing Office, 1972). Data for 1980 and 1984 represent women sixteen years and over. All other data are for women aged fourteen and over. Additionally, data for 1980 and 1984 are not strictly comparable to 1970 statistics as a result of changes in the occupational classification. Data for 1980 and 1984 have been reorganized to match prior occupational categories. Data for 1984 are from: U.S. Department of Labor, Bureau of Labor Statistics, *Employment and Earnings*, Vol. 31, No. 12, (Washington, D.C.: Government Printing Office, December, 1984), Table A-23. Data for 1980 are from: U.S. Department of Labor, Bureau of Labor Statistics, *Employment and Earnings*, Vol. 29, No. 1, (Washington, D.C.: U.S. Government Printing Office, January, 1982), Table A-22.

offices of Black doctors and filled other positions within the Black community. In the North, rigid racial barriers also promoted the development of Black social welfare agencies, hospitals, churches, and *de facto* segregated schools (Osofsky, 1971; Spear, 1967). And again, Black women working as professionals would fill the slots in these internal colonies.

It was difficult for Black women to seek professional employment outside of these restricted sectors. This was particularly true in the North, where many cities lacked predominantly Black institutions. There Blacks faced a severe job ceiling and discriminatory barriers prohibiting competition with whites in the public sector. This was the case in Cleveland. In the 1920s, the city hospitals of Cleveland served Black patients in segregated wards, but "no hospital admitted blacks to nurses' training or internship programs" (Kusmer, 1978:266). Unlike New York City or Chicago, Cleveland never developed a Black hospital, even though there was a movement to build such a facility. Instead, Blacks appealed to public officials, over the protests of white hospital administrators, and demanded changes in the discriminatory policies of the tax-supported city hospital. "In September, 1930 five black women were admitted to the hospital's nurses' training program. In the following year, the first black intern was admitted to the staff. The hospital's policy of segregating Negro patients also came to an end at this time" (Kusmer, 1978:267–68). Private hospitals remained unchanged until a later period, but opening public facilities to Black professionals was certainly monumental.

The history of nursing in Cleveland is illustrative of an important fact. Public sector discrimination made professional employment problematic for Black women. They were concentrated in occupations more dependent upon employment in this sector than were Black professional males. Jane Edna Hunter, a nurse, arrived in Cleveland and was unable to practice her profession. There was no place for a "nigger nurse," because both private and public sector hospitals did not hire Black women in these capacities. Therefore, Hunter devoted her life to human service work in the Black community. She founded and operated the Phyllis Wheatly Society, a residence and job training center for Black girls (Kusmer, 1978). During this era, other Black women with college degrees and professional skills found their employment options were shaped by the nature and degrees of discriminatory policies in the public sector of their city.

In the South, a number of public sector jobs were set aside for Blacks, because Jim Crow policies dictated segregated facilities. This was especially true in the teaching field, where Blacks had a monopoly on the jobs, even though they were paid less than white teachers and taught larger classes in deteriorating facilities (Myrdal, 1962). Yet in the North, urban policies with regard to public sector employment for Black professionals was more mixed. *De facto* segregation was frequently the rule for designating where children were schooled, but cities varied in whether or not they hired Black faculty to staff those facilities. Philadelphia, Gary, Indianapolis, Cincin-

nati, Columbus, Dayton and other cities hired Black teachers and administrators to work with Black pupils (Tyack, 1974). While this practice had
many drawbacks, it did foster employment options for Blacks. In New York
and Chicago, Blacks had to fight for teaching opportunities, but were able
to make serious inroads into these professions. Many taught in predominantly Black institutions, but a few were found in integrated and predominantly white schools. Many other cities hired white teachers to in-
struct Black children, even though they staffed *de facto* segregated facilities.
The presence of discrimination and the Jim Crow policies had a direct impact on the numbers of Black professionals.

Given that the majority of employed Black professional women were
teachers, they could either find work or not depending upon the specific
school policies. This helps to explain Myrdal's (1962) finding in 1930 of
only 4.5 percent of full time employed Black women in professional, technical, and kindred workers. Myrdal noted the regional variations in employment options:

> In the South, more than 5 percent of the Negro female workers were in
> professional occupations. The corresponding figure for the North was less
> than 3 percent. The main reason, of course, is that the Negro's chances in
> the teaching profession are much smaller in the North than in the South
> (p. 318).

Doxey Wilkerson identified the number of Black teachers and administrators employed in the public school systems of several major northern
cities. He found that the municipalities with the best record for hiring
Blacks were those who had instituted a policy of hiring Black teachers to
teach Black pupils. He also highlighted cities with particularly poor
records. For example, Detroit had a nonwhite population of 150,790 in
1940, but had only 80 Black professionals in the public school system.
Chicago, whose nonwhite population was 282,244 had nearly four times as
many Black teachers and administrators as Detroit. Pittsburgh was another
city with rigid discriminatory policies. They had only three Black faculty in
the public school system with a Black population of 62,423 (Tyack,
1974:226).[4]

Black professional women were at the mercy of such policies. Even if
they secured teaching credentials, they could be blocked from public school
teaching jobs in Northern cities. This was also the case for social workers.
There were only a few Black social welfare agencies (many of them supported by white philanthropists), which meant there were a limited number
of positions for Black social workers. The expansion of the welfare state
(during the Depression and the New Deal) meant new options for Black social workers. But the availability of these jobs to Blacks varied according to
the individual cities' labor policies.

In the nursing profession, Black women worked with Black physicians
and as public health nurses who served the Black community. They were

frequently barred from private predominantly white hospitals that delivered health care to white people. Myrdal's research indicates that there "were only 5,600 Negro nurses in 1930, constituting less than 2 percent of the total number of nurses in the United States" (1962: 325).

The minority of Black women able to secure professional employment do merit our praise. But their lives were not without difficulties. The histories reveal a tale of economic success relative to less educated Black women and men. But compared to their white peers, they found their situations lacking. This was evident in both early research and later sociological studies. In his 1938 study, *The Negro College Graduate*, Charles Johnson (1969) surveyed 5,512 men and women with college degrees. The subjects were all plagued by racial barriers of the age, but women had additional problems. In their jobs as teachers, nurses, and social workers they were routinely paid less than Negro men and white women who held the same positions. Race and sex compounded the barriers they faced to promotions and higher salaries.

THE CONTEMPORARY SCENE

World War II saw the beginning of a slow but steady growth of a significant Black middle class (Wilson, 1978). This meant increases in the number of Black women in professional occupations (refer to Table 4.1). This growth can be attributed to two major sources: the expansion of the welfare state and the Civil Rights movement. As federal government grew and provided its citizens with new services, Blacks were able to secure a proportion of those jobs. While their numbers in the higher ranks of the federal apparatus are still below par, this is a significant sector of employment for Blacks (Newman, et al., 1978). City, county, and state government has also expanded to address the needs of a growing and mobile population. Services were expanded to accommodate the baby boom cohort. Black professional and managerial women have benefited from the need for more teachers, nurses, counselors, and other human service workers. Also the Civil Rights movement demanded access for qualified Blacks to positions which corresponded with their educational attainment. This was especially significant for college educated Blacks, who had been routinely denied access to many areas of professional employment. The increase in Black workers in professional, technical, and craft positions were considerable (Wallace, 1980). This segment of the Black work force grew from 11 percent in 1960 to 21 percent in 1980 (Westcott, 1982). The growth of a Black middle class has not been without a unique set of problems. Sharon Collins (1983) comments on the precarious position of middle class Blacks:

> Growth since 1960 within the black middle class is the result of race oriented policies which have created new mechanisms to address black needs. Seen from this perspective, I believe that researchers have presumed, rather than demonstrated, the market integration of the black middle class. Re-

searchers have paid little attention to the types of organizations in which
income is earned, black workers' functional relationship to black consumers
networks, and the dependency of class mobility on government rather than
free market forces. The assumption that the accumulation of human capital
has assured black middle-class advancement underestimates the dependence
of the black middle class on both political relationships and the organization of work roles (p. 370).

Her comments are particularly relevant for Black professional women,
who have benefitted some from public relations positions in the private sector, but the majority of Black women have benefitted from Affirmative Action and new employment policies in the public sector. Their entrance into
many jobs has changed the racial composition of the staff of many elementary and secondary public schools, public and private hospitals, social
welfare agencies, libraries, and other employment settings.

Employment patterns which were evident earlier in this century, are still
demonstrated in the sector distributions of professional Black and white
women. While the private sector has expanded to include more professional
Blacks, the majority of Black professional women continue to secure employment in the public sector. This is evident from Table 4.2 , which presents the percentages of Black and white professional, managerial and administrative women in public, private, and other employment sectors
(self-employment and unpaid family labor) for 15 Standard Metropolitan
Statistical Areas (SMSAs) in 1980. These metropolitan areas were selected
because they each have a large Black population.[5] In 14 of the 15 SMSAs,
the majority of Black professional women are found in public sector employment, while in every city the majority of white women are found in the
private sector. Across the 15 SMSAs, the average concentration of Black
women in public sector professional employment was 57.9 percent. White
professional and managerial women were less likely to be found in this sector ($\bar{x} = 31.2\%$). Instead, the highest concentration of white women was in
the private sector ($\bar{x} = 63.5\%$), while Black women were less concentrated
in this sector ($\bar{x} = 40.3\%$).

Los Angeles is the only major SMSA with more Black professional
women in the private (49.3 percent) than in the public sector (47.6 percent).
Los Angeles is also distinctive because 3 percent of the Black professional
and managerial women in this metropolitan area are self-employed. Across
the 15 SMSAs the concentration of Black women who are self-employed
and unpaid family workers is minimal ($\bar{x} = 1.7\%$). More white professional
women are found in this category ($\bar{x} = 5.2\%$), the majority of which are self-
employed. But Black women are having a more difficult time establishing
themselves in this sector.

Overall, we find that Black women continue to depend upon public sector employment to realize their professional aspirations. This is particularly the case in Baltimore and Memphis, where 72.3 and 71.7 percent,

Table 4.2. Sectoral Distribution of Women Managerial and Professional Specialty Workers by Race for 15 SMSA's

	% Public		% Private		% Other[1]		Sample Total and %[2]			
	Black	White	Black	White	Black	White	Black	%	White	%
Atlanta	55.7	35.0	42.5	60.2	1.8	4.8	18,479	(18.6)	81,039	(81.4)
Baltimore	72.3	40.5	26.9	55.0	.8	4.5	19,902	(20.4)	77,606	(79.6)
Chicago	53.8	26.7	44.8	68.8	1.4	4.5	44,066	(13.9)	251,971	(79.4)
Cleveland	53.8	30.0	44.0	66.0	2.1	4.0	10,835	(14.5)	63,946	(85.5)
Dallas	54.8	32.2	42.6	62.0	2.6	5.8	11,308	(8.7)	119,083	(91.3)
Detroit	59.3	33.9	39.1	61.9	1.5	4.2	24,257	(15.9)	124,187	(81.3)
Houston	55.5	31.0	42.4	63.2	2.1	5.7	19,418	(15.1)	109,102	(84.9)
Los Angeles	47.6	26.8	49.3	65.2	3.1	8.0	36,119	(10.1)	260,742	(73.0)
Memphis	71.7	34.5	27.0	60.4	1.3	5.0	9,040	(25.5)	26,362	(74.5)
Miami	60.3	26.8	38.2	66.8	1.5	6.4	9,679	(11.6)	56,701	(68.0)
Newark	55.2	33.7	43.6	61.8	1.2	4.5	14,208	(15.8)	75,425	(84.1)
New Orleans	65.8	31.5	32.8	63.7	1.4	4.8	11,446	(23.5)	35,659	(73.3)
New York	49.3	26.6	48.8	66.5	1.8	6.9	67,026	(16.2)	346,470	(83.3)
Philadelphia	56.0	29.3	42.2	66.1	1.8	4.6	25,273	(13.6)	160,761	(86.4)
St. Louis	58.2	29.4	40.3	66.3	1.4	4.3	12,939	(13.8)	80,958	(86.2)
X̄ Percentage	57.9	31.2	40.3	63.5	1.7	5.2				

Source: All data from U.S. Bureau of the Census, 1983c.

[1] Other includes self-employed and unpaid family workers.

[2] Totals less than 100% in some SMSAs due to presence of other minority populations.

respectively, of the professional Black women are in the public sector. In Baltimore, Black women are about one-fifth of the professionally employed women in the area, but only 26.9 percent are found in the private sector. This is the employment sector for 55 percent of the white professional women in this city. In Memphis, Black women are about one-quarter of the professional and managerial women in that SMSA, but only 27 percent are in the private sector, while this is the employment source for 60.4 percent of white professional women. The Los Angeles and New York metropolitan areas have a better balance of public-private sector employment for Black women, but even in these areas Black women lag behind white professional women in securing employment in the private sector.

Black professional women continue to be dependent upon public sector employment for two major reasons. First, they are clustered in predominantly female occupations which are overwhelmingly dependent upon the public sector for employment. And secondly, they continue to face discriminatory barriers in the private sector. This chapter only suggests these as dimensions worthy of exploration, based upon a preliminary analysis of the census data. We will briefly discuss these two points beginning with the occupational distribution of professional Black women. Black males and females are found in the labor force in about the same proportions, but there are 78 managerial and professional Black males for every 100 managerial and professional Black females. But Black males are directed into predominantly male occupations which are frequently more prestigious and they can sustain themselves as independent entrepreneurs. Black females, while they are a majority of the professionals in the race, are overwhelmingly still teachers, nurses, social workers, and so forth. For example, for every 100 Black women in nursing, there are six Black males. Males are only 26 percent of the Blacks engaged in preschool, primary, and secondary teaching. Black women have made significant gains in postsecondary education, where they are on par with Black males. Yet, despite their gains in a few areas, Black women, like their white counterparts, are underrepresented in the more prestigious and financially rewarding professional occupations. Among Blacks working as lawyers and physicians, there were 218 and 316 males, respectively, for every 100 Black women in these fields (Matney, 1983).

The continued concentration of Black professional women in a few occupations is evident from an examination of Table 4.3. For the 15 SMSAs, 40 percent of all Black women, managerial and professional workers are employed as teachers, counselors, and librarians. Less than a third ($\bar{x}$ = 30.8%) of white professional women hold these occupations. New York is the only metropolitan area where teachers, counselors, and librarians are not the largest professional occupation for Black women. In this metropolitan area, 29.1 percent of professional Black females are found in health assessment and treating occupations, especially nursing. In this case, they are employed in both public and private hospitals and other treatment

Table 4.3. Teachers As a Percent of Women Managerial and Professional Specialty Workers and Sectoral Location of Black and White Teachers

	Teachers As % of PMS's		% Teachers in Public Sector		% Teachers in Private Sector		Number of Teachers	
	Black	White	Black	White	Black	White	Black	White
Atlanta	41.7	29.0	79.8	72.2	19.9	25.1	7,703	23,469
Baltimore	40.2	30.4	91.0	70.8	8.7	27.1	8,005	23,590
Chicago	37.0	29.1	80.9	64.6	18.9	32.8	16,330	73,258
Cleveland	37.2	31.8	77.3	67.8	22.0	34.1	4,036	20,331
Dallas	44.9	31.3	84.1	73.3	15.5	23.7	5,084	37,285
Detroit	36.1	33.5	84.9	71.6	14.4	26.2	8,765	41,664
Houston	45.4	32.1	84.4	73.6	15.2	23.3	8,815	35,054
Los Angeles	29.8	25.5	77.8	67.7	22.2	28.8	10,784	66,583
Memphis	53.2	32.9	88.1	63.0	11.9	33.5	4,810	8,663
Miami	42.0	25.5	86.9	66.3	13.1	31.1	4,065	14,461
Newark	34.1	34.7	82.1	70.3	17.6	27.3	4,852	26,199
New Orleans	53.5	33.9	84.8	56.9	14.9	40.8	6,122	12,090
New York	23.0	26.5	79.3	62.6	20.1	35.0	15,431	91,930
Philadelphia	39.8	32.9	80.0	60.3	19.8	37.5	10,073	52,880
St. Louis	41.4	33.4	76.3	59.4	23.3	38.7	5,360	27,031
X̄ Percentage	40.0	30.8	82.5	66.7	17.2	31.0		

Source: All data from U.S. Bureau of the Census, 1983.
Teachers include librarians and counselors.

centers. Many of their white sisters have moved out of sex-segregated occupations into other areas of employment, especially administrative and managerial positions in the private sector. Meanwhile, Black women continue to be employed in a limited number of occupations.

The picture of employment for Black professional women also indicates continued discrimination in the predominantly white private sector. Looking again at Table 4.3, we see that even when both Black and white women work in the same traditionally female occupations, there are significant differences in the sector where they can secure employment. A larger percentage of white women in these occupations are able to find employment outside the public sector. While nearly one-third ($\bar{x} = 31\%$) of all white professional women employed as teachers, counselors, and librarians are employed in the private sector, only 17.2 percent of these Black professional women are privately employed. And the vast majority of Black professional women ($\bar{x} = 82.5\%$) in these occupations are employed in the public sector, while only two-thirds ($\bar{x} = 66.7\%$) of their white counterparts are employed in the public sector. There are several cities where over 30 percent of white teachers are found in the private sector—New Orleans, St. Louis, Philadelphia, New York, Cleveland, Chicago, and Miami. These are metropolitan areas with large Catholic populations and consequently significant parochial school systems. And Memphis, with 33.5 percent of the white teachers, counselors, and librarians in the private sector, lacks a sizable Catholic population, but the desegregation of public schools spurred the development of many all-white Baptist academies. In each case, there are employment options, especially in education, for white teachers in both the public school system as well as private and parochial systems. Some Black professionals are also employed in private and parochial settings, particularly in St. Louis, Los Angeles, Cleveland, New York, Philadelphia, and Atlanta, but they are more frequently employed by local, state and the federal government.

CONCLUSION

Many people have applauded the progress of Black professionals, especially women, but we also must be clear on the extent to which their entrance into professional and managerial occupations represents major alterations in the nature of racial and sexual oppression. No one will debate that is it better to work as a nurse, with fringe benefits and compensation for overtime, than to do private household work. And there is equally no debate about the opportunities that public school teaching presents, especially in terms of adequate salaries and many vacation days. It is a sharp contrast to many clerical jobs, where individuals make minimum wage and get two weeks paid vacation per year. At the same time the continued clustering of Black professional women in the public sector is indicative of the nature of the racial stratification in the professions.

Black women do get to work in professional occupations, but they are limited to serving clients who are predominantly Black or other people of color. Their clients are also generally poor and working class people. Employment in the public sector is also problematic for professionals in this sector, as well as their class coworkers, because both groups are vulnerable to policy shifts. In this sector, "the fiscal health of federal, state and local governments affects wage levels" (Malveaux, 1984:26). These factors not only affect wages, but working conditions, fringe benefits, and pensions. While there was once a premium on employment in the public sector (at least in the North) people can now enjoy better work environments and conditions in the private sector. For example, high school teachers in many urban areas fear for their physical well-being on the job.

The history of racial oppression which has shaped a Black professional group and the current reliance on the public sector for a livelihood has to generate questions about the supposed success of Black professional women. It has to temper our tendencies to celebrate the achievements of Patricia Harris, Shirley Chisholm, Phyllis Wallace, and Alice Walker. Looking at these "exceptions" detracts us from the serious inequities which exist even among those Black women who have attained heights of which their Black sisters, who lack many advantages, can only dream. The history of racial discrimination and the current restrictions should remind us that we need to identify and explore the ways that racial stratification continue to affect the labor market. This should be an area of concern which is equal to attending to the number of women entering traditionally male occupations and the struggle for comparable work within agencies and businesses.

We must learn from those researchers who have discussed the segmentation of the middle classes of racial minorities. Sharon Collins highlighted the limits of the progress of the Black middle class because their stability rests upon a government commitment to the public sector and enforcement of antidiscrimination legislation.[6] Both of these trends are jeopardized by the Reagan administration with its new definition of government responsibility. Thus, the growth of public sector employment for Blacks will be minimal and few efforts will be made to support Affirmative Action efforts on the part of the private sector.

In addition to its precarious future, the patterns of employment among Black professionals, especially females, have perpetuated a segmentation of the Black middle class. This is similar to Barrera's observations among Chicanos in the Southwest. There, the Mexican American middle class were also members of the internal colony and shared cultural issues with others in the Chicano community. Barrera notes:

Chicanos also constitute a colony with a certain coherence across class lines in the sense that they are liable to be in frequent contact with each other. Thus, the bilingual Chicano teacher, a member of the professional-managerial class, comes in contact with Chicano parents from the working class. Chicano social workers are liable to have a largely Chicano clientele, as are other Chicano professionals (1979:216).

The pattern for Blacks is very much a mirror image, except that many females as well as males in the Black community participate in the professional labor market. Additional research is needed to document specific trends and policies which result in the continued clustering of Black women in traditionally female occupations and their heavy reliance upon the public sector for employment. These are critical but the least discussed characteristics of this population of professional women. The patterns of employment for professional Black women must be discussed. Otherwise as we pass through the 1980s and into the 1990s, we will continue to find Black women teaching in public schools, nursing in public hospitals, and coping with heavy caseloads as social workers for the department of welfare. They will still be colonized professionals, caught in either public sector jobs or the few occupational opportunities in the private sector of the Black community. Maybe then researchers will cease to sing the praises of the tiny minority of Black women in formerly traditional male professions who are able to secure employment in the private sector.

NOTES

1. Following the model of Braverman (1974) the middle class is defined here as those who do mental rather than manual labor. This division roughly corresponds to the census categories of professional, technical and kindred workers, and managers, officials, and proprietors.

2. The nonwhite population for Chicago in 1940 was 282,244 (U.S. Bureau of the Census, 1943). Thus only a tiny minority of Black women were able to secure these white collar jobs.

3. In rural Black communities, earlier in this century, nonfarm employment options for Black women were limited to private household work, where women were frequently subjected to sexual exploitation. Only higher education could provide significantly different options for rural Black women. Meanwhile, Black males had more farm and nonfarm employment options and faced less sexual harassment. Thus E. Wilkin Bock (1971) posits that rural Black families encourage schooling more for daughters than sons as a means of insuring their mobility.

4. In his research, Doxey Wilkerson used the figures from the 1930 census and collected data on Blacks in the public school systems in 1940. This paper uses figures for the nonwhite population in cities from the 1940 census (U.S. Bureau of the Census, 1943).

5. The District of Columbia is omitted because the majority of its residents are employed in the public sector.

6. After an exploration of current data, Collins notes:

My findings contradict arguments that the growth of a black middle class is evidence of a decline in racial inequality in the United States. Rather, the evidence suggests the existence of race-regulated systems. Although members of the middle class are not necessarily restricted by occupation, income, or residence, they remain segregated in institutions dependent on federal government subsidy and concentrated in functions created to serve the black consumer and community. Race is implied within the black economy independent of class position. Public sector employees are most likely to be found in federal, state, and local government functions that legitimize and subsidize black under-class dependency. Blacks employed in the private sector remain concentrated in economically underdeveloped areas, or in intermediary positions between white corporations and black consumers, manpower, or policy issues (1983:379).

CHAPTER 5

Women, Labor Migration and Household Work: Japanese American Women in the Pre-War Period

Evelyn Nakano Glenn

INTRODUCTION

Women make up a large segment of the flow of labor from the often rural economic periphery to metropolitan centers. Recognition of women's role in labor migration is only recent, however. Until the mid 1970s women were ignored in the literature on labor migration, which focused almost exclusively on male migrant workers. When women were considered, they were viewed as appendages or dependents of male migrants, rather than autonomous actors.

Since the mid 1970s the increasing interest in women's work and a sharp rise in the proportion of women in the movement of labor have stimulated research on contemporary women migrants in Western Europe and the United States (*e.g.*, Phizacklea, 1983; Mortimer and Bryce-Laporte, 1981). This research has contributed much needed descriptive detail on the employment status or family situations of specific groups of migrant women. Still, much empirical and conceptual work remains to be done.

Most of the research on women migrants presents only partial views, for example focusing on women's personal lives in the family or examining aggregate data on labor force activity. In order to develop an adequate understanding of women's relationship to labor migration, we need to take a broader perspective, simultaneously considering women's relation to the family, the labor market and the larger political economy in which both family and employment are embedded. We also need more adequate historical grounding, so that the situation of contemporary women migrants is viewed as part of longer-term developments in capitalist economies and shifts in their labor market needs, rather than as isolated phenomena, unconnected to other historical processes. By taking a more holistic and historical approach, we may then begin to understand how the experience of migration differs for men and women and how these different experiences interrelate. Such an understanding is a first step in developing a theoretical framework that incorporates gender into the overall analysis of labor migration and settlement.

Though the recruitment of labor from economically dependent former colonies was accelerated by the demands of advanced capitalist economies, this type of migration is not an exclusively post-World War II phenomenon. It has been going on since at least the late eighteenth century in Europe (*e.g.*, Irish migration to England) and since the mid-nineteenth century in the United States (Bonacich and Cheng, 1984). Starting in that period, hundreds of thousands of workers were drawn from impoverished areas of Asia and Latin America to fill the demand for labor in the developing economies of the U.S. West and Southwest. Women's participation in these earlier labor migrations has remained largely invisible, however, perhaps because most women were not recruited as independent contract workers, but arrived as members of male migrants' families or as prostitutes, who are not seen as 'workers'.[1] Irrespective of the circumstances of their entry, wives and daughters of male migrants became wage laborers as well, and played a similar role in the economy. Like their male counterparts, female migrants filled jobs that were deemed too low paying, degraded or insecure for native workers of their own sex. Moreover, the same forces that pulled male migrants also drew the women to follow: namely the demand for cheap and malleable labor. This demand was a promise that if they came, they would be able to work to support themselves and their families.

Most importantly, the conditions governing women's labor migration were identical to those governing men's movement. Like their male counterparts, women migrants came from areas whose economies had been disrupted by colonial incursions, so that a large portion of the population was torn from its usual means of livelihood. They were recruited strictly to meet labor needs and were expected to come as temporary workers, not as permanent settlers, so family formation was discouraged. While in the "host" country, they were put into a special legal category that exempted them from the usual rights and protections. Finally, they were hemmed in by administrative and legal barriers, including being bound by long-term contracts, to ensure that they remained in the undesirable jobs for which they were recruited and did not compete with native workers.[2] In short, women migrants were part of the same historical processes and should be treated within the same conceptual framework as male migrants.

At the same time, however, migrant women's situation requires separate analysis, because their relationship to market and nonmarket work is distinct. Their work is shaped by gender as well as by their statuses as immigrants and racial/ethnic minorities. First, their place in the labor market is defined by stratification along all three axes, which interact to create a distinct labor market. In the pre-World War II period in the United States this market was made up principally of domestic service, agricultural labor, other service and manual occupations, and unpaid work in family enterprises. Second, their work diverges from that of men, including men in their groups, in that it subsumes a great deal of reproductive labor; this is labor that maintains the current labor force (*i.e.* feeding, clothing, and cleaning services for male workers) and creates the next generation of workers (*i.e.* caring for, nurturing, and socializing children) (Sokoloff, 1980). Maintaining family ties and transmitting cultural values are central elements of reproductive work for all women, but these tasks are more arduous for migrant labor women. Keeping the family together and building community solidarity are more difficult and essential in the face of stratified labor markets, poverty, and assaults on their cultures and community institutions.

The remainder of this paper presents a case study and analysis of one group of pre-World War II migrant women, Japanese American (issei) women in Northern California. This case is examined in terms of a larger historical context, which includes the structure of the local labor market and the recruitment and treatment of Asian labor during the first decades of the century. I look at the meaning of gender in the immigration process by focusing on women's work in the family and how it was affected by the transformation of the family economy that occurred with migration and women's entry into the urban labor market. I argue that the reshaping of gender politics in the family was a complex process involving contradictory elements: some traditional family features were retained because of their usefulness in the new situations, while other features underwent change. Some changes meant greater inequities in the division of labor while others involved reallocation of power favorable to women. In the conclusion, I address the issue of incorporating gender into theoretical models of labor immigration by pointing to some implications of focusing on women and their work in the family for the conceptualization of labor immigration and labor migrants.

ISSEI WOMEN'S MIGRATION

Issei women's migration took place almost solely within a 15 year span between 1908 and 1924. The first date marks the beginning of a "Gentleman's Agreement" between the governments of Japan and the United States that terminated all further immigration of "laborers" but left openings for relatives of resident Japanese. The latter date marks the cutoff of all immigration from Asia with the passage of the 1924 Immigration Act. The 35,000 women who entered during this brief interlude followed on the heels of nearly 100,000 men who migrated between 1890 and 1908.[3] They came, for the most part, as recent brides of men who had resided for some years in the United States.

This brief stream of women migrants was part of a larger international movement of labor from Asia to the western United States that took place between 1850 and the 1930s. During this period, hundreds of thousands of Asian workers, often male, left China, Japan, Korea and the Philippines to work in Hawaii and California. They came in response to the call for "cheap" labor required by capitalists to build the economic infrastructures and exploit the region's resources. Native labor was scarce, expensive and militant, in part because of abundant opportunities for natives in independent mining and farming. The U.S. presence as a power in Asia made that region a logical source of more malleable labor. Dislocations in the political economies of Asian countries had left a substantial portion of the peasantry with their means of livelihood disrupted and therefore detachable from their roots. As an imperial power the United States could exact conditions that permitted recruitment of labor under terms that made Asian immigrant labor highly vulnerable and therefore malleable. For example, Asian laborers were denied naturalization rights and were sometimes bound by long-term contracts (Bonacich and Cheng, 1984).

The cheapness of Asian labor was further ensured by restricting immigration for the most part to prime age males. The cost of reproduction devolved on wives and other relatives in the home village, who engaged in subsistence farming, maintained the household, raised children, and took care of the sick, elderly and disabled. They stretched the meager remittances sent by male workers abroad.

Legal and administrative practices prohibited or discouraged the entry of women and children. These practices, as well as racist treatment, reinforced the sojourner orientation of Asian male immigrants, most of whom planned to work for a few years and return home with a nest egg. The majority of Asian men did precisely that. Ironically, the restrictions designed to keep Asians subordinated in the labor market made it difficult for them to earn enough to accumulate capital to return home. Men who were therefore the least successful economically predominated among those settling permanently, despite being parted from wives and children or forced to remain single. Only among the Japanese did substantial numbers of women immigrate, through a peculiar loophole in the law, and then only for a few years and in smaller number than men.

The first to be recruited were the Chinese, who began entering in the 1850s. When their entry was cut off by the Chinese Exclusion Act of 1882, the Japanese took their place, and after 1924 the Filipinos replaced the Japanese. The experience of the Chinese was critical for the succeeding groups because the restrictive measures developed to handle the Chinese became the model for the treatment of all Asians. The peak years of Chinese immigration saw the entrenchment of a race-stratified labor system (Saxton, 1971). Henceforth, only the most demeaning and dangerous jobs were deemed appropriate for Asians, who were also paid on a separate and lower wage scale, because of their "lower standard of living."

The vast majority of issei women, like their husbands, came from rural farm or small town entrepreneurial families. They were drawn almost exclusively from the four southern prefectures of Hiroshima, Yamaguchi, Kumamoto, and Fukuoka, among the poorest in Japan. Most were in their twenties, and (due to *Meiji* era reforms) most were literate, with six to eight years of schooling. They were recruited to come to America through arranged marriages, sometimes contracted in person and sometimes at a distance via an exchange of photographs. Leaving their villages for the wilds of California, Washington, and other parts of the U.S. West was somewhat of a hardship, but it was consistent with Japanese patrilocal practice. Wives left their parents' household to join her husband in his native village. Moreover, it was a demographic necessity that some women marry men abroad, since so many men had left for various parts of Asia and the New World. The move was seen as temporary in any case: at most 5 or 10 years of work abroad would enable them to return with the prospect of a comfortable future.

ISSEI WOMEN'S LABOR MARKET WORK

The marriages were instigated by male sojourners at a point when they had decided that they were not going to make their fortune and return home as quickly as they originally hoped and felt the need of a wife's help. What I am suggesting is that quite apart from any sentimental desire for family life, there were hard, practical reasons for a man to send for a wife. A wife would provide much needed labor, in the form of services at home and income producing activities outside.

Therefore, though they were not independent migrants, women were indirectly recruited to fill labor needs. They were quickly absorbed into the labor market. As early as 1915 an observer of the Japanese in California noted:

> The great majority of wives of farmers, barbers and small shopkeepers take a more or less regular place in the fields or shops of their husbands, while a smaller number accept places of domestic service, or in laundries or other places of employment. Thus a larger percentage of those admitted find a place in the labor supply (Millis, 1915:20).

The 1920 census shows 20.8 percent of all Japanese women over 15, nearly all of whom were married, were gainfully employed, more than twice the proportion of employed among married women in the population as a whole. Even this rate is an underestimation, given the concentration of Japanese men in agriculture and small enterprises. Their wives performed unpaid labor, usually not enumerated by census takers. In the San Francisco Bay area, where I conducted interviews, elderly issei reported that virtually all women engaged in income producing activities.

The labor market for Japanese immigrant women was closely related to that for Japanese men, and it varied by locale. Agriculture employed over half of all issei employed women in 1920, while 40 percent of the remainder were drawn into domestic service. Most of the rest were in personal services, primarily in laundries and retail trade. In the Bay area the majority of issei women were employed as private household workers. The local economy also provided opportunities for women to engage in informal market work not covered by the census, including taking in laundry and manufacturing small goods at home. (Occupational distributions reported in the U.S. Census for 1900 to 1940 are shown in Table 5.1.)

Whether in the formal or informal market, the occupations in which issei women specialized share several common characteristics. Issei women's jobs were seasonal, irregular or part time. They involved female-typed activities (e.g. housecleaning, laundry, sewing.), especially "women's work" that was physically taxing, low waged, and degraded in status, so that native white women shunned it. They were in positions where language difficulties and racial discrimination did not constitute barriers to employment. Finally they were in industries outside the advanced sectors. They were often employed in the interstices of capitalism, where long hours and low pay substituted for capital investment, as was the case with small service and retail establishments. That these occupations formed a distinct labor market for Japanese immigrant women in confirmed in the job histories of 15 issei women interviewed in depth. All had worked in domestic service, which was why they were included in the study in the first place: in addition, however, 11 of the 15 had worked in other jobs at various times, including farming, laundry work at home or in a commercial laundry, plant nursery work, garment manufacturing, dressmaking, home manufacture, midwifery, and unpaid labor in a family-run shop or hotel.

THE FAMILY ECONOMY IN SOUTHERN JAPAN

The entry of women into the labor market represented a major shift in the family economy of the immigrants. The profundity of the change can be appreciated by considering the family system in which the immigrants were raised.

The fundamental social unit of the towns and villages of late nineteenth and early twentieth century Japan was the household or *ie*. The *ie* was a

Table 5.1. Occupational Distribution of Employed Japanese American Women, 1900-1940[a]

	1900	1920	1930	1940[b]
Agricultural workers	4.9%	34.0%	30.3%	37.7%
Servants	56.8%[c]	26.6%	17.7%	10.3%
Other personal service workers	21.4%	18.0%	21.7%	23.6%[d]
Trade	3.4%	7.0%	14.0%	10.2%[e]
Dressmakers, seamstresses and tailors	8.6%	2.3%	1.8%	—[f]
Other manufacturing pursuits	3.0%	7.1%	5.2%	12.0%[g]
Professionals	1.9%	2.7%	4.9%	3.2%
Clerical workers	—[i]	1.4%	4.0%	—[h]
Other	—[i]	0.8%	0.4%	3.0%
Total Employed	(266)	(5,289)	(6,741)	(6,693)

Sources: For 1900: U.S. Bureau of the Census, *Special Reports. Occupations of the Twelfth Census* (Washington, D.C.: U.S. Government Printing Office, 1904, table 35: "Distribution, by Specified Occupations, of Males and of Females in the Chinese, Japanese, and Indian Population Gainfully Employed, 1900." For 1920: U.S. Bureau of the Census, *Fourteenth Census of the United States, Taken in the Year 1920,* vol. 4: *Population. Occupations* (Washington, D.C.: U.S. Government Printing Office, 1923), table 5: "Total Persons 10 Years of Age and Over Engaged in Each Specified Occupation." For 1930: U.S. Bureau of the Census, *Fifteenth Census of the United States: Population,* vol. 5: *General Report on Occupation* (Washington, D.C.: U.S. Government Printing Office, 1933), table 6: "Chinese and Japanese Gainful Workers 10 Years Old and Over by Occupation and Sex, for the United States and Selected States, 1930." For 1940: U.S. Bureau of the Census, *Sixteenth Census of the Population, 1940: Population Characteristics of the Non-white Population by Race* (Washington, D.C.: U.S. Government Printing Office, 1943), table 8: "Non-white Employed Persons 14 Years Old and Over by Major Occupation Group, Race, and Sex, for the United States, by Regions, Urban and Rural, 1940."
[a]Data for 1910 are omitted because occupational figures for Japanese and Chinese were combined in the census report.
[b]Only foreign-born (issei) women are included in the figures for 1940. The 1940 census for the first time reported separate figures for native and foreign-born. The figures for 1930 include some native-born (nisei) women, but they probably constitute only a small proportion of the total. Because of immigration patterns, most nisei were born after 1910.
[c]Includes some waitresses.
[d]Made up of "proprietors, managers, and officials, except farm" and "service workers, except domestic."
[e]Named "clerical, sales and kindred workers" in the 1940 census.
[f]No longer separately reported; presumably these occupations are included below under "manufacturing."
[g]Named "operatives and kindred workers" in the 1940 census.
[h]Included under "trade," above.
[i]Not applicable.

residential unit consisting of all members living together, whether related by blood or not. Like peasant households everywhere, the *ie* operated as a corporate economic body for property ownership, production, and consumption. Land or business was held in common. Profits accrued to the household, not individuals, and each member was provided for out of the joint production. In return members contributed unpaid labor to the household enterprise, whether farming or trade (Nakane, 1967).

The *ie* was hierarchically structured according to gender, age, and insider-outsider status. Males took precedence over females, elder over younger, and those born in the household over those born outside (Beardsley *et al.*, 1959; Nakane, 1967). Authority, work assignments, and privileges were assigned according to these three axes of stratification. The head of the household, the eldest male born in the household was accorded ultimate authority. He was the recognized representative of the household to outside institutions, and the manager of the family enterprise. The eldest son (*chonan*) was the most favored offspring, for he assumed the headship upon the death or retirement of his father. He inherited the common land or business and the main house. He carried on the family occupation, took care of elderly parents, and was responsible for worshipping ancestors. Younger sons moved out to form separate households upon marriage. Daughters joined the households of their husbands (Watanabe, 1977).

In contrast to the formal rules governing the authority of the male head, the position of the mistress of the household was ill-defined. According to the social ideal, women were subordinate and denied any formal role in the public domain. A woman could, nonetheless, exert considerable leverage if she was politically capable, contributed a great deal to family income through skill or hard work, or had a forceful personality. A woman gained power as she moved through the life cycle, culminating in the period when she was a mother-in-law and ruled over the other females in the household (Watanabe, 1977).

A woman was at her lowest ebb as a daughter-in-law in a stem household. As a young female outsider, she fell at the bottom of the hierarchy. She was assigned the most menial and onerous tasks and waited on every one else, all under the critical supervision of her husband's mother.

The value of women's labor has been hypothesized to be a variable in women's relative status. Embree, an American sociologist observing a southern Japanese village in the mid-1930s, commented:

> In farm work man and wife are equal, so that in a farmer's household a woman has comparatively higher status than in a shopkeeper's house. If a man did not get along with his wife on the farm, his own income and food supply would be endangered (Embree, 1939:13).

In addition, farm women seemed to have greater freedom than suggested by the ideal. Women participated regularly in village festivals and were involved in female work groups in cooperative ventures such as manufacturing hair oil. Older women, especially, seemed to have considerable freedom to drink, joke, and tell ribald stories (Smith and Wiswell, 1952).[4]

WAGE EARNING IMMIGRANT FAMILIES

When they immigrated, the issei entered an industrialized economy in which wage labor was becoming the predominate mode. Though many issei families found preindustrial niches in farming and small enterprises and retained the family as a production unit, others, including most in the Bay area, adapted to the urban economy by turning to multiple wage earning. Husband and wife, and sometimes older children, were individually employed in marginal low paying jobs. While each worker's wage was small, the pooled income was sufficient to support a household and generate some surplus for remittances and savings. Tilly and Scott (1978) call this pattern, found among working class urban families in the nineteenth and twentieth centuries, the "family wage economy."

In some ways the family wage strategy was congruent with the Japanese *ie* system. Because the household relied on multiple wages, the strategy preserved economic interdependence among family members. At the same time, women's employment enabled women to retain their traditional role as active contributors to the family economy. In other ways, however, the strategy contradicted traditional values. Under a wage labor system, the individual, not the household, was the unit of production, and work and household were separate, rather than integrated spheres. Finally, when women were employed outside the household, husbands no longer exercised direct control over wives' labor.

These contradictions are expressed in a division among issei men in their attitudes toward wives' employment.[5] Some men vociferously opposed their wives' working outside, claiming their services were needed at home. Other men demanded that their wives assume financial responsibility by taking a job, irrespective of the women's own desires. Mr. Amano and Mr. Togasaki represent the two poles. Mrs. Amano reports that she went out to work in defiance of her husband's wishes:

> Mr. Amano was sickly when he was young, so he didn't want the children left alone. He said, "What if the children get hurt. You couldn't get their lives back. The children are worth more than a few dollars. Just as long as we have enough to eat, that's enough"

In contrast, Mrs. Togasaki reported that she felt compelled to seek employment:

> My husband didn't bring in enough money, so I went out to work. I didn't even think twice about it. If I didn't take the job, people would have started to call me "madam" (Interviewer interpretation: presuming she thought she

was too much of a lady to work.) It was like a race; we all had to work as hard as possible.

The contradictions of women's wage work extend to its impacts on women's status in the family. On the one hand, as long as an unequal allocation of household labor and male privilege persisted, wage work increased women's burdens. On the other hand, outside employment reduced women's economic dependence and circumvented husbands' control over their labor, thereby freeing them from the more extreme constraints imposed by traditional gender roles in the family. Both tendencies can be seen in issei women's accounts of family life.

Not unexpectedly, issei women uniformly reported that they, rather than their husbands, bore the major burden of household work and child care, regardless of employment status. Fourteen of the fifteen interviewed said their husbands contributed little or no housework. The sense of privilege assumed by issei men was vividly conveyed by Mrs. Nishimura in her description of her husband:

> No, my husband was like a child. He couldn't even make tea. He couldn't do anything by himself. He was really Japan-style. Sometimes I had too much to do, so although I would always iron his shirts, I might ask him to wait awhile on the underwear, but he'd say no. He'd wait until I would iron them. People used to say he was spoiled. He was completely a Japanese man. Some people divorce their husbands for not helping around the house, but that never entered my mind. I thought it was natural for a Japanese.

Mr. Nishimura might be considered extreme even by issei standards, but all the women reported that their husbands expected to be waited upon by their wives. The term "Japanese" was used frequently to describe husbands. The use of the term signified the difference issei women saw between issei men and other men, (i.e., Caucasian Americans), whom they saw as much more domesticated. Issei women viewed their husbands' obstinance as peculiarly Japanese. They attributed that intransigence to their husbands' early upbringing, which had permanently molded their personalities. One detects in Mrs. Nishimura's account a perverse pride in her husband's stubborness and in her ability to fulfill his demands, no matter how unreasonable. When asked whether they wished their husbands helped more around the house, women typically responded in the affirmative, but added that it was a baseless hope. Mrs. Kono, for example, replied: "If he would, it would be good, but—indeed—they don't do it—men folk won't." Another typical response was Mrs. Togasaki's: "Right from the beginning he never did it, so I thought that's the way it was. People from Japan are that way. Nisei are different. Issei men usually don't do any housework."

Male privilege was so firmly entrenched that even when the wife was the sole earner, as sometimes happened due to a husband's ill health or unemployment, she continued to do most of the housework. In a culture that so emphasized male prerogative, unemployed men may have had a special need to avoid losing status by taking on devalued "women's work." The complement of male privilege was female overload. Though issei men typically performed heavy phyical labor and worked long hours, their work days had defined limits, ending when they reached home. In contrast, women's work spanned the clock. Their duties started before other members of the household arose, with the preparation of a morning meal, and continued after the others retired for the night, with the cleaning up and preparing of food and clothing for the next day. Some women complained of being constantly overextended and exhausted. Mrs. Togasaki confessed to having to let her housework slide: "My house was a mess. I went to work in the morning, and when I came back from work, I'd cook a little and then go sleep, and that's about all."

Other women managed numerous responsibilities by sleeping very little . Mrs. Nishimura was blessed by a high level of energy, which is apparent even today. She had seven children, a full-time job, and managed to sew all of her own and children's clothing. She described a typical day when she lived in Alameda and worked as a garment operative in Oakland:

> Since I had so many children, I asked my mother-in-law to take care of the children. I would get up at 5 o'clock to do the laundry. In those days we'd do it by hand—and hang up the laundry, then go to Oakland. I would come home, and since my husband didn't have much work then, he'd get drunk and bring the children home. I would cook and eat, and then go to sleep. They all asked me how long I slept at night. But since I was in my twenties, it didn't affect me too much.

Mrs. Nishimura's account reveals an additional complication created by wage employment that did not exist when the household functioned as a production unit. With women working outside the home, special provision usually had to be made for child care. Interestingly enough, some issei owners of laundries and nurseries operated under the traditional household model and employed couples, allowing them to bring infants or small children to work. Mrs. Nishimura reported that her employers, brothers who ran a large commercial laundry, set aside space for infants and gave her time off to nurse. Employers of domestics occasionally allowed household workers to bring a child to work. More often, however, separate arrangements had to be made; husbands and older children were called upon to babysit. Older daughters might be forced to drop out of school to help care for younger siblings. Once all her children reached school age, a woman might cope by arranging work hours to coincide with school schedules. When children were small and women had to work full time, however, some issei families resorted to sending their children to Japan to be raised by relatives. Three of the issei women interviewed did so. Mrs. Taniguchi, a laundry operative, had stopped working after her second child was born. Soon afterwards her husband became seriously ill and could not work. She asked her father-in-law, who was returning to Japan, to take the two children with him so she could return to her job in the laundry. The Taniguchis, like other issei, hoped to return someday to Japan and felt their children would benefit from a proper Japanese upbringing and education. Their children's presence in Japan would also commit them to returning. However, as with many other issei families, the Taniguchis never went back and eventually sent for their children to rejoin them in the United States.

The other twelve issei families managed to raise their children in the U.S. even with the mother employed. Instead of relying on extended kin, families shifted responsibilities internally. Even though male privilege persisted, roles were partially redefined as a result of the pressures created by a wage labor system and women's employment. Although hubands rarely undertook housework, they were more willing to assume some responsibility for child care. Even Mr. Nishimura, the completely Japanese man, transported and minded his children when his wife worked and he was unemployed. Mrs. Sugihara reported that her husband did quite a lot of housework and didn't mind doing the dishes. She noted that he was unusual in that:

> He was considerably Americanized. He was young when he came over and he was a schoolboy, so he was used to the American way of doing things. Even when we quarreled, he wouldn't hit me, saying it's bad in this country for a man to hit a woman, unlike Japan. In Japan, the man would be head of the family without question. "Japan is a man's country; America is a woman's country" he often used to say.

Though not found among the issei who were interviewed, nisei respondents (American-born Japanese, children of issei) and community informants reported cases of role reversal among issei couples, in which the wife took on sole responsibility for breadwinning while the husband assumed all household tasks. Such reversals seemed to occur most easily when the husband was considerably older than the wife. Many issei men had remained bachelors for years, trying to accumulate a nest egg; when they finally decided to marry, they nonetheless chose much younger women as wives. In such instances they might be in their fifties, the typical age of retirement in Japan, by the time their children reached school age. Many of these issei men were employed in manual jobs that required physical strength, so their employment prospects dimmed as they got older. Their younger and more vigorous wives could easily secure positions in domestic service. Mrs. Tanabe was the only child of just such an issei couple. She recollected that her father was already retired when she was quite young. Perhaps embarrassed by her parents' situation, she exclaimed:

> The Hiroshima men in Alameda were the laziest men! Their wives did all the work. My dad raised me while my mother went out and did domestic

work. He did the cooking and kept house and did the shopping and took me when I went to school. So he didn't do much really. But in Alameda they're known for being the lazy ones—most Hiroshima men are—so no one's rich.

In addition to limited opportunities to work and attitudes about retirement, another reason for role reversal may be that domesticity, though considered inappropriate for men in their prime, was viewed as suitable for older men. Evidence confirming this interpretation is found in Mrs. Yamashita's account. She reported that her issei father, a widower, lived with her family and acted as housekeeper and baby sitter while she and her husband were both employed: "Oh, yes he babysat the children. And he cooked and cleaned and everything. So that's why I was able to work."

Immigration, settlement and the shift to the family wage economy also affected women's nonwork time and activities. As is true of agricultural labor everywhere, the work of Japanese farm families was governed by seasonal rhythms. They worked long hours during peak times, but they also enjoyed periods of relief from toil. Seasonal and religious festivals were occasions for emotional expression and release. In addition, much work was convivial. Men and women in the village often formed work groups to carry out a communal project. For example all the women got together once a year to manufacture hair oil for everyone's use. Such projects combined work and socializing. In the United States the issei experienced an unceasing round of labor, seldom interrupted by leisure or socializing. Spurred on by a drive to get ahead as quickly as possible and return to Japan, yet hampered by discrimination from succeeding, the issei toiled harder and more constantly than they would have in Japan. When asked about how their life might have differed had they stayed in Japan, issei women replied that they would not have had to work as hard, though they might have been less well off materially. There were community activities, but few women participated. Women also found fewer opportunities to engage in communal projects with other women and less seasonal variation in the amount of work to be done. None of the issei had ever taken a vacation before World War II, and few had money or time for entertainment. Mrs. Yoshida who lived in Alameda was asked whether she had ever gone to Oakland (a 10 minute car ride) or San Francisco (a 30 minute bus ride); she responded:

No, not once did I ever go! When the children were small I never went anywhere. When we lived on Encinal, there was a very large movie house. It was only a half block away, but I never saw it. Not once. I didn't have that kind of money. If I had any money I had to buy the kids things. I lived there ten years, but never once went when they were kids. That was a very hard time.

Because many immigrant families never had time for recreation, they remained uninvolved in community life. They did not belong to organizations or contribute to them. Church on Sunday was their only nonwork activity.

Scarce leisure time was rarely shared by husbands and wives. Issei couples retained the segregated pattern characteristic of the rural Japanese (*c.f.* Bott, 1957). Though the household was unified for economic purposes, sleeping and working together, behavior in public was governed by strict separation. Embree, observing a rural village in the 1930s noted:

> Man and wife are never seen to walk down the street talking together. The man will go alone or with a group of men, the wife alone or with some other women. Both man and wife, however, usually come to strictly family affairs such as weddings and funerals, though even here, men and women are seated on opposite sides of the room (Embree, 1939:95).

This description fits the issei, who retained the traditional pattern of segregation, especially in public life. Most community organizations, such as district associations, athletic clubs, and credit associations were open to men only. Many activities, such as a dinner for contributors to the Japanese school, were attended solely by men, who went as representatives of the household. When men and women attended affairs together, they congregated with others of their own sex. Separate sections were set aside for men and women at church services. In general women's orbits were much smaller than men's. Aside from infrequent outings for weddings, funerals, or special church functions, their socializing was restricted to informal encounters with other women in the course of daily shopping or running errands. Men had many more opportunities for socializing with other men. Some men regularly gambled or drank with their male friends. Mrs. Nishimura complained that she sometimes stayed up until two in the morning, serving snacks and drinks to her husband's friends when they came over to play cards, even though she had to get up at five to go to work.

Drinking was perhaps the most common pasttime of issei men, many of whom turned regularly to alcohol as a solace from the daily grind. While some men imbibed in the company of friends, engaging in horseplay and storytelling, many drank alone at home. Men's drinking was a source of discord in many families, leading to financial problems and conflict. Two women's lives were scarred by tragedy as a result of their husband's drinking. Mrs. Takagi's husband was often out of work, and he refused to turn over much of what he did earn. He got into frequent accidents and she recalls the constant worry of waiting for him to come home. Once she had to borrow money from a friend to bail him out of jail. Mrs. Shinoda's husband was killed in a judo mishap while intoxicated, and she was forced to take her two sons to Japan to be cared for while she worked as a live-in domestic to support herself. Perhaps a more typical story is Mrs. Kayahara's. Her husband continued to work, but his health deteriorated as a result of regular heavy drinking. When asked what kind of person her husband was she replied:

Not so much nice, but not so bad. (Interviewer questioned: Was he old fashioned?) Just like a Japan boy! So I did everything—cook, wash, keep house. My husband drank. He drank so much his stomach went bad. Once we married, he would have 5 or 6 drinks every day—sake. All his life he did that. But he did work hard.

Money spent on alcohol or going out with the men was a drain on family income. The contention over men's drinking thus reflected a larger conflict over control of family resources. Many wives did not know exactly what their husbands earned, since most were gardeners or otherwise self-employed and could keep their earnings secret. Some husbands chose to treat their wages as their own property, giving their wives some portion while withholding some for their own expenses: the amount they contributed did not increase as the actual expenses of the household rose. Women were expected to make up the difference through their own earnings.

The frequency of drinking among issei men is revealed by the fact that women whose husbands did not drink heavily made a point of mentioning it without being asked. Mrs. Sughihara describes her husband as unusual among issei men. Though we may doubt whether he was quite the paragon that she describes, it is noteworthy that she focussed on his not drinking as evidence of his virtue:

Yes, I've been lucky. I worked, of course, and encountered social problems (*interpreted by interviewer to imply discrimination*) but I didn't suffer at all with regard to my husband. He didn't smoke, drink or gamble. Very serious Christian with no faults. Everyone else was drinking and gambling. Park Street was full of liquor stores and so they'd all go there. But my husband led such a clean life, so I was lucky.

A more down-to-earth assessment is made of Mr. Adachi by his wife, who is grateful that he was not a problem, even when he did drink: "He was not quarrelsome; he didn't gossip about other people. He didn't get drunk, that is, not knowing what day it was or falling down. If he drank, he fell asleep."

Despite these conflicts issei marriages were extremely stable; the divorce rate was only 0.6 percent according to Kitano (1976). Yet, the marriages ought not to be romanticized. Nor should harmony or unity of interest be assumed. To be sure, economic interdependence and shared cultural values bound members together. Yet, members were also separated by gender divisions: the discrepancy in power and privilege, the unequal division of household and child care labor, and the disjunction of male and female social and emotional worlds. These divisions meant that men's and women's interests were fundamentally different. Overwork and poverty intensified conflict. Far from responding passively, many women actively contended with their husbands. Mrs. Taniguchi, who had to send her three children to Japan and work in a laundry to support her sickly husband, reports:

My life in the U.S. was very hard in the beginning because my husband was ill so much and we had such totally different personalities. We were both selfish, so we had many problems. But after I started going to church, I became more gentle. So we had fewer quarrels. I think that is a gift from God.

Mrs. Nishimura also noted that she frequently quarreled with her husband. She explained:

Well, he was rather short-tempered . . . there were times when I thought he was stubborn, but we were far apart in age, so I would attribute our differences to that. Being apart in age does create quite a lot of differences . . . but I bore it all.

What is the significance of the age difference? Quite likely Mr. Nishimura attempted to exercise patriarchal authority; he expected her, as a younger female, to acquiesce to him, an older, more experienced male. That she did not, led to constant contention. Thus, though both Mrs. Taniguchi and Mrs. Nishimura express the proper Japanese attitude that women must bear difficulty and hardship stoically, it is evident that they did not do so silently. They were willing to challenge their husbands and engage in daily struggle.

CONCLUSIONS

Migration from economically underdeveloped regions to more advanced urban centers is often assumed to have a liberating effect for women as traditional patterns of family life, such as the authority of the larger kin network, give way to individualism, and as women gain economic independence through outside employment. The experience of Japanese immigrants in the pre-World War II period indicates that the degree and kind of change depends on the economic strategy that migrants adopt in the host economy. Issei who continued household-based production by going into family farming or small enterprises reproduced traditional Japanese household structures. In contrast issei, including those of the domestic workers in the study, who adopted a new economic strategy, (namely multiple wage earning), experienced greater change in household relationships. The changes that accompanied the shift to a family wage economy had contradictory impacts on women's reproductive work and their position in the family.

The sojourner strategy of working hard and sacrificing short-term comfort for long-term goals; the entry of women into the labor market to further the economic goal; and the traditional expectation that women both contribute economically and assume responsibility for domestic labor all served to increase the overall burden on issei women. The tradition that women contribute economically was easily adapted to the urban wage economy, in that women simply transferred their productive activities to the labor market. The tradition of male privilege and female service was harder to alter. One suspects that buttressing the ideology, which was deeply internalized, was the implicit threat of physical domination. Therefore, it is only under special circumstances that the weight of household labor was shifted. One such circumstance was the not infrequent case where the husband was considerably older than the wife, so that he was in his fifties or sixties while the wife was in her prime working years. In that case he might take on some or all of the housekeeping chores, while she assumed the main income earning role.

Involvement in wage work instead of household based production also created some new problems that did not exist when women were part of the household production unit. The most notable of these was the lack of built-in care and supervision of children. Under the family production system in Japan children were surrounded by a group of caretakers: parents, grandparents, older siblings, and sometimes other relatives and servants. The change in work rhythms and organization of labor from the farm village to the urban economy (in combination with the economic pressures on immigrants) altered patterns of work and leisure in ways that were largely unfavorable. The immigrants, particularly immigrant women, probably had less relief from the grinding work load than they would have in the village. There was less seasonal variation in the amount of work, fewer occasions for participating in communal projects with other women that combined work and socializing, and less frequent community festivities to provide periodic release of emotion.

The gains that women made with migration and entry into the urban labor force are more subtle than the costs. There was, of course, the tangible benefit of added income, part of which could be retained for individual savings or spending. A less tangible but perhaps more significant gain issei women made was to attain some degree of control over their economic circumstances. In Japan women were ultimately at the mercy of their husband's ability or willingness to provide support. Mrs. Takagi's mother suffered extreme poverty as a result of her father's irresponsibility and heavy drinking. His debts eventually led to the loss of their family farm. Her own husband drank and rarely contributed to the family income. Mrs. Takagi feels less victimized than her mother because in the U.S. she was able to work to support herself and her children. The ability to provide for their children fulfilled issei women's deeply engrained belief in *oya-koku*, the reciprocal obligation that existed between parent and child. Sacrifice and hard work for the sake of children enhanced issei women's self esteem and also their reputation in the community. According to Kitano, "The story of an aging parent living practically on bread and water in order that his children could gain a college education is not an unusual one in issei culture" (Kitano, 1976:76). Though Kitano uses the male pronoun, his statement is probably more appropriately applied to women, who were much more likely to sacrifice and stint themselves for the sake of their children than their husbands. Mrs. Nishimura recalls the years spent working and planning for her children's future with satisfaction:

> This is my best time, but my happiest time was then, when my children were small. I was poor and busy then, but that might have been the best time. It was good to think about my children—how they'd go through high school and college and afterwards.

The very difficulty of their circumstances and their ability to bear it all was a point of pride for many issei women. Looking back at what they accomplished, they express amazement at their own energy and fortitude.

THEORETICAL IMPLICATIONS

I turn now to more general implications of this analysis of issei women for the conceptualization of labor migrants and their families. First, and most basic, the analysis of women migrants draws attention to the fact that migrants are not just individual workers in the labor market, but are also members of family groups. Moreover, the experience of women migrants' work in the market and at home highlights the connection between migrants' position in a stratified labor market and the structure of their family life.

Models of labor migration based on the analysis of male migrants treat migrants as individual units of labor (*e.g.,* Piore, 1979). According to these models, migrant workers are of value to the host society precisely because they are unencumbered by family ties. Detachment from family makes them cheaper sources of labor because reproductive costs are saved, and it makes them more flexible, because they are free to be moved about as needed. The host society discourages or prohibits migrant workers from forming or reforming families in order to keep them more exploitable and to prevent permanent settlement.

Family life of migrants therefore ends up getting ignored or seen primarily as a "social problem". Despite the invisibility of and hostility to migrants' family ties, migrants are nonetheless members of families, in the home country, if not in the receiving society, and sometimes in both. Even in the case where an individual migrates alone, migration is typically a family strategy rather than an individual one, as remittances from sojourning members is the means for supporting the household at home. For the migrant who succeeds in forming a family in the host society, the economic strategies adopted to cope with the stratified labor markets are similarly family survival strategies, whether they involve cooperating in a family enterprise or pooling multiple wages.

Ironically, the very difficulties placed in the way of migrants getting ahead and accumulating a nest egg often make family formation, and therefore permanent settlement a necessity. Because migrants cannot make it on their own in a short time, they willy-nilly become long-term settlers, establishing ethnic communities and raising children. Migrants, moreover, do not passively acquiesce to the restrictions imposed on family formation, but attempt in a variety of ways to use legal and extralegal means to get spouses and relatives into the host country. They strive to reconstruct family life in whatever way possible.

The analysis of changes in issei women's role and work in the family points to a further implication: namely the way we conceptualize the migrant family. The family is obviously an important resource in migrants' ability to survive in a hostile environment. It is united in opposition to the forces arrayed against it. However, the interests of individual members within it are not synonymous. Divisions and inequality along gender lines create conflicts and generate struggles between men and women. The issei family was simultaneously a unity, bound by economic interdependence and the struggle for survival, and a segmented institution in which men and women struggled over power, resources, and labor.

POLICY IMPLICATIONS

What relevance does this historical case study have for current policy? Can any implications be drawn for the situation of contemporary migrant and immigrant women?

At the global level the issues raised are still current for millions of migrant and immigrant workers in societies ranging from South Africa to Scandinavia. Migrant workers are still prevented from bringing family members or forming households in the metropolitan centers of western Europe and in the white designated areas and labor camps of South Africa. Women in these situations, whether they are the ones left behind in the homeland or the ones who migrate to find work, carry a tremendous weight. They either bear the whole brunt of reproductive labor without assistance or give up any semblance of normal family life, through prolonged separation from husbands, children, and extended kin. A world economic order that simultaneously devours "cheap" human labor, while tearing the source of the labor from its roots, is supported by inhumane state policies that are buttressed by force.

Since 1965 official immigration policy in the United States favors the formation of families, even among non-European immigrants. Reunification of family members is one criterion for entry. Nonetheless certain kinds of labor are still recruited as "individual units" outside that official policy. Recently in response to intense lobbying by corporate agricultural interests, the U.S. Congress reinstituted the Mexican *bracero* program. Once again temporary detached workers, in this case males, can be recruited legally as low wage farm labor to undercut permanent native and immigrant labor. Concomitantly women are being drawn to urban centers to fill the demand for domestic labor—to become maids, baby sitters, and housekeepers in New York, Los Angeles, and other large cities. Frequently, especially if they enter *sub rosa*, these women are isolated and vulnerable, bereft of any legal protections, as well as the support of kin and community.

Current Asian immigrant women, Korean, Chinese, Southeast Asian, and Filipino, arrive as members of family groups. Like earlier Asian immigrant women, they are forced into unpaid labor in marginal family enterprises or into the wage labor force. Because of their extreme vulnerability (problems with language, unfamiliarity with their legal rights, etc.), they are often exploited. Chinese women are paid subminimum wages in the garment industry, and pressured to falsify time cards or to do illegal home work to keep their jobs. They suffer from the same lack of institutional services that issei women did earlier. Their children must be left on their own while both they and their husbands work at low wage jobs.

Immigrant women are trapped in such marginal, seasonal, low wage work. They cannot improve their prospects, because of discrimination and because they have no time to learn English or to develop alternative job skills. Thus the kinds of supports that all working class women need—affordable, extended-day child care, job training, and health and social services—are needed by immigrant women. Additionally, immigrant women require special services, such as legal assistance with immigration and employment problems, translation services, and bilingual instruction. All such services should be tailored to the unique cultural and economic circumstances of particular groups, and located in the communities in which they live, so that they are accessible. Thus a policy for women's employment must be sensitive not only to issues of race and class, but also to the additional concerns of immigrant women.

NOTES

1. It is conceptually consistent to see the recruitment and migration of prostitutes from colonized areas as part of the overall recruitment and exploitation of cheap labor: the women were exploited economically and they generated huge profits for those who controlled their labor. See Hirata, 1979.

2. These conditions differentiate labor migration from other types of migration and immigration. Thus, the history of groups that entered as labor migrants is fundamentally different from the history of other groups, particularly those of European origin. The various European immigrant groups did not confront the above conditions: the countries from which they originated were not usually colonial dependencies. They were viewed as permanent or potentially permanent settlers, rather than as temporary laborers. They were not placed in special legal categories, and the barriers to mobility were not nearly so systematic or impenetrable. Hence, the analysis developed in this paper focuses on the relationship of women to a particular type of migration, and may not be applicable to other cases, such as the experience of European immigrant women.

3. These figures are for the mainland U.S. only, and do not include migration to Hawaii. They are based on figures presented by Ichihashi, 1932.

4. For a detailed description of the latitude allowed women see pp. 73–84 of Smith and Wiswell, 1982.

5. The quotations in this section are drawn from interviews with 15 issei women living in the San Francisco Bay area, and were carried out by the author between 1976 and 1977. All the names used in this chapter are pseudonyms.

CHAPTER 6

Young Women's Choice of Nontraditional Occupations

SUE E. BERRYMAN AND LINDA J. WAITE

This research was prepared with the support of Grant Number 820-0408 from the Urban Poverty Program, The Ford Foundation.

THEORETICAL PERSPECTIVE

Economists routinely attempt to explain the economic *consequences* of occupational choices, such as earnings distributions or human capital investments, but only rarely do they try to model the process of choice. Sociologists are more apt to model the determinants of the socioeconomic status of occupational choices (as in Sewell and Hauser, 1975; or Rosen and Aneshensel, 1978), but to ignore factors that have traditionally caused occupations to be regarded as typically male or female.

Although there is some literature on the gender typicality of choice, much of it is descriptive; little structural analysis has been done. The descriptive literature identifies historical and developmental trends in occupational preferences (*e.g.*, Lueptow, 1981; Herzog, 1982; Mason, Czajka, and Arber, 1976; Hewitt, 1975; Frye and Dietz, 1973; Maccoby and Jacklin, 1974; Gettys and Cann, 1981), and discusses correlates of these preferences, such as sex role attitudes or attitudes toward the characteristics of jobs.

In this paper we develop a theoretical perspective on the sex typicality of young women's occupational choices. We draw hypotheses from this theoretical perspective and test them using data from the *National Longitudinal Survey of Youth Labor Market Experiences,* a large recent survey of young men and women 14 to 21 years old. The relegation of women to a small number of 'female' occupations has been identified as an important reason for women's earnings being lower than those of comparable male workers. Access to and retention in a larger number of occupations— especially those professional, managerial, craft, and operative occupations usually held by men—would obviously increase women's earnings.

A few studies (*e.g.,* Almquist and Angrist, 1970; Polachek, 1975; 1979; Aneshensel and Rosen, 1980; and Blakemore and Low, 1984) have begun to illuminate the conditions under which young women choose traditionally male occupations. However, other studies that purport to model occupational choice often explain different choices by simply listing attributional differences among people doing the choosing; they do not theorize about the structures or processes that generated those differences. Still other studies assume that traditional choices, by definition, do not require explanation. However, cultural traditions retain their influence only if the factors that initially generated or maintain them remain relatively unchanged. Those factors can change, of course, and when they do, both women and men may begin making nontraditional occupational choices— whereupon explanation is called for.

We agree with authors such as Mincer and Polachek (1974), Polachek (1975; 1979), and Aneshensel and Rosen (1980) that a key to the typicality of a young woman's occupational choice is how she expects to allocate her time during her adulthood to the labor force, home responsibilities, and leisure.[1]

We assume that young men plan on working careers, with limited time commitments to the home. If women entertain similar expectations, they should evaluate occupational alternatives in much the same way as men, and therefore make similar choices.[2,3]

HYPOTHESES

Our theoretical perspective implies several hypotheses that we test.

Hypothesis 1. A woman who expects to allocate more time to the home is more likely to expect intermittent labor force participation and therefore to select a typically female occupation. This relationship could arise either because women think that typically female occupations combine better with the roles of wife and mother than other occupations, or because women who prefer to spend more of their adult lives exclusively in familial roles hold traditional views of sex roles and for this reason select typically female occupations. (For expository simplicity, we will henceforth usually refer to *typically* or *traditionally* female and male occupations merely as female and male occupations. No sexism is implied, nor, we are sure, will the reader infer any.)

Qualifying Hypothesis

Aneshensel and Rosen (1980) find that socioeconomic class affects the occupational choices of women who have the same expectations regarding their stay in the labor force. Specifically, they find that among women who expect to remain in the labor force, working class women are more likely than middle class and upper middle class women to select female occupations—usually white collar occupations, such as teacher or nurse.

We assumed earlier that women who expect to stay in the labor force will use the same calculus as their male contemporaries in selecting occupations. If so, one interpretation of the Aneshensel and Rosen finding is that young women will continue to choose female occupations *if the rewards are comparable to those sought by their male counterparts.*

Occupations within the sets of male and female jobs vary in status, working conditions, and wages, but there is more homogeneity in the female set. As measured by these dimensions, certainly the best jobs and probably the worst jobs are underrepresented in the female set. For both sexes, educational and occupational progress tends to be moderate from one generation to the next. Ambitious children of working class parents, whether boys or girls, will tend to aspire to middle level jobs and moderate, not high levels of education. Accordingly, daughters of working class parents who plan to stay in the labor force can get wage and status payoffs commensurate with their ambitions and education *without leaving the domain of traditional choice.* They can simply choose a female job that offers moderate status and pay. If they choose nontraditional occupations, they may face more resistance from the males in their lives than would the daughters of middle class parents.

By the same reasoning, daughters of middle class and upper middle class families who plan on working careers are more apt to aspire to high level jobs and higher education, and consequently to range beyond the domain of traditional choice in search of the rewards they merit.

We can test this idea in hypothesis 2.

Hypothesis 2. Among women who expect to remain in the labor force, daughters of working class families are more likely than daughters of middle class or upper middle class families to select female occupations.

Effects of Academic Ability.

We propose that a girl's academic ability affects the range of alternatives open to her. As an adult, a woman can find support by marrying someone who will support her, by relying on government transfers, or by working. Superior academic ability opens the way to higher levels of education. Since both ability and education are rewarded in the labor force, but not necessarily in marriage, higher ability women are more likely to plan on working careers than lower-ability women. They also enjoy more access to those traditionally male professional and managerial jobs that have been opening rapidly to women over the past decade (Beller, 1984). Many of these jobs require college degrees—now held by far more women than in the past.

Hypothesis 3. Women with higher academic ability than other women are more likely to select a traditionally male occupation.

Intergenerational Transmission of Labor Force and Occupational Preferences.

We propose that people—usually parents—who are significant in the young woman's life affect the occupational alternatives that she considers and their utilities for her. Both our data and the results of other studies confirm that the mother—either alone or in combination with the father—is the person that daughters name most frequently as having the most influence on them. The next task, then, is to determine what Keniston (1964) calls the "lessons of the mother's life." Earlier studies (Almquist and Angrist, 1970; Angrist, 1972; Etaugh, 1974; Hoffman, 1974) indicated that the mother's occupation was key to the daughter's employment and occupational choices, a working mother having positive effects on a daughter's labor force commitment and choice of an atypical occupation.

However, D'Amico, Haurin, and Mott (1983) conclude:

> There is a strong tendency for mothers to transmit intergenerational educational behavior patterns to daughters and sons. There is also considerable evidence that mothers can transmit non-traditional values and career orientations to their daughters. There is very little evidence that the employment of mothers per se has any pervasive effect—positive or negative—on the educational, family, or career paths of their sons or daughters. (p. 167)

As those authors and Macke and Morgan (1978) observe, a daughter can draw *negative*, as well as positive, conclusions from the "lessons of the mother's life," depending on the mother's attitude toward the choices she makes—or has to make—and how successfully she executes them.

We assume that mothers have chosen a single role (family only) or a dual role (work and family) and that daughters can perceive maternal choices as positive or negative. We hypothesize that the mother's choice and the daughter's perception of the attractiveness of that choice define the set of family, labor force, and occupational alternatives that the daughter considers. Since they have not yet formed families of their own, daughters can entertain three alternatives: family only, work only, or a mixture of the two.

D'Amico, Haurin, and Mott (1983) found that mothers who work, and say that they would continue to work even if they did not need the money, are more apt to have daughters who, at the ages of 24 to 27, plan to be working when they are 35. It seems plausible that girls whose mothers apparently enjoy their work are more likely to look with approval on their mothers' labor force choices, and repeat them.

Although we have no direct measures of these young women's evaluations of their mothers' choices about work and family, we do have measures of two factors that could affect what conclusions daughters draw from their mothers' lives: the mother's occupation and the composition of the household in which the daughter grows up (female-headed or intact).

Studies of how mothers who work in low status and low wage occupations affect their daughters' labor force commitment report contradictory results (e.g., Macke and Morgan, 1978; D'Amico, Haurin, and Mott, 1983). One explanation of these contradictions is that, even if daughters negatively evaluate their mothers' low status and low wage occupations and reject their mothers' choices, *we do not know what alternatives daughters select.* They can reject working or reject working at an unrewarding occupation.

Hypothesis 4. If their mothers work in low wage, blue collar or service occupations, daughters are less likely to plan to repeat their mothers' labor force commitment and occupational choices.

Although Hypothesis 4 assumes that the mother's occupation will affect the traditionality of the daughter's occupational choice, it does not predict direction. The choice may be more traditional, by virtue of a reduced commitment to the labor force; less traditional by virtue of an increased commitment to occupations more rewarding than traditionally female occupations; or, as we suggested earlier, more traditional through use of the female professions as avenues of upward mobility for daughters of working class parents.

A second factor is family structure: their being members of either intact or female-headed households should affect daughters' labor force, home, and occupational plans.

D'Amico, Haurin, and Mott (1983) examined the effects of belonging to a female-headed household (the result of divorce or death) on educational and career outcomes for boys and girls who were 14 to 17 years old in the late 1960s. They found that such a background *depressed* the occupational status of the *sons'* 1976 jobs and expected occupations at age 30, but *increased* the status of *daughters'* expected occupations at age 35.

We suspect that daughters in female-headed households may see their mothers either as negative models or as male models, with similar implications for the traditionality of their own occupational choices. Most female-headed households being financially stressed, daughters may resolve to find ways of not ending up like their mothers, whether their mothers are on welfare or work in low wage occupations. If a girl rejects welfare, the structure of her adolescent home should make her less likely than girls in intact families to select marriage and home as an alternative. This leaves a higher wage occupation as a solution. Most single mothers also work—for example, 57 percent of the female heads in our population of 14 to 17-year-old girls in 1979. These mothers, as heads of household and primary breadwinners, are examples of women who operate like men. Thus, whether the daughter sees her mother as a negative model or a male model, we hypothesize the following.

Hypothesis 5. Coming from a female-headed household will increase the chances that daughters will choose traditionally male occupations.

SAMPLE, VARIABLE DEFINITIONS, AND STRUCTURE OF THE ANALYSIS

Sample

Our analysis uses data from the *National Longitudinal Survey of Youth Labor Market Behavior* (NLS). This survey began in 1979 with a national probability sample of youth 14 to 21 years old on January 1, 1979, and living within the United States or on active military duty outside of the United States. The sample excludes those permanently institutionalized. A total of 12,686 persons completed interviews in 1979, with an oversampling of Hispanics, blacks, economically disadvantaged nonblack non-Hispanics, and a separate sample of 1,280 persons on active duty in the military.

In the baseline interview year, the respondents provided detailed information on their family background; schooling and training history; work history; marital and fertility status; characteristics of their current job; earnings and income; their attitudes toward their current job; and educational, training, occupational, marital and parenting preferences and expectations.

Our analysis of the gender typicality of occupational expectations uses a subset of the data described above. We restrict our sample to males and females 14 to 17 years old at the baseline interview in 1979. We selected this age group because choice at these ages is less affected by the realities of labor markets, postsecondary educational experiences, and marital and parenting responsibilities than is choice at older ages. Thus, it is a good age for investigating the gender typicality of *initial* occupational *expectations*, as opposed to changes in expectations as a function of post-high school experiences. The latter is an important question, but requires a separate study.

Variable Definitions

Table 6.1 defines all of the variables used in the models. Most of the measures are straightforward and require no explanation. We define our central predictor variable, the traditionality of the occupation, as the proportion female in that census three-digit occupation in 1979. The occupation is that named by the respondent as the one she would like to have when she is 35 years old. We do not assume that she will actually achieve it, nor does the validity of this study depend on our being able to make that assumption. In any case, that expectation affects other major choices, such as educational choices.

The questions about plans for age 35 first asked the young women's occupation for that age. If she replied that she wanted to be "married, keeping house, raising a family" (about 20 percent), then she was asked what sort of job she would prefer if she were to work at this point. Thus, all young women named an occupation in response to this series of questions.

We experimented with various functional forms of the traditionality variable, including a linear form that measures proportion female and ranges from 0.0 to 1.0 (TRAD35), and a dummy variable that divides the continuous form into two categories: a traditionally male occupational choice and all other choices (MALEOCC35). We coded an occupation as traditionally male if the workforce was less than or equal to 25 percent female.

The independent variables include several scales. The measures SEX ROLE 1 and SEX ROLE 2 result from our factor analysis of a series of seven items measuring the respondent's attitudes about the proper family and work roles of men and women and the consequences of a wife's working.

A factor analysis of scores on the ten subtests of the Armed Services Vocational Aptitude Battery (ASVAB)[4] produced three factors: ASVAB1, ASVAB2, and ASVAB3. The factor structure was the same for both sexes. Five subtests load most heavily on the first factor: general science, mathematics knowledge, arithmetic reasoning, word knowledge, and paragraph comprehension. ASVAB1 obviously measures the individual's verbal and quantitative skills. ASVAB2, a stronger factor for boys than for girls, is associated with the general science, auto and shop information, mechanical knowledge, and electronic knowledge subtests. ASVAB3 is associated with coding speed and numerical operations, reflecting skills with clerical and routine operations.

The independent variables include several measures of the respondent's perceptions of how the person that the respondent identifies as most influential in his or her life decisions would feel if the respondent made particular educational, career, marriage, and parenting choices.[5] We wanted to

Table 6.1. Names and Definitions of Variables for Analysis of Occupational Choice

Variable Name		Variable Definition
Occupational preference		
TRAD35		Proportion female in occupation preferred at age 35, 0.0 to 1.0
MALEOCC35	(D)	Occupation preferred at age 35: 25 % female
Home and labor force preference		
FAMILY35	(D)	Respondent's preferred activity at age 35 is marriage and family
EARLY MARRIAGE	(D)	Respondent wants to marry before age 25
NO CHILD	(D)	Respondent wants no children
EARLY CHILD	(D)	Respondent wants first child at 19
FAMILY SIZE		Desired number of children
SEX ROLE 1		Sex role attitudes 1: beliefs about proper labor force and home role for women (High = traditional attitudes)
SEX ROLE 2		Sex role attitudes 2: expected consequences to the family of a working wife (High = positive consequences of work)
MOM TRAD WORK	(D)	Mother worked when respondent age 14 in an occupation 90% or more female
WORKING	(D)	Respondent currently has paid job
RESERVE WAGE		Average of wages respondent would accept for 7 different occupations (Scale 1-4; High = 4)
Ability		
ASVAB 1		Verbal and quantitative skills
ASVAB 2		Mechanical, electronic, and auto knowledge
ASVAB 3		Clerical/administrative skills
Influence of significant others on occupational choice		
MOM EDUCATION		Mother's educational attainment in years

DAD EDUCATION		Father's educational attainment in years
DAD BLUE COLLAR	(D)	Father's occupation when respondent was age 14 = blue collar, but not craft
DAD CRAFT	(D)	Father's occupation when respondent was age 14 = craft
DAD MALE OCC	(D)	Father's occupation when respondent was age 14: 75% male
MOM NON-TRAD WORK	(D)	Mother worked when respondent age 14 in an occupation 90% or more male
MOM SERVICE	(D)	Mother's occupation when respondent was age 14 = laborer or service
MOM BLUE COLLAR	(D)	Mother's occupation when respondent was age 14 = craft or operative
FEMALE HEAD	(D)	Respondent lived in female-headed household at age 14
		Respondent (R) thinks an individual significant to R would approve if R:
CARPENTER	(D)	Chose to become a carpenter
ENGINEER	(D)	Chose to become an electrical engineer
MILITARY	(D)	Chose to join the Armed Forces
COLLEGE	(D)	Chose to go to college (indeed, would disapprove if R chose not to go)
CAREER	(D)	Chose to pursue a career and delay marriage
PARENT	(D)	Did not have children
Controls		
AGE		Respondent's age at 1979 interview in years
KNOWLEDGE TMJOB		Knowledge about typically male occupations (Scale 0-4; High = 4)
DROPOUT	(D)	Respondent has no high school degree and is not enrolled in school
ED EXPECTATIONS		Respondent's expected educational attainment in years
CONTROL		Locus of control (Scale 0-16; 16 = internal control)
BLACK	(D)	Respondent = black
HISPANIC	(D)	Respondent = Hispanic
VOCATIONAL ED	(D)	Respondent's high school curriculum = vocational

Note: (D) = dummy variable.

include six of the significant other variables in the model, and factor-analyzed the data for these dimensions to see if we could substitute one or two factors for the six variables. However, the factor structures differ for boys and girls and, although interpretable, are relatively complex.[6]

The other scales listed in Table 6.1 are simple additive scales. For example, RESERVE WAGE represents the average of the respondent's responses to seven ordinal scales.[7] The only exception is CONTROL, which weights each response on the internal/external locus of control scale by the strength with which it is held.

Table 6.2 presents the means and standard deviations for the variables in the model, weighted to reflect the 1979 population of young women 14 to 17 years old. Clearly, most young women name an occupation generally filled mostly by females; the average percent female in their choices is 62.

Occupational Choice	Percent
Traditionally female	47.2
Mixed	33.3
Traditionally male	19.5

The next section discusses the analytic strategy that we used to test our hypotheses with the data just described.

Analytic Strategy

We used ordinary least squares regression to estimate the models for the continuous form of the dependent variable (TRAD35). Since the dummy form of the dependent variable (MALEOCC35) receives codes of only zero or one, we estimated the model for this form of the dependent variable with *logit*, a maximum-likelihood technique appropriate for the analysis of dichotomous dependent variables (Goodman, 1976).[8]

Our analysis treats missing data in two ways. We excluded from the analysis any case with missing information on the dependent variable or with incomplete responses to any of the questions that the respondent should have answered. However, where information was incomplete because of the questionnaire skip patterns (*e.g.*, no data on father's education for those with no father in the household), we set that variable equal to a predetermined missing-value code and included a dummy variable coded 1 to identify observations with that missing value. We do not present coefficients for missing-value indicators.

We estimated the models with weighted data. The NLS substantially oversamples certain subgroups, and we used weighted data to eliminate composition effects from the specification process. However, the tests of significance (*t*-ratios) for the regression coefficients are corrected for these weights.

Table 6.2. Means and Standard Deviations of Variables For Analysis of Occupational Choice

Variable	Mean	Standard Deviation
Occupational Preference		
TRAD35	0.616	0.331
MALEOCC35	0.197	0.398
Home and Labor Force Preference		
FAMILY35	0.202	0.402
EARLY MARRIAGE	0.687	0.464
NO CHILD	0.072	0.259
EARLY CHILD	0.082	0.274
FAMILY SIZE	2.587	1.580
SEX ROLE 1	−0.074	0.933
SEX ROLE 2	−0.048	0.948
WORKING	0.088	0.283
RESERVE WAGE	2.249	0.762
Ability		
ASVAB1	0.344	1.000
ASVAB2	0.238	0.955
ASVAB3	0.265	0.942
Influence of Significant Others on Occupational Choice		
MOM EDUCATION	11.597	2.625
DAD EDUCATION	11.875	3.473
DAD BLUE COLLAR	0.231	0.421
DAD CRAFT	0.212	0.409
DAD MALE OCC	0.753	0.431
MOM TRAD WORK	0.198	0.399
MOM NON-TRAD WORK	0.364	0.481
MOM SERVICE	0.160	0.367
MOM BLUE COLLAR	0.116	0.320
FEMALE HEAD	0.148	0.355
CARPENTER	0.573	0.495
ENGINEER	0.651	0.477
MILITARY	0.403	0.491
COLLEGE	0.254	0.436
CAREER	0.732	0.443
PARENT	0.337	0.473
Controls		
KNOWLEDGE TMJOB	2.403	1.033
AGE	15.601	1.079
DROPOUT	0.041	0.198
ED EXPECTATIONS	14.070	2.152
CONTROL	10.935	2.397
BLACK	0.139	0.346
HISPANIC	0.064	0.244
VOCATIONAL ED	0.131	0.337

RESULTS OF OCCUPATIONAL CHOICE ANALYSIS

Table 6.3 presents regression and *logit* coefficients for both forms of the dependent variable for young women.

Hypothesis 1 states that women who expect to allocate more time to the home are more likely to expect intermittent labor force participation and therefore to select a female occupation. Testing Hypothesis 1 requires indicators of the respondent's expected commitments to home versus labor force.

Although we lacked direct measures of these preferences, we assume that, relative to other girls, a girl values time spent in the home more than time spent in the labor force if she: (1) expects to marry earlier (EARLY MARRIAGE), bear children earlier (EARLY CHILD), and have a larger family (FAMILY SIZE); (2) prefers at age 35 to be married with a family than working in the labor force (FAMILY35); (3) has traditional sex role attitudes; (4) is not working at the time of the survey; and (5) has a lower reservation wage.

The results confirm Hypothesis 1, although not all variables that we thought would predict a traditionally female occupational choice have statistically significant effects. Girls who prefer to marry earlier (EARLY MARRIAGE), who prefer to be homemakers at age 35 (FAMILY35), and who do not think that wives' working outside the home benefits the family (SEX ROLE 2) are more likely to select a female occupation. Preferred timing of childbearing (EARLY CHILD), family size, beliefs about the proper home and labor force roles for women (SEX ROLE 1), and reservation wages (RESERVE WAGE), do not have statistically significant effects on TRAD35.

When we examine predictors of picking a traditionally male occupation at age 35 (MALEOCC35), we find a stronger confirmation for Hypothesis 1. In addition to the variables found to be significant for TRAD35, SEX ROLE 1 is statistically significant at $p = .03$ for a one-tailed test, and for RESERVE WAGE, at $p < .04$ for a one-tailed test.

The reader should note that the two measures of occupational traditionality run in different directions, with MALEOCC35 scored 1 if the young woman expects a typically male occupation, (0 otherwise), and TRAD35 (percent female in the occupation) scored 1 if she expects a wholly female occupation. Thus, the signs of the coefficients must change over the two equations to show an effect in the same direction.

Hypothesis 2 states that for women who expect to remain in the labor force, those from lower socioeconomic status (SES) families are more likely than those from middle class and upper class families to select gender typical occupations. Testing this hypothesis requires estimating the effect of the interaction of SES and labor force expectations on the traditionality of the occupational choice. Since a significant number of respondents did not know their father's education and occupation, we used MOTHER EDU-

CATION as an indicator of SES. We used FAMILY35 to indicate labor force expectations.

The analysis (not presented here) does not confirm Hypothesis 2, in that the interaction term, MOTHER EDUCATION x FAMILY35, was not statistically significant. In other words, among those girls who are committed to the labor force, and controlling for other variables that affect choice, *the SES of the girl's family does not affect the traditionality of her occupational choice.*

Certainly girls from lower SES families, as measured by their mothers' education, select occupations that are more traditionally female than do girls from higher SES families.[9] However, it is the positive relationship between SES and labor force commitment that accounts for the negative relationship between SES and the traditionality of occupational choices observed in other studies. Girls whose mothers have less than a high school diploma are less committed to the labor market: 24.2 percent choose homemaker at age 35, versus 18.3 percent of girls whose mothers completed high school and 17.8 percent of girls whose mothers had 13 or more years of education. As we have already shown, when girls who prefer homemaking are forced to work instead, they choose female occupations.

Hypothesis 3 states that women with higher academic abilities are more likely than those with lower abilities to select male occupations. Using ASVAB1 as a measure of verbal and quantitative ability, we find strong confirmation for the hypothesis. Higher skills reduce the traditionality of the occupation selected and increase the chances of choosing a male occupation. On a scale of −2.86 to 2.91, a one point increase in ASVAB1 reduces the traditionality of the selected occupation by 6 percentage points. It increases the chances of selecting a male occupation by 5 percent.

Higher clerical skills (ASVAB3) increase the traditionality of the occupation selected and decrease the chances of selecting a male occupation. On a scale of −3.09 to 2.54, a one-point increase in ASVAB3 increases the traditionality of the selected occupation by 2 percentage points and reduces the chances of selecting a male occupation by 2 percent.

Since our models control for expecting or not expecting to work at age 35 (FAMILY 35) and for sex-role attitudes, these results point to some effects of high ability that increase the probability of choosing male occupations apart from the effects of ability on labor force commitment. Among these effects, we suggest the increased access to the better paying, higher status, professional and managerial occupations recently opened to women.

Hypothesis 4 predicts that mothers in less attractive occupations will affect the traditionality of the daughters' occupational choices, but does not predict the direction of the effect. We test Hypothesis 4 with MOM BLUE COLLAR and MOM SERVICE (MOM WHITE COLLAR being the omitted category). We assume that blue collar and service jobs are less attractive than white collar jobs.

The results for TRAD35 disconfirm Hypothesis 4, in that the mother's

Table 6.3. Regression and *Logit* Coefficients From Models of Traditionality of Occupational Choice (Men and Women, Ages 14–17)

Variable	TRAD35		MALEOCC35	
	Regression Coefficient	T Ratio	Logit Regression	T Ratio
Home and Labor Force Preference				
FAMILY35	0.0874	5.0946	−0.0625	−2.2912
EARLY MARRIAGE	0.0438	2.9155	−0.0626	−3.1321
NO CHILD	−0.0224	0.8195	0.0382	1.0664
EARLY CHILD	−0.0063	0.2470	0.0507	1.2860
FAMILY SIZE	0.0021	0.4748	0.0028	0.4418
SEX ROLE 1	0.0097	1.2591	−0.0207	−1.8823
SEX ROLE 2	−0.0134	−1.9005	0.0216	2.2002
WORKING	0.0039	0.1629	0.0217	−0.6014
RESERVE WAGE	0.0108	−1.2000	0.0221	1.7746
Ability				
ASVAB1	−0.0607	−5.9692	0.0485	3.4874
ASVAB2	−0.0065	−0.7900	−0.0015	−0.1276
ASVAB3	0.0244	2.8701	−0.0234	−1.9513
Influence of Significant Others on Occupational Choice				
MOM EDUCATION	−0.0050	−1.4582	0.0072	1.5115
DAD EDUCATION	−0.0025	−0.9496	0.0018	0.4979

	(1)	(2)	(3)	(4)
DAD BLUE COLLAR	−0.0064	−0.315	−0.0144	−0.4911
DAD CRAFT	−0.0048	−0.2425	0.0170	0.6084
MOM TRAD WORK	0.0208	1.0864	−0.0416	−1.5509
MOM NON-TRAD WORK	−0.0190	−1.005	−0.0303	−1.1703
MOM SERVICE	0.0145	0.6671	0.0294	0.9411
MOM BLUE COLLAR	−0.0364	−1.3874	0.0812	2.4383
FEMALE HEAD	−0.0593	−2.3131	0.0758	2.1256
CARPENTER	−0.0268	−1.7319	0.0265	1.2138
ENGINEER	−0.0438	−2.7055	0.0661	2.7749
MILITARY	0.0236	1.6893	−0.0396	−2.0206
COLLEGE	0.0237	1.4957	0.0437	−1.7864
CAREER	0.0156	0.9967	−0.0396	−1.6786
Controls				
KNOWLEDGE TMJOB	0.0173	2.5069	−0.0086	−0.8812
AGE	−0.0023	−0.3467	−0.0124	−1.3555
DROPOUT	−0.1054	−2.9714	0.0375	0.6838
ED EXPECTATIONS	−0.0321	−8.2041	0.0377	6.9215
CONTROL	0.0010	0.3525	−0.0082	−2.0419
BLACK	0.0338	1.4959	−0.0242	−0.7564
HISPANIC	−0.0381	−1.3222	0.0765	1.9877

occupation (blue collar, service, or white collar) does not affect the traditionality of girls' occupational choices. However, the results differ for MALEOCC35: girls whose mothers work in blue collar jobs have an 8 percent greater chance of selecting a male occupation.

We need more analyses to explicate these results. We do not believe that we have a good test of Hypothesis 4, although it may be the best that we can do with our data base. For example, the three occupational categories tested are very gross; the *intra*-category variation in wages and working conditions may produce variable and ultimately cancelling responses in daughters. We also cannot predict the direction of the effect of mothers' occupations on their daughters' choices. Daughters could respond to their mothers' work situation by reducing their commitment to the labor force—tilting them in a traditionally female occupational direction—or by rejecting their mothers' low wage occupations, tilting them in a traditionally male direction. If our respondents *differed* in their responses to their mothers' choices, the effects could cancel one another, leaving no net effect in either direction.

We also need to explicate the positive effect of mothers in blue collar jobs on MALEOCC35. This could be simply a methodological artifact of some variety. At the same time, the positive effect for MALEOCC35 may say less about the attractiveness of occupations than about the intergenerational transmission of knowledge about them. Blue collar occupations are less traditionally female than the white collar or service occupations. The positive effect for MALEOCC35 may simply signal that daughters know about and repeat their mothers' less traditionally female occupations.

Hypothesis 5 predicts that girls from female-headed households are more likely to select a male occupation than girls from intact families, either because they see their mothers functioning as male models, or as negative models of traditional female roles. We expect our measure of living in a female-headed household, FEMALE HEAD, to affect TRAD35 negatively and MALEOCC35 positively. Estimates for both TRAD35 and MALEOCC35 confirm Hypothesis 5. All else equal, being in a female-headed household at age 14 decreases the traditionality of girls' occupational choices by 6 percentage points and increases the chances of choosing a male occupation by 8 percentage points.

This finding is potentially very important. What has been a major structural change in household composition in our society[10] may generate a change of similar magnitude in daughters' home, labor force, and occupational choices.[11]

To explicate this finding, we examined whether the effect of living in a female-headed family differed by family composition, race/ethnicity, and daughters' occupational preferences at age 35. (See Table 6.4).

As Table 6.4 shows, the effect of female-headed households on occupational choice is limited to Hispanic and non-Hispanic white girls. The effect is greatest for non-Hispanic white girls, increasing the chances of selecting a male occupation from less than one in 5.5 to almost one in 3.4—

Table 6.4. Traditionality of Occupational Choice by Household Structure and Race/Ethnicity

Race/ Ethnicity	Household Structure	MALEOCC35	MIXEDOCC35	FEMALEOCC35	Total
All girls	Intact	18.6	33.5	47.9	100.0
	FHH	25.1	31.8	43.1	100.0
White girls	Intact	18.2	34.8	47.0	100.0
	FHH	29.6	33.5	36.8	100.0
Black girls	Intact	19.3	28.1	52.6	100.0
	FHH	18.6	30.3	51.1	100.0
Hispanic girls	Intact	20.9	26.1	52.8	100.0
	FHH	26.7	20.5	53.0	100.0

FHH: Respondent was living in a female-headed household at the age of 14.

an increase of 61 percent. It does not affect choice of a mixed occupation, but reduces the chances of selecting a female occupation from one in 2.1 to one in 2.7. For Hispanic girls, a female-headed household increases the chances of selecting a male occupation from one in 4.8 to one in 3.8. It does not affect selection of a female occupation, but reduces the chance of choosing a mixed occupation.

Household structure does not affect the traditionality of black girls' occupational choices.[12] Although female-headed households substantially increased in the last decade among blacks, it has always been a more common household form among blacks than among whites or Hispanics. Whatever it is about this kind of household that affects daughters' occupational choices may have already diffused within the black community, affecting the occupational choices of all black girls, whatever sort of household they were raised in. Perhaps more important, even when married, black women have participated in the labor force at higher rates than their white and Hispanic counterparts (Smith and Ward, 1984). In other words, they have traditionally taken on economic roles that white and Hispanic women have assumed more often under conditions of the female-headed household.

Some of the other results in Table 6.3 are worthy of brief comment. If the respondent reports that the significant other would approve if she became a carpenter or an engineer, she selects a less traditional occupation at age 35. As noted earlier, support for nontraditional occupational choices could increase the chances of such a choice, or girls who prefer these occupations may assume that individuals whom they generally find supportive will approve of their preferences. The measure of knowledge of traditionally male jobs, KNOWLEDGE TMJOB, *increases* chances of preferring a female job, net of other factors. We speculate that girls in lower SES families are both more likely to pick female occupations and to have male relatives in highly traditional male occupations, such as machinist. This reasoning suggests that knowing about nontraditional occupations is not enough to induce choosing them.

Being a high school dropout strongly and negatively affects TRAD35, reducing the percent female of the preferred occupation by 11 points. It increases the probability of choosing a male occupation (MALEOCC35) by 0.04. We do not know why dropping out reduces the traditionality of the occupation selected. However, the effect persisted through all specifications of the models, and it deserves more analytic attention than we have given it.

Educational expectations also negatively affect TRAD35. Every additional year of education that the respondent expects to attain reduces the percent female of the preferred occupation by 3 points. It increases the probability of choosing a traditionally male occupation by 0.04. These results are consistent with our initial theoretical expectations. We assumed that the more highly educated young women are, the more likely they are to prefer market work over homemaking. We also assumed that young women with strong attachment to the labor force are more likely to consider occupations with greater educational requirements—an occupational set that includes many traditionally male occupations. Educational expectations should therefore be positively associated with, although not necessarily causal of, entry into female-male occupations.

The continuous variable TRAD35 shows two more results of interest. Relative to non-Hispanic whites, Hispanic ethnicity increases the chances of selecting a male occupation by 8 percentage points—but if the respondent believes that the significant other would approve if she enlisted in the armed forces, she is *less* apt to select a male occupation.[13] The effect is small, reducing the probability of choosing a male occupation by 0.04. However, of interest here are the relationships among expected approval of enlistment, enlistment expectations,[14] and occupational preferences at age 35. The military is overwhelmingly male; men perform almost all jobs, including those that have been traditionally female in the civilian sector. However, exploratory analyses do not support an assumption that military enlistment for girls represents a traditionally male occupational choice.

SUMMARY AND CONCLUSIONS

Summary

We predicted that high school girls' expected allocation of time between the labor force and homemaking is key to the traditionality of their occupational preferences at age 35. We expect that the more definitely they plan on working careers, the more their occupational choices will resemble those of men. This argument implies that planning for a continuous attachment to the labor force will move women *in the direction* of men's jobs. We confirmed these hypotheses for different forms of the dependent variable, and with ordinary least squares regression and *logit* models. As girls increase their planned commitments to the labor force relative to home, they weaken the traditionality of occupational choice and increase the likelihood of choosing male occupations.

For girls committed to the labor force, earlier studies suggest an interaction between the socioeconomic status of their families and the traditionality of their occupational choices. Specifically, these studies suggest that among such girls, working class girls are more likely to select traditionally female—albeit higher-status—occupations than are middle class and upper middle class girls. Our results do not confirm this hypothesis: the interaction observed in earlier studies does not survive the multiple controls of regression models.

We tested several hypotheses about factors that affect girls' commitment to the labor force. Since ability is rewarded in labor markets, but not necessarily in marriage markets, and because high-ability women now have easier access to traditionally male professional and managerial jobs, we predicted that higher-ability women are more likely than others to select a male occupation. The analyses strongly confirm this hypothesis: each point increase in the scale of verbal and quantitative skills reduces the traditionality of the selected occupation by 6 percentage points.

The literature on the intergenerational transmission of behaviors and attitudes indicates the importance of the "lessons of the mother's life" for daughters' home, labor force, and occupational choices. We expected that a daughter's negative appraisal of her mother's choices would cause her to choose differently from her mother; a positive appraisal, a repeat of her mother's choices. Assuming that girls regard blue collar and service occupations as less attractive than white collar, we predicted that daughters of blue collar mothers would be less likely than daughters of white collar mothers to plan to repeat their mothers' labor force and occupational choices.

We could not predict the direction of the effect of mothers' occupations on their daughters' choices. Daughters could respond to their mothers' work situation by reducing their commitment to the labor force—tilting them in a traditionally female direction—or by rejecting their mothers' traditionally female roles, tilting them in a male direction.

Although we find that daughters of blue collar mothers are 8 percent more likely to select a male occupation, we find no effect for service occupations and no effect for service or blue collar occupations on the continuous form of the dependent variable. We do not consider the hypothesis confirmed or well tested, although the test may have been the best that we could do with our data base. For example, the fact that we could not theoretically predict the direction of the effect of mothers' occupations on their daughters' choices allows respondents to differ in their responses to their mothers' choices. Opposing effects cancel one another, leaving no net effect in either direction.

A second test of the intergenerational transmission of behaviors involved family structure. We predicted that living in a female-headed, as opposed to an intact, household would predispose daughters toward male occupations.

Estimates for both the linear form of the dependent variable and for the categorical form confirm this hypothesis. All else equal, being in a female-headed household at age 14 decreases the traditionality of girls' occupational choices by 6 percentage points and increases the chances of choosing a male occupation by 8 percent.

Conclusions

These analyses suggest that changing young women's occupational choices requires changing their expected time allocations to both the labor force and the home. Policies that address the occupational choice alone—ignoring women's planned tradeoffs between labor force and homemaking—may achieve only limited effects.

The effect of female-headed households on occupational choice is important in two ways. First, it indicates the intergenerational transmission of behaviors and attitudes and highlights the importance of understanding how mothers' home, labor force, and occupational choices and attitudes affect those of their daughters. Second, the major changes in family structure in this country may eventually generate a change of similar magnitude in the educational, labor force, and occupational choices of our young women.

NOTES

1. As Roos (1983) observes, human capital theorists propose dual career theory to explain gender differences in occupational choices and wages. The theory assumes that actual or anticipated family responsibilities affect the jobs that women enter by limiting their investments in education and on-the-job training, the number of hours they work, their labor force continuity, and the advancement opportunities they pursue.

2. Women can plan to minimize domestic responsibilities in several ways—for example, by planning to delay marriage or childbearing, by planning not to marry or not to have children, by planning a small family, by expecting a future spouse to contribute substantial time to the home, or by planning to purchase services that a housewife normally provides *e.g.,* laundry, food, childcare, and cleaning services.

3. Using data from the *National Longitudinal Study of the High School Class of 1972,* Blakemore and Low (1984) estimate choice of college major separately for males and females. They find that as much as 50 percent of the substantial gender differences in choice is attributable to gender differences in the mean values of characteristics (*e.g.,* mathematics scores, values such as community orientation), not to differences in the effects of a particular characteristic (*i.e.,* not to the coefficients) on the choice of a major. In general, as gender roles and expectations converge,

theoretically we can expect most male and female behaviors to converge. We already see that happening in several behavioral domains—for example, in criminal behavior. Girls show crime rates increasingly similar to boys' rates; are committing increasingly violent crimes that were previously associated almost entirely with males; and show increasingly similar criminal histories, *i.e.*, their criminal careers have cycles increasingly like those of males' careers.

4. The ASVAB was administered to the sample in the first NLS followup survey in 1980. The weights for the ASVAB variables take account of the fact that not all respondents to the 1979 baseline survey took the ASVAB in 1980. The military services administer the ASVAB to all enlistment applicants to determine their eligibility for service and for particular occupations. It consists of 10 subtests: general science, mathematics knowledge, arithmetic reasoning, word knowledge, paragraph comprehension, numerical operations, coding speed, auto and shop information, mechanical comprehension, and electronics knowledge.

5. The 1979 baseline questionnaire asked all 14 to 17 year olds to select, from a list of types of individuals (*e.g.*, parents, male peer, female peer), that person who had most influenced their thoughts about school, marriage, jobs, and having children. Each respondent was then asked his or her perception of whether the person named would approve if the respondent decided: to become a carpenter, to join the armed forces, to become an accountant, to become an electrical engineer, *not* to go to college, to move far away from home, to never have children, and (for female respondents only) to pursue a full-time career and delay starting a family.

6. The factor analyses suggest that an *approval* dimension runs through the variables—in other words, that respondents expect that the significant other will approve of whatever they choose. There is also a suggestion, especially for girls, that their perceptions of the significant other's attitudes toward choices that they might make in the educational, career, and marital/parenting domains are somewhat inconsistent with each other. If we assume that the observed attitude structure is valid, *i.e.*, not a methodological artifact, the structure probably reflects career versus family cross-pressures on young girls.

7. Each respondent was asked what wages he or she would accept for each of seven different jobs. There were three wage options. If the respondent accepted the lowest option, he or she received a score of one. If the respondent rejected the lowest option, he or she was asked if the next option was acceptable. If the individual rejected the highest option, he or she received a score of four for that job.

8. To make the results easier to interpret, we transform the estimates of log odds coefficients by multiplying each by $(P)(1-P)$, where P is the mean of the dependent variable (see Hanushek and Jackson, 1977). These transformed coefficients can be interpreted in the same way as regression coefficients—they show the estimated effect of a one-unit change in an independent variable on the probability of job turnover, evaluated at the sample mean.

9. On average, girls whose mothers completed less than 12 years of education selected occupations whose percent female is 67; girls whose mothers completed high school, 63 percent; and girls whose mothers completed 13 or more years of education, 59 percent.

10. In 1950, 9 percent of all families were female-headed; in 1983, 16 percent (*Statistical Abstract of the United States, 1982-83*, Table 60; Johnson and Waldman, 1983). A much larger proportion of families have female-headed episodes during the period in which children grow to maturity. In the early 1970s, white children had a

0.33 probability and black children a 0.60 probability of experiencing the divorce of their parents before they themselves were 18 years of age (Bumpass and Rindfuss, 1979). Since children usually reside with the mother after a divorce, the probabilities of divorce translate into the probabilities of living for some period of time in a female-headed household. These probabilities represent the lower limit on the chances of a child's living in a female-headed household because they do not take into account children of never-married mothers.

11. As male-headed, single-parent families become more common, it will be important to monitor what, if any, effects the gender of the single parent has on children of the same and opposite sexes.

12. Household structure may affect dimensions of black girls' occupational choices other than traditionality, such as occupational status.

13. In the TRAD35 model, MILITARY is statistically significant at $p = 0.10$ for a two-sided test.

14. Respondents are asked if, in the future, they think they will try to enlist. The four response options range from "Definitely will try to enlist" to "Definitely will not try to enlist."

Part Two

POLICY AND CHANGE
STRATEGIES

CHAPTER 7

Union Stewards and Women's Employment Conditions

PAMELA ROBY

I thank the rank-and-file labor leaders whom I interviewed for their perspectives and time, and the Academic Senate of the University of California-Santa Cruz for financial assistance. I appreciate the generous advice and other assistance of Chris Bose, Alice Cook, Arlene Daniels, Valerie Dennie, Myra Marx Ferree, Kathleen Kinnick, John Kitsuse, Chalsa Loo, Joyce Miller, James Mulherin, Jim Potterton, Patricia Sexton, Rusty Smith, Glenna Spitze, George Strauss, Gail Sullivan, Barbara Wertheimer, and Norma Wikler. Lynet Uttal and Mike Webber contributed much by conducting fourteen of the interviews; Marcy Howe ably did much of the coding.

INTRODUCTION

Although women are a growing segment of the labor force, they remain underrepresented as members and leaders of unions. Increasing women's participation in unions is an important women's employment strategy because organized labor has unique powers and potential for maintaining and improving women's employment conditions.

In this paper, I will examine factors that help and hinder women in taking on and carrying out rank-and-file labor leadership as union stewards. Union stewards occupy an influential position within the workplace. Stewards are union members and employees of private enterprises or government agencies who are elected by union members in their unit (office or shop) or appointed by the union to represent their coworkers and the

139

union.[1] Stewards' importance to women's employment conditions derives from their daily handling of workers' grievances and enforcement of the contract and laws relating to workers' rights. Working side by side with others in the steno pool or the factory, stewards represent their coworkers before management, communicate between the members and the union, serve as relatively independent leaders of their constituents and, in handling grievances, interpret and extend the negotiating process and contract (Cook, 1962).

Stewards' understanding of workers' problems, their decisions to act or not to act, and their ability to represent workers effectively significantly affect women's everyday employment experiences. A good steward can make a big difference in areas of particular interest to female employees such as termination practices related to workers' absences involving the care of sick children, the distribution of overtime, the allocation of promotions and special job assignments, the scheduling of work days, and sexual harrassment. In addition to the importance of women serving effectively as stewards to their constituents (who are generally women given the sex segregated labor force), service as a steward is a step toward higher level positions in unions and workplaces (Wertheimer and Nelson, 1975; Cook, 1984; Koziara, Bradley and Pierson, 1982). Furthermore, by working as a steward, women gain leadership skills which they may use in reshaping their unions, developing new workplace organizations, or attaining other employment goals of their choosing.

UNIONS AND A WOMEN'S EMPLOYMENT POLICY

Women's increasing participation in the labor force[2] is occurring within the context of broad changes in the United States' and the world's economic structures. The increasing movement of capital between regions of the nation and the world and between industries, the centralization of ownership and managerial control of capital in multinational corporations, and increased global competition and underutilization of human and material resources are affecting women and workers throughout the world. In the United States, declining economic growth, deindustrialization, increasingly high military expenditures, and the attempt by corporations and the Reagan administration to restore profitability to big capital by restructuring the economy have disproportionately affected women, workers, and people of color (cf. Power, 1984; Miller and Tomaskovic-Devey, 1983; O'Connor, 1984; Bluestone and Harrison, 1982; Piven and Cloward, 1982; and Sweezy, 1984). The administration's cuts in child care, Aid to Families with Dependent Children, and job training programs have particularly affected low paid working women. Corporate and governmental actions have simultaneously made trade unions' organizing and increasing or maintaining workers compensation more difficult (Mercury News, 1984; San Jose Mercury, 1985; and Wrenn, 1985).

In this context, the fate of unions is important to women and all workers in the United States and throughout the world. In the United States, no other institution, as Alice Cook points out, is "prepared or authorized to represent workers in collective bargaining for wages and working conditions" (1984:12). Despite union setbacks, organized women workers in all industries continue to earn more and have more substantial health care, retirement, vacation and other fringe benefits than their female counterparts who are not covered by union contracts (U.S. Department of Labor, 1986a:Table 84).[3]

Nearly six million women were union members in 1985 and another million working women were covered by union contracts (U.S. Department of Labor, 1986a:213). These female employees are obviously affected most directly by the health of unions and the nature of union leadership, policies, and practices, but the conditions of unorganized women are also influenced by the state of unions. Gains which unionized workers attain in wages, benefits, and working conditions affect those of unorganized workers in the surrounding area (Freeman and Medoff, 1985; Kahn, 1978). In addition, the healthier unions are and the greater the role women play within them, the more likely unions will be to devote resources to organizing unorganized women workers, the more reason unorganized women will have to join unions, and the greater their reward will be when they do so.

Historically, although significantly advancing concerns of women, unions have also excluded or ignored women (Milkman, 1980). Since the founding of the Coalition of Labor Union Women (CLUW) in 1974, numerous changes have occurred. Many old-time union women have commented that members attending union meetings are now addressed as "sisters and brothers" rather than "you guys" and that union letters are generally signed "in unity" rather than "fraternally yours" (Nelson, 1984). In 1980, Joyce Miller, president of CLUW and vice president of the Amalgamated Clothing and Textile Workers Union, became the first woman to be appointed to the AFL-CIO executive council. The following year, Barbara Hutchinson of the American Federation of Government Employees was elected to the executive council. Many unions have established departments for women and a number have filed court cases concerning pay equity, pregnancy disability, wage discrimination, and other issues of concern to women (Wertheimer, 1984).

The percentage of union members who were women in 1985 (33.7 percent) was more than double that in 1960 (18 percent: U.S. Department of Labor, 1986a:213; LeGrande, 1978), but while growing, remained considerably lower than women's representation in the labor force (43.7 percent in 1985:U.S. Department of Labor, 1986b:12–13). Women also remain underrepresented among union officers and staff (Koziara and Pierson, 1980; LeGrande, 1978; Bergquist, 1974; Raphael, 1974; Wertheimer and Nelson, 1975; and Hartmann, 1976).[4] Predominantly male sectors of the labor force which have been most heavily represented by unions, such as manufacturing and construction, have declined and are expected to continue to decline relative to other sectors. The predominantly female service sector, only 10 percent of which is organized, accounted for 90 percent of all new jobs in the 1970s and is expected to employ nearly three-fourths of the labor force in 1990 (AFL-CIO, 1985).

These structural shifts in the labor force and the decline in union membership have caused unions, to ask new questions. The 1985 report of the AFL-CIO's Committee on the Evolution of Work states, "It is not enough merely to search for more effective ways of doing what we always have done; we must expand our notion of what it is workers can do through their unions" (p. 13). Given women's increasing representation in the labor force, this is a time for unions to direct attention to learning more about women's concerns.[5] Given unions' stated openness to new methods of advancing the interests of workers, this may be an opportune time for women to place their concerns before labor organizations. Women's taking on and effectively carrying out rank-and-file leadership is one way the interests of unions and women converge.

Since the important research of 25, 30, and 35 years ago, little attention has been devoted to the study of union stewards within the United States (Mills, 1948; Peck, 1963; Sayles and Strauss, 1953). Not only do changing labor market and union conditions call for new studies in the United States, but the few women who were stewards in the 1940s and 1950s were largely ignored by the earlier studies. In addition, over the ten year period following the founding of the Coalition of Labor Union Women, in which annual trade union women's institutes were held in all regions of the nation and labor union women became increasingly organized, there was no major study of women in unions or of women rank-and-file labor leaders in the United States.

This paper is based on in-depth structured interviews which were conducted in 1983 and 1984 with rank-and-file labor leaders. The following sections will describe my research methods and findings concerning ways women become union stewards, their experience as rank-and-file leaders, their mentors, and the influence of their families on their steward work. Each section will address the following questions: What factors help and hinder women in taking on and carrying out their responsibilities as rank-and-file leaders? How is female stewards' experience similar to and different from that of male stewards? How might unions further facilitate women's leadership?

METHOD

This paper is based on data from 35 structured interviews with rank-and-file trade union leaders, focused interviews with two dozen union staff and labor studies program directors, and participant observation at the first New York and the second and third West Coast Trade Union Women's Institutes, at local and national meetings of the Coalition of Labor Union Women, at union meetings and conventions, and at community college labor studies classes. The interviews with rank-and-file leaders averaged three hours in length. There is no national baseline data for union stewards upon which to base a stratified sampling plan. I chose to interview women and men from the public and private sectors who were as diverse as possible in terms of race, age, unions, occupations, and industries. My first set of interviews was conducted during the 1983 West Coast Trade Union Women's Summer Institute. From the 48 women who volunteered to be interviewed, I selected 14 from throughout the state of California. My second set of interviews was conducted in Fall 1984, with 21 rank-and-file leaders who were or had been students in San Jose City College's Labor Studies Program.

The 35 leaders who were interviewed included 26 women, 6 blacks and 4 Hispanics who were 26 to 61 years of age and from 16 unions (the male stewards were an average of two-and-a-half years older than the female stewards, with the average age of the men being 39½ and the women being 37).[6] The inclusion of nine men in the sample provides a comparative perspective from which to analyze the women's experiences. Sixteen of the leaders were public sector and nineteen private sector employees. They had an average of 14½ years of schooling; six had no college and two had masters degrees (nationally, 21 percent of union members have completed college degrees as compared with 16 percent of the U.S. population: AFL-CIO, 1985). The family of origin was described as poor by 17 percent, as working class by 6 percent, as middle class by 50 percent, and as upper middle class by 22 percent.

FINDINGS

Paths to Leadership

On the average, the women we interviewed joined their unions seven years ago as compared with the men who had joined eleven years ago and who were about two-and-a-half years older than the women.

All the stewards we interviewed had at least one family member who was or had been a union member; half had two or more union members within their immediate family. A surprisingly high proportion of the stewards— over half of the women and nearly three-quarters of the men—had relatives who had served or were serving as union *officers*. When asked why they joined their union, the leaders' most frequent response was family influence combined with their family's exposing them to unions. One, a steward whom I will call Sara, said, "Why did I join? My mother! I was supposed to. It was expected like buying a car when you get out of high school. I'd been involved with union parties and strikes with my mother since I was five."[7] When joining, Elizabeth recalled, "I remembered my father being in the

Teamsters, and my brothers were too." Pat's story was similar. She had joined the international union to which her father had belonged. He had been active as a steward and a secretary of a neighboring local. Her mother was currently a business agent for her (the mother's) union. Being required to join their union because of a closed shop agreement and a union member talking with them about the union were the reasons the leaders interviewed gave the next most frequently, after the influence of family members, for joining their union.

When asked, "Do you always, sometimes or never think of yourself as a leader," a slightly higher proportion of women than men replied always or sometimes, but men reported being encouraged to take leadership or to think of themselves as leaders at a considerably younger age than women (men reported being first encouraged at the average age of 17 and women at 24). Women most frequently cited the family as the place where their first leadership experiences occurred. One observed, "I think I was a leader before it was apparent to me . . . The first time it struck me that what I said mattered to someone was when my little sister was having problems at home and came to me. I knew what I said would make a big difference in her life. She was 14 and I was 21. This was a big responsibility." Another chuckled, "I had three little sisters and used to organize them in work and play. I was the spokesperson when we were in trouble." Men most frequently cited the army as the place of their first leadership. One recalled, "I was a medic in Viet Nam with responsibility for 30 men in the platoon. They had confidence in me and treated me as special."

Most of the women and the men first started thinking of themselves as leaders well before they joined their unions, but a few said that their union was responsible for their starting to think of themselves as leaders.

Grace is one of the stewards who began to think of herself as a leader *after* joining her union. Her mother and younger brother were union members, and her older brother had been a steward and "very, very active for several years" in his union. She became a steward the first day on the job. Grace explained, "The guy who was the steward was moving to Sacramento and he tried desperately to find somebody to do it. He asked me if I would, and he told me that one of the people who had been helping him would stay on at least for a period of a year, that transition period. So I thought that with her help, I would do it. I would give it a try." It was as a steward that Grace began to think of herself as a leader. "Before that I thought of myself as a follower. But when people come to you with questions, you almost naturally acquire a leadership quality. You find yourself leading them in a sense because you find answers they wouldn't ordinarily know how to get. You lead them by giving them a better understanding of the situation."

Knowledge of how these stewards came to be union leaders gives us clues as to how others might be assisted in becoming leaders. Over one-third of both the women and the men reported that one or more family members had encouraged them to be active in their union. Pat, for example, reported that both of her parents had encouraged her but that her mother had done so more than her dad. "She's worked in a medical records department like mine so she knows there are a lot of problems. I think she thought I would be a good person to get involved in that so she kind of encouraged me before I was elected. She just said she thought I should try and become a steward, try to get elected. This was mostly because I was complaining about problems." Pat was also helped and encouraged in her leadership by her union business representative.

> I've had a lot of problems to handle as a steward. He basically lets me know I'm doing a good job. Generally it's when I ask him about things and he'll say that was a good thing to do or advise me. He's assisted me in various ways and given me a lot of encouragement and reassurance that "you are doing ok" (laughs) or letting me know that "you might have done something wrong" and correcting me along the way. It's not any one particular incident but if I've had a problem that I'm not quite sure how to handle, then I let him know and he leads me along and gives me some answers.

Family and union were intimately related in the case of Sara and Elizabeth. Sara's mother, Elizabeth, was a vice-president of the local to which Sara belonged. When Sara's building needed a steward, "Mother gave me the opportunity to be a steward."

The majority of stewards who came to think of themselves as leaders prior to becoming union members were encouraged to do so by a wide range of people—parents, spouses, rabbis, aunts, teachers, grandparents. Nonetheless, similar threads ran through their accounts of how these people had offered them encouragement. Over and over, they described how these people had let them know that they "could do it" and had stuck by them, often through crises. With an air of appreciation and pride, Denise reported, for example, "My Aunt instilled confidence in me; she also told me I could do anything I wanted to do. When my parents kicked me out of the house at age eighteen, she'd say, 'Hey, don't get in the dumps, you're capable of anything!'" Such reminders were important to men as well. Gerald who grew up black and poor in Texas recalled, "My mother passed away when I was five. So sometimes you had to make the right decision as to what to do or not do because there was no one to ask. . . . I had one teacher who was my elementary teacher (laughs). She was handicapped with polio and I thought she was just mean and evil but she would always say 'I know you got it, and I know you can do it, and I expect it out of you!' Even after I got into high school, this lady would call me at home. . . . "

Approximately three-quarters of the female and half of the male stewards reported that their parents had been in organizations when they were growing up (church groups, PTA, and scouts were most frequently cited); and a substantial majority of both the women and the men said that they themselves had had organizational experience prior to taking on union leadership. An equal proportion of women and men, one-third in each case, had had *leadership* experience in formal organizations prior to joining their union, and three-quarters of the women as compared with half of the men had had supervisory experience on their job before they became union leaders (*cf* Izraeli, 1982). Approximately three-quarters of the women and two-thirds of the men said that the women's movement had made a difference to them personally. Most, but not all, mentioned positive consequences. Women's positive responses included:

- It is easier to be outspoken because you know support is out there from other women.
- The women's movement has been all my life and my mother's. Black women always had to struggle. Nothing's won without a struggle.
- It's enabled me to be doing what I'm doing now. They've overcome the obstacles for me. I salute those who've worked for this in the past.
- It came into being about the time when I started becoming aware. It's made a difference to me in that I don't consider myself any less or any more than any man. I never felt that I had to get married and have babies like a lot of women before me.
- It's given me an awareness that women are doing things.

Although most women responded positively about the effect of the women's movement, a few were negative. One stated, "It's degrading. Women have always been able to do what the women's movement said they cannot do."

THE STEWARD EXPERIENCE

The women whom we interviewed had served as stewards for an average of two-and-a-half years as compared with the men who had served an average of four. The women typically began serving as stewards during their fourth year in the union as compared with the men, who began in their seventh. More women than men were appointed to their steward position as opposed to being elected. That only a small proportion of stewards are elected raises questions to be explored in future research concerning the legitimacy which they are granted by their constituents. Over half of the women who were appointed to their positions were appointed by men. This finding is probably the result of more males than females being in a position to appoint people to office, but it is also evidence that today a number of men are willing to appoint women to at least rank-and-file positions. Their actions signal a considerable change from the "woman's place should be in the home" attitude that Sid Peck found characterized male union leaders in the 1950s.

A number of findings suggest that the female leaders we interviewed are at least as involved, if not more involved, in their unions as their male counterparts. According to their reports, these female stewards were directly responsible for over twice as many members as the men (an average of 181 members as compared with 85). These differences reflect the different steward structures of unions to which the women and men belonged, but they also are an indicator of the greater leadership responsibility assumed by these female stewards and may explain why women reported that they had put in a half hour more work, on the average, as stewards than the men during the last day they worked. Women also reported spending more time with coworkers outside work (an average of 20 as compared with 17 hours last month) and knowing more stewards by name in their workplace and in their local. When asked what portion of their friends worked at their workplace, over two-fifths of the women and none of the men replied "most." In addition, over twice as many women as men said they held one or more union positions in addition to that of steward, always attended union meetings, participated in union activities in addition to meetings, and had been a delegate to an international union convention. Three-quarters of the women and half of the men said that they would be somewhat or very interested in holding another union job.

Many people have some fears when they take on a new job, and I asked the stewards what fears they had when taking on rank-and-file leadership. Most of the women and a number of the men named fears centering around whether they could do the job or whether management would be more repressive toward them. "Whether I could do a good job and help, not hinder," "I had no confidence that I could adequately fill the job," and "I had no confidence that I could perform," were some of their responses. Several of those who worried about whether they would be adequate stewards, cited fears about working with management. One with such fears said, "It's hard to get used to feeling that you're equal to them as a steward;" another remembered, "I was petrified when talking to the supervisor about the grievance." The women who feared that becoming a steward would make things more difficult between them and their bosses all reported that indeed this had happened, but they are now less afraid of and more satisfied with how they handle problems with their supervisors. A number of women cited lack of knowledge about the contract and other matters as a source of their fear. Sally, for example, said she feared she wouldn't do a good enough job in representing her members because she didn't know what questions to ask.

A number of these reported fears raise questions concerning the type of training these rank-and-file leaders had for their jobs. Half the women and two-thirds of the men said that they had not received training specifically for their steward job either before or on the job. Most of the women and all of the men said that they thought they would benefit from additional training. One woman who did not feel that she would benefit from more training explained, "Having a support person to ask questions of is what you need. You can't be trained in it. You have to encounter it." The training which stewards did report receiving varied from an hour orientation session about the contract and grievance procedures to week-end long steward training classes with CSEA. CWA stewards reported being sent to steward school when they signed up to be stewards. One described a CWA course she took after becoming a chief steward. It was "not about the contract but how to get facts and how to deal with people. It was helpful." Another, not a CWA member, who was dissatisfied with her training complained, we learned "how to fill out forms, how to look at the contract. That doesn't make a steward. You need to know how to *question* people."

What do stewards consider to be their most important responsibility? A substantial number of both female and male stewards cited insuring workers' rights and handling grievances as their most important responsibility, but one-third of the women and none of the men said that listening was most important. When asked what they had done most effectively as a steward, most told of resolving grievances. Several told of preventing coworkers from being laid off or fired from their jobs. Others cited proving the need for an interpreter for deaf postal workers, empowering workers by getting them to be more vocal and less intimidated, and improving workers' image of the union.

The stewards most frequently cited their satisfaction in helping and working with people as what they liked best about their steward work. Denise observed, "It's not that hard to get things changed so they'll be better for everyone," and Sandy said, "It's satisfying helping people." Others mentioned the fulfillment and challenge their union work offered as well. Pat commented:

> I figure people need to know that there's somebody looking out for them. You know even if I don't know the answers, I have a lot of resources. The work I do (on the job) generally is real mundane. My steward work is a little extra thing that makes the job more interesting. Being a steward has built my self-confidence because when you do something you get a little praise and you want to do a lot more . . . and I don't really get that in my job. . . . People relying on you is a challenge.

Two women, now technicians, who said that at age twelve to fourteen they had wanted to be social workers both said that their work as a steward was much like social work. Denise exclaimed, "I *am* a social worker, believe me! But I didn't have to have the college, and I get paid a lot more and have more job security!"

MENTORS, ADVISORS, AND FRIENDS

We learned that many of the stewards interviewed said that encouraging family members and supportive union members were important reasons for their joining and becoming active in their union. Approximately four-fifths of the women and three-fifths of the men we interviewed said that now that they are stewards they count on one or more people in the union for help or advice about union matters. Three-quarters of both the women and the men said they count on someone outside of the union for such help and advice. Perhaps because more men than women are in senior union leadership positions, somewhat over half of the women said that the key person they count on for advice in their union is a man. The female stewards' responses to questions concerning why they count on this person, how they came to know and count on them, and what is the most important thing s/he has helped you do, indicate that today union men as well as women can be counted on, sometimes within limits, sometimes without limits, to support women as they learn the ropes of union leadership.

What qualities did these union members have that enabled the women to count on them? A number cited their advisor's availability and encouragement.

- She's available to talk. She answers questions and is encouraging. She's a hard worker for our cause. During the strike and with contract negotiations, I saw how hard she worked and wanted to help out.
- His faith in me. I can count on his support at all times. He persuaded me and pushed me. He'd tell me, "I know you've got it. I know you can handle management."

Other women counted on others specifically for their knowledge. Marlene observed:

The General Manager of my union knows the most. I intentionally established a close relationship with him because I knew I could learn a lot from him. Whenever anything happens, I call him up, ask him to go out for coffee and pump him with questions about what's happening and how to handle it. He says he learns a lot from me too, so I don't feel bad about asking. The other person I count on understands the issues of people in my unit. I call her up often to test out ideas. I believe in having mentors.

A few women noted that those they count on have limitations. Nancy cautioned: "He can only be counted on to a certain point, that is, you can't do things new and different. We represent a lot of women in our local. He is for the women's movement, but he has to have the last say."

Many women mentioned the importance of having a mentor. On the other hand, some named the lack of such assistance as what hindered them most in taking on their new responsibilities when they first became a steward. Cherise, for example, said, "There was no communication, feedback, answers." Denise recalled. "I felt that they all abandoned me and wondered why weren't they welcoming me and telling me what it was all about."

FAMILY, WORK AND UNION

Today, American women typically juggle two jobs, one in the paid labor force and one in the home. Nearly half of the women interviewed had three jobs. They were full-time employees in the paid labor force, mothers to children under age sixteen, and trade union stewards.

These women had their first child at an average age of 20. For most, marriage had been an ever-changing phenomenon. At the time of the interview, 14 were divorced or separated, 8 married, 3 were single and never married, and 1 was widowed. Of the 8 currently married, 5 had divorced and remarried.

How do these working women handle union work as well as family responsibilities? A number indicated that their spouse's attitude toward their union work is or was, for better or for worse, a significant aspect of their relationship. These women have generally not been passive victims within the institution of marriage. Rather, they have sought and sometimes found partners who effectively support their union work and goals. Some of these active women, like many of the active men, are considerably aided by partners who listen at the end of the day to their trials and triumphs.

Patricia, one of the remarried respondents, reported that her first husband was "very jealous of any outside interest. My present husband," she continued, "gives me drive. I pull him in and ask for his input. We were married when I ran for office. After I was nominated, I had some doubts as to whether I could perform the duties and thought of dropping out of the race. He was the one who kept encouraging me. He told me, 'You're ready for it.'" Debbie, another remarried respondent, became a union activist after her second marriage. Her present (second) husband's work as a musician takes him away from home for several weeks at a time. Since he is often absent and her only child is now grown, she has considerable time to work with the union.

Dale, who is divorced and has not remarried, said of her present partner who is also a member of her local, "My man's not only my total support but the recipient of all my anxieties when I come home. He's a little jealous when I go out of town (on union business), but he never tries to talk me out of it. If he did, it would destroy our relationship."

Several of the women who are divorced volunteered that their spouse's lack of support for their union work was a factor in their decision to divorce. Maria recalled that her ex-husband had asked her "Who comes first—me or the union?," and that she replied: "It's something I enjoy and need. If I wasn't active in the union, I'd be active in the PTA or something else." Dorothy who had been a steward for over eight years reported that she became a union activist during her second marriage and that her husband, also a member of her local, chaired her successful campaign for treasurer of their local. Then:

During my term as treasurer, our marriage began to go down the road, partially because of the union, partially because of everything else. A lot of it
was because of my awakening. Finally I had found something that was important to me. He couldn't deal with it. All of a sudden he wasn't one hundred percent my focal point. . . .

The union is not the only reason our marriage broke up, but when I told
him that I was thinking about running for vice-president, and he said, 'I
thought you might be. . . . Well let me tell you something now. If you
decide to run for vice-president, you also decide to terminate our marriage.'
It was not an easy decision. . . .

It was three months of hard soul searching. I finally said, I'm running. It
didn't matter whether I won or lost. I have to live, and I have to live with
myself as a person. Since I don't have children, I needed something. If it
hadn't been the union, it would have been something else.

By 1984 when I reinterviewed her, Dorothy had a new partner, had served for three years as vice-president of her 20,000 member local as well as
continuing as a union steward, and had just been elected to another three-
year term as vice-president. Her new partner is also a member of her local.
Unlike her second husband, her third partner entered into a relationship
with Dorothy knowing about and supporting her union activism. She commented, "He's great. He spends time with his friends when I'm off at con-
ferences, and at night when I come home he's there as I let off steam. For
two months he had to be away because of work, and I realized how much I
depend on him to be there as I unwind."

Two of the four respondents who are still married to their first spouses,
said that their husbands were initially and are currently "very supportive"
of their union work. Sheila's husband is a union member himself and discusses her union work with her as a "colleague." On the other hand, Sara
reported that her husband is very unsupportive and that she didn't expect
her marriage to last much longer, and Janet, who was recently married said,
"Part of him resents labor and politics, but he knows better than to get between me and the union. He helps me with thinking about union
problems."

Half of both the female and male stewards said they had developed special arrangements or ways of doing things that made it easier to handle all of
their family, job, and union responsibilities. In a number of cases, family
members actively contributed to their union efforts. Cherise, who has two
boys in their late teens, said laughingly, "I'm just not domestic. I've always
given my boys jobs. I raised them to be very independent. When they were
old enough, their responsibilities increased. They help me with union stuff
and housekeeping. They host at union meetings held at my home." Geraldine, who is divorced and has two children under age five, takes them to
union social activities. "They feel part" of the union, she said. At other
times, her mother and ex-husband look after the children. Shirley, who is

separated, started teaching her teenagers skills for caring for themselves when she went back to school. Now they help her stuff envelopes for the union and host at union parties.

Many of the arrangements the women had for handling their three jobs did not happen automatically but were the result of their persistently educating and sometimes struggling with their spouses and children. Judith, who has three children between six and sixteen, said that although her husband was supportive of her union activism in the beginning he told her that "he personally would never get involved in his union. . . . The next thing I said to him," she went on, "was, 'Are you saying I shouldn't do this?'" Laughing, she mimicked his squealed "Noooo". Now, she reported, he runs the family and holds "the household down when the union requires me to be out or to be separate from the family with a phone call from an anxious worker. He picks up the ball and runs with it. He's supportive too in that we'll talk about specific cases (worker grievances) and that's very helpful to me." Judith also reports that her husband cooks 60 percent of their meals, does 90 percent of the clean up after meals, 10 percent of the laundry, 60 percent of the routine general housekeeping and all the grocery shopping.

HUMAN AGENCY: WOMEN TAKING CHARGE

One of the highlights of the interviews was hearing women tell of the many ways they take charge of their lives in order to achieve various goals. Within their families, workplaces, and unions, they have worked around limitations by recognizing both the limits and possibilities various situations have offered, and by acting so as to minimize the limitations and maximize the possibilities offered by their social environments. I have described above several examples of women making decisions and acting with regard to spouses, union officials, and managers so as to maximize their chance of achieving their goals for themselves and others. Susan provides another example.

Shortly before the interviews, Susan had accepted the chairship of her local's Health and Safety Committee knowing that the previous chair had been unable to get the committee's members together more than once over the previous year and a half. Susan decided to try a new approach. Rather than asking members to meet after a tiring day at the plant, she planned a Saturday picnic party, including a brief meeting at her home for the members, their wives, and children. She said she loves to cook, so this would be fun for her, but she was also looking forward to everyone getting to know each other. At the time of the interview, she had talked with each member individually about the picnic meeting, and the response had been good.

Another example is Rosa, a single mother with two young children. Their development and relationship with her is important to her. She knows that at this stage in their development she wants to spend considerable time mothering them. At the same time, Rosa wants to offer leadership in her union and, over the long run, to improve her job conditions and affect social change through her union. Coworkers, mostly men in an auto plant, suggested that she serve as a steward, but she chose to be an alternate steward for this period of time. As an alternate steward, she is gaining leadership skills, learning about her union, learning how to work with a wide variety of people in her local, and is becoming known within her local.

In these and other interviews, women repeatedly gave evidence of taking charge of their family and union circumstances rather than being passive victims. In a portion of the interviews which I will report on in a future paper, the stewards told about their goals for their unions, the nation and the world. When asked, "Do you think people like you can do anything about achieving goals like those you have for the world?", 92 percent of the women and 83 percent of the men said "yes."

CONCLUSIONS

Facilitating women's taking on and carrying out stewardship responsibilities is an important strategy for improving women's employment because stewards significantly influence women's employment conditions by enforcing and extending the contract. In addition, stewards' recruiting new members, communicating with members, and organizing members for strike action strengthens unions in collective bargaining for wages, benefits, and working conditions. Finally, service as a steward affects the employment of many of those who so serve by providing training in leadership skills and by being a step toward higher level positions in unions, companies and government agencies.

In this study I examined women's experiences as rank-and-file labor leaders and compared them with those of men. I also investigated factors that help and hinder stewards in taking on and carrying out their leadership roles.

The findings of this study suggest ways that unions through officer mentoring, training programs, and family activities may assist women in taking on rank-and-file labor leadership. Within their unions, a significant support person and steward training, not only in the particulars of grievance procedures but in leading and working with constituents, facilitated women's taking on and carrying out new leadership roles. Stewards we interviewed who lacked such assistance cited their need for it and in some cases said that its absence resulted in their becoming less involved in their unions or in their having to learn how to fulfill their steward responsibilities in an inefficient trial-and-error manner. Finally, I found that these women stewards had developed numerous creative arrangements to not only facilitate their juggling their union, family, and work responsibilities but to have each enhance the other. In future research involving interviews with over a hundred female and male stewards from nine major northern California unions

I will examine the goals of women and men who are stewards, the relationship of their steward activities to the accomplishment of their goals, and the bearing of varying union structures on their taking on and carrying out rank-and-file labor leadership.

NOTES

1. In many unions, a steward's primary role is to handle the initial step or steps of worker grievances. In most unions, stewards also have political, educational, and organizational responsibilities. In some unions, the steward watches for company violations of the contract but does not actually handle grievances. A grievance is a complaint made by a worker to a union steward or representative about her or his employer's violating the contract or a law, acting unfairly, or jeopardizing the workers' health or safety (cf. Nash, 1983; Peck, 1963; Cook, 1962; Miller and Form, 1951). For descriptions of the historical roots of the union steward see Peck and Nash.

2. Women comprised 25.4 percent of the U.S. labor force in March 1940, 29.1 percent in April 1950, 33.3 percent in April 1960, 38.1 percent in April 1970, and 43.7 percent in 1985 (U.S. Department of Labor, 1986b, pp. 12–13). 28.9 percent of women 16 years of age and over were in the labor force in March 1940, 33.0 percent in April 1950, 37.4 percent in April 1960, 43.2 percent in April 1970, and 53.6 percent in 1984 (U.S. Women's Bureau, 1975, Table 2:11; U.S. Department of Labor, 1986b, Tables A2 and A3: 16–17).

3. Full-time female wage and salary workers who were covered by union contracts earned 30 percent more than their female counterparts who were not covered by a union contract in 1984. The median usual weekly earnings of the former were $326 as compared with $251 of the latter; men covered by a union contract earned a median usual weekly wage or salary of $444 and those not covered earned a median wage of $362. (U.S. Department of Labor, 1986a, Table 54; cf U.S. Department of Labor, 1979:2–4; cf. Raphael, 1974).

4. Since 1983, the data on union membership have been derived from U.S. Bureau of the Census Current Population Household Surveys. Data have never been gathered on the numbers of women who hold local union posts across the country, and union locals do not calculate the percentage of their members or stewards who are female. With computerization, an increasingly large minority of locals are developing up to date, unified lists of stewards. It is generally agreed that over the past decade women have comprised an increasing proportion of most unions' stewards. For those northern California locals from which I have obtained lists of stewards, I have found that female members continue to be underrepresented among stewards. (In one local women were approximately 2 percent of the stewards and 7 percent of the membership, in a second local women were 55 percent of the stewards and 68 percent of the membership, and in a third local 86 percent of the stewards and about 92 percent of the membership was female).

5. Women offer unions not only large numbers of potential members but new approaches and skills. David Montgomery suggests, for example, that the issues and tactics of the Yale strike offer new models for strikes of the future (Cerullo and Feldberg, 1984). The international women's liberation movement, women's common experience nurturing young ones, and the impoverishment of a large propor-

tion of the world's women, may provide a vision and base for women to take decisive leadership in shaping their workplaces, unions, and world.

6. The unions are the Amalgamated Transit Union; American Postal Workers Union; Communication Workers of America (CWA); California Nurses Association; Engineers and Scientists of California; Glass, Pottery, Plastics and Allied Workers; International Association of Machinists and Aerospace Workers; International Brotherhood of Electrical Workers; International Chemical and Atomic Workers Union; International Brotherhood of Teamsters, Chauffeurs, Warehousemen and Welders of America; International Typographers Union; National Association of Letter Carriers; Service Employees International Union (SEIU); Sheet Metal Workers; United Automobile Workers; United Brotherhood of Carpenters and Joiners of America.

7. All names have been changed in order to protect confidentiality.

CHAPTER 8

Equitable Compensation: Methodological Criteria for Comparable Worth*

RONNIE STEINBERG AND LOIS HAIGNERE

INTRODUCTION

Equal pay for work of comparable worth achieved national visibility in 1979 under Eleanor Holmes Norton, chair of the Equal Employment Opportunity Commission (EEOC) during the Carter administration. Among her actions, Norton contracted with the National Research Council of the National Academy of Sciences (NRC/NAS) to form a committee to examine the feasibility of implementing a comparable worth policy. She no doubt reasoned that, for comparable worth to move from a political demand to a legitimate policy, it would be necessary to operationalize the concept of wage discrimination.

One important step toward operationalization involved identifying the institutional features likely to embed wage discrimination. These are found in mechanisms that established wage structures. Pay is commonly assigned

---

* For comments on this chapter see Feldberg (pp.245-250) and Hartmann (pp.251-258) in this volume.

to jobs through classification and compensation systems. Most of these use some variant of job evaluation procedures. These are essentially measurement procedures designed to establish pay differentials between jobs. Treiman and Hartmann (1981:71) report that well over two-thirds of all employees in the United States are subject to some form of job evaluation. After assessing existing job evaluation systems, the NRC/NAS cautioned that they are likely to contain sex bias. Nevertheless, they concluded that job evaluation plans "provide measures of job worth that, under certain circumstances, may be used to discover and reduce wage discrimination for persons covered by a given plan" (Ibid:95). They went on to suggest methodologies, which, if refined, could provide empirical estimates of the extent of wage discrimination on a job title by job title basis. They discuss as well some of the problems with the state of the art in job evaluation.

The next step in building a methodology for identifying wage discrimination is to move from these general statements to a more specific and systematic understanding of the ways in which wage discrimination is embedded in job evaluation methodologies and classification and compensation systems. It also involves delineating the methodological standards that will help eliminate this discrimination. This paper is an attempt to develop operational criteria for achieving comparable worth.

It is especially important to develop these methodological standards at this time. Legislative task forces and labor management committees are allocating hundreds of thousands of dollars to undertake comparable pay studies. In most cases they are selecting the very management consulting firms that have been using biased job evaluation systems for decades. They are also doing comprehensive overhauls of classification and compensation systems when all they might need to do is (less costly) adjustments of specific components of it. Through our personal communication with many of these policymakers, it is clear that they have an incomplete understanding of how to select an evaluation system that has the least sex bias and the greatest methodological rigor. They will thus fall short in achieving pay equity. To assist those policymakers at this critical point in the reform process, it is important to extend and ground existing knowledge on the feasibility of job evaluation in identifying wage discrimination.

The discussion that follows is based on ten years collective experience of the authors. This has included serving as the director and assistant director, respectively, of the New York State Comparable Pay Study.[1] It has also involved work in four political subdivisions in New York State.[2] In addition, it has resulted from providing technical assistance on drafting comparable worth legislation, on designing pay equity studies, and on developing plans for implementing pay equity adjustments.[3] Examples from classification and compensation systems used below are largely drawn from the jurisdictions in which we have worked.

COMPARABLE WORTH AND
JOB EVALUATION PROCEDURES

Comparable worth policy broadens the earlier policy of equal pay for equal work which prohibited wage discrimination if women and men were doing the same or essentially similar work. It requires, instead, that dissimilar jobs of equivalent worth to the employer should be paid the same wages. Theoretically, the policy goal of equal pay for work of comparable worth involves the issue of whether work done primarily by women and minorities is systematically undervalued because the work has been and continues to be done primarily by women and minorities.[4] Systematic undervaluation means that the wages paid to women and men engaged in historically female or minority work are lower than they would be if these jobs had been and were being performed by white males. At the most simple level, *operationally,* comparable worth involves correcting where it is found to exist the practice of paying women and minorities less than white men for work that requires equivalent skills, responsibilities, stresses, personal contacts, and working conditions.[5]

Most public and private sector employers build their wage structure through job evaluation procedures. Typically, these involve three major components: description of characteristics, evaluation of characteristics, and salary-setting.[6]

Description

Description of jobs has often been called job content analysis. The general purpose of job content analysis is to describe the individual incumbent positions so that they may be grouped into job classes or titles. These classes can then be categorized by job families and, within families, into appropriate promotional tracks.

To meet these objectives, the content of each position must be accurately described in terms of the range of tasks, and behavior or functions associated with it (Beatty and Beatty, 1984). Commonly, this information is collected through desk audits (in which an observer records what an incumbent does), interviews, or open- or closed-ended questionnaires administered to incumbents, supervisors, or both.

Job characteristics may be described in terms of skills, effort, responsibilities and working conditions. Alternatively, they may be defined more specifically to include items such as job related experience, formal training time required, frequency of review of work, total number of personnel an employee is responsible for, impact on and responsibility for budget, physical stress, time spent working under deadlines, time spent in processing information and so on. (Appendix A provides an illustration of closed-ended and open-ended questions commonly used in job description.)

After job content information is collected, it is almost always transferred to what is called a job specification. The job specification is based on a grouping of responses on individual positions. It is usually organized in a format or outline, with sections listing job content factors relevant for hiring and evaluating the job. It is also common for promotional series of a particular job title, such as Typist I, II, and III, to be included on the same specification. Categories found on job specifications include qualification at hire or minimum qualifications, examples of common duties, supervision received, supervision exercised, working conditions, and differences between the levels in the series.

In most job evaluation systems, job specifications provide the link between analysis and evaluation. This is because they are the informational basis for hierarchically ranking jobs in relation to one another, either by assigning points or a less precise measure of value.

Evaluation[7]

The purpose of evaluation is to assign relative worth to job content in order to rank jobs in relation to one another. This may be done either within job families or across all jobs in a specific internal labor market. In most cases, these hierarchical rankings become the method for directly translating a set of job characteristics into an appropriate wage or salary rate.

To meet these objectives, most approaches include some procedure for weighting job content characteristics as more or less valuable to the employer. At its most precise, value is defined in terms of points. There are two major approaches to obtaining the weights in a system: an *a priori* approach, using a predetermined system of characteristics (or factors) and weights (or factor weights) to evaluate jobs within a specific firm, and a *policy-capturing* approach, using a statistical analysis of the individual firm as the basis for creating factors and factor weights to apply to jobs in that firm. Typical *a priori* systems define work content in terms of broad categories such as skill, effort, responsibility, and working conditions. The selection of *a priori* factors and the weighting of the factors is usually made by the consultant whose services are being retained. An employer can modify the factors and factor weights to more closely represent organizational goals or preferences. In the public sector, the employer could be a personnel director, or a task force or committee. In some, albeit unusual, circumstances, the employer will retain a consultant to construct a customized *a priori* factor and factor weighting scheme in accordance with the job characteristics to be valued in that firm.

Once the factors and weights have been selected, they must be applied to each job title. In general this is accomplished through the use of several small evaluation teams. Most teams are composed of personnel administrators with experience in the job evaluation process. Sometimes, however, teams contain individuals from diverse occupations, who differ by gender, race, age, and interest group affiliation. The rationale behind the use of nonpersonnel teams is that evaluations conducted by teams of diverse individuals result in greater occupational consensus over the final wage structure. Whatever the composition of the team, training is likely to be conducted to assure within-team consistency in applying points to jobs.

Jobs are commonly assigned to evaluation teams in the following way. Each job family is assigned a team. Then, beginning with the highest job in the series and working backward to the lowest, the evaluation criteria are applied by the committee to a job. For example, the Stenographer V would be assigned job worth points first, followed by Stenographer IV and so on.

By contrast, the more recently developed and less frequently used *policy-capturing* approach develops a compensation model which statistically captures the relationship between current wages paid for a job in a firm and the content of the job. In this approach, specific job content features such as the number of persons supervised, type of training needed to work with machines, and extent of traveling overnight on the job become the basis for describing job content. Then, through statistical analysis, factors and factor weights can be determined by determining which elements of jobs are best correlated to existing pay practices for that firm. These will vary, of course, from firm to firm. For example, a public sector jurisdiction may value supervision, responsibility for budgetary decisions, and writing skills. By contrast, a manufacturing firm may value supervision, cost effective production monitoring, and manual dexterity.

Each of the two systems of job evaluation has technical strengths and limitations, and both must be tempered by political realities (see Remick and Steinberg, 1984 for a fuller discussion). For example, *a priori* systems, especially when customized, have the advantage of making explicit the values used in the evaluation of jobs. The systems provide employer and employee alike the opportunity to study the underlying value system of the evaluation instrument in an accessible, nonmathematical framework. The major limitations of these systems are their resistance to modification, general lack of flexibility or responsiveness to firm-specific factors, and probable bias. On the other hand, procedures labelled as *policy-capturing* make fewer assumptions than *a priori* about what the firm should value because they build an evaluation system that is firm-specific. Yet, because they require sophisticated statistical analysis, they seem less accessible to those who must implement the evaluation results.

The level of objectivity in measurement by either kind of system should not be confused with a mistaken vision that there is or can be objectivity in values. Both approaches are ways of systematizing value systems, and both potentially include or remove more or less of the discrimination embedded in an existing classification system. Both kinds are geared to describe *what is* in the firm or in some other labor market. *Neither* start from scratch in prescribing *what should be.*

Salary Setting

Once jobs have been ranked through evaluation, they are assigned a wage rate or salary level. In assigning wages, there is an attempt to balance internal and external equity. By internal equity, we mean "the value of one job (in relation) to another within a firm." By external equity, we mean "the value of each job with respect to prevailing labor market practices" (Beatty and Beatty, 1984:59).

For internal equity, a legitimate job evaluation system will result in a wage structure in which: (1) all positions within a title are paid the same, except for differences resulting from seniority; (2) higher job titles within a promotional track or job family are paid more; and (3) wages across job families or occupational groups, if they are at all compared, are regarded as plausible. In *a priori* evaluation systems, this internal equity is aligned to prevailing wages in the appropriate labor market through a process called benchmarking. Key job titles, considered representative of a particular job series, family, or occupational group, are selected as so-called benchmark titles. These are job titles easily found in other nearby corporations or public jurisdictions. In general, seven or eight employers are used in matching benchmarks. Firms selected are those geographically proximate or functionally similar to the firm conducting the job evaluation. Ideally, the internal salary for a benchmark title should be at least as high as most of the external comparisons. Once the competitive salary is established for the benchmark title, other salaries are set in relation to it in terms of where the title fits in the hierarchy.

Other salaries are set through a procedure establishing a pay policy line. A pay policy line is drawn by arraying the jobs on a graph with evaluation points on the horizontal axis and salary or salary grades on the vertical axis. For any particular job, the salary or grade is then determined by its evaluation points in a straightforward practice. Frequently, several pay policy lines are drawn, one for each broad occupational group. On occasion, for firms placing a high value on internal equity, one pay policy line is drawn for all jobs.

In *policy-capturing* evaluation, the evaluation and salary setting are interrelated. Job descriptions are regressed against salaries to obtain the line which best establishes the relationship between what incumbents do in their work and what they are paid. Salaries may be those currently existing in the firm or prevailing wages in the external labor market. The regression procedure generates a set of factors and factor weights. This equation is then used as the basis for estimating a predicted salary or salary grade for each title. As with *a priori*, this procedure can be followed for each occupational group or for all titles in the firm.

While we have presented a general overview of the typical job evaluation methodology, in our experience, no two systems are exactly alike, even if they have been developed from the same management consultants. Differences are a function of organizational policy, external labor market constraints, and political considerations. Systems also vary as a function of the size and status of the employer. In the following section, we highlight how these varied systems are designed in ways that perpetuate wage discrimination.

WAGE DISCRIMINATION AND METHODOLOGICAL CRITERIA FOR COMPARABLE WORTH

In the last section, we described the basic steps in carrying out job evaluation in firms and public jurisdiction employers. Job evaluation need not lead to sex- and race-based wage discrimination. It is, after all, a set of techniques for making the values operating in a specific internal labor market explicit in terms of what people do on their jobs. It also provides a procedure for systematically ordering jobs into a relative wage structure based on the values articulated.

In practice, however, the way job evaluation is designed creates pervasive salary inequities, because sex and race typing of jobs are implicit compensable job content characteristics that depress the wage rate. The fact that current job evaluation approaches embed broader cultural assumptions about the value of activities performed by women and minorities should not be surprising. Until recently, assumptions of the differential worth of activities performed by women and minorities were part of the taken-for-granted cognitive organization of reality for the society as a whole. Why wouldn't they, then, find their way into job evaluation systems?

Shepela and Viviano (1984:47) report, "there is considerable anthropological and sociological data to indicate that the value of an activity or characteristic can be lowered simply through its association with women (or minorities)." The NRC/NAS Committee arrived at the same conclusion: "it is possible that the process of describing and evaluating jobs reflects pervasive cultural stereotypes regarding the relative worth of work traditionally done by men and work traditionally done by women" (Treiman and Hartmann, 1981:81). Uncovering these pervasive cultural assumptions was a function of the improved position of women reflected in economic and political pressure to eliminate the impact of stereotypes on wages.

Prior to the new system presently being designed for New York State, their classification and compensation process provided a characteristic illustration of the way in which many systems embed wage discrimination in the description and evaluation of jobs. New York State used a job evaluation system which grouped particular positions into job classes like Secretary I, Secretary II, Cook, or Carpenter. Classes were then assigned to one of 85 job families or occupational groups, such as tax administrators and technicians, parks and forestry, general clerical and food preparation. Within each occupational group, classes were arranged hierarchically from highest to lowest in terms of job content characteristics. No points were assigned to the characteristics. Each occupational group was attached to a general grading scheme independently. This means that there was no comparison with other occupational groups that may have had similar job content characteristics. Because there were no checks for internal equity across job families, the New York State system carried 85 metrics—one for each occupational group. This was especially troublesome because occupational groupings are highly sex and race segregated.

This way of designing job evaluation has been labeled the multiple plan problem by Hartmann and Treiman (1983). It occurs when major sex and race segregated occupational categories like clerical jobs, manual labor jobs, and managerial jobs are treated independently of each other. Descriptions are frequently based on dissimilar job content features. Evaluations are based on different factors. Similar factors used in different occupational groups are given different weightings. Salaries are set in relation to different external firms. It is troublesome for comparable worth because it prohibits comparisons across categories.

A second example is drawn from Massachusetts. Like many other jurisdictions, Massachusetts uses collective bargaining to establish wage rates in all nonmanagerial jobs. Because of this, salary setting for nonmanagerial jobs occurs through the labor relations process, while salary setting for managerial jobs is handled by the personnel department with legislative approval. This difference in locus of responsibility made it easier to implement a new classification system for managerial employees in the early 1980s. Nonmanagerial positions are compensated based on pre-1976 job descriptions and evaluation standards. Thus two systems operate. One is outdated and the other up-to-date. Moreover, because women and minorities are primarily found in nonmanagerial positions, the use of two systems has a disparate impact. This remains the case despite the increase in the number of women entering management positions over the last two decades.

The goal of pay equity requires the elimination of multiple plan job evaluations within a firm or public jurisdiction. Indeed, Helen Remick (1984c:99) has defined comparable worth in precisely these terms, "the application of a single bias-free point factor job evaluation system within a given establishment, across job families, both to rank order jobs and to set salaries." In other words, comparable worth requires *consistent* treatment of all job titles in every component of job evaluation. In addition, it requires the bias free application of procedures. For example, as we will develop below, it is not acceptable to ignore job content characteristics common to traditionally female or minority jobs even if this content is consistently ignored for all job titles.

Thus, for job evaluation to result in classification and compensation systems meeting comparable worth standards, two criteria of consistency and bias free application must be met in each of the three major components of job evaluation.

Description

Job content analysis frequently ignores or overlooks compensable job content characteristics of female-dominated and significantly minority jobs. A first example is drawn from a study of the third edition of the *Dictionary of Occupational Titles* (DOT) (Witt and Naherny, 1975). The DOT, compiled by the U.S. Department of Labor, contains a list of almost every job title along with a rating of the job in terms of a skill-complexity code. These researchers noted that the ratings for certain historically female jobs compared to certain historically male jobs did not carry face validity. At that time, for instance, dog pound attendant and parking lot attendant were rated more highly than nursery school teacher, and zookeeper more highly than day care worker.

Independently evaluating these historically female jobs, the researchers found their ratings differed substantially from those of the Labor Department evaluators. When examining why the differences emerged, they found that the Labor Department evaluators had overlooked important characteristics of the female-dominated jobs, especially those associated with taking care of children. The evaluators did not regard these as job related *skills*, but rather as *qualities intrinsic to being a woman*. Because of this, the job evaluators were confusing the content and responsibilities of a paid job with stereotypic notions about the characteristics of the job holder. We find this happening with fine motor coordination, rapid finger dexterity skills, and with the noisy and public working conditions associated with female-dominated blue collar and clerical work.

A second example of distortion in job content analysis comes from a review of 16 job analysis/evaluation frameworks conducted as a preliminary step to developing a job content questionnaire for New York State. Our purpose in reviewing these plans was to include, in early drafts of the survey instrument, *every* category of job content included. We also noted the levels or degrees within a characteristic that had been used in these other systems. Even the resulting 100 page item list proved incomplete as we began both reading over job descriptions for major female-dominated job families and conducting preliminary field testing with incumbents. Either important job characteristics were overlooked or questions were formulated so that incumbents regarded them as inapplicable.

For example, questions about record keeping would be listed among a series of content items relevant primarily to clerical and administrative work. Instructions preceding the question would use an example from an office job. Because of this, institutional caretakers (in correctional facilities, state and municipal hospitals, youth facilities) did not answer record keeping questions, even though when they were probed, they acknowledged that the task was an important part of their job. While some of the problem here is methodological, we note as well that we added an item on record keeping because it was not included in our 100 page item list. As we will indicate below, there are skill, responsibility, stress, and working condition characteristics prevalent in female-dominated jobs that rarely show up in job descriptions. If an employee is not asked about specific job content or is asked incorrectly, she/he cannot respond. If there is no response, wages for that job will be less because it was not considered in the subsequent evaluation.

This is especially troublesome when interviews or open-ended job questionnaires are used to collect job information from employees with no training in job analysis. If these employees are simply asked to "Describe the major or key duties and responsibilities of their work," their responses may be constricted by limited verbal and conceptual skills. It is easy to overlook many tasks and responsibilities. Moreover, Remick (1979) has written at length on the tendency for women to underdescribe and men to overdescribe their jobs. If jobs are described incompletely and inaccurately on a systematic basis, existing specifications become nothing more than job content-based justifications for perpetuating undervaluation of female-dominated or significantly minority jobs.

A third example builds on the earlier discussion of the multiple plan problem between managerial and nonmanagerial jobs. Different questionnaires are frequently used to collect content information for managerial and nonmanagerial jobs. For instance, in one state, information concerning time stress or the stress of meeting deadlines was gathered concerning managerial jobs but no information on time stress was collected for any of the nonmanagerial positions. Because of this, time stress demands in nonmanagerial jobs could not be compensated, although it was a compensable factor for managerial job titles.

The way in which job information is translated from the data instrument to the job title specification can also involve inconsistencies and bias. There is considerable judgment involved in deciding what information about a title to emphasize on the specification. Information selected will have a considerable impact on how a job will be rated on the subsequent evaluation component. Unless those writing job specifications are given training in awareness of sex and race stereotypes and bias, they may unintentionally incorporate these into the specifications. An example is taken from a job evaluation manual comparing the rating of experience for a typist and truck driver (Treiman, 1979: 52–53). To score the job knowledge factor of this system, it was necessary to determine how much prejob and on-the-job experience would be needed to perform the job duties under normal supervision. The typist was judged to require one month of training time and the truck driver was judged to require twelve months of training time. As Treiman notes:

> It is easy to speculate that this difference may result from cultural stereotypes since both positions involve skills usually learned prior to entry into the labor force, sometimes by means of formal instruction and sometimes by quite informal means. Were typists judged to require the same training time as truck drivers, it would mean an increase of two full pay grades.

Another illustration of faulty job specification procedures is provided in one jurisdiction in which we found a higher number of repetitive statements under *Qualifications Required at Hire* for male-dominated than female-dominated jobs. In this instance, for male titles, the same characteristic was listed twice, once as an "ability" statement and once as a "willingness" statement. The following three pairs of statements occurred in at least four male-dominated occupational series (labor, skilled labor, carpenter, and painter). At hire, incumbents of these jobs had to have:

- the ability to lift and carry heavy objects;
- the ability to stand for prolonged periods of time;
- the ability to climb and work from ladders and scaffolds;
- the willingness to lift and carry heavy objects;
- the willingness to stand for prolonged periods of time; and
- the willingness to climb and work from ladders and scaffolds.

By contrast, for typists and stenographers, willingness statements did not duplicate ability statements, perhaps because few if any working conditions features of their jobs (such as the ability or willingness to sit for long periods of time) were included in their job specifications. Instead, they were described as having "no unusual working conditions." Several human relations abilities which could have been repeated as willingness statements were not included. These were:

- the ability to establish and maintain harmonious working relationships with others;
- the ability to deal tactfully with others; and
- the ability to exercise discretion in handling confidential information.

The redundancy for male titles becomes of even greater concern when we note that the characteristics cited above were repeated under a separate section on *Working Conditions*. For female titles, no special working conditions were noted. Nor was there a separate section on *Human Relations Requirements*. It was only after we remarked upon these redundancies to the personnel staff involved that they became aware of the inconsistency and bias involved.

A number of steps need to be taken to correct the way in which job description procedures result in wage discrimination.

All jobs must be described fully and consistently and not differentially by the sex or race of the typical incumbent. The questionnaire or other information gathering methods must give incumbents of all jobs an equal opportunity to report the work they do. These instruments must be comprehensive as well as consistent, giving incumbents the chance to report work done on the same universe of job content characteristics.

If questionnaires are used, reading level must be kept as simple as possible. Open-ended questionnaires should not be used if at all possible with employees with limited verbal skills and/or no training in job analysis. It would be unclear, for example, whether responses to a question such as, "Describe the major duties and responsibilities of your work," are a function of the variation among the jobs or the variation in incumbents' education levels and verbal abilities. In other words, the information must be collected in a way that minimizes variations that are a function of incumbent differences in providing information. In the public sector, this can especially be a problem for people in institutional and facility human service settings (largely women and minorities).

Further, to minimize bias, the job content characteristics used must include ones associated with female-dominated work. Frequently ignored female characteristics include: *job stress,* such as the number of individuals from whom one receives direction, doing the same task over and over for a long time, and working around people who are sick and disabled with no hope of recovery; *working conditions,* such as cleaning up other people's dirt and garbage, and physically handling sick or injured people; *responsibility,* such as scheduling meetings or appointments, coordinating meetings, and showing new workers who make more money how to do their job; and *skill,* such as creating a record-keeping system, writing standard letters, and reading forms. Indeed, we have compiled the following preliminary checklist of items as a starting point for developing a more comprehensive list.

LIST OF FREQUENTLY OVERLOOKED JOB CONTENT
IN FEMALE JOBS

- Fine motor movement skills like rapid finger dexterity
- Special body coordination or expert use of fingers and hands (*e.g.,* typing, giving injections, sign painting)
- Scheduling appointments
- Coordinating meetings
- Record keeping
- Filing
- Writing standard letters
- Reading forms
- Protecting confidentiality

- Working office machines
- Cleaning up after others
- Sitting for long periods of time
- Time stress
- Communication stress (dealing with upset people)
  — gathering information from upset or ill people
  — calming upset people
- Stress from distractions
- Stress from concentration (*e.g.*, from video display terminal)
- Stress from exposure to the sick and disabled with no hope of recovery
- Stress from multiple demands (receiving work from lots of people)
- Stress from multiple role demands (being asked to do work quickly and to provide better service to several people)
- Working with constant noise
- Working in an open office setting: with room dividers; without room dividers
- Answering questions for the public on the phone or in person
- Answering complaints from the public
- Responsibility for inmates, patients, or residents of institutions
- Degree of severity of problems of inmates, patients, or residents of institutions
- Degree to which new or unexpected problems on the job arise
- Damage to equipment from a mistake

Evaluation

The process of job evaluation involves using specifications as the information base for assigning relative worth to jobs in terms of characteristics identified as more or less valuable to the employer. Inconsistencies and bias may be present in the selection of which job content is valued, in the weighting of exactly how much they are to be valued, and in the way the process itself is conducted.

First, as we noted for descriptions, job content factors primarily found in historically female and significantly minority jobs may be ignored or weighted very lightly. For example, working with mentally ill or retarded persons may be overlooked as a stressful working condition, while working with noisy machinery may not. Poor working conditions such as lifting heavy weights or working out-of-doors may be given a high point value, while the eyestrain associated with working on VDT's may be entirely ignored.[8] Or, nurses who supervise employees and care for patients only receive points for supervision, because the way "human relations know-how" is defined largely excludes skills necessary in working with people other than those supervised.

Second, the distribution of points among job factors may result in a weighting system oriented to job characteristics predominating in white male jobs. For instance, managing money or responsibility for heavy equipment frequently receives a higher percentage of overall points than responsibility for clients and human relations skills. In the Hay Guide-Chart System, one of the major *a priori* job evaluation systems available to firms, one set of charts is constructed so that the number of points in the "Managerial Know-How" scale is *five times* as great as the number of points in the "Human Relations Know-How" scale. On the same chart, "Technical Know-How" can receive *seven* times the number of points as "Human Relations Know-How." Human relations skills are disproportionately found in women's and minorities' jobs. Fiscal responsibility, heavy machinery, and management/supervision are disproportionately associated with white male jobs. As a result, the point values contained in the charts may reflect a traditional bias against the content of female and minority jobs. For example, if you are a registered nurse responsible for patients, the fact that you work with patients is likely to increase your know-how points from 175 to 230. However, if you are a carpenter or electrician who is promoted into a supervisory position, your know-how points might increase from 230 to 400.

Third, the process of assigning job worth points to jobs can also be done inconsistently, resulting in a sex and race biased application. At the extreme, one finds the use of different evaluation systems for different occupational groupings. For instance, negotiations between American Telephone and Telegraph and the Communication Workers of America over the classification of telephone operators revealed the use of separate factor weighting schemes for nonmanagerial and managerial employees. The managerial job evaluation system assigns a high point value to customer contact. By contrast, the evaluation system for telephone operators assigned only a few points for customer contact, even though the company randomly screens the operators' calls to assess quality of assistance. After negotiations, the job of telephone operator was upgraded to acknowledge the importance AT&T places on customer contact. This is a specific variant of the frequently observed decision to weight human relations skills high for managerial, as opposed to nonmanagerial jobs.

It is also common to find the use of different procedures in conducting an evaluation for different occupational groups and especially between managerial and nonmanagerial jobs. For example, we have examined systems in which evaluation teams made up of managers were used to evaluate both managerial and nonmanagerial positions. While this may appear neutral on its face, in practice, it means that managerial jobs are evaluated by incumbents and nonmanagerial jobs are evaluated by supervisors. A consistent approach would mean that the evaluation team for clerical titles would include incumbents of clerical positions, for example. It would also mean that diverse teams would be given a set of jobs to evaluate that would cross all major occupational groupings and levels of hierarchy.

It is rare that job titles are assigned to evaluation teams in a random fashion. Rather, as indicated earlier, a single team is likely to evaluate a total bargaining unit, and within that unit, to consider all jobs in a series together. Since most job series and even most bargaining units are sex and race segregated, this format for job evaluation significantly increases the likelihood of *halo* effects. By halo effects, we mean that global impressions, or halos, of the value of the work are formed by an individual group, and spread to other assessments. For instance, the second point in the following statement represents a halo effect of the first point. "This job is a highly responsible position; therefore, it must require great technical knowledge." Halo effects in evaluation are well documented. They make valued jobs seem even more valuable, and less valued jobs seem even less valuable. The greatest concern in relation to comparable worth is the gender halo, characterized, in the extreme, by statements such as "this job is performed by women, therefore, it must involve few skills. . . . or little responsibility . . . or good working conditions." If sex or race segregated occupational groups and job series are considered by the same evaluation teams at the same time, gender halo effects may influence the rankings. It is also quite possible that the same factors may be weighted more heavily for male than female jobs.

In adjusting for the inconsistencies and biases associated with evaluation, it is important, as a first step, to develop an explicit set of compensable factors and factor weightings. As a second step, whichever method is used to create factors and factor weightings, job characteristics which "are regarded as worthy of compensation by an employer should be equally so regarded irrespective of the sex, race, or ethnicity of job incumbents" (Treiman and Hartmann, 1981:70). This, in effect, prohibits the use of multiple pay plans across job families, or between managerial and nonmanagerial jobs.

If evaluation teams are used, they should be comprised of individuals who differ by sex, race, age, and occupation. It may also be helpful if representatives of unions, management, women's and other interested groups are included on the teams. Diversity will decrease the likelihood of systematic bias in reaction to specific groups of jobs.

Furthermore, to minimize gender halo effects, the rating committee or evaluation teams should use a random procedure to determine the order in which job titles will be evaluated. If several rating teams are used, job titles should be assigned to teams randomly. Moreover, raters should rate all jobs on one chart before rating any jobs on the next chart. Alternatively, a rater or group of raters should make ratings on only one chart. This is especially important for systems in which the score on the chart influences the score on the next.

When there is any question about the consistency, validity, or reliability of the job evaluation procedures, additional checks of evaluation results should be made. Such checks should be made across jobs in different occupational groups, in different bargaining units, paying particular attention to comparing male- vs. female-dominated and minority vs. nonminority jobs.

In one jurisdiction examined, we compared points assigned for job skill for three traditionally male and three traditionally female jobs. These comparisons indicated inconsistencies in the ranking of educational requirements, technical skills, requirements for manual dexterity, and human relations skills.

Salary Setting

Salary setting characteristically uses some combination of external and internal wage information to assign a level of wages to job titles. Even when carried out using consistent procedures, it can result in lowering the wages that are assigned to female and minority titles. In describing problems of salary setting, we will assume that whatever the methodology, the description and/or evaluation components are completed without the problems discussed in the last two sections. We will further assume that, if the job evaluation component is completed, evaluation points have been assigned to the job titles.

The first set of inconsistencies arises in the way in which key jobs are benchmarked to the external labor market. Recall that benchmarking involves matching titles to ostensibly similar jobs in other firms. Based on these comparisons, a salary is assigned that is the average of the salaries paid by other employers for that job. Benchmarking can be done in a variety of ways.

One commonly used procedure involves skipping the evaluation component entirely and moving, instead, directly from job specifications to the external labor market to determine a wage rate. In this variant, the value of the job becomes an implicit acceptance of the average value assigned to the job by other employers. As a result, if these other firms ignore or weight lightly a job characteristic found disproportionately in women's jobs such as fine motor skills, then this market bias will be incorporated into the classification and compensation system in question.

A related procedure involves benchmarking to the external market only a percentage of job titles for which point evaluations have been made. Salaries are obtained for benchmarked titles. Typically, this approach to salary setting involves further separating jobs into occupational groups and achieving internal equity only within the group. Although the link to the external market is a weaker one, it nonetheless involves carrying external market wage discrimination into the firm.

Transferring external market discrimination into the firm is exacerbated if different employers are used to benchmark titles in different occupational groups. For instance, one county which we examined selected a set of public jurisdictions as the basis for assigning salaries for clerical titles while using both public and private sector employers as the basis for assigning salaries for laborers and managers. It is well known that the salaries for blue collar and managerial jobs are higher in the private than the public sector. Thus the way the external firms were chosen would tend to widen the internal wage gap between clerical and other, traditionally male titles.

Indeed, benchmarking can even be designed in a way that results in incorporating market wage discrimination into salaries assigned to traditionally male jobs. In Maine, for example, all nonmanagerial job titles were aligned to a sample of benchmark titles, which were selected to include primarily lower paying clerical and institutional service job titles like nurse's aide. Craft and operational jobs were noticeably absent among benchmark titles. Consequently, to the extent that the market pays less for the female-dominated benchmark titles, this was reflected in lower wages for craft and operative jobs.

A second, problematic feature of the salary setting process is the way in which evaluation points are arrayed against salaries to obtain a pay policy line. Typically, as indicated earlier, salary setting is carried out separately by occupational group, with one pay policy line per job family. Similarly, in jurisdictions and corporations where different unions negotiate different salary increments, there is a tendency to divide jobs by bargaining unit, and array the jobs for each on a separate graph with its own pay policy line. Individual bargaining units, however, are likely to be organized by job family and thus to be sex and race segregated. Consequently, comparisons between male and female titles within bargaining units will not bring about pay equity. If unionization and relative market power of different unions have historically had a discriminatory impact on wages, these inequities can only be removed by consolidating all bargaining units into one pay policy line.

This is equally true where management confidential titles are concerned. Typically, as noted above, job evaluations for managerial and nonmanagerial jobs have been conducted independently. The line dividing these two classes of jobs is so thick that we have developed different terminology to characterize the wage contract. Commonly, managers are exempt employees who earn a salary. Nonmanagers are nonexempt employees who earn a wage. While this carries significant status distinctions, it also carries serious consequences for the wages assigned to nonmanagerial titles. The exclusion of managerial titles, in effect, lowers the slope of the pay policy line.

When salary setting is based on one pay policy line, that line must be adjusted to remove potential sex- and race-based discrimination embedded in market wages. Indeed, the failure to adjust the pay policy line for this discrimination is perhaps the most frequently observed problem in jurisdictions that have established point factor systems. In fact, jurisdictions such as Idaho and San Jose, California claim to have established comparable worth in their classification and compensation systems, but have used an unadjusted pay policy line as the basis for making pay equity adjustments. Not only are pay equity adjustments lower, but average wages paid for white, male jobs are depressed.

The procedures for benchmarking and establishing a pay policy line have been fraught with inconsistencies that result in sex and race bias. Solutions to these problems, interestingly enough, are likely to be much simpler methodologically than they are politically.

First, benchmarking can be used to ground the salary setting process to the external labor force without incorporating bias if the following criteria are met:

- the same sample of external firms are used for all benchmarked titles;
- the firms selected accurately represent the external labor market, in terms of demographic as well as economic characteristics such as per capita income and proportion of private and public sector employers;
- a representative cross section of male-dominated positions are included among those used for benchmarking purposes;
- the pay policy line is adjusted for market discrimination embedded in salaries for female and minority titles.

Second, salaries for *all* job titles in a firm or public jurisdiction should be established on the basis of one pay policy line. That line should be based on a comprehensive and representative sample of titles in a firm, crossing job families, salary grades and sex and race categories. This line must be adjusted to correct for possible discriminatory bias in one of three ways. One way is to use only those jobs that have been traditionally held by white males in establishing the pay adjustment line. The second approach is a statistical manipulation which in essence holds sex composition constant. In other words, the resulting equation removes the impact of the proportion of women in the job. A third approach uses only the coefficient of percent female from the preceding equation.

Theoretically, it is possible that these approaches to removing bias from the pay adjustment line could have no effect. If this were the case, the adjusted pay line would be the same as the unadjusted pay line. If this happened, we would conclude that there was no discriminatory pay bias against traditionally female jobs in the labor market from which salaries were drawn.

Moreover, when examining the pay policy line for potential discrimination, we would also expect to see as many female-dominated jobs above as below the unadjusted pay line. No studies to date have resulted in such a finding.

Treiman, Hartmann, and Roos (1984:149-152) tested these adjustment formulas, and the unadjusted market line on 1970 Census data. They found a "straightforward" effect of each procedure on the predicted adjusted earnings for female jobs. The uncorrected market equation did result in some adjustment to mixed gender and female-dominated occupations, but less so than the other three formulas. The unadjusted pay line also lowered average male job wages, confirming the suggestion that discriminatory female wages are indeed being embedded in the average. But the adjustments were larger using the other three models because each statistically removed the impact of sex composition on earnings, albeit in different ways. On average, these latter procedures created nearly equivalent average earnings for male-dominated and mixed occupations—as would be expected, given the essential similarity between these two groups of occupations with respect to their characteristics. They also reduced the earnings gap between male-dominated and female-dominated occupations by about two-thirds—again as would be expected, given differences in the average levels of the compensable factors that account for about one-third of the gap.

The three adjustment models yielded different results, however. As yet, there has been no political consensus about which adjustment model is preferable. Minnesota and Oregon are using the male policy line. Iowa used the adjusted female line. The female coefficient was used by the American Federation of State, County and Municipal Employees in its case against the state of Washington. In New York State, we provided labor and management with two undervaluation estimates, using both the white male and the average line adjusted for females and minorities.

In the next few years, we expect that a consensus will emerge over which pay policy line will represent a nondiscriminatory standard of job worth. In our judgment, either the white male line or the adjusted average line is consistent with comparable worth policy as generally defined. The white male line is based on the assumption that, by definition, wages paid for historically white male jobs are nondiscriminatory. The adjusted average line derives from the position that wage discrimination is that portion of the wage differential that cannot be accounted for by any job content characteristics other than the degree of sex or race segregation. Practically, the white male line is easier to understand. By contrast, since the adjusted average line includes factors and factor weightings that are based on female and male and minority and nonminority job titles, it includes job content characteristics associated with historically female and significantly minority jobs.

DESIGNING JOB EVALUATION TO MEET
COMPARABLE WORTH CRITERIA

For a job evaluation study to have incorporated gender equity concerns into its research design, it must meet the following criteria:

(1) All jobs must be *described* fully and consistently and not differentially by the sex or race of the typical incumbent. This means that jobs must be viewed in terms of the same possible range of job content characteristics, including ones associated with female-dominated or significantly minority work. The information must be collected in a way that insures that variations are not a function of incumbent differences in providing information.

(2) All jobs must be *evaluated* and assigned points according to a uniform set of factors and weights. It does not matter whether the factors are obtained from an *a priori* system or from a policy-capturing model. Factors must include characteristics associated with all types of jobs, including those often associated with female-dominated and significantly minority work. The evaluation framework must be applied consistently across all titles.

(3) *Salary setting* in a firm should be completed on the basis of one pay policy line established on the basis of a graph including an agreed upon set of jobs in the organization. This line must be adjusted for possible discrimination in market rates using a formula recommended in Treiman and Hartmann (1981) or Treiman, Hartmann, and Roos (1984).

One way to maximize consistency and minimize bias in an employment system is to rely heavily on statistical procedures for data collection, for establishing factor weights, and for constructing a pay policy line to obtain predicted wage rates for female-dominated and significantly minority jobs. This can be done through a policy-capturing job evaluation approach like the one used for the New York State and Florida studies. Because policy-capturing regresses job content on current salaries, job content information must be carefully collected and the pay policy line must be adjusted.

To meet the first criterion of describing all jobs fully and consistently, we developed a questionnaire customized to the range of job content characteristics found in most public sector employment. To design the questionnaire, we examined over 18 job analysis or job evaluation approaches. We included additional potentially compensable characteristics which were not a part of other systems but which might be relevant to public sector policies. We wrote the questionnaire at a seventh grade readability level. For each question, employees had to choose one from a number of possible closed-ended responses, to minimize the impact of differential abilities to express ideas in writing and to eliminate any sex and race/ethnic differences in word usage or comprehension of job content factors.

Thus, we designed the job content questionnaire so that we could ask exactly the same questions of employees in many different job titles. In the New York State study, the questionnaire contained 110 specific items.

We carefully pilot tested the questionnaire in New York State to assure its readability, reliability, and validity. We gathered information on all job titles with four or more incumbents. The final sample included over 37,000 employees working in over 2,800 job titles.

The questionnaire asks people specific questions such as:

- How often do people in your job have to travel overnight on the job?
- How much control do people in your job have over spending money within a set budget?
- How much do people in your job do the same thing every day?
- How many people do you supervise directly as a regular part of your job?

Primary objectives in designing and pilot testing the questionnaire include: (1) asking questions that would predict the current wage structure; (2) asking questions that would be highly related to female-dominated jobs and negatively related to current pay policy; and (3) asking questions that would allow for comparisons across job titles differing by sex and race. In meeting these objectives, we increase the likelihood that compensable features of women's jobs will be made visible and thereby incorporated in equity adjustments. These may include items such as coordination and planning responsibilities, human relations skills, time and communication stresses, and working with machines and equipment. Additionally, it would provide information about uncompensated dimensions of female-dominated and significantly minority jobs that could lead labor and management to change the compensation policy of New York State.

The policy-capturing model was derived directly from the data collected from these employee self-administered questionnaires. This eliminated the possibility that consultants or evaluation committees impose stereotypes on job descriptions. To be sure, employees carry these stereotypes as well. Yet, wherever possible, we asked specific and factual questions about jobs. In addition, we averaged incumbent responses to obtain a composite job description. This averaging process, combined with a detailed questionnaire, provides, to our knowledge, the best available methodology for accurately capturing job content information on an employee population of this size.

The second criterion is that all jobs be evaluated and assigned points according to a consistently applied and uniform set of factors and weights. In order to meet this criterion, we statistically derived a set of factors and weights by analyzing the data collected from our employee questionnaires in relation to current state salaries. Using data from incumbent responses averaged by job title, we statistically sorted the data from the questionnaire using factor analytic statistical techniques to group together items of similar job content, like questions on supervision, data entry, group facilitation and so on. Weights for job content factors were assigned in relation to the current wage structure using multiple regression analysis. In New York State and Florida, the resulting compensation model was applied to each female-dominated and disproportionately minority job title to obtain a predicted salary grade, indicating what the wages for these jobs would be in the absence of discrimination.

These policy-capturing procedures rely heavily on statistical analysis performed by computers. The use of standard statistical procedures and computer analysis ensures that the set of factors and weights are applied consistently, eliminating the possibility that consultants or committees impose subjective stereotypes in their selection and application of factors and weights in relation to particular female-dominated and disproportionately minority jobs.

CONCLUSION

This paper has examined how compensation systems based on job evaluation embed and perpetuate inconsistencies and sex biases which result in gender and race-based wage discrimination. It has proposed a set of criteria for designing job evaluation to maximize consistency and minimize bias. As such, it has focused on technical considerations in implementing the policy of equal pay for work of comparable worth.

If comparable worth is to move beyond a political demand, it is necessary to unravel the oftentimes complicated ways in which assumptions about race and sex impinge on the ways in which wages are set. This could involve as seemingly innocent a decision as establishing lower paying female titles as benchmarks for all jobs. At the other extreme, it could involve intentionally paying female titles 80 percent of the wages paid to male titles with the same number of evaluation points. Whatever the source, comparable pay studies must examine existing classification and compensation systems in a comprehensive manner.

Serious discussions of acceptable methodologies for conducting applied studies of wage discrimination have been all too few. Treiman and Hartmann (1981) and the articles contained in Remick (1984a) are notable exceptions. Unfortunately, treatment of comparable worth tends to remain at the ideological level. Proponents and opponents debate over the extent of the wage gap due to segregation-based wage discrimination, over the economic consequences of implementing pay equity adjustments, and even over the availability of methodologies for conducting pay equity studies. This paper represents an attempt to move beyond these debates. By specifying operational criteria for achieving comparable worth, we hope to contribute to a more fruitful and constructive dialogue on how to eliminate systematic wage inequality that cannot be accounted for in any way other than the sex or race of the typical incumbent.

NOTES

1. The New York State Comparable Pay Study was being conducted by the Center for Women in Government under a contract with New York State. The Center's Comparable Pay Team included: Carol Possin, Ph.D., Research Associate; Cynthia Chertos, Ph.D, Director of Research and Implementation at the Center; Nancy Perlman, Executive Director of the Center; Donald Treiman, Ph.D., Professor of Sociology at U.C.L.A.; Richard Maisel, Ph.D., Director of Graduate Studies, Department of Sociology, New York University; Wendy Essex, Research staff; and Sharon Stimson, Research staff.

2. The Comparable Pay Study of four political subdistricts is being conducted by the Center for Women in Government under a grant from the American Federation of State, County and Municipal Employees. The sites include four locales of the Civil Service Employees Association, AFSCME, New York State. They are: Dutchess County, Three Village School District, Erie County, and the City of Schenectady, New York.

3. States and municipalities to which assistance has been provided by one or both of the authors include: Arizona; Arlington, Virginia; California; Florida; Iowa; Louisiana; Maine; Maryland; Massachusetts; Monroe County, New York; Nevada; New Jersey; New York City, New York; North Carolina; Ohio; Oregon; Pennsylvania; Philadelphia; Portland, Oregon; Stockholm, Texas; Vermont; West Virginia; and Wisconsin. In addition, the senior author has worked with Congress and the General Accounting Office on achieving pay equity in federal employment.

4. Although comparable worth policy originally focused almost exclusively on undervaluation due to gender, it is becoming associated with race-based wage discrimination as well. In the New York State Comparable Pay Study, for example, estimates of undervaluation will be made for such job titles as youth division aide, window washer, elevator operator, janitor, cook, barber, and bus driver. This is because processes perpetuating undervaluation are the same, whether the source of differential treatment is race or sex or ethnicity.

5. Comparable worth policy is directed at closing *only* that portion of the wage gap between women and men due to systematic undervaluation. Not all of the wage gap is a function of this undervaluation. Some differences are legitimately derived from differences in job prerequisites, requirements, and responsibilities (Milkovich, 1980; Roos, 1981). However, women have also been segregated into lower paying jobs that require the *equivalent* amount of skill, effort, and responsibility as male jobs. The policy of comparable worth is concerned with salary differences between women and men that cannot be justified in terms of productivity-related job content characteristics.

6. Critics of comparable worth contend that it cannot be achieved because there is no absolute worth that can be assigned to jobs. Comparable worth is not concerned with job worth in a metaphysical sense. Instead, worth or value is defined in the classification and compensation systems that currently operate in most firms and public jurisdictions.

7. For the purpose of this paper, we differentiate classification and compensa-

tion systems, job evaluation, and the evaluation component of job evaluation. Classification and compensation sytems are the policy basis for the wage structure, including fringe benefits and other nonwage compensation policies. The classification and compensation systems are typically built from some type of job evaluation study. Within a job evaluation, there is a component which involves ranking jobs from higher to lower based on the presence or absence of valued job content characteristics. In addition, job evaluation involves job description and salary setting components.

8. In policy-capturing approaches, it is very likely that characteristics associated with historically female and minority work will receive a low factor weighting. This is one of the disadvantages of policy-capturing. One way to circumvent this problem is to perform a customized policy-capturing, in which policymakers can change the factor weightings after the regression has been performed. This could increase the beta weights for factors associated with female-dominated or significantly minority titles.

9. More precisely, the population of New York State employees from which we drew the sample consisted of all incumbents of these positions, excluding those who were selected for the pilot study, those who work part-time or who have held their positions for less than one month, positions earmarked to be eliminated through attrition, positions whose salaries are not set through Civil Service procedures, and individuals in eight so called "quasi" agencies like the Thruway Authority.

10. New York State is defining female-dominated and significantly minority job titles differently than other studies. Our definition does not involve an arbitrary cutoff point, but is rather based on the average number of women and minorities employed by New York State. The formula for calculating the cutoff point is $x + (.4)x$, where x is the mean percent female or minority. This means that, in this study, a female-dominated job title is one with 67 percent or more female incumbents; a significantly minority job title is one with 31 percent or more minority incumbents. In addition, we will be estimating undervaluation for titles which do not make the statistical cutoff but are in direct line of promotion from entry-level female and minority jobs. This is because New York State has historically aligned direct line of promotion title salaries to the entry level positions with which they are associated. Wage discrimination thus could spill over into the salaries of direct line of promotion titles.

Appendix A

Sample Job Content Questionnaire Items: Description

I. *Open-ended Questions:*

1. Briefly state the main purpose of your job.

2. List duties you perform regularly. State clearly *what* you do and *how* you do it. In the space at the left, estimate the amount of time you spend on each main group of duties.

3. List any machines, tools, and equipment used in your work and show time spent using each.

4. In what work do you make the final decision?

5. Describe the knowledge, skills and abilities you need to do your work.

6. Describe the physical hazards you are exposed to. How much of the time?

7. If you were promoted, what type of education, training, job-related experience and other qualifications would your replacement need?

8. Do you supervise other employees? If yes, how many people do you supervise? What are the job titles and primary duties of your subordinates?

II. *Closed-ended Questions:*

A. *Computer Usage:* (Steinberg, *et al*, 1984)

In some jobs people use a VDT, CRT, computer, word processor or photo composition equipment. Do people in your title do any of the following or teach others to do any of the following? Check YES or NO.

	NO	YES
1. Editing data	1☐	2☐
2. Entering data	1☐	2☐
3. Verifying data	1☐	2☐
4. Word processing or operating a photo composing machine	1☐	2☐
5. Developing computer runs using software packages like SPSS or SAS	1☐	2☐

6. Writing original computer programs .... 1☐ 2☐

7. Systems programming .... 1☐ 2☐

8. Systems designing .... 1☐ 2☐

B. *Practices and Planning:* (Steinberg, *et al*, 1984)

1. Which statement best describes the role that people in your job
   have in setting operating practices? Check one.
   No role .... 1☐
   They are asked about practices that have to do with
   their unit, but someone else has the final say ...... 2☐
   They set practices for their unit but have no
   involvement with other units .... 3☐
   They set practices for their unit and participate
   in setting practices that affect several units .... 4☐
   They have the final say on practices that affect
   several units .... 5☐

2. Think of the work activity in your job that is planned the
   farthest in advance. How far in advance do people in your job
   plan this activity?
   They do not plan their work schedule .... 1☐
   Planning less than a day ahead .... 2☐
   A day or two ahead .... 3☐
   A week or two ahead .... 4☐
   One or two months ahead .... 5☐
   Three to six months ahead .... 6☐
   More than six months ahead .... 7☐

CHAPTER 9

Sex Bias in Job Evaluation: A Comparable Worth Issue*

Joan Acker

Job evaluation occupies a central place in the comparable worth strategy for achieving greater sex equity in wages. Job evaluation is a process of assessing the worth of particular job categories on a number of dimensions or compensable factors usually including knowledge and skill, effort, responsibility, and working conditions. A numerical score is assigned for each factor and a total score for the job is computed. Jobs are then ranked according to their scores and the wages of jobs with similar scores are compared to determine the presence or absence of pay inequity. Female-dominated and male-dominated jobs with similar scores are the particular focus of comparable worth analyses. Plans for pay equity involve strategies for equalizing the pay for job classes that have the same scores. If the job evaluation process is itself flawed with gender bias, its use will underestimate sex-based pay inequities. For that reason, the question of whether or not job evaluation systems are free of sex bias is critical to the comparable worth effort.

In the past few years, a number of researchers have looked at sex bias in traditional job evaluation systems (Treiman, 1979; Schwab, 1980; Remick, 1979; 1980; 1984c; Treiman and Hartmann, 1981). Also called *a priori* systems, these methods have been in existence for many years and are now used widely in both the public and private sectors (Steinberg, 1984). *A priori*

---

* For comments on this chapter see Feldberg (p. 245–250) and Hartmann (p. 251–258) in this volume.

systems are sold by large management consulting firms for the purposes of job classification and salary setting. "As Remick (1979), Schwab (1980), and others have pointed out, job evaluation systems are designed to reflect prevailing wages in their choice of factors, weighting of factors, and salary-setting practices" (Remick, 1984c:100). Therefore, it is not surprising that high correlations between scores and prevailing wages have been found for some systems (Remick, 1984c:112). To the extent that prevailing wages reflect historically produced discrimination against women, point factor scores may also reflect this discrimination. As Treiman and Hartmann (1981:81) suggest, "it is possible that the process of describing and evaluating jobs reflects pervasive cultural stereotypes regarding the relative worth of work traditionally done by men and work traditionally done by women."

In spite of the concern that *a priori* methods may contain biases that undervalue women's jobs, such approaches have been successfully used in a number of states and localities to establish claims for pay equity for women (see, *e.g.*, Cook, 1983). These methods consistently demonstrate that certain female-dominated clerical and service jobs are underpaid according to their point factor scores. Indeed, it is that fact that makes job evaluation so useful in efforts to raise the low wages of women. Contemporary comparable worth strategists recognize that measurement of worth always involves value judgments, and thus some "bias," but maintain that "existing systems can be used with bias minimized as new and better systems, reflecting new values, evolve" (Remick, 1984c:100).

In this paper I explore the problem of sex bias in job evaluation using qualitative data from a comparable worth study in which efforts were made to minimize bias. I will address two questions: 1) accepting the assessment that *a priori* systems are not bias-free, what can be done to reduce the social judgment bias in these procedures? and 2) how is it that job evaluation systems that have been constructed to predict and justify prevailing wage structures nevertheless show that female-dominated jobs are not paid equitably with male-dominated jobs with identical point factor scores?

THEORETICAL FRAMEWORK

The following description and analysis draws upon and intends to contribute to the ongoing efforts of feminist scholarship to understand the persistence of the subordination of women. Cultural conceptions of appropriate work for women and men and differing evaluations of female and male typed work are integral to a symbolic system that helps to maintain male dominance. Judgments about the relative value of female-dominated and male-dominated jobs are ideological statements that justify action and may be practical guides to action in setting wages. Ideology and action are, in this view, organically linked in the wage determination process. Comprehension of this process must include clarity about the value assumptions embedded in it (see *e.g.*, Hartmann, 1984:8). Job evaluation systems are well developed methods for making explicit the implicit assumptions that underlie prevailing wage determination practices. As Remick (1984c:113) argues " . . . job evaluation systems primarily measure how cultural values are compensated in the marketplace . . . "

Feminist analysis would point out that these are not just generalized values of the culture, but values of those who have the power to define. The location of the power to define, to create meaning, is critical to understanding the situation of women. The power to define has historically, in capitalist societies, been held by males who are in positions of economic and political control (e.g., Smith, 1979). In the case of wages, the immediate definers are employers and managers. Unions have challenged that power with some limited success, raising the wages of unionized workers above those of the nonunionized. But, these have usually been gains for male unionists, even though the earliest comparable worth successes were achieved by organized labor (Portman, Grune, and Johnson, 1984). The social movement for comparable worth that challenges the male employer monopoly over the power to define must engage organizational practices and structures that include male workers and their unions.

Thus, the movement for comparable worth may be a ground on which class and gender interests both conflict and intersect. Gender interests cut across class boundaries (see, e.g., Smith, 1977). Moreover, the interests of working-class men and working-class women may not be identical, at least in the short run (see e.g., Hartmann, 1976). As a consequence of these considerations, comparable worth projects provide an opportunity to examine theoretical issues of how gender and class inequalities are interrelated (Acker, 1983).

An intensive study of a comparable worth application of job evaluation should help us to decode the structures and images of gendered work that contribute to wage inequity. Attempting to eliminate sex bias from the process should reveal old assumptions about female work and male work making them increasingly available for scrutiny and analysis. The structural arrangements of class and gender differences in organizations should also become more open to examination.

SOURCES OF SEX BIAS IN *A PRIORI* SYSTEMS

Sex bias may enter job evaluation at any, or every, point in the process (Remick, 1979; 1984c; Treiman and Hartmann, 1981). These include the choice of factors and factor weights (Treiman, 1984). Job content found primarily in women's jobs, but not in men's jobs, may be excluded from factors and factor definitions (Remick, 1979). In addition, the indicators chosen to measure various factors may reflect male jobs but not female jobs (Beatty and Beatty, 1984; Hartmann and Treiman, 1983:411). The range of values on a particular factor may not reflect the full range of variation in the organization (Hartmann and Treiman, 1983:422). In packaged systems, factor weights have usually been preassigned and have usually been determined on the basis of their contribution to predicting actual wage rates of firms. Those wage rates most likely reflect the general wage gap between the sexes. Those who buy such a system are buying the factors and factor weights and the values that are implicit in these measures.

The job descriptions or documentation used as the basis for evaluation may also contain biased material. The actual process in which job descriptions are scored on each factor may be carried out with implicit stereotypes of female-dominated and male-dominated jobs influencing decisions (Remick, 1984c:107). Thus, even an unbiased system, if such existed, may be used in a biased way, undervaluing female jobs. In spite of widespread recognition by experts on comparable worth that multiple sources of sex bias probably exist in traditional systems, there is very little literature that documents this in any detail. The following account of the Oregon case describes efforts to deal with sex bias in job evaluation and offers one answer to the question of why female-dominated jobs are found to be undervalued using such systems.

THE OREGON CASE

Date sources: This description is developed from data I collected from November, 1983 to January 1985 as a member of the Oregon State Task Force on Compensation and Classification Equity. This paper is based primarily on analysis of public documents and records of public meetings. The data include tape recordings of Task Force meetings, written minutes of those meetings, field notes on the study and evaluation process— including notes on my participation on a job evaluation team during a test of the system, and preliminary results of Benchmark evaluations.

Importance of the Oregon Case: The Oregon project was probably unique in a number of ways. First, the legislative mandate directed the use of a bias-free, sex neutral point factor evaluation method. Thus, to carry out the legislative intent, the Task Force had to be concerned with sex bias. Second, the Task Force responsible for the project had a majority of members who were feminists. They had the advantage of being able to consult with other feminists who had had considerable experience with comparable worth and job evaluation. Thus, they were alert to the sources of possible bias in *a priori* methods and were committed to eliminating such bias if at all possible. Third, although the system chosen had been used in a number of other public jurisdictions for comparable worth purposes, to our knowledge, modifications of that system to deal with possible sex bias had not previously been attempted. We were in uncharted territory. For all these reasons, the Oregon case is of interest historically in the effort to modify existing systems.

Background to the Oregon Case: The Oregon Comparable Worth Task Force was established by the Oregon Legislature in 1983 and mandated to: "1) Establish comparability among state jobs by application of a single point-factor job evaluation system. 2) Determine where inequities exist in the compensation and classification systems, 'giving primary consideration to identifying and correcting inequities between female and male dominated classes.' 3) Report to the 1985 Legislature findings and recommendations on establishing a comparable worth pay plan" (Hallock, 1984). The Task Force hired a major consultant, Hay Associates, to provide a job evaluation system and technical direction in its use. The personnel division of the Executive Department of the state carried out most of the work of the project with a large staff on temporary assignment from other state agencies. The Task Force was responsible for overall direction of the project and the making of all policy decisions. The Task Force was, thus intimately involved in the project and its chair was a member of the project steering committee that supervised daily operation. The Task Force decided to complete a study in one year in order to report to the 1985 Legislature. It also decided to do a complete review of the state job classification system because the old system was inadequate as a basis for applying a point-factor job evaluation method. Following a work plan that would allow completion in one year, the Task Force, personnel staff, and consultants designed and tested a questionnaire, developed modifications of the Hay factors and tested the evaluation process, had questionnaires completed by approximately 32,000 state employees, sorted the questionnaires into job groups and wrote job composite descriptions for these job groups, evaluated the job composites using the Hay Guide-Chart Profile Method of job evaluation, analyzed the results, and prepared a final report. Delays occurred in constructing the new classification system and implementation of pay equity was also delayed to the end of 1986.

Efforts to modify the Hay Guide-Chart Profile method of job evaluation: Oregon Task Force members were aware that all *a priori* systems contain certain values and that these systems had been criticized as sex biased. However, budget, time, and legitimacy considerations led us to choose an *a priori* system, that of Hay Associates. We understood that a new system, reflecting a consensus on what is valued by the State of Oregon, would be impossible to build, validate, and use within a year with the amount of money the Legislature had allocated. Moreover, Hay Associates is perhaps the most prominent consulting company doing comparable worth studies and is highly respected in both the public and private sectors. Equally important in our choice of this consultant was the experience of their staff and their willingness to make some modifications of factors and factor definitions to accommodate some of our concerns about possible sex bias. In this paper, I deal primarily with efforts to modify factors and factor definitions.

The Hay system has been described elsewhere (*e.g.*, McAdams, 1974; Treiman, 1979; Farnquist, 1983). Briefly, it involves assessment of job content on three major factors—Know-How, Problem Solving, Accountability, and one additional factor, Working Conditions. Each factor contains several subscales. Scores for each factor are summed to provide a total score for a job. Although the factors and factor weights are predetermined, operational definitions must be given to the factors; Know-How, Problem Solving and Accountability could be examined for sex bias implicit in their definitions. This the Task Force intended to do in its public meetings with Hay consultants. The following paragraphs are a detailed examination of efforts by feminists on the Task Force and its Advisory Group to examine and alter the measurement of one aspect of the Know-How factor—Human Relations skills. This case study of an attempt to reduce sex bias in job evaluation reveals how such bias is deeply embedded in organizational structure.

Human Relations is a subscale of Know-How, the knowledge and skill factor. Two other scales are involved in Know-How, Technical and Professional Knowledge, and Managerial Knowledge. Human Relations points vary with levels of these other scales. In the Hay Guide-Charts used for evaluations in other states, Human Relations had only three levels of skill, as contrasted with other scales in the Guide Charts that have many more levels. Some Task Force members wanted to expand Human Relations to better reflect components of many female jobs in the public sector. This would have the effect of giving some additional weight to Human Relations. The consultants had varied responses to the first suggestion that Human Relations be expanded and redefined.

In Hay experience, one consultant pointed out, jobs with a large human relations component were never undervalued. Another said that in experiments with different numbers of levels of Human Relations, it was more difficult for evaluators to make distinctions between five levels than between three. The consultants also argued that human relations knowledge would be counted in the scales on Technical Know-How and reflected in Problem Solving points, as well as in the Human Relations scale. In sum, the consultants advised the use of their usual three-level scale.

Some Task Force members were unconvinced and continued to press the question of possible bias, reflected in the Human Relations scale, toward the values of employers. The discussion continued, consuming most of two day-long meetings, and shorter portions of several other meetings. The consultants explained that job evaluation must be separated from decisions about how to pay for evaluated points. Moreover, they contended that there is no bias in the evaluation process itself, although bias could sometimes be found in resulting pay plans; female-dominated jobs might be paid on a different scale than male jobs, resulting in two salary ranges for jobs with the same point scores.

The problem of the meaning of human relations skills kept coming up in the discussion. The primary problem had to do with "common courtesy." The lowest level on the scale was defined by a consultant as "overt friendliness or ordinary courtesy." Application of the notion of common courtesy to hypothetical jobs revealed difficulties with this definition. Does this represent the level of human relations skills needed for work in an ordinary office? Some Task Force members argued that this definition would undervalue the skills used by many clerical workers. Courtesy is a skill, especially needed in dealing with the public. This should be reflected in the scale; courtesy should be given more points, they maintained. A consultant countered that Hay had looked at the possibility of a zero level on the scale for jobs that do not require any courtesy, as well as a fifth level for jobs that require an extraordinary amount of skill. He indicated that a job with that high level of skill probably did not exist in the State of Oregon.

While Task Force members defined Human Relations to include mediating relationships with coworkers, supervisors, and the public as well as maintaining cooperative processes with irate clients and disturbed patients, consultants focused on supervisory and managerial tasks of motivating and training. Hay definitions of levels of Human Relations seemed linked to levels of bureaucratic function. According to our consultants the first level requires personal interaction dealing essentially with facts; the second level, persuasion and influence to change behavior; the third level, motivating behavior. The second and third levels differ in intensity in the need to use interpersonal skills to cause behavioral changes in another individual or a group of individuals. In level two, it is an important part of the job; in level three, it is critical. Several Task Force members still maintained that these definitions did not adequately reflect the skills needed for human service and clerical jobs.

As discussions continued, the consultants revealed two concerns about increasing the number of levels in the Human Relations scales. First, because the Human Relations scale is a subscale of Managerial Know-How, increasing Human Relations scores would result in a higher value placed on human relations relative to managerial skills. This would be problematic, because it might change the rank order of some jobs. Second, additional levels of Human Relations might decrease the point spread between managerial and nonmanagerial jobs. This is a problem, they indicated, because in the public sector, in general, management jobs have a lower salary differential relative to nonmanagement jobs than in the private sector. Anything that might reduce that differential even further could have a negative impact on state employment, causing even more difficulties in recruiting and keeping good managers. To this, a Task Force member countered that Human Relations skills include supervisory skills, so perhaps there would not be this problem.

The differing positions on the issue of how to count Human Relations skills are reflected in the following interchange:

> TF (*Task Force member*): In any organization, in terms of meeting the objectives of the organization, whether or not it's successful depends a great deal on human relations skills. That kind of a value is important in terms of meeting the goals of the agencies. I would support five levels.
>
> Ex (*Executive Department personnel*): If five levels were used, human relations skills would be too high relative to other factors.
>
> Con (*Consultant*): I have concerns. It would not just be creating five levels of Human Relations skills, they would be devaluing the relationship of Management Know-How to Human Relations skills.
>
> TF: In view of the fact that the Hay system was heavily weighted toward management skills, would it really be such a big down-sizing? Because there is still a tremendous amount of weight placed on Management Know-How skills, particularly in the Human Relations component. In some ways, I feel they are double counting management by doing that.

The consultants tried repeatedly to convince the Task Force that Human Relations could be adequately rewarded with points by using a three-level scale. In sum, the consultants argued that: 1) Human Relations were never undervalued in the Hay system; 2) evaluators cannot make distinctions between more than three levels of skill; 3) increasing Human Relations to five levels would result in "over counting" relative to managerial skills; 4) it would reduce the point difference between managerial and nonmanagerial jobs leading to problems in management recruiting; and 5) there is no sex bias in the Hay method. Nevertheless, the majority of the Task Force voted to compare a five-level and a three-level scale in the pretest of the evaluation process. Task Force members suggested wording for a five-level scale that would reflect human services and clerical job content as well as managerial supervisory job content. However, these suggestions were not followed and different definitions were used in the actual pretest. The pretest showed that use of a five-point scale altered the rank ordering of some jobs as the consultants had predicted.

The number of levels in Human Relations became a political issue for the Task Force. The Task Force was split on the issue of five versus three levels, while its Advisory Group voted to recommend five levels. Management representatives sided with Hay on three levels; union, worker, and women's movement representatives voted for five. A compromise was finally reached to use four levels of Human Relations skills. The Task Force suggested definitions for the first three levels and asked the consultant to draft language for all four levels, reflecting Task Force intent to give points for the handling of human interactions by office and service workers. A comparison of different definitions of human relations skills proposed and finally adopted demonstrates the complexity of the concept and the difference in meanings attached to it by some Task Force members and by the consultants.

DEFINITIONS OF HUMAN RELATIONS SKILLS

HAY—3 LEVEL

Suggested at Project Beginning

1. *Basic:* ordinary courtesy and effectiveness in dealing with others through normal contacts, and request for, or providing information.
2. *Important:* understanding, influencing, and/or serving people are important considerations in performing the job; causing action or understanding in others.
3. *Critical:* alternative or combined skills in understanding, developing and motivating people are critical to successful job performance.

TASK FORCE MEMBERS—5 LEVEL

Suggested March, 1984

1. *Minimal* skills
2. *Ordinary:* ordinary office courtesy.
3. *Good:* dealing with people is part of the job.
4. *Sensitive:* dealing with people in emotionally demanding situations is part of the job.
5. *Highly sensitive:* human relations
5. *Highly sensitive:* human relations are of primary importance in the job.

TASK FORCE—4 LEVEL

Adopted April, 1984

1. *Incidental:* human interaction is incidental to nature of work being performed.
2. *Basic:* effectiveness in working with others is specifically related to the nature of the work.
3. *Important:* understanding, influencing or serving people are important considerations.
4. *Critical:* understanding, influencing or serving people are critical considerations.

FINAL DEFINITIONS USED IN PROJECT

1. *Incidental:* communication skills are incidental to the nature of the job duties performed.
2. *Basic:* skills in communicating factual information are necessary in the job.
3. *Important:* skills in understanding and influencing, motivating, counseling or training people are important job components.
4. *Critical:* skills in motivating, developing, understanding, persuading, and/or counseling people are critical for effective job performance.

In spite of the many hours of discussion in Task Force and Advisory Group meetings and in spite of the majority decisions in both groups that a broadening of the Human Relations scale should be the policy of the State of Oregon, in the Benchmark[1] evaluations, the consultant's definition of three levels of Human Relations skills prevailed. The consultants achieved this outcome in the training they gave in the use of the four-level scale. They defined Level One to include only those jobs in which practically no human contact occurs. "Incidental" came to refer to the person who sits in a room all alone and gets direction from pieces of paper shoved under the door. Because there are practically no jobs that are so isolated, the Incidental level was rarely used by the evaluators. This left a three-level scale that did not allow discrimination between, for example, a typist and a receptionist, or a clerical worker who must interact with several bosses in the office and a highway maintenance worker who must get along with the other workers on the work crew. At the same time, decision rules developed that gave a "true supervisor" an automatic four on Human Relations skills. A "true supervisor" is one who supervises five or more employees in a job in which 75–80 percent of the tasks are supervisory.

Some job evaluators were uncomfortable with the three-level scale and a struggle over the definition of human relations skills developed in one of the job evaluation teams. Clerical worker evaluators attempted to recreate a four-level scheme in order to differentiate between types of clerical jobs and between clerical and blue collar jobs. They did this by giving the maximum points possible, within the Guide-Chart limitations, to jobs deemed to have heavy human relations obligations. This effort was only partly successful, as the final scores reveal. In the Benchmark evaluations, Level One on Human Relations was used for only 11 out of 346 job classes evaluated. Clerical jobs were all evaluated at Level Two, with the exception of the Executive Administrative Secretary which was Level Three. Level Three on Human Relations was given to lead workers and many human service jobs. All higher level managerial jobs and human service professional jobs dealing with sensitive emotional problems rated at Level Four, the highest level.

Task Force members also modified, with the help of the consultants, the Working Conditions factor. A number of critics had pointed out that measures of working conditions usually reflect male jobs and heavy manual labor (Remick, 1979). As one Task Force member said, "most of the current jobs are sedentary which pose many types of new physical problems compared to the hard physical labor which had been more common in the past" (Task Force minutes, April 25, 1984). Consequently, physical effort was defined to include rapid and continuous hand movements as well as heavy lifting. Sensory effort, such as frequent use of a microscope, was added to physical effort. Job stress was another concern of the Task Force. However, "stress" was rejected as a suitable word, because it referred to the reactions of individuals, not the content of the job. The term "psychological demands" was offered as a substitute, but this too seemed to refer to the occupant of the job rather than to the job itself. Finally, the consultants suggested "Work Demands" as the term to use to get at those aspects of jobs that put particular sorts of strains on workers, strains that are not compensated for under other factors.

Work Demands were defined as "mental alertness and mental energy required by the intensity, continuity and complexity of work being performed." They were further specified as "Time Demands: the build up of work that must be accomplished under generally inflexible timelines. Frequent interruptions, if characteristic of the job, may contribute to time demands; Role Loading: having to perform in multiple, critical roles, or two or more incompatible roles; and Emotion Loading: the provision of direct services to individuals experiencing physical or emotional distress." There was considerable opposition to including this factor in the evaluation of working conditions. One argument was that the Work Demands factor would lead to double counting of certain job components already given credit under Human Relations skills or technical Know-How. Another argument was that giving points for stress related aspects of jobs would be taken as evidence that certain jobs are stressful in worker's compensation cases and might, thus, put the state in greater jeopardy of such suits. Ultimately, the Task Force split on the Work Demands issue, and it was included in the Working Conditions chart by a majority vote.

As with Human Relations, however, the interpretation of this factor in the training of the job evaluators determined how it was used in the job evaluation process. Work Demands were interpreted as a way to add points for only the most severe conditions. For Time Demands, the criterion, in general, was "is this a drop dead situation?" For example, a hostage negotiator in a prison riot situation would experience Time Demands. Moreover, if, in any way, credit was given elsewhere for an aspect of a job, it was not to be given under Work Demands. Role Loading was defined in private sector, managerial terms, as, *e.g.,* a job in which the incumbent was required to do long-term planning for a company and at the same time be responsible on a daily basis for production. The suggestion that many workers in human service jobs experience role loading or conflict when they have to act as an enforcer of laws on the side of the state and a supportive/helper on the side of the client was not adopted in the definition of role loading. Emotion Loading was defined as applying to jobs in crisis medical care or treatment of extremely difficult psychiatric problems.

The use of Work Demands in the Benchmark evaluations was consistent with the definitions provided in the training sessions. Points for Work Demands were given to only 20 of the 346 jobs. These were primarily jobs dealing with people under severe physical or emotional strain. Some Task Force members had hoped to pick up the stress inherent in many clerical jobs, but this did not occur. Although these attempts to allocate evaluation points to often invisible job content characteristics of women's work were only minimally successful, this study revealed pay inequalities between female-dominated and male-dominated jobs. The inequalities were similar in magnitude to those found in other applications of *a priori* methods.

Obviously these methods provide a way of correcting part of the wage gap. In the Hay method, Know-How, "the sum total of every kind of skill, however acquired, required for acceptable job performance" (McAdams, 1974:406), is the most heavily weighted factor. Therefore rating on this factor is critical in the production of the total score. Job evaluators disagreed often about the level of knowledge and skill needed for female-dominated jobs, particularly those at the lower end of the occupational hierarchy. They worked toward consensus on a score through detailed discussion of job content, repeatedly returning to the criteria established in the training process by the consultants. The consultants instructed the evaluators to think of the job, not the gender of the job holder. If a team member used "he" or "she" to refer to the job incumbent, he/she had to pay a fine. Thus, gender attributions were made conscious in the job evaluation process. This may have supported the effort to apply the criteria consistently across female and male typed jobs. Ultimately, the consistent application of the same criteria seems to have been crucial in the final assignment of scores for Know-How that brought, for example, skilled clerical jobs total scores similar to those of skilled blue collar jobs. Thus, the evaluation process appears to correct for cultural assumptions that women's jobs, such as clerical work or food service work, require little knowledge and skill and present few challenges or problems to the worker.

CONCLUSIONS

I have spent considerable space in describing the battle over Human Relations skills, Working Conditions, and their measurement for two reasons. First, this effort at change bears on the question of how modifiable are *a priori* methods. Second, the interchanges on Human Relations skills reveal the underlying assumptions of the system and suggest implications for questions of both class and gender.

What are we to conclude about the possibility of minimizing sex bias, here defined as possible neglect of compensable aspects of women's jobs, in existing job evaluation systems? This case example is, of course, only suggestive, but some lessons can be drawn from it. It is technically possible to slightly modify even such a complex system as the Hay Guide-Charts. A five-point scale could have been devised; the definitions of the levels of a four-point scale could have been constructed in such a way that all four levels could have been used in the evaluations. Evaluators could have been trained to interpret human relations skills in different ways. They could also have been given different instructions about the meaning of Work Demands. A rank order of jobs different from the one the study produced would have resulted. How different is impossible to estimate. This did not occur because the consultant was in control of the job evaluation instruments and the training for the evaluation process. The consultants were hired because they had the knowledge and experience to do this. Thus, they were carrying out their commitment to the project.

The analysis of the consultants' reactions to efforts to expand Human

Relations suggests a concern with the effect that such an expansion would have on the hierarchical ordering of jobs and on the distance in points between managerial and nonmanagerial jobs. As one consultant said, "the Guide-Charts were developed over time by working with a number of different managers in different organizations. The Guide-Charts represent a composite of the value systems of managers from various organizations. They are reflective of traditional organizational designs. The question is, incrementally how large the jump is as you go from one layer of management responsibility to the next layer, and to what degree the Task Force wants to differ from that kind of concept" (Task Force minutes, April 25, 1984:8). Although the majority of the Task Force wanted to differ from that concept, there was not unanimous support. Managers of state agencies on the Advisory Group were also concerned about upsetting existing organizational stratification. The consultants may have been responding to these differing stances on the problem as they proceeded to implement definitions of Human Relations that were little different from those that they brought to the project from other applications where there were no feminists involved in trying to change their system. Implementing the new Work Conditions subfactor, Work Demands, also apparently threatened the hierarchy.

This attempt to alter the Hay method illustrates an ongoing process of reproducing the managerial orientation of the system (Treiman, 1979). The attempt to increase the points allocated for Human Relations skills and for stressful working conditions to clerical and service female-dominated jobs was undermined in the interests of the integrity of the hierarchical structure of the organization. Class interests won out over gender interests. Or, to put it differently, in order to value job stress or to allocate more value to the interpersonal skills required in many female-dominated jobs, it would have been necessary to achieve a consensus on a goal of reducing the overall inequality in the state as an employing organization. No such consensus existed.

At the same time, the use of the Hay Guide-Chart Profile method did reveal that many female-dominated job classes had similar scores to male-dominated classes, but much lower pay scales. The Task Force recommended pay equity adjustments on the basis of the study. Although some of the adjustments will be at the professional lower managerial levels, they are primarily adjustments between working class jobs of men and women.[2] Thus, this comparable worth project should produce substantial gains in pay for many low paid women workers, decreasing gender differences in the distribution of income within the working class sector of this state labor force.

This suggests a number of questions about the interaction of class and gender in the comparable worth process. How do working class men respond to this reduction in income difference? Under what conditions will there be solidarity across gender lines for these gains for working class women? Will pay raises for low paid women result in pressures by supervisors and professionals above them in the hierarchy for pay raises to keep the class differential in pay from also being reduced? Will there be gender solidarity across class lines? Will cultural images of women's work change as their pay increases?

Finally, what policy conclusions can we draw about the problem of sex bias in the application of *a priori* job evaluation methods? Attempts to minimize sex bias will be met with powerful and sophisticated opposition if these attempts threaten the internal stratification of organizations. The elimination of sex bias is potentially subversive of existing hierarchies. A reasonable strategy may be to work for small changes in traditional job evaluation methods, recognizing that they do identify and provide a way to reduce large pay inequities. New job evaluation methods should explore more complex definitions of skills in working with and understanding other people, skills that mediate organizational processes (Glenn and Feldberg, 1979). More work should also be done on assessing new hazardous and stressful working conditions that are a result of the use of new technologies. However, in the long run, it would seem that the elimination of sex bias depends upon an overall attack on inequality.

NOTES

1. In the Oregon use of the Hay method, job evaluation was done by teams of employees, representing a variety of occupations, organizational levels, and including both women and men. The teams each had a facilitator and a recorder who documented the reasons for each decision. The teams evaluated 349 benchmark jobs that were selected to cover the entire range of salary classes and job families. The benchmark evaluations were then used as a framework within which to evaluate the remaining over 1500 job groups. Consensus is the goal in the evaluation process. Evaluators work from descriptions of jobs and draw on other information if necessary. Often the discussions are long and detailed and agreements may not be easily reached. The consultants provided a total of approximately six days of intensive training to the job evaluation teams.

2. Working class, as used here, includes most clerical jobs and many service jobs, as well as the more traditional blue collar, working class occupations.

CHAPTER 10

On The Edge: Marginal Women Workers and Employment Policy

DIANA M. PEARCE

The majority of women workers (52 percent) work part-time or part-year, or both, and thus do not fit the 'regular' worker model. Among women maintaining households alone, only 37 percent fit the regular worker pattern of full-time, year-round work (see Table 10.1). These women workers experience extensive low and poverty-level incomes, and high levels of economic and health insecurity. This is in part because women workers who do not fit the regular worker model find themselves not only economically marginal, but marginal as well to many of the policies and pro-

Table 10.1. Labor Force Status, for Employed Civilian Labor Force 16 Years and Older, as of July 1985

Labor Force Status	Men		Women		Women Heads	
	Number	Percent*	Number	Percent	Number	Percent
Full-time	56,995	85	37,422	67	4333	69
— year-round	43,836	66	26,587	48	3777	60
Part-time	9,518	14	18,174	33	1920	31
—part-year	6,343	10	11,400	21	—	—
Total workers	66,513	99%	55,596	100%	6253	100%

Source: U.S. Bureau of the Census, 1985.
*Column does not total to 100% because of rounding-error.

197

grams explicitly addressed to the inequities and insecurities experienced by all workers.

This chapter will be divided into three parts. First, a profile of the marginal woman worker, including full-time, part-time, unemployed and 'discouraged' workers, will be detailed. For each group, the economic consequences for women workers of not matching the regular worker model, in terms of low income and poverty rates, as well as the patterns of economic and health insecurity, will be described. Second, public policies in five areas that directly impact marginal workers will be discussed, with emphasis on trends in the 1980s. Finally, alternative policies in each area will be outlined.

THE MARGINAL WOMAN WORKER

Whether employed, unemployed, or not in the labor force, which includes discouraged workers, women workers are disproportionately disadvantaged by almost every criterion of economic status.

Employed Women Workers

Many women workers work full time (about two-thirds: see Table 10.1), but few women work overtime. While one-third of black and 45 percent of white men workers average at least five extra hours per week, only 2 percent of white and 2 percent of black women work that much overtime (Duncan, et al., 1984.) At any one time, then, we would expect that perhaps 95 percent of those working overtime would be men. Many women are limited to 40 hours per week (including being unable to take jobs that have compulsory overtime) because of domestic obligations. Ironically, it is women's performance of these same domestic chores that facilitates the overtime work of men; without women's unpaid labor—the meals, cleaning, shopping, housekeeping, child care, laundry, car repair, etc.—many men workers would not be able to work long hours at overtime or a second job.

More than twice as many women work on part-time schedules, accounting for more than one-fourth of woman workers. And the numbers are likely to increase; one-third of new jobs in 1985 were part-time, and estimates of job growth over the next decade are that three-fourths of new jobs will be in the services and trade sectors. It is no secret that it is precisely these industries and occupations which have high proportions of their jobs part-time. Thus, the 'personnel supply business' better known as temporary help, was one of the fastest growing industries in 1984 (Devens et al., 1985).

According to the Labor Department, most women take part-time jobs 'voluntarily', with only one-fourth of women on part-time schedules (but almost one-half of black women working part-time) doing so for 'economic' reasons—that is, because they are unable to find full-time work, or because their employer has cut back on their hours, etc. (U.S. Department of Labor, 1985). But since voluntary part-time workers include those whose jobs are 35 hours or less per week and are 'full-time for this job', (*i.e.,* they are workers who 'voluntarily' took a job knowing it was part-time), the distinction between economic and voluntary part-time is not a meaningful one. More importantly, the economic consequences of part-time work for women are equally disastrous, whether one's choice of part-time was voluntary or not.

For women, the 'choice' to work part-time is as much a measure of limited child care opportunities and the structure of other institutions, such as schools with short hours, frequent holidays, and long vacations, as it is a measure of preference and/or lack of economic necessity.

In addition to working part-time, many women work only seasonally. One fourth of full-time, and two-thirds of part-time women workers work less than 50 weeks a year. As can be seen in Table 10.1, while two-thirds of men worked full-time, year round, less than half of women workers did so. One of five women workers worked both part-time and part of the year, while less than 10 percent of men workers did so. Among women maintaining families, the proportions were even less: only three-eighths of all women household heads—and only 31 percent of black and Hispanic women heads—worked full-time year-round in 1984.

The economic consequences of not fitting the 'regular worker' model are great. The familiar '59¢' (now 63.6¢) applies to full-time year-round workers. The differences in hours worked discussed above for full-time workers are even more extreme for part-time workers and preclude a similar gender comparison for part-time/part-year workers generally. But the consequences for families can be seen: while 21 percent of female-headed families have incomes below the poverty level when the head works, this increases to 33 percent if the head works all year, but part-time, and 45 percent if the head works only part of the year. For black women household heads, the percentages are even higher: 33, 49, and 60 percent respectively (U.S. Bureau of the Census, 1985).

One of the reasons that poverty rates are so high, even among those who are working substantially to support their families, is that more women work at the minimum wage; 18 percent of female, versus 8 percent of male workers earn the minimum wage. One million women household heads earn the minimum wage. Three-fourths of household workers earn the minimum wage, and 40 percent of minimum wage workers are found in retail sales and restaurants (Pavetti, 1985). While most people think of the minimum wage as being a minimum living wage, it has eroded steadily in the 1980s, and this is no longer true. A worker in 1985 earning the minimum wage, even at a full-time, year-round job, does not bring in enough to support even one adult and one child above the poverty line.

Part-time, seasonal, and minimum wage workers, disproportionately women, not only have lower earnings, but they are less protected against income loss. They are less likely to have either employer-provided protection in the form of fringe benefits such as health insurance, sick leave, and disability, or public insurance, such as unemployment compensation. In many instances, fringe benefits are limited to those who are permanent, full-time workers, creating a two-tier wage force distinguished not only by the level of earnings, but also by the level of economic insecurity. For women maintaining households alone, the availability of family coverage against medical costs is crucial; a single emergency room visit—for child or adult—with a broken bone or ear infection can easily cost a week or even two weeks' wages. Yet many such women find themselves between a rock and a hard place, as the jobs available to them do not provide health insurance coverage for their families, nor earnings enough to buy it. At the same time, their earnings are too high for eligibility for Medicaid; in half the states, in fact, you can only get Medicaid if you are on welfare, and few workers qualify for welfare because even small amounts of earnings put one's income above the eligibility limits.

A growing but unknown number of women workers whose workplace is the home are particularly economically vulnerable. They include day care providers, people operating computer terminals, simple assembly (e.g., costume jewelry), as well as the cottage-industry entrepreneurs and self-employed professionals. They rarely have health insurance, sick leave, paid vacation, workers' compensation, or unemployment compensation coverage. For example, the women entering data from Blue Cross-Blue Shield reimbursement forms on their home computers do not have health insurance coverage themselves. Although theoretically these homeworkers have the advantages of independence and flexibility, the use of piecework payment systems and keystroke monitoring make a mockery of this independence. In some ways, the total assumption of risk by the worker is a repeat of the sweatshop system, compounded by the isolation of individual workplaces which precludes worker organization and unionization to win protection against income loss and workplace and materials hazards.

By virtue of their part-time and part-year status, as well as workplaces such as the home, many women workers not only lack private fringe benefits such as health insurance, but they also are frequently not covered by unemployment insurance. Many women workers, for example, do not earn enough or work long enough before losing their jobs, to establish eligibility for unemployment insurance, for it was established to help only the 'regular worker' (Pearce, 1985). While it is difficult to estimate the exact numbers because each state sets its own eligibility criteria, a rough estimate is that about 10–20 percent more jobless women than men did not work the required minimum hours and/or earn the wages required for unemployment insurance eligibility. In addition, women are more likely to work for the small marginal businesses, family enterprises, and/or in occupations—such as household service or child care—which either are not covered by unemployment compensation, or illegally do not pay into the system.

Unemployed Women Workers

Historically, women workers have suffered unemployment rates higher than those of men. This reversed during the recent recession, but once again it is higher among women—7.9 percent of female workers, versus 7.0 percent of male workers in July 1985 (U.S. Department of Labor, 1985). Among women maintaining families alone, the rates are generally one-third to one-half higher, standing at 10.2 percent in July 1985 (U.S. Department of Labor, 1985; figures are not seasonally adjusted).

While women workers generally have shorter spells of unemployment, this fact masks several important differences between unemployed men and unemployed women. First, women are much more likely to leave the labor force altogether—that is, stop looking for work—and this is particularly true during recessionary periods. They end their unemployment not with a job, but with giving up on seeking employment. Whether they are then defined as discouraged workers depends on several factors discussed below. A second difference between unemployed men and women is that twice as many women as men (44 percent versus 22 percent) come into unemployment from outside the labor force. At the same time, unemployed men are more likely to be laid off from a job while women are more likely to lose jobs altogether.

A third difference between unemployed men and women workers occurs among those who have lost a job, and that has to do with the reasons for job loss. Two sources of job loss are almost exclusively found among women: sexual harassment and domestic quits. Domestic quits—99 percent of which are by women (Dahm and Fineshriber, 1980)—basically means leaving because of irresolvable conflict between domestic responsibilities and work requirements and includes such reasons as inability to arrange child care (*e.g.*, for night shift), need to care for a sick child or dependent, to enable one to join spouse at his/her new job location, etc. As with sexual harassment, domestic quits are usually considered 'voluntary' on the part of the worker, with the narrow exception being when the employer changes unilaterally a work condition that violates the contract. If the change, such as working the night shift sometimes, was accepted by the worker at the time of employment, to leave under those circumstances is 'voluntary'.

Mainly because of the expansion and extension of unemployment compensation, poverty is not the inevitable consequence of unemployment. In addition to the growth of unemployment insurance (UI) in coverage and amount, the economic costs of job loss may be cushioned by income from other employed family members. Unfortunately, women are less likely to have either the cushion of another employed family member, or to be adequately covered by unemployment insurance.

As more and more families put both parents, as well as other adult and/or teenage members to work, the consequences of one person's unemployment is lessened. For married women, this is common; three out of four unemployed wives were in families with another member still at work. For women maintaining families alone, however, the percentage who have another household member at work is much less, averaging about only one out of five unemployed women household heads (Klein, 1983).

Women, especially women who head households alone, are less likely to receive unemployment insurance, and when they do, they receive less. This is a direct consequence of their marginal labor force participation with its higher rates of part-time, part-year, intermittent and low-wage work. Unemployment insurance was developed and enacted during the Depression explicitly to help regular workers—meaning full-time, steady workers, who through no fault of their own, lost their jobs. Thus, although there are state-to-state variations, all state requirements aim to limit unemployment compensation payments to those workers who: (1) had a recent and substantial work history, *i.e.*, were recently and steadily employed; and (2) had not left their jobs 'voluntarily'. Because women are more likely to work part-time or seasonally, they are less likely to fit the requirements of the first test, and when they do, are likely to receive smaller payments, as benefit levels are a function of previous earnings; because women are more likely to leave 'voluntarily', to fulfill domestic obligations, or to escape sexual harassment, they are less likely to meet the second test of involuntary job loss. Put another way, failure to meet both of these eligibility requirements is in fact failure to fulfill the 'regular worker' requirements of full-time, year-round work.

In sum, unemployed women workers are much less likely than men to be cushioned against poverty, particularly if they are family heads, by either family or public programs. Only one in five unemployed women heads has another family member at work, and only one in six receives unemployment compensation. And neither employed family members nor UI provide them much protection against poverty: while less than one-fourth of households with an unemployed male householder had poverty level or below incomes, over two-thirds of the households in which the woman head experienced unemployment, had incomes at or below the poverty level (U.S. Bureau of the Census, 1985).

Women Out of the Labor Force: Discouraged Workers

Two out of three discouraged workers are women, though most people not in the labor force, including most women not in the labor force, are not counted as discouraged workers. To be a discouraged worker, one must want a job now (which eliminates 90 percent of those not in the labor force), and not be looking only because one believes one cannot find a job. If one states that one has entered school because one does not think he/she can get a job now, one is not a discouraged worker. Because of this strict definition, only 3.7 percent of men and 2.6 percent of women not in the labor force are labelled discouraged workers (U.S. Department of Labor, 1985). However, whenever private market jobs or job training slots in public programs open up, the numbers applying far exceed the number expected based on the discouraged worker count. Particularly in times of recovery, the number of people moving directly from non-labor force status to employed exceeds estimates derived from survey-based numbers of discouraged workers; this is especially true of women as well as teenage and minority workers (Wool, 1978). Virtually all of the officially touted decrease in discouraged workers at the end of the 1982 recession was accounted for by women (Devens, 1985).

An Estimate of the Numbers of Marginal Women Workers

Table 10.2 provides an estimate of the number of marginal women workers. If we assume that twice as many women outside of the labor force are discouraged workers as are now counted, and combine that with the number of women who are officially unemployed, or working on a part-time or part-year basis, then over one-third of women workers are marginal at any one point in time. If we look at the entire year, which adds all those who experience unemployment or underemployment for some of the year, the percentage rises to over half, or 54 percent. At any one point in time, 19 million women workers are marginal, and over a year, about 31 million women workers experience unemployment and/or underemployment that makes them marginal workers.

PUBLIC POLICIES AND THE MARGINAL WOMAN WORKER

This section details how each of five public policies impinges on the marginal woman worker. In some cases, the consequences are more a result

Table 10.2. Estimate of Number of Marginal Women Workers (15 years and older).

Category	Number	
	Current	Over the Year (1985)
Unemployed	4,077,000	—
Underemployed:		
Part-time	12,796,000	18,174,000
Part-year	—	10,835,000
Discouraged workers	1,100,000	1,100,000
Discouraged workers -		
uncounted	1,100,000	1,100,000
	19,073,000	31,209,000
As percentage of all		
women workers	35.6%	54.0%

of the disproportionate numbers of women workers subject to the policy, and in others the consequences can be traced to the marginal worker's lack of fit to the regular worker model. But regardless of the sources of inequities, these public policies have important negative consequences for women workers that suggest employment policy reforms, which are detailed in the third section.

The Minimum Wage

As described above, the minimum wage, while it has never been formally indexed, has in the past been raised frequently; each time it has been eroded by inflation, it was raised, approximately to the poverty threshold of a family of three. In spite of high inflation in the early 1980s, the minimum wage has not been raised since 1981, which is the longest period without change since its inception. It is an important public policy, affecting millions of workers, yet it is not publicly debated. Ironically, while policymakers discuss establishing a subminimum wage for youths, the main minimum wage, particularly for those trying to support families, has become subminimum.

Anti-job Creation Policies

The structure of tax incentives and cost structures mitigates against employers creating new jobs. Instead, investing in capital is encouraged via the tax laws and subsidy programs. In addition, when the employer wishes to expand production, the costs of adding a regular worker, in the form of fringe benefits (including both present costs and future obligations such as pensions) are quite high, even before factoring in the risks of a new person not working out. An employer averages one dollar in nonwage costs for every three dollars in wages. Thus it is both cheaper and less risky to either hire present workers overtime, or bring in 'temporary' workers, even if the latter must be constantly replaced. The Targetted Jobs Tax Credit program addresses this problem by reimbursing employers for the costs of hiring disadvantaged workers, but it is narrowly focused and tiny in scale, particularly when compared to capital subsidies such as accelerated depreciation, tax credits, etc.

'Indirect' Subsidy Programs

For many women workers, the problem is that they are unable to garner adequate resources both to provide for their families economically and to protect their families against income losses or drains. For these families, subsidies obtained outside of employment are essential to their families' well-being. For example, subsidized day care, or access to low cost health care through a public program or clinic, enable single mothers to get by on low earnings—even minimum wage. Unfortunately, many of these subsidies have been reduced or eliminated in the last few years. Thus one-third of subsidized child care places were eliminated under OBRA (Omnibus Budget Reconciliation Act of 1981). Child care deductions for working welfare recipients were also capped at $160 per month, affecting particularly mothers in high cost metropolitan areas (Sarri, 1984).

Besides child care, reductions in food stamps and other nutrition programs (particularly WIC—Women, Infants, and Children—which provides in-kind high nutrition supplements to pregnant women and very young children), further squeezed the woman worker's budget. Important as each of these programs are, the single most important area of cutbacks has been housing. At the same time as the private market began decreasing the number of rental units available to families with children—through condominiumization, through restriction or exclusion altogether of families with children—and raising the rents for the rest, federal rent subsidies, rehabilitation programs, and subsidies for low cost family housing were reduced drastically. Particularly for the marginal worker, whose jobs do not provide the fringe benefits of health insurance, employer-provided or subsidized child care, or UI coverage, the cutback in these public programs has greatly increased their poverty (Center for Budget & Policy Priorities, 1984).

Direct Income Support for Unemployed and Underemployed Workers

Public policy changes in the 1980s have decreased income support to workers who have lost their jobs or are working part-time in two ways. First, in contrast to previous recessions, during the 1982 recession, unemployment insurance was cut back rather than expanded. The state unemployment rate required to trigger federal supplementary benefits to the long-term unemployed was so high that few states qualified. And because it was tied to the insured unemployed, that is, those currently receiving unemployment benefits (limited to six months in most states), even states with very high rates of unemployment found that they did not qualify, for many of their unemployed no longer were insured (*i.e.,* they had exhausted their benefits) or never qualified. As a result, the number of unemployed receiving unemployment compensation payments dropped in the 1980s from one-half to under one-third. Whereas almost a third of unemployed women heads of households received unemployment insurance during the 1975 recession, less than one in six did so in 1982, and the percentage of women heads of households receiving unemployment insurance who were thereby lifted above the poverty level fell from 62 percent in 1975 to 16 percent in 1982 (Burtless, 1983).

Before the 1980s, many women household heads both worked and received welfare in small amounts. In addition, welfare receipt in half the states is the only way to qualify for Medicaid, an important subsidy for many marginal women workers who have no other access to health care

costs coverage. The 1981 OBRA reduced or eliminated benefits disproportionately for this group of poor but working women heads of households, affecting about 500,000 women and their families. The rule changes were
such that, in half the states, after the four months grace period, women
heads of households with average work expenses and wages were better off
not working than working (Joe, 1982). Nevertheless, the majority reacted
not by quitting work, but by trying, unsuccessfully for the most part, to
make up the lost income and benefits by working more hours, taking a second job, etc. Almost all suffered income losses in substantial amounts, went
hungry, borrowed money, etc. (Sarri, 1984). In sum, where welfare once
subsidized marginal women workers through provision of the nonwage
fringe benefits their jobs lack (child care, health insurance), today's welfare
mother faces an impossible choice at the end of the grace period (which has
been extended to twelve months). Either she must try to survive on her earnings (perhaps by increasing her hours), and "run bare", hoping she will
not need expensive health care, or she can leave her employment, reducing
her income below the limit, and become completely dependent on welfare,
but no longer have to worry about the costs of a health crisis, or try to find
an affordable day care slot.

Work Training Programs

One of the potential means out of poverty for marginal women workers is
via job training programs that give them access to jobs with better wages
and opportunities. Programs that aid marginal workers, such as the Job
Training Partnership Act (JTPA) or the Work Incentive Program (for
welfare recipients), discriminate against women workers in several ways.

Table 10.3. JTPA participants and wage rates (October 1983–June 1984)

			Enrollees Obtaining Employment		Wages		
			---	---	---	---	---
Program	Number Enrollees	Percent Women	Percent of Enrollees	Percent who are women	Overall	women men	f/m ratio
Classroom Training	234,000	58	32%	54	$4.60	$4.31 4.94	.872
Work Experience	40,500	62	26	48	4.10	3.85 4.35	.885
Job Search Activities	123,100	44	47	43	4.45	4.13 4.66	.897
On the Job Training	130,300	41	46	40	4.67	4.22 4.97	.849
Total	585,800*	50	38	46	—	— —	—

Source: Jarboe, 1985
*Columns do not total because some enrollees are in 'other' programs.

JTPA is the successor to CETA (the Comprehensive Training and Employment Act), but is both much smaller, and provides no jobs per se. For not even half of its approximately half million enrollees, JTPA results in employment; for women enrollees, the rate is 35 percent. Perhaps even more discouraging is how poorly women are served by the program, even when it results in employment. As can be seen in Table 10.3, women are found in larger numbers in the longest lasting programs (Classroom Training), the ones which are least renumerative (Work Experience which is not paid), and the ones with the least success rates (*i.e.,* percentage of enrollees getting jobs—Classroom Training and Work Experience). Thus, On the Job Training, which is paid, is 59 percent male, and Work Experience, which is not, is 62 percent female. Overall, women are half the enrollees, but only 46 percent of those obtaining jobs. Likewise, especially in the female-dominated programs, women's wages are lower, averaging about 85 percent of those of men.

What these figures do not show is the minimal aid given by this program, or similar training programs, to those enrolled. Many of the jobs are minimum wage, and many are dead-end. For example, the largest number of JTPA placements in Chicago were in McDonalds, and the second largest, in Jewel Foods, a grocery store chain. Few programs provide auxillary services, such as child care, language training for non-English speakers, or remedial math and English classes. Some are inaccessible by public transportation, though accessible sites are available.

The Work Incentives program, even though ostensibly targeted to a population that is predominantly female with primary responsibility for their family's support, nevertheless has a statutory preference for the 'principal wage earner' and the few men on welfare (Law, 1983). Women with young children (under six) are exempted from the program, rather than given child care and a meaningful opportunity to participate. The Supported Work Demonstration Program for long-term welfare recipients, often cited as an example of a well-designed program, exempted mothers of young children from the program, rather than provide the option to participate through offering child care.

All of these programs, whether targeted to disadvantaged workers or welfare mothers, are built on the regular worker model. They presume that all participants need is a full-time job. They have low rates of "success" at best, and even when employment does result, it rarely solves the problems faced by marginal women workers, who need decent wages, fringe benefits, income security, supportive services, and subsidies, such as child care, health care, housing, etc.

ALTERNATIVE EMPLOYMENT POLICIES
FOR THE MARGINAL WOMAN WORKER

The policies outlined below incorporate several basic principles. First, employment should provide workers with the minimum adequate resources needed to provide for a family. This would include both income and fringe benefits, as well as public insurance against income loss. Second, employment policies and programs should not discriminate against the part-time and seasonal worker. Third, employment policies should value the work that women do as homemakers and rearers of children, and not force women to make impossible choices between their domestic obligations and their jobs. Fourth, employment programs and policies, while recognizing the distinctive nature of subgroups of workers, should be as far as possible universal in application. As the English social welfare theorist, Richard Titmuss, often stated, services for poor people exclusively are often poor services.

Employment policies that would specifically help the marginal woman worker include the following.

Raise and index the minimum wage: In the early 1970s, Social Security was indexed, with the result that poverty among the aged has been drastically reduced. Few would disagree that a person who works full-time and year-round should receive at least enough to support him-herself and one or two children.

Develop pro-worker rather than pro-capital tax credit and subsidy programs: In particular, if the costs of hiring a new worker made it more economical than putting on temporary help, or overtime, a substantial number of new jobs could be created. Using Duncan *et al.* (1984) estimates, if all the hours of those working overtime or on second jobs were redistributed as 'new' jobs, it would amount to over 10 percent of present workers, or enough jobs and more, for all the unemployed.

Expand fringe benefits: This should include in particular health insurance and child care to all workers requiring them. Child care could be in the form of subsidies and programs for child care providers, including aid in developing child care associations for in-home providers, that makes health insurance, sick leave, paid vacation, etc., available to these workers. Health insurance could be in the form of national insurance, but a more realistic and workable model might be auto insurance or home insurance. In the latter instances, society declares that it is in the interest of the public generally that everyone have coverage against loss but leaves the choice of insurance carrier to the individual. Likewise, it makes sense that all workers be insured against the income loss due to illness or injury, for society has to cover the costs in some way, or pay the costs of untreated illness. Furthermore, universal coverage of the costs of health care, as with child care, is more desirable than one system for the middle class (the insurance model), and another (the charity model) for the poor only.

Expand the coverage of unemployment insurance:

UI should include:

1. new or reentering workers, including displaced homemakers and new graduates of school who cannot find work; the only test should be willingness to work.
2. women on welfare; 90 percent have worked, many recently.
3. those who left their jobs because of domestic obligations or sexual harassment.

The lack of coverage by unemployment insurance for these groups of workers forces them to take jobs too quickly, which may not be viable in the long run leading to high turnover, low productivity, and unstable incomes. Lack of coverage under UI also excludes one from programs providing job placement, job training, and relevant labor market information.

Reinstitute and expand programs providing income support: This should be targeted for workers with insufficient earnings, including the "thirty and a third" program in welfare that permitted women to keep the first $30 and a third of the remaining wages, in addition to welfare benefits. Likewise, short-time compensation programs that supplement the wages of workers partially laid off, should be expanded to include the many women workers who can only work 'short-time' (*i.e.*, part-time).

Reform job training: Training programs should be effective for women workers, and so should include the following:

1. require the provision of appropriate support services as needed, including child care, transportation, rehabilitation for disabled workers, etc.
2. mandate that program outcomes be equal for men and women, including placement rates and wages. This might be done by weighting program achievement measures in favor of more disadvantaged workers.
3. institute personal assessment procedures that match the person to the appropriate level program, and allow for individual choice.

Provide for parental leave: Leave programs should reward rather than punish those who devote several years to childrearing. If a young man contributes two or three years out of the beginning of his career to his society in the form of military service, he is rewarded then and later with educational benefits, health care, and employment opportunities. If a young woman does the same for childrearing she is castigated for her lack of commitment to work, is given no special access to education or training when she reenters employment, and is given to believe that her career will suffer for having taken that time out. This is especially true if she returns to part-time employment. While mothers returning to full-time employment quickly return to their preleave earning levels, those returning to part-time work suffer long-term earning losses (Corcoran, Duncan, and Ponza, 1984). A very different message would be conveyed if young parents were supported as parents, e.g., through children's or family allowances; if parent preference points (a la veteran preference points) were given to those seeking employ-ment after a hiatus at home; if special training and education opportunities were offered to those returning to the work force.

CONCLUSIONS

Unemployment and underemployment are serious problems, not only for those women experiencing them, but for all women workers. The low wages and economic insecurity disproportionately born by marginal work-ers also pulls down the wages, and increases the insecurity of all women workers. There are noneconomic costs as well, as mothers take full-time jobs against their better judgment, compelled by economic necessity which precludes working part-time, with all its disadvantages.

The economic costs, the low income, insecurity, and poverty experienced by marginal women workers is neither immutable nor inevitable. It is the result of policies, built on a regular worker model, that many women workers do not fit. But what private and public policy has created can be changed. Indeed, by standards in force 75 years ago, today's full-time workers would be part-time. By developing policies for all women workers, and hopefully blurring the more invidious distinctions, between 'real', regular, full-time, and marginal, irregular, part-time/temporary, we can create comprehensive employment policies that will reduce the poverty and inequality experienced by all, but disproportionately, by marginal women workers.

CHAPTER 11

Undoing Discrimination: Job Integration and Comparable Worth*

WILLIAM T. BIELBY AND JAMES N. BARON

This research was supported in part by a grant from the National Science Foundation (SES 79-24905). We thank Joan Smith and Deborah Rhode for comments on an earlier version of this chapter.

INTRODUCTION

Sociologists have been somewhat reluctant to draw strong policy conclusions from what is now a large body of research on women and work. Economists, in contrast, are not nearly so shy. They have both an explanation for gender inequality and a prescription for policy. Solomon Polachek, the most enthusiastic of the "supply siders," concludes that the human capital model is "the only viable approach for which there is more than adequate empirical support" (1984: 34). In this view, paychecks and career prospects differ by sex because of rational, optimizing decisions made by men and women, given their respective skills, experiences, home responsibilities, and intentions regarding future work and family activities. Workplace discrimination exists only in those sectors of the economy shielded from the forces of competition. The only legitimate policy interventions in the

*For comments on this chapter see Smith (pp. 233-238) in this volume.

workplace are those that eliminate barriers to competition among firms. Anything else—including everything from comparable worth to enforcement of Title VII—creates inefficiencies and inequities (Polachek, 1984: 51-52).

The human capital explanation—coherent, logical, and internally consistent—has a certain elegance to it. It seems to have been accepted in its entirety of late by federal officials charged with enforcing EEO laws, and it turns up in countless editorials pointing to the folly of affirmative action, comparable worth, and other egalitarian reforms. However, the human capital explanation is at odds with much of what sociologists and other behavioral scientists have learned about patterns of segregation, organizational practices, and processes of choice, perception, and attitude formation.

Below, we summarize our recent research on determinants of sex segregation in organizations. That research is based on data describing staffing patterns, job requirements, and personnel policies in over 400 California establishments, which were studied between 1959 and 1979 by the U.S. Employment Service. Details on sample representativeness, procedures of data collection, and the like can be found in Bielby and Baron (1984; 1986). Here, we emphasize findings that call into question human capital explanations. Then, drawing on other research, including micro-level studies of organizational behavior, we suggest some implications for policy that are very different from those offered by supply-side economists.

WHAT WE KNOW ABOUT SEGREGATION AT WORK

Job Segregation is the Immediate Cause of
Sex Differences in Earnings and Career Prospects.

For a variety of reasons, men and women end up working in different occupations. Most craft occupations, for instance, are overwhelmingly staffed by males, while men are rarely found in most clerical occupations. Within the professions, teaching in elementary schools is done primarily by women, and engineering work is performed mostly by men. However, occupational specialization explains only part of the sex difference in earnings. For example, differences in the employment distribution of men and women across over 400 detailed (census 3-digit) occupations accounts for no more than 40 percent of the gender gap in earnings (Treiman and Hartmann, 1981; Polachek, 1984). Most of the sex difference in earnings (and presumably other dimensions of socioeconomic achievement) occurs *within* detailed occupations, and, according to Polachek, nearly all of it can be attributed to sex differences in human capital acquisition.

But considerable sex segregation occurs within detailed occupational categories as well. Figure 11.1 reports evidence of the extent of segregation

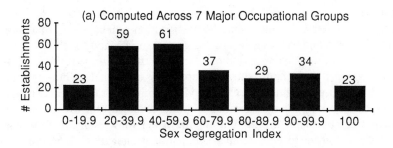

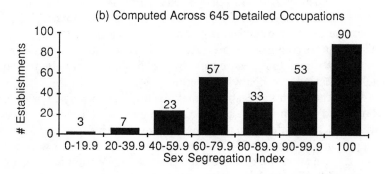

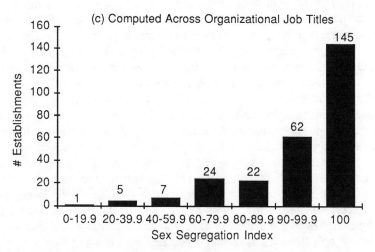

Figure 11.1. Distribution of Establishments by Level of Sex Segregation, Computed across: (a) Major Occupational Groups; (b) Detailed Occupations; and (c) Organizational Job Titles (N = 266 Establishments)

by occupation and job title for 266 establishments studied by the U.S. Employment Service between 1964 and 1979. For each establishment, we computed three segregation indexes.[1] The first assesses the degree of segregation across seven major occupational categories, the second is computed across 645 detailed occupations (a classification scheme somewhat more detailed than one based on census 3-digit categories), and the third is computed from the sex composition of official job titles within establishments. The top panel of the figure shows a more or less uniform distribution across establishments, ranging from those having roughly the same ratio of men to women in each major occupational group to those that are completely segregated by major group. The middle panel shows considerably more segregation at the level of detailed occupational categories. Over a third of the establishments have no mixed detailed occupational categories, and the majority have segregation indexes over 80. Finally, the bottom panel shows that at the level of establishment job titles, over half of the 266 establishments are completely segregated (that is, *no* job title has members of both sexes assigned to it), and most other establishments are almost completely segregated (see Bielby and Baron, 1984; 1986 for further details).

Within-occupation segregation comes about in several ways. For example, men and women in the same occupation often work for different employers, and, more often than not, those employers hiring men provide better opportunities (Blau, 1977). Moreover, even when men and women in the same occupation work for the same employer, they often have distinct job titles, with different duties, responsibilities, and opportunities for training and advancement. Indeed, we found that only 10 percent of the nearly 61,000 workers in our sample of establishments were in job titles that had both men and women assigned to them (Bielby and Baron, 1984; 1986). Furthermore, sex segregation was nearly as extreme when we excluded from our analysis jobs in detailed occupations that were more than 80 percent male or more than 80 percent female. Consequently, sex segregation— by establishment or by job title within establishments—is almost always the mechanism generating sex differences in pay, promotion opportunities, and other career outcomes. Unequal pay or promotion prospects for the same job are rarely the issue, since men and women rarely share the same job title in an establishment. Moreover, this is true even when men and women work in the same detailed occupation. To account for pervasive intraoccupational sex segregation, the human capital model would have to explain why even women who have chosen to enter sex-atypical occupations only "invest" in certain segregated job titles and employers.

Human Capital Theory Does Not Account for This
Pattern of Sex Segregation in Job Assignments.

So far, we have shown that job segregation by sex is the *proximate* cause of gender differences in socioeconomic opportunities. Of course, human capital theory might still be able to explain why men and women end up in different firms or in distinct job titles in the same firm. For example, men and women may choose to specialize in different jobs or firms. Even within the same detailed occupation, it might be easier to combine work and family responsibilities in some settings than in others. Or, even if men and women do not deliberately choose different firms or job assignments, their experiences and training might not qualify them for the same jobs, even when men and women are in the same line of work.

We put the human capital explanation to a test. We examined the factors determining the sex composition of all establishment job titles in our sample that were classified into a mixed occupation (that is, the job title was in an *occupation* that was no more than 80 percent male or 80 percent female). In particular, we examined whether the staffing of particular jobs reflected factors stressed by economic orthodoxy: training time, various job skills and requirements, and the cost of replacing a worker who leaves the job. Presumably, more experienced workers are in jobs with high turnover costs, since employers have an incentive to retain workers who are costly to replace.[2] The specific measures are listed in Table 11.1; complete details appear in Bielby and Baron (1986). Our analyses revealed two things: first, skills, training, and turnover costs have a remarkably weak impact on how men and women in seemingly integrated occupations get distributed across organizations and across specific job titles within establishments. Our statistical model explained just 14 percent of the variance in the sex composition across establishments for men and women in the same occupation, and only 16 percent of the variance in the sex composition of specific titles in the same occupation within establishments. In short, a remarkably rich collection of measures of training and human capital requirements of jobs failed to explain the degree to which women occupy the same jobs as men in mixed lines of work.

Second, the same set of variables *did* allow us to determine conclusively whether or not women are excluded altogether from a given job title in a mixed occupation. Our measures allowed us to correctly predict whether or not women were excluded from jobs in mixed occupations for over 82 percent of the cases. Moreover, coefficients of a *logit* analysis, reported in Table 11.1, show that two measures—Employment Service analysts' ratings of *physical demands* and *finger dexterity requirements*—had by far the greatest impact on whether women were excluded from a job. Other measures of training and human capital requirements were of secondary importance (see Bielby and Baron, 1986). Our results strongly suggest that decisions about allocating men and women to jobs in mixed occupations are not based on a specific candidate's qualifications for that position. If, for example, the job is viewed as physically demanding, it is typically deemed inappropriate for *all* women. Conversely, jobs viewed as requiring finger dexterity are typically seen as inappropriate for men.

In short, we have considerable evidence that employers practice *statistical*

Table 11.1. Logistic Regression Coefficients for Likelihood That Women are Excluded From a Job in a Mixed Occupation (N=2997)

Independent Variable (and Metric)		Coefficient[a]
z_1 Organizational scale	(log employment)	.20**
z_2 Union or bidding arrangements	(0-1)	.59**
x_1 Specialization[b]	(log workers)	.60**
x_2 Training time	(1-7)	.29**
x_3 Numerical aptitude	(1-4)	.33**
x_4 Verbal aptitude	(1-4)	−.70**
x_5 Finger dexterity aptitude	(1-4)	−1.13**
x_6 Clerical perception	(1-4)	−.58**
x_7 Spatial skill	(1-4)	.52**
x_8 Eye/hand/foot coordination	(1-4)	.52**
x_9 Physical strength, lifting 25 lbs.		
or more	(0-1)	1.45**
x_{10} Varied duties	(0-1)	−.27
x_{11} Repetitiveness	(0-1)	−.39**
Likelihood Ratio Chi-square = 1001.4 with 22 d.f.		

*p <.05
**p < .001
[a]Maximum likelihood estimate.
[b]Sign reversed so that high scores correspond to specialized jobs.

discrimination: they reserve some jobs for men and others for women, based on perceptions of group differences between the sexes. Economists claim that employers rationally rely on group differences when it is difficult and costly to determine the qualifications and likelihood of turnover for specific job candidates. Yet our results suggest that statistical discrimination is neither as rational nor as efficient as the economists believe. Variables most directly related to the turnover costs of jobs had only small effects in our statistical model. The two variables that did distinguish between male and female jobs (in *occupations* pursued by both men and women), finger dexterity and the ability to lift at least 25 pounds, are relatively easy to assess for individual men and women. Since failing to hire a qualified applicant is usually costly to an organization, these results are difficult to reconcile with the notion that sex operates as an efficient screen utilized by rational, efficient, unbiased, profit-maximizing employers. Instead, it seems that stereotypical notions of "men's work" and "women's work" play a more decisive role than the technical qualifications of individual applicants and skill requirements of jobs. We return to this issue again below.

*Sex Segregation is Imbedded in Organizational Policies
and Sustained by Organizational Inertia.*

The impact of physical demands showed up in our qualitative analyses of organizational policies as well. Our evidence suggests that the statistical effects described above come about because of employers' *deliberate policies* restricting women's access to jobs perceived to be physically demanding. Court decisions in the early 1970s invalidated the legal basis for these policies, and, not surprisingly, we found fewer references to such policies in organizations studied since 1971. However, court decisions barring the use of physical demands as a criterion for excluding women from specific jobs appeared to have had little effect on employers' practices in the early to mid-1970s. In our statistical model, we allowed the effect of physical demands to differ between establishments studied prior to 1971 and those studied since 1971. The effect of physical demands on the likelihood of excluding women from a job was actually slightly larger for the organizations studied more recently (Bielby and Baron, 1986:785).

Table 11.2 lists examples of policies regarding the employment of women in jobs perceived to be physically demanding. References to such policies appeared in about 40 percent of the narrative reports prepared by Employment Service analysts. The examples in Table 11.2 illustrate the diversity of organizational and industrial contexts in which physical effort provided a rationale for segregation, and several of these examples show how these policies limit women's opportunities for advancement. Furthermore, in many instances detailed job analyses were available for the specific positions to which these policies referred, and they revealed that the jobs actually required *no strenuous physical exertion.*

The organization chart in Figure 11.2 illustrates how a policy of excluding women from physically demanding jobs is one element of a system in which sex segregation gets built into an organization's formal structure. The chart is based on the Employment Service's analysis in 1970 of the production department of an establishment engaged in the manufacture of ordnance for the federal government. There are two entry level production jobs in the department, Production Worker and Assembler. According to Employment Service job analyses, these jobs are classified into the same detailed occupational category and have virtually identical job requirements and duties. The only difference between the two jobs is that the position staffed by men occasionally requires lifting more than 25 pounds, the limit (in 1970) that women could legally lift without a special permit. Segregation at entry is sustained throughout the hierarchy. The Production Worker and Assembler positions promote to and are supervised by male Leadmen and female Leadladies, respectively. While the ratio of men to women is 3:1 in the two "lead" classifications, it becomes more skewed in favor of men as one moves up the hierarchy: the ratio is 10:1 in the Foreman

Table 11.2. Policies Regarding Employment of Women in Physically Demanding Jobs

The job of *UTILITY WORKER, FEMALE* could be considered a dead-end job. Women are restricted to that title due to physical demands and working conditions (1964, brick and tile manufacturing).

The employment of women is primarily confined to the home economics and clerical classifications because of the physical nature of other jobs (1964, natural gas utility).

Employment opportunities for women are limited in the production sections due to the physical requirements of many of the jobs (1971, felt goods manufacturing).

The nature of the work (medium to very heavy) does not lend itself to employment in production of either women or the handicapped, although these people are hired for office positions (1973, wire manufacturing).

Normally they [women] are excluded from jobs requiring heavy physical exertion such as *DRIVER, PUTPOST INSTRUCTOR,* and *SWIMMING INSTRUCTOR.* They are specified for the job of *ARTS AND CRAFTS INSTRUCTOR* (1965, coeducational summer camp).

Women are hired for office work classifications in all divisions. Women are also hired exclusively to fill *HOSTESS,* hostess supervisory, and training and cabin cleaning positions. They are preferred applicants for positions in reservations and counter sales. They are generally excluded from the passenger service counter, cargo service, and terminal operations because of the physical labor involved. Women are not hired as maintenance or flight crew personnel primarily because those jobs have been traditionally filled by men and because workers are often required to lift or carry objects in excess of the 25 pound limit set by state law for women (1964, commercial airline).

Males are hired as *FLOOR REPORTERS* and females as *CLERKS, GENERAL.* Both entry jobs are on the trading floor. *FLOOR REPORTERS* stand and walk constantly and *CLERKS, GENERAL* stand and walk about 50 percent of the time. . . . According to a stock exchange executive, the *FLOOR REPORTER* classification is a "training ground" for young men starting a career in the securities business (1968, securities exchange).

Women are hired in clerical occupations and in other plant areas where the physical requirements of the tasks involved do not preclude it (1968, pharmaceutical manufacturing).

Policies Regarding Employment of Women in "Detail" Work

Female employees perform work of repetitive nature under exacting standards and must possess the temperament for confining work at one station (1970, [firm 1708]).

Women are used almost exclusively in Packing and Carton Departments where the work is somewhat routine. The work requires considerable standing and walking, and demands a high degree of finger dexterity, close attention to details, and near acuity or color vision (1969, bottle manufacturing).

Table 11.2. (*Continued*)

Women perform all of the assembly operations, since the work is light and merely requires good hand and finger dexterity and a willingness to perform monotonous work (1965, wooden box manufacturing).

The workforce of this establishment is predominantly female, as the employer feels they are best suited to this type of work (1967, jewelry manufacturing).

When hiring new employees the company favors older women because of increased stability and favorable attitudes toward job responsibility. Women are employed for practically all production jobs (1970, electronics manufacturing).

Only women are hired for packing and inspection duties, because various aptitude tests indicate that women are more manually adept at this type of work. However, according to the employer, in company plants in other countries throughout the world, the reverse has been found (1966, chewing gum production).

Source: Narrative Reports Prepared by Employment Service Analysts for Selected Establishments

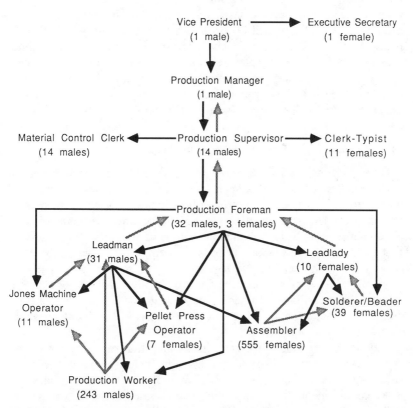

Figure 11.2. Organization Chart, Production Department of Ordnance Establishment (1806 Employees), 1970. (Solid arrows denote supervision relationships; halftone arrows denote promotion paths.)

position, while none of the 14 Supervisors was a woman. This example illustrates patterns we saw throughout our sample: women in supervisory
positions rarely supervise men, and their opportunities for further advancement up the hierarchy are much more limited than those for men in otherwise comparable positions (Baron and Bielby, 1985; Baron, Davis-Blake
and Bielby, in press).

Statistical analyses we performed also showed how sex segregation is sustained by formal organizational structure. In attempting to explain why
some organizations are more segregated than others, we found that small,
entrepreneurial firms were often completely segregated by sex. In these establishments, women are either excluded altogether or confined to just one
or two job classifications, such as Receptionist. Among the remaining
organizations, we found that levels of segregation were higher in larger establishments, those with more specialized jobs and a proliferation of job
titles, and in settings with unions and/or formal bidding procedures governing promotions (Bielby and Baron, 1984). In short, instead of promoting
universalistic standards in personnel matters, bureaucratic rules, procedures and job titles seem to have been implemented in a way that sustains
the segregation of jobs and opportunities by sex (Baron and Bielby, in
press). Moreover, longitudinal analyses of a subset of establishments (those
analyzed twice by the Employment Service, typically four to six years
apart) revealed that large, bureaucratic firms were least likely to show any
change in the level of segregation *in the absence of any sustained, deliberate effort to bring women into jobs previously closed to them.*

Sex Segregation is Sustained by Behavior as Well as Structure.

Human capital and other explanations for sex segregation based on
market forces are limited in part by naive, one-dimensional views of
organizational structure. Structures are seen as efficient responses to
technical problems in economic organization; those that are inefficient simply do not survive the forces of market competition. We have argued above
that this view is substantially at odds with empirical evidence about the
structures that sustain sex segregation. In this section, we argue that
economists' views of human behavior are equally naive and one-dimensional. Understanding and undoing sex segregation in the workplace requires a balanced analysis of structure, behavior, and their interrelationship.

Economists are certainly correct in insisting that specialization by sex
comes about in part because of choices individual men and women make
regarding work and nonwork roles. How individuals form attitudes and
make commitments, perceive others, and choose among alternative activities influences the roles men and women play in the workplace (Marini
and Brinton, 1984). However, orthodox economists' explanations of sex
segregation rely on a model of individual behavior that has little empirical

content, since it is uninformed by recent research on perception, attitude formation, and choice behavior.

For example, social psychologists have gained considerable insight into the process of person perception. They have discovered that stereotypes seem to be an essential feature of human perception, a cognitive shorthand invoked to achieve economy in processing information (Ashmore and Del Boca, 1979; 1986). This research suggests that even employers have limited cognitive capabilities and are not immune from the use of stereotypes. According to the model of statistical discrimination, employers base decisions on their perceptions of group differences when it is difficult and costly to determine the true qualifications of individual applicants. It is not difficult to see how the phenomenon that social psychologists call "expectancy confirmation sequences" (Darley and Fazio, 1980) can turn this seemingly efficient behavior into a self-fulfilling prophecy: employers expect certain behaviors from women (*e.g.*, high turnover) and therefore assign them to routine tasks and dead-end jobs. Women respond by exhibiting the very behavior employers expect, thereby reinforcing the stereotype. Moreover, we know that individuals are more likely to attend to and retain information that confirms stereotypes. We have a remarkable capacity to ignore information that fails to fit our expectations (Hamilton, 1981). Even when confronted with exceptional cases, we maintain our belief systems by creating subtypes (Deaux, 1985). Social psychologists have consistently elicited and isolated stereotyping, expectancy confirmation, and subtyping processes, even in the contrived environs of the laboratory. These processes certainly operate in the workplace as well, where long-term interactions among employers and employees allow such patterns of behavior to stabilize and become taken for granted. Unfortunately, empirical evidence from the workplace is limited to a handful of case studies, although at least one, Kanter's (1977) *Men and Women of the Corporation*, provides a vivid illustration of the microbases of sex segregation.

Of course, there is a dimension present in the workplace that is largely absent in the social psychologists' laboratory experiments: the stakes individuals and groups have in existing social arrangements. Employers who benefit by crowding women into a narrow range of occupations, and male employees who view job integration as a potential threat to their paychecks and statuses, are both likely to find a belief system that presents sex segregation as rational and efficient particularly appealing. Social psychologists have also vividly demonstrated that we are most prone to biases and distortions, including stereotyping, in situations having greatest personal relevance (see Cooper and Fazio, 1979:150-153).

In summary, sex segregation at work is rooted in organizational structures that tend to remain stable unless deliberate efforts are made to change them; the tendency for organizational arrangements to be inert in the absence of profound environmental shocks is well-documented (Hannan and Freeman, 1984). In addition, segregated structures are reinforced by—and in turn reinforce—belief systems that are also rather inert and that allow us to accept existing workplace policies as rational, efficient, and legitimate. Only recently have we developed alternative theories and accumulated empirical evidence about why work roles are segregated by sex. Our findings lead us to conclude that: (1) much of the disparity between men and women in economic well-being and career prospects is due to segregation at work; (2) intervention can make the workplace more equitable; and (3) to the extent that job assignments are based on inaccurate stereotypes and structural barriers, intervention may actually make workplace arrangements more efficient as well. It is time to think about effective intervention strategies.

UNDOING DISCRIMINATION: JOB INTEGRATION AND COMPARABLE WORTH

Some readers may find a grim message in what we report on the organizational bases of sex segregation. Our research shows the pervasiveness of sex segregation in the workplace in the 1960s and 1970s, even in what should be the most "enlightened" sectors of the economy—large, professionally managed organizations. Such work settings typically have specialized subunits to deal with personnel matters. Employee recruitment, selection, and development procedures are usually codified and standardized. There should be little room in these organizations for interjecting personal prejudices into job assignments. Yet we found large, bureaucratic organizations to be among the most segregated establishments in our sample. Furthermore, their staffing patterns typically changed very little over time. Have we painted a picture of inevitable and immutable sex segregation in the modern workplace?

Segregated job assignments are pervasive and persistent *in the absence of deliberate efforts to undo sex segregation.* Such attempts were rare among the firms in our sample, although we encountered several successful efforts (Bielby and Baron, 1984). More importantly, identifying the organizational mechanisms that create and sustain sex segregation provides a roadmap for successful intervention. In fact, work in this direction is well under way. We have touched upon just a few specific mechanisms in summarizing our findings. Roos and Reskin (1984) offer a more comprehensive review of organizational practices restricting women's access to sex-atypical jobs, while others have evaluated the efficacy of various procedures for changing those practices (*e.g.,* Shaeffer and Lynton, 1979; O'Farrell and Harlan, 1984). Instead of covering the same ground, we offer a more general discussion of how organizational systems for selecting, evaluating, advancing, and rewarding employees can be used both to open opportunities for women in male-dominated jobs and to eliminate pay inequities between male and female jobs with comparable work conditions and responsibilities.

To many, job integration and comparable worth are viewed as *alternative* strategies for undoing discrimination. We reject that notion. They can be viewed as *complementary* policies—one to provide opportunities to women in areas heretofore closed to them, the other to redress the devaluation of work done by women. However, we go one step further. Given what we have learned about sex segregation and organizational dynamics, we view job integration and comparable worth as part of a single, *unified* approach to gender equity. The most productive way to undo discrimination is to approach it as a problem of organizational design: devising effective ways of using the very mechanisms that have sustained sex segregation in the past as tools to both integrate jobs and reassess their worth.

Large, bureaucratic firms typically have a personnel function to manage human resources with a selection and development system, a measurement or appraisal system, and a compensation or reward system. Judging from the policies regarding employment of women we encountered in our sample, it is possible that the formalization of these personnel procedures institutionalizes whatever discriminatory practices exist at the time. Baron *et al.* (1985), for instance, found that older agencies in the State of California were more segregated than otherwise comparable (but younger) ones, reflecting the legacy of their founding conditions. Similarly, the cross-sectional relationships we found between sex segregation and measures of bureaucratic formalization probably reflect the cumulative impact of policies implemented for diverse reasons over the course of organizational life cycles (Stinchcombe, 1965).

Entrenched personnel procedures are unlikely to change unless there is a firm commitment to change them by top management, and top management rarely develops such commitments unless substantial costs are imposed for maintaining the status quo. During the 1970s, organizations vulnerable to costly EEO lawsuits did develop commitments to change and successfully modified personnel practices, providing opportunities for women in male-dominated jobs (Shaeffer and Lynton, 1979; O'Farrell and Harlan, 1984; Smith and Welch, 1984; Burstein, 1985). In the face of internal or external EEO pressures, dramatic reductions in levels of sex segregation have been accomplished in both private firms (Shaeffer and Lynton, 1979) and public administration. For instance, Baron *et al.* (1985) have documented very sizeable declines in segregation between 1979 and 1985 in some California state agencies, including several that are large, old, and organizationally complex and therefore supposedly resistant to change.

No doubt, any attempt at organizational change meets resistance from groups who perceive that their power will be undermined. Moreover, belief systems strongly support existing arrangements. In the absence of external pressure, managers remain committed to past practices; indeed, managers responsible for implementing existing procedures find themselves *identified* with them. On the other hand, the ease with which executives in some targeted companies developed strong commitments to EEO supports our finding that mechanisms sustaining segregation are not inevitable. When the incentives to change personnel practices are strong enough, managers' commitment will follow; an assertion consistent with social psychologists' notions of rationalizing or retrospective commitment to actions (see Salancik, 1977).

The advances of the 1970s were confined primarily to changes in selection and development systems (*e.g.*, opening new recruitment and advancement channels to women) and secondarily to appraisal systems. Apart from remedying gross violations of the Equal Pay Act, we have seen little change in organizational compensation systems. This is hardly surprising. Given the pervasiveness of sex segregation in large firms and the absence of any clear legal mandate for pursuing comparable worth, there has been little pressure to change compensation practices.

Nevertheless, the elements exist in most large organizations for a united approach to reversing discriminatory personnel practices. Editorials in the business press notwithstanding, such an effort can be viewed as simply rationalizing existing practices, not as a massive disruption of our economic system. Indeed, at least some segments of the business community apparently share this view. According to a report in *Business Week*, the National Association of Manufacturers' EEO panel has taken a stand in opposition to the Reagan administration's plans to further relax EEO standards. According to the article, the group "passed a ringing endorsement of affirmative action as a social policy that has worked and should be kept" (Moskowitz, 1985). If managers dislike government intervention, they dislike volatile intervention even more, and many resent the onslaught against egalitarian reforms that had started to become standard operating procedure. Given such evidence, we dare to sketch an optimistic (but hopefully realistic) scenario for progress.

Executives will probably develop a genuine commitment to job integration and comparable worth only when it proves very costly not to do so. Pressure might come from either of two directions. First, comparable worth may become part of EEO policy through further reinterpretation of existing legislation by the courts or through new legislation. Of course, organizational vulnerability to actions under EEO laws and regulations is nonexistent without vigorous enforcement, something that has not been seen for several years and that is unlikely to be seen for the next few years. It is more likely that employers will become vulnerable through collective bargaining. It appears as though comparable worth will advance first in female-dominated industries: the public sector, services, finance, and the like. In our limited experience with several large California firms, we have discovered some organizations seriously considering the threat of litigation, organizing, or strikes over the issue of comparable worth. At the same time that they publicly declare comparable worth to be illegitimate and unproductive, they are carefully reexamining their own job evaluation and compensation procedures and realigning the wages of men's and women's jobs. In essence, the threat of comparable worth litigation or legislation may be fostering some—if not all—of the change that litigation or legislation would require.

Given commitment at the top, design and implementation of egalitarian reforms can be reasonably straightforward. Most large organizations utilize Management By Objectives (MBO) or similar performance evaluation systems. Using these systems, managerial performance is evaluated against preestablished financial and nonfinancial goals. Often, part of a manager's compensation is determined by performance relative to MBO goals. Once mechanisms that facilitate job integration are introduced into personnel procedures, line managers can be evaluated explicitly with respect to their success in: (1) disseminating information about these mechanisms; and (2) getting subordinates to take advantage of these mechanisms. Thus, a subordinate's request to transfer between departments in order to enter a sex-atypical job classification would register progress toward EEO goals, instead of indicating a failure to reduce turnover in the manager's subunit. A program like this does more than offer an incentive for managers to attain EEO objectives: it also demonstrates to the manager that top executives are sufficiently committed to EEO to make it a part of the organization's performance evaluation system (see Shaeffer and Lynton, 1979).

While most organizations purport to include EEO goals in management evaluation, fewer actually do so effectively. For instance, few performance appraisal forms that we have seen display a prominent or extensive section for assessing managers' progress toward egalitarian goals. In addition, the performance appraisal process in many organizations, even if formalized, is haphazard, a low priority, done under severe time pressures, and is loosely coupled to tangible rewards. Under circumstances like these, simply formalizing and quantifying mangers' accountability is by no means sufficient to induce changes in their behavior.

A firm using job evaluation techniques as part of its compensation system already has a mechanism for realigning wages and salaries to ensure internal equity. Job evaluation is typically used for just that purpose, but usually not specifically for eliminating inequities between the compensation of men's and women's jobs. Three conditions must be met in order to use job evaluation as a mechanism for implementing comparable worth. First, the same job evaluation system must be applied to men's and women's jobs. More often than not, firms use different schemes for blue and white collar jobs or for clerical and managerial jobs. Indeed, many firms seem all too aware of the implications of a unified approach to job evaluation for the compensation of women's jobs. Although there is no systematic evidence, it has been charged that some personnel managers carefully avoid organization-wide approaches to job evaluation for fear of the expense involved in realigning women's wages and the uses to which the data generated might be put in future litigation.

Second, employees and employers must come to agreement on the specific dimensions of skill, effort, responsibilities, working conditions, and the like that constitute legitimate compensable factors for pricing jobs. They also must agree on a procedure for assigning weights to those factors. Large organizations with internal labor markets and idiosyncratic job tasks price jobs internally, even if the pricing procedure is not an explicit company policy. Using job evaluation to achieve pay equity requires employers to make explicit their criteria for setting wages, and it almost certainly requires that representatives of employees participate in setting compensation policy (Lawler, 1981:Chapter 7). If sex composition of jobs is associated with wages after controlling for accepted criteria, then the burden of proof would be on employers to specify and quantify any legitimate unmeasured factors, such as supply and demand, that might account for the relationship between wages and gender composition.

The third condition necessary in applying job evaluation to comparable worth is to mitigate so far as possible, biases in procedures for describing and rating jobs that cause women's work to be undervalued. This is probably more difficult than we are willing to admit (McArthur, 1985). Nevertheless, once agreement is reached on the issues of compensation policy described above, minimizing bias becomes a tractable technical issue that can be informed by a burgeoning social science research literature (Treiman and Hartmann, 1981; Hartmann, 1985).

There are other reasons for linking job integration and comparable worth. The use of separate evaluation schemes for men's and women's jobs is one more example of how segregation gets built into the structure of organizations. Basically, it provides two different standards of internal equity: men's jobs are rewarded according to their standing within the hierarchy of men's work, and women's jobs are rewarded according to their standing within the hierarchy of women's work. The legitimacy of this system is easy to sustain in a segregated workplace. With little movement from men's to women's jobs (and vice versa), women themselves compare their compensation primarily to what other women are making (and likewise for men), exacerbating the well-documented tendency for individuals to evaluate their performance relative to others in the same social group (Smith, 1973: Chapter 2; Major *et al.,* 1984). When significant numbers of women avail themselves of opportunities to move to sex-atypical jobs, such a system becomes more difficult to sustain. Women who are aware of the requirements, working conditions, and rewards of male-dominated jobs are less likely to accept a dual reward system. Ultimately, employee support for a single reward system should help both those women who choose to enter sex-atypical work and the vast majority (at least for now) who remain in the jobs typically held by women. Dismantling the sex segregated structure of work is thus a necessary element in recalibrating the rewards traditionally allocated to women's work.

Linking job integration to comparable worth can also help to keep job assignment and compensation systems *flexible*. Our research has shown that formalized bureaucratic rules and procedures may sustain sex segregation rather than mitigate it, and there is a danger that rigid job evaluation systems might further institutionalize existing wage disparities between men and women (Treiman and Hartmann, 1981:Chapter 4; Rosenbaum, 1985). Similarly, job integration requires continuous scrutiny of job assignment policies in order to eliminate barriers to women's career mobility; short-sighted and overly rigid efforts to desegregate can backfire by creating "solos" or "tokens" out of individuals in sex-atypical jobs, impeding long-term progress. By monitoring compensation systems and job integration at the same time, employers and employees can work to ensure that personnel policies remain responsive to changes in both workforce composition and the business environment. For example, efforts to achieve integration targets in particular jobs may require temporary or permanent adjustments to the job evaluation or compensation system, while efforts to achieve comparable worth may alter the gender composition of specific jobs in the short run. Hence, desegregation and pay equity must be pursued *in tandem*, with enough flexibility that: (1) the pursuit of one does not jeopardize the other; and (2) neither management nor labor perceives the long-term pursuit of gender equality as seriously compromising other important organizational objectives. At a time when employee involvement and participation are increasingly viewed as strategies for making large organizations less rigid and more competitive, we think that flexible approaches to pay equity and job integration with widespread employee involvement makes sense from the standpoint of management *and* labor.

Our overview of job integration and comparable worth has ignored some important issues. First, we have said nothing about the costs and employment effects of comparable worth policy, basically because our research does not bear directly on these issues. Economists are certainly right in the *direction* of their predictions: raising the wages of women's work is likely to increase women's unemployment, and reducing the wage disparity between men's and women's work creates a disincentive to leave women's jobs for men's jobs. We need empirically-based estimates of the magnitudes of the employment and incentive impact. The only systematic evidence is from Australia. It shows that the effects are in the direction that economists predict, but whether the magnitudes are trivial or substantial has been a matter of considerable debate (Gregory *et al.*, 1985; Killingsworth, 1985; Hartmann *et al.*, 1985:15). We certainly require more research on this.

Second, we have stressed the importance and viability of linking job integration and comparable worth efforts in rationalizing workplace personnel policies. We think it productive to link organizational selection and development systems, appraisal systems, and reward systems in order to improve women's employment prospects. However, we may have slighted other factors that will make significant progress difficult to achieve. For example, the demography of organizations in a slow-growth economy suggests that it will be difficult to move sizeable numbers of people (of either sex) into more rewarding jobs. Moreover, most projections show that the jobs that will increase most in employment over the next several decades are the ones that are already female-dominated (Cain, 1985). Unfortunately, what little success we have achieved in moving women into male-dominated jobs has not been duplicated in the other direction. Men are no more likely to aspire to female-dominated jobs today than they were 20 or 30 years ago (Cain, 1985). We suspect that it will take more than just a realignment of pay scales to turn this around. In short, the demographic realities for the rest of the century suggest that a sexual division of responsibilities at work will be a reality for many people for years to come.

Third, we have said nothing about the division of labor, responsibility, and power in the household and how it reinforces segregation and wage inequality at work. We have sidestepped that issue simply because the tools of our trade—organizational analysis—are much more useful for changing workplaces than for changing families. We also neglected the one area where family and organization clearly intersect: in employer policies for child care, parental leave, and the like.

Fourth, we have stressed issues of organizational internal equity, particularly in large firms. We have said nothing about the mechanisms that channel women into marginal firms or industries or how to intervene effectively in small firms where the disadvantages women face are not so clearly identifiable in the organization's formal structure. These issues too deserve further discussion. Our bias is to focus first on areas where change is not only possible but visible to others. Mobilizing support for change in large organizations has the potential for altering attitudes and practices beyond the specific workplaces where changes are implemented. Of course, it would be a mistake to simply assume that gains will automatically diffuse to peripheral sectors of the economy.

Our research shows that pay disparities and segregation by sex are largely the outcome of organizational arrangements. Gender inequality is sustained by organizational structures and procedures and reinforced by the beliefs employers and employees have about men's and women's work. As organizational problems, segregation and pay inequity require organizational solutions. Job integration alone does not address problems faced by women who have neither the resources nor the inclination to move into male-dominated jobs. Job evaluation applied rigidly can institutionalize existing pay disparities and may even create disincentives to job integration. Applied jointly, however, as part of a unified approach to equal employment opportunity for women, we believe these policies can prove effective (and flexible) in reducing, if not eliminating, organizational inequities.

NOTES

1. The segregation index (index of dissimilarity) measures the percentage of workers of one sex that would have to be reclassified in order to equalize the ratio of men to women in each category (occupation or job). For example, an occupational sex segregation index of 70 indicates that 70 percent of the women (or men) in the sample would have to change occupations to equalize the sex ratio in all occupations.

2. Furthermore, employees have an incentive to stay with the organization when their skills are firm specific.

Part Three

COMMENTARY

CHAPTER 12

Comparable Worth, Gender, and Human Capital Theory

JOAN SMITH

The paper by William Bielby and James Baron (this volume) offers a rich opportunity to open up for consideration several unexamined aspects of comparable worth programs and the economic theory of wage allocation.

Bielby and Baron's work is a major—perhaps the first—empirical refutation of the human capital thesis. This is no narrow academic achievement but in fact represents a major political breakthrough. Let me first sketch out what that thesis entails in the briefest possible terms for the purpose of argument.

Neoclassical economists argue that discrepancies between male and female earnings, job opportunities and the like are the effects—indeed, unintended effects—of rational decisions reached by both employees and would-be employees on how to best maximize their rewards. Because they marry and rear children, women tend to make smaller investments in work related human capital. Since the chance of training paying off is restricted by their nonwork related roles, women choose jobs that require little training or on-the-job experience. Thus they enter jobs that are characterized by low rates of productivity, low wage rates, and little upward mobility.

On the other hand, employers need to distinguish between employees who will remain in the labor force, repay costly training, and contribute more in productivity by virtue of their labor market commitment. But because such rational discrimination is costly if applied individually to each and every prospective employee, employers practice what has come to be called within the neoclassical enterprise statistical discrimination. That is, employers will treat all members of a group as though they are endowed with the attributes of its average member. Let me offer an example. I find soccer games on average horribly boring and pass them up whenever I get a chance. But by doing so I forego the one or two games that are packed with excitement. Nevertheless, the cost of foregone excitement is considerably less than the cost I would incur if I either went to every single game or if I tried to determine which games were likely to be sufficiently less boring to warrant my presence.

Since it is assumed—a major assumption these days—that women on average have less labor market commitment, it is reasoned by neoclassical economists that employers quite rationally avoid the expense of sorting out which ones are more likely to stay in the labor force and which ones are not by discriminating against the group as a whole.

While it all looks quite silly—not one of us has ever met either an employer or a woman who actually acts this way—the political implications have been absolutely deadly since the schema neoclassical economists employ has become the reigning ideology. It has provided the necessary legitimitization for right-wing cutbacks of all sorts of regulatory programs.

Here is what is so very dangerous and here is why Bielby's and Baron's work is such a major contribution. The neoclassical argument is theoretically coherent and airtight. It starts with the assumption that long standing economic practices are rooted in the most efficient ways of doing business. Otherwise, given competitive markets, they would have long ago been eradicated. Thus, attempts via government policy to change these practices would produce inefficiencies that the national economy could ill afford. These neoclassical economists do not deny that there are vast and even unfair differentials between men and women, but what they argue is that these differentials have their origins in sources other than the market itself. Any tampering with the market would in the long run not only fail to solve the problem but would cause altogether unacceptable inefficiencies.

Feminists and radical economists have made virtually a sport out of refuting the neoclassical model on logical and historical grounds. But Bielby and Baron's work is the first that I know of that refutes it on empirical grounds. It is worth risking repetition to lay out just where that refutation lies. In their paper, Bielby and Baron show that *occupations* are not the cutting edge of sex segregation but in fact it is *firm specific jobs* and *organizational structures* that are the real culprits. Occupations are creatures of the culture and the Labor and Commerce Departments. They are bundles of all sorts of different jobs. So, for example, one major occupational classification is that of "manager" but the jobs which get the managerial title are so vastly different that in the end *all* they share is the name. Consider for example the difference between being the manager of a bank and the manager of a beauty salon. Of course the people at the Labor Department understand the difference and break down occupations into component parts. Thus the birth of the DOT. However, even these do not correspond to the *jobs* to which people are assigned in specific firms. What Bielby and Baron are able to show is that gender segregation is vastly *undercounted* if one considers just the major occupational groupings but if one looks closely at firm specific *job titles*, gender segregation is almost total.

Why is this so important? There are two reasons: one, on the simple level of empirical adequacy and the other, the adequacy of the model itself. First, neoclassical economists look at *occupations* and not *jobs*. Thus they miss by far the largest proportion of gender segregation. But second, and much more importantly, women do not and cannot self-select for jobs that are totally esoteric and peculiar to individual firms. The relevant question to most working class women is *not* "what do you do?" but "where do you work?" As Bielby and Baron are able to demonstrate, the difference between jobs as far as their gender composition goes is peculiar to individual firms. A cook in one firm is always a woman, in another always a man. A beautician in one establishment always a woman, in another always a man. In short, training, productivity and the like—the totems of neoclassical economists—play only a minor role in differentiating men's and women's jobs within firms and, with most jobs, very little between firms. Whether or not a firm will be characterized by a high or low degree of gender segregation is a function of specific aspects of the organization itself and its operating environment.

Those features of jobs that are primarily responsible for sorting out women from men are related to gender stereotypes rather than to job specific skills. Thus, neither women's rational choices nor employers' rational decision making can account for job segregation by gender—the principle form of gender discrimination in organized economic activities.

Let me turn very quickly to what I consider to be Bielby and Baron's second major contribution.

I suspect few working women have been convinced by human capital theory. Neither, however, would they hesitate to question the more radical approach to the issue—what has come to be called labor market segmentation theory. While that theory may be right in the most global sense, it is so nonspecific that it hardly helps in either scholarly work or in the formulation of strategies or of policy alternatives. These theorists point out that labor market segmentation is intimately linked to the dynamics of monopoly capitalism. Nevertheless, the theory tells us nothing about the intricate nature of those links. We are told merely that labor market segmentation arises because it is functional—it facilitates the operation of capitalist institutions. Since criticisms of such an approach are legion, let me simply say what we all know: What is functional does not always persist and what persists is not always functional. Simply an assertion of its functionality for capital hardly helps explain the origins of occupational segregation *in specific organizational practices*. This is where Bielby and Baron make their major contribution. Their paper is specifically about the set of organizational arrangements, practices, and procedures that guarantee the continuation of almost complete gender segregation of jobs in most of the firms they studied.

Last, these two authors raise the most serious consideration concerning the adequacy of government-sponsored research into the extent of gender segregation since that research rests on occupational level groupings rather than in firm specific job titles. By going beyond just occupational titles and beyond cross-firm aggregation, Bielby and Baron's measurements show that in spite of all the rosy predictions, gender segregation is probably as prevalent today as it was 20 years ago. The extent it appears to be reduced is as much or more a function of definitional artifact than a real change in what women can expect in the world of paid work.

As much as I admire the paper, however, there are problems which in the long run I suggest raise serious questions about comparable worth strategies.

Advocates of comparable worth recognize that in the short run women are destined to work in highly gender segregated jobs. Under these circumstances, equal pay for equal work, while worth struggling for, makes little sense for the majority of women workers. It is only by recalibrating the value of women's jobs to match that of comparable men's jobs that any measure of pay equality can be achieved in the immediate future. Bielby and Baron's work on job segregation certainly adds considerable ammunition to this approach. If it is job segregation that is at the bottom of women's disadvantaged condition and if job segregation is as prevalent as their data clearly show—and more importantly if the technical differences between jobs with different titles are as negligible as they argue—policies emphasizing comparable worth make the most sense in at least the short run.

But increasingly women's low pay is less a function of simply job segregation than it is of *sector* segregation. The vast majority of recent entrants into the labor force have found jobs in the two lowest paying industrial sectors—business and personal services on one hand, and in retail and wholesale trade on the other. These industrial sectors are certainly highly segregated but aside from managerial level employees, the pay of *all* the employees whatever their gender is abysmally low; career mobility for both men and women virtually nonexistent. Comparable worth programs in these settings would be close to meaningless since there is little distinction between men's and women's jobs in terms of either wages or opportunities. While the pay for women would increase in these settings if it was recalculated to match that of men the resulting wage would still be less than adequate. In addition, policies which would integrate women into managerial positions in these firms would be almost equally meaningless for the vast majority of women since one of the outstanding features of these firms—features which distinguish them from traditional firms—is the extraordinarily high ratio between nonsupervisory personnel and supervisors.

Further, this kind of employment structure, with many Indians and precious few chiefs, is the wave of the future. Compare, for example, the vast differences between IBM's employment structure and that of McDonald's. The former is finely tuned, composed of clearly demarcated job ladders; career profiles; seniority rungs and the like. McDonalds offers to the vast majority of its personnel none of these features of employment. It is the difference in their employment and organizational structures that distinguishes the most rapidly growing service sector jobs, jobs that are chiefly offered to women.

What I am arguing is that as rich as Bielby and Baron's methods are as vehicles for policy formulation, they are going to be quickly outmoded by changes in the basic structures of work. We may get comparable worth precisely at the moment when it is no longer applicable to the changing mechanisms of employment discrimination. I will return to this point in my final comments.

The second problem I have with the paper is certainly a problem in all of our work—mine no less than anyone else's. It can be summed up in a question. Why women? Why are women the group whose major form of discrimination is found in occupational segregation. Indeed people of color are to be found in segregated occupations, of that there is no question. There are black jobs and Hispanic jobs and so on. But even within these jobs there are strict boundaries between women's work and men's work. While I don't have definitive data, my guess is that it is much more likely that a Puerto Rican woman would be found working alongside an anglo woman than a Puerto Rican man! I do not think that there can be any satisfactory policy implemented for ending this sort of segregation or its effect on pay and opportunity structures unless that question is answered.

For all of its problems, and they are legion, neoclassical-economists attempt to join women's experiences at home with those in paid labor. In rejecting these neoclassical models, Bielby and Baron may be throwing out the baby with the bath water. In other words, it may not be totally inconceivable that women's work trajectories *are* overdetermined—shaped both by organizational and administrative dictums *and* by the set of forces that shape and reshape their unwaged labor activities.

The third set of problems is related to Bielby and Baron's strategies for change. I have absolutely no quarrel with their overall intent, although I have some with how these may be implemented given the rapidly changing structures within which the vast majority of women wage workers are finding employment. As I mentioned above, the very organizational mechanisms that are the target for changing women's labor force experiences identified by Bielby and Baron are *precisely* the ones that are increasingly irrelevant to more and more women workers. Let me offer just two examples. Bielby and Baron identify highly complex personnel procedures as a particular target; yet, increasingly, women work in settings where personnel procedures are considerably less complex and considerably more massified, to use the authors' very nice phrase. More and more women work in units that hire directly and there is a clear absence of centralized procedures for selecting new employees. It is a catch as catch can system in an increasing number of cases.

Secondly, and related to this first point, women are increasingly finding waged work in dramatically decentralized units. And this is, in my view, no accident. That is to say the decentralization of production has become both technically possible and, from the point of view of employers, the most advantageous. I am thinking here not only of increasing utilization of the franchise system but as well much, much smaller production units even in the most sophisticated manufacturing systems, such as computer parts, a considerable proportion of which are now being assembled in private kitchens two counties away from us. Because this is so, in the not so distant future the pressure points for creating radical reorganization in women's work lives will have to be considerably different than what Bielby and Baron suggest and what is commonly assumed in comparable worth policies. In other words, I think that Bielby and Baron are right when they suggest that "identifying the organizational mechanisms that create and sustain sex segregation provides a roadmap for successful intervention." Unfortunately, those organizational mechanisms, not coincidentally, are being revised. It is the process of those revisions which must also be our target.

CHAPTER 13

Changes in Labor Force Opportunities: An Appraisal

FRANCINE D. BLAU

The papers by Barbara Reskin and Patricia Roos and by Marta Tienda and Vilma Ortiz (this volume) raise the issue of whether recent changes in women's employment represent real progress. Before examining how the papers address this question, it may be helpful to summarize what the recent changes have been and when they have occurred.

Looking first at occupational segregation, we find on the basis of census data a trend toward integration of occupations dating to the 1960s; a trend which further appears to have accelerated during the 1970s (Blau and Hendricks, 1979; Beller, 1984). Moreover, while the decline in segregation during the 1960s was associated with women's movement into traditionally male clerical and sales jobs (as well as the entry of men into the traditionally female professions), during the 1970s women made considerable progress toward increasing their representation in predominantly male managerial and professional occupations. Nonetheless, the degree of segregation remains substantial. Further, while there is some evidence of a decline in the earnings gap dating from the late 1970s or early 1980s, the gains in this area have been even more modest (Blau and Ferber, 1986). As of 1984, even women working full-time, year-round earned only 64 percent of their male counterparts' earnings.

The paper by Reskin and Roos seeks to assess this progress by asking how much improvement in opportunities the decline in occupational segregation really constitutes. Their focus is upon the *quality* of the opportunities women have found in the male sector. Tienda and Ortiz examine the nature of and earnings pay-off to occupational and industrial shifts over the 1970s, and, in particular examine the consequences of restructuring for the male/ female earnings differential.

Looking first at the Reskin and Roos paper, the authors point out that there exist a number of mechanisms whereby women's entry into male occupational categories can end up producing little if any real improvement in their economic status. First, women may encounter internal segregation within more detailed occupational categories or across employment sectors or firms. As an example, although women have increased their representation among bus drivers, they have been concentrated among school bus drivers, with few obtaining the higher paying jobs in metropolitan transit systems.

Second, deskilling may occur so that, as women are entering the occupation, the job itself may be changing so as to require less skill and thus command lower monetary rewards and status than previously. Such appears to be the case among insurance adjusters where computerization seems to have reduced the judgment and knowledge necessary to perform the job.

Finally, they point out that when women enter a job, it may not become permanently integrated. Rather, resegregation may occur as has been the case historically for primary school teachers and clerical workers, and more recently for insurance adjusters and examiners.

Reskin and Roos have developed a very useful framework for analyzing women's progress. Their typology is important not only from a research perspective, but also from the vantage point of policy in that they have identified pitfalls that must be avoided if efforts to improve women's occupational attainment are to succeed.

They present some compelling evidence based on case studies of specific occupations that internal segregation, deskilling, and resegregation do indeed occur, to the detriment of women. While case studies cannot establish how prevalent these problems are, their findings are impressive in that these phenomena are uncovered in a fairly heterogeneous group of occupations which I assume were not preselected to make this point.

However, I would like to raise some questions about where this leaves us, based on the admittedly preliminary evidence available so far. A crucial issue is whether or not women have achieved real progress to date. To answer that question, I believe it's necessary to distinguish between the notion of incremental improvement—having things get better, perhaps not as rapidly as one would have hoped, perhaps not as rapidly as one could have reasonably expected—and basically not getting anywhere at all. Due to their focus on the mechanisms that may prevent women's entry into male occupations from enhancing their economic status, the work of Reskin and Roos may leave the impression that perhaps after all, when the changes are inspected carefully, women are not actually getting anywhere. I would like to challenge this impression on two grounds.

First, internal segregation, deskilling, and resegregation are not new processes. If they have been going along at about the same pace over time, they could *not* account for the *increase* in apparent occupational integration that occurred during the 1970s. Unless opportunities for internal segregation, deskilling, and (eventual) resegregation *increased* during the 1970s, it seems reasonable to conclude that some, perhaps a substantial portion of the observed decline in segregation that occurred during the decade did represent progress for women. (It may be noted that resegregation only gives a false impression of declining segregation before the process is complete whereupon a segregated female job replaces a segregated male job). Of course it may indeed be the case that the very pressures toward increasing women's representation in nontraditional fields may have increased the use of the mechanisms to thwart women's actual progress. A final conclusion on this awaits more data and analysis. However, it is important to bear in mind that, even when internal segregation, deskilling, and resegregation occur, it is possible, even likely, that women are finding opportunities that are superior to those previously available to them in the female sector.

This brings me to my second point, the proof of the pudding is in the eating. That is, to fully resolve this issue we need to know whether or not women have benefited economically from these shifts in occupations. Reskin and Roos do not address this question because they are waiting for the availability of compatible data from the 1970 and 1980 censuses to examine changes in reward structures. We do, however, have some information from other sources. For example, Andrea Beller and I (1984) have examined this issue using the 1972 and 1982 Current Population Surveys. Our preliminary findings indicate that the payoff to being in a male job (70 percent or more male) or an integrated job (40 to 70 percent male)—defined in terms of 1970 sex composition of occupation—increased for both men and women over the decade. This suggests that entry into such occupations continued to represent enhanced opportunities for women over the decade. However, the returns to being in a male or integrated job increased more for men than women, possibly due to the factors Roos and Reskin identified.

Tienda and Ortiz have also directly tackled the returns issue. They use census data and focus on 11 major occupational categories. They first decompose the 1970 to 1980 changes in the occupational distributions of men and women into three components: 1) *Industry shifts*, by which, for example, an occupation may increase in relative size because industries which use a disproportionately high proportion of workers in such jobs expanded in relative terms; 2) *Intraindustry occupational shifts*, which occur when, for example, an occupation increases in relative size because industries use an increasing proportion of such individuals. This would be the case if, say, manufacturing employed a higher proportion of semiprofessionals in 1980 than in 1970; and 3) *Interaction effect*, which is essentially a manifestation of the "index number problem." It may be interpreted as being occupational changes due to the combined effects of industry and (intraindustry) occupational shifts.

This is an instructive analysis that highlights a number of interesting points. For women over this period there was little relative change in clerical employment. But this was the outcome of two counterbalancing effects: a large positive industry shift effect, on the one hand, and a sizable negative occupation shift effect (as well as negative interaction effect), on the other. That is, among women, clericals held their own because industries which typically use a relatively high proportion of them increased. But, *within* industries there was a decrease in the relative importance of clerical workers in the occupational distribution. The latter may be due to technological change and is important information for those trying to predict the consequences of the telecommunications revolution for clerical employment. It could also reflect the upgrading of clerical workers into managerial and supervisory positions. Or, it may reflect, at least in part, the "title inflation" that has been alleged to have occurred in some firms due to government antidiscrimination pressures. In any case, this and other of the findings of the shift-share analysis are of considerable interest and are worthy of further analysis.

Tienda and Ortiz then turn to an examination of the consequences of these shifts for the earnings of men and women. As they point out, the impact of these shifts on wages and on wage differentials between men and women is unclear *a priori*. If the increase in relative employment is due to increased demand, a positive effect on earnings is anticipated. However, this effect may be counterbalanced by an increase in the supply of workers. In the presence of occupational segregation, an increase in the supply of women may exert downward pressure particularly on women's earnings.

Tienda and Ortiz find that, overall, women benefited from industrial and (intraindustrial) occupational shifts over the period in terms of higher earnings. However, since men also gained from occupational upgrading during this time, the effect on the gender earnings gap was less than one might have expected. They also present evidence that the impact of restructuring on earnings is dependent on the sex composition of occupational employment. They suggest that this in turn implies that the benefits of restructuring are mitigated by new patterns of gender typing. This may well be the case. However, their analysis proceeds at such an aggregate level, it is difficult to evaluate the implications of their findings. Having laid valuable groundwork with this overview study, I would like to see them follow up with a more detailed analysis.

While I may have some points of disagreement over the methods of analysis or the conclusions reached by these authors, I believe that both these papers break new ground and provide considerable food for thought as well as identify potentially interesting topics for future investigation. Despite their very different approaches, it is notable that their conclusions are remarkably similar. The potential for change over the 1970s was not fully realized due to the continued effects of occupational segregation by sex and the processes whereby it tends to reestablish itself in the face of change.

CHAPTER 14

Comparable Worth: The Relationship of Method and Politics

ROSLYN L. FELDBERG

The theory of comparable worth, its ideological struggles and its legal strategies continue to attract considerable attention. In contrast, as the chapters by Acker and Steinberg and Haignere in this volume point out, methods of implementing it have been largely ignored. No longer. These chapters begin to redress the balance, describing and analyzing the methods by which comparable worth is assessed. This close attention reveals not only biases in current methods but also difficulties in improving them.

Much said in these chapters is of great interest, and will be discussed below. But despite the importance of these chapters, one connection remains unexplored: the politics of method. For what these chapters highlight, beyond the specific flaws in existing job evaluation systems, are two critical links between method and politics. First, an analysis of methods unveils the political dimension of knowledge—the power of the researcher or expert. As with other forms of power, we must ask who exercises it, and in whose interests or within what taken-for-granted context. Ultimately, the questions asked in job evaluation studies reflect both the assumptions of the researcher and the outcome of a struggle over how work is defined and whose definitions count. Second, accurate job evaluations expose the political gap between knowledge and implementation. It is not enough to establish the worth of a job or its comparability to other jobs. The appropriate political body must then be convinced to pay what the job is worth. Thus the politics of knowledge and the politics of the purse stand between the theory and practice of comparable worth.

At the same time, even the biased systems now available are of use. For example, the Oregon case as described by Acker is very instructive. It shows how job evaluation systems can be used to challenge the undervaluation of women's work. At the same time it shows how difficult it is to reduce both gender and class bias which are built in to the very instruments of evaluation. Moreover, class and gender bias are interrelated: complete elimination of sex-based inequity cannot be accomplished without challenging class-based definitions of the meaning and value of specific kinds of work. On these grounds I argue that an unbiased system can only be developed when proponents are prepared to offer a political challenge as well. The political challenge addresses the question of comparability: Who can be compared to whom? Which jobs are included in the range of comparison? In the most fundamental way, these simple questions address the issue of power, the power to hold some groups of workers to one standard and other groups to another in both evaluation and compensation.

Looking at Acker's chart on Definitions of Human Relations Skills helps in summarizing the dilemma. The Oregon Task Force saw human relations skills as involved in understanding, influencing and serving people. This definition, in contrast to that of the Hay system, acknowledged "emotionally demanding situations" as part of clerical jobs. If we think of clerks in social welfare or unemployment offices, we can easily picture them in the difficult position of explaining the rules and procedures of public agencies to distraught or angry members of the public. But the Task Force, composed of representatives of women's groups and feminist lawyers and scholars, was only one component of the complete Oregon evaluation team which included representatives of employed men and women at all levels of state government, managers from state administration, and consultants from the Hay company. In the end, the Task Force was unable to convince the others of the appropriateness of its definition. The evaluation teams therefore used a definition which acknowledged only the least demanding of the human relations activities found in most clerical jobs: "skills in communicating" and "factual information are necessary in the job."

The question is why was such an inadequate definition the end result of discussions which included the Task Force? Here I think the political dimensions of the process emerge most clearly. The Hay consultants and the state management personnel on the team placed a different and higher value on human relations skills involved in supervising and managing other peoples' behavior from a position of authority than they did on motivating people from the position of a peer. The decision rule which gave "true supervisors" an automatic four on Human Relations skills, thus placing them in a grade different than other workers whose jobs involved sensitive interactions with the public, illustrates the differential evaluation quite clearly. Yet one could easily argue that mediating with the public from a position without formal authority may actually require greater human relations skills that motivating the performance of subordinates over whom one has authority and sanctions. To me, it is not self-evident that one form of influence is more crucial to the successful operation of a public agency than the other—but that too appears to have been assumed in the final skills chart. Assumptions about the greater value of managerial work were sufficiently embedded in the thinking of most participants of the larger group that members of the Task Force were unable to dislodge them.

Acker points out that, "in order to (have) value(d) job stress or to (have) allocate(d) more value to (the) interpersonal skills required in many female-dominated jobs, it would have been necessary to achieve a consensus (on the part of the whole evaluation team) on a goal of reducing the overall inequality in the State as an employing organization." Since it is unlikely that such a consensus will be reached, what happened in the Oregon case is likely to happen again. Definitions and standards of human relations and working conditions are being developed that effectively separate managerial and nonmanagerial jobs. *The political question of how to shift the power to define out of the hands of management turns back into a methodological question of how to develop definitions that do not assume greater skill in managerial jobs than in jobs without authority over others.* The link between methods and politics is strong, and is revealed here as one aspect of the politics of knowledge.

The Steinberg and Haignere chapter reveals another aspect of the politics of knowledge in job evaluations. It matters a great deal what methods are used to gather job descriptions. Asking people to describe their jobs is disadvantageous to those who are less articulate and/or who have been devalued as people and as workers in the past. Yet the alternative of giving people a fixed choice questionnaire captures only those aspects of the job that the person designing the questionnaire has recognized. If the kinds of human relations skills practiced by clerical workers are not listed on the questionnaire in the terms clerical workers use to describe their work, most clerical workers will probably not check the listed skills as ones required in their jobs. For example, if a skill is listed as "motivates compliance of subordinate," clerks who "motivate" the public to follow the rules are unlikely to check this item. If a more appropriate item does not appear, this aspect of their work will remain hidden. The examples indicate that whichever method is used, designing a job evaluation system gives the designer considerable power over the values which are embedded in the evaluation. Furthermore, since decisions about hiring experts to design and conduct job evaluations are usually made by managers, it is not surprising that consultants are reluctant to tamper with systems that managers have accepted as legitimate.

Finally, Steinberg and Haignere draw directly on the Hay system to illustrate how the award of points for different kinds of skills favors those in managerial jobs. Being at the highest level of Human Relations skills cannot move a job into the highest ranks on points if it does not have managerial content on the know-how dimension. As the Hay Chart shows, the highest level of Human Relations skill is worth more points when combined with Managerial Know-How than it is under any other conditions. As long as that managerial bias is present, managers will be paid substantially more than other categories of employees. Since most managers are white males, this means that the salaries of white women and minority men and women will continue to be lower than we might expect if all compensable components of nonmanagerial jobs were recognized and compensated equitably.

This analysis does not imply that job evaluation should be abandoned. Even within the limits of established job evaluation systems, female- and minority-dominated jobs are being ranked in ways which permit comparison to white, male-dominated, nonmanagerial jobs for the first time. And even here the pay inequities are substantial and worth eliminating. For example, in Minnesota (1981) nurses and vocational education field instructors received equal job evaluation points. Yet the latter, male-dominated job paid an average $537 more per month—or 31 percent more than the average wages of nurses. Similar examples could be offered throughout the job structure. They show that even the present, biased systems of job evaluation offer some opportunities to reduce one part of the pay discrimination that has lowered the wages of all workers in female-dominated and minority-dominated jobs.

Within the limits of established job evaluation systems, female- and minority-dominated jobs can be compared to white, male-dominated nonmanagerial jobs. This represents an advance over previous approaches to job evaluation. But comparable ranking does not insure comparable pay. It is one part of the strategy for achieving pay equity, but only one part.

Establishing the worth of female-and/or minority-dominated jobs will not automatically win equitable wages for the women and men in these jobs. What it will do is to make clear the contribution of work which has historically been undervalued and taken for granted. Job evaluation will not translate directly into wages because employers are resisting. Although I agree with Steinberg and Haignere that a system of job evaluation involves three areas: description, rating of jobs, and salary setting, the heart of the current resistance is in salary setting.

Bradford Reynolds of the Justice Department declared that he does not believe it is discriminatory to pay different salaries to men and women whose jobs have been comparably evaluated; i.e., that employers are not bound to pay the same salary to all jobs with the same points. On the face of it, that is blatantly unfair. Yet that position is familiar to us in the form of "prevailing market wages" or "distinct labor markets."

Hay Associates, the consultants whose evaluation system has been used most widely, advanced the position in their 1984 statement to the Civil Rights Commission that there is no reason to assume that distinct labor markets should be paid on the same scale. As evidence they cite *Briggs vs. City of Madison.* As they present this case, the court agreed that the nurses met requirements as high or higher than those of the sanitarians but ruled that the city was not discriminating when it paid higher wages to sanitarians, because market studies presented by the city showed convincingly that it could not hire and retain the latter unless it paid them higher wages. By implication, nurses were "willing" to work for less, because they do. It is clear that employees are not paid what their work is "worth," but what they demand for doing it.

This example highlights two issues involved in moving from unbiased evaluation to equitable wages. First is the technical issue that Steinberg and Haignere refer to as the conflict or balance between "internal" and "external" equity. Internal equity implies that all jobs should be treated the same way according to an internal standard: *i.e.,* all jobs with the same points get the same pay. External equity refers to the value of the job in the marketplace: *i.e.,* the same jobs in different firms should be paid roughly the same amount. As far as I can see, maximizing external equity would maintain the status quo—the inequitable wages for female- and minority-dominated jobs—since prevailing market practices led to these inequities in the first place. Methods for determining the proper balance remain rudimentary.

Second is the political issue of what kind of struggle workers are prepared to undertake to insure that they do get equitable wages. Even unbiased methods cannot guarantee that workers are paid what their work is worth. Only those who are organized to demand equity and ready to struggle in support of that demand are likely to be paid fairly.

IMPLICATIONS: THE POLITICS OF KNOWLEDGE, THE POLITICS OF STRUGGLE

These chapters show how bias can be incorporated into job evaluation. Steinberg and Haignere argue that this can occur at each stage: description, rating of jobs, and salary setting. Both chapters argue for close attention to the methods of job evaluation since bias will lead to continued undervaluing of the work done in female-dominated and minority-dominated positions.

I agree with them. I think their evidence is clear and convincing. To me, it suggests that those of us committed to pay equity need to become involved in the process of developing and applying job evaluation systems. We also need to educate workers, especially those who work in undervalued jobs, about the availability of less biased evaluation systems. Such evaluations offer an opportunity for those working in female-dominated and minority-dominated jobs to learn to value their own work fully. In this way, job evaluation can contribute to both self-respect and organizing. Struggles to gain pay equity will require both.

There is, however, a political problem that is not adequately addressed in these papers. Establishing the worth of female- and/or minority-dominated jobs will not automatically win equitable wages for the women and men in those jobs. Developing unbiased methods of job evaluation is essential in establishing the legitimate value of jobs, but it is only a first step in achieving equitable wages. Wages reflect political strength. Job evaluation provides an arena in which to contest wage levels, but it does not, cannot guarantee them. Instead, job evaluation provides evidence for a struggle over wages. To get pay equity on the basis of even improved, unbiased job evaluations, workers in female-dominated and minority-dominated jobs will have to struggle for it. One aspect of that struggle is ideological, involving the definition of what is fair or equitable. Another aspect of that struggle is tactical. Once the values of jobs are established, how can pay equity be advanced when employers resist? In San Jose workers went on strike after the city refused to negotiate wage settlements which reflected the findings of the job evaluation that had been conducted. In the State of Washington, workers waged a court battle after years of negotiation proved fruitless. While their legal victory was overturned by a higher court, they won a substantial out of court settlement.

This brings me to my final points. Acker raises the question of working class unity. It is an important question, but in some sense a side issue. I think we should fight for pay equity because it is just. Those in female- and minority-dominated jobs should not put aside their struggles for equitable wages until attitudes change and workers in white, male-dominated jobs come to understand and support pay equity. Indeed, I think the struggle around and the application of job evaluation systems and comparable worth in particular could offer exciting opportunities for the development of a new appreciation to each others' work among all nonmanagerial workers. In addition, working for pay equity offers new insight to workers in male- as well as female-dominated jobs because it makes explicit and challenges many employment practices. But even if those possibilities were not present, I think the struggle around comparable worth should go forward as a matter of economic justice.

In conclusion I want to emphasize the link between methods and politics. First, methods work only as well as people are prepared to fight for them to work. Only when people are organized politically to oppose bias in job evaluation systems can the methods serve us well. Second, although unbiased, carefully used methods are a valuable resource, their contribution to pay equity depends crucially on politics: on the willingness of undervalued workers to make it clear that they will no longer work for less than equitable wages.

CHAPTER 15

Comparable Worth and Women's Economic Independence

HEIDI I. HARTMANN

Comparable worth is a strategy that is central to women's achievement of economic equality with men; in seeking to raise the wages of "women's jobs"—those jobs in which women predominate—to equal the wages of those "men's jobs" that are comparable in skill, effort, and responsibility, it seeks to increase women's incomes. Women with higher incomes, earning perhaps as much money as men, will most likely become more equal politically and socially with men as well. In fact, women might be able to become economically independent, able to support themselves and their children at a decent standard of living primarily through their own earnings. Because it contributes to this end, comparable worth is a politically controversial strategy, one that has both strong adherents and strong opponents.

Both chapters discussed here, by Steinberg and Haignere and Acker (this volume), seek to advance the comparable worth strategy by providing tools that will help adherents achieve the goal of pay equity. Both these chapters provide useful and thoughtful discussions of the practical details of implementing comparable worth policies from the viewpoint of participant observers. Steinberg and Haignere served as director and assistant director of a project identifying potential bias in compensation in the civil service system of the State of New York and offering remedies. Joan Acker served as a member of the Oregon State Task Force on Compensation and Classification Equity.

The Steinberg and Haignere chapter provides a good overview of the technical procedures of the two major types of point-factor job evaluation plans (*a priori* and policy-capturing), analyzes their sources of sex and race bias, and provides many helpful suggestions for eliminating bias in the job evaluation process. Steinberg and Haignere illustrate their criticisms of job evaluation with examples from several different jurisdictions, many of which they have worked with and many of which are in New York. In discussing one application of an *a priori* point-factor system, in Oregon, Joan Acker's chapter discusses a few sources of bias in some detail. Both chapters are especially valuable to those who conduct job evaluations or are involved in working for comparable worth and seek to understand the role of job evaluation techniques. To the non-expert, Acker's chapter is the more accessible.

In the course of relating her case study, Acker raises deep and complex issues of class and gender conflict. In doing so, Acker's chapter deals directly with some of the political issues that arise in attempting to compare women's and men's jobs; she discusses how resistance to change in the evaluations of traditionally "female work" was expressed by consultants, managers, and some workers throughout the evaluation process. In contrast, Steinberg and Haignere, though well aware of the political debates both in and beyond the workplace, stick closely to the technical aspects of job evaluation. Indeed they hope to move the debate beyond its well-worn political tracts by providing the technical know-how to develop objective, bias-free job evaluation tools. They seem to be arguing implicitly that the debate has focused on broad issues because participants have not been aware of the technical solutions that are available to actually achieve pay equity. Steinberg and Haignere succeed in providing much needed information which many practitioners will find very useful, but practitioners will find equally useful the analysis of the political debates, and particularly the description of the way they occurred in the job evaluation process itself, that Acker provides. Perhaps some of the opposition to comparable worth results from inadequate technical knowledge and understanding. But some of the opposition may actually result from full knowledge and understanding; some opponents undoubtedly resist comparable worth because they resist the economic equality and independence of women.

Both Steinberg and Haignere and Acker point to the same general job factors that are left out of most standard job evaluation plans and that are especially important to jobs that women tend to hold disproportionately: human relations skills and related forms of stress, or work demands, including stress from time pressure and from communication (such as working with unhappy, unhealthy, or angry people). Although both chapters focus on the ways in which job evaluation plans can be improved to make them more useful in implementing comparable worth, Acker points out that even traditional job evaluation plans, uniformly applied, tend to indicate that wages in women's jobs should be increased (*i.e.,* that women's jobs are paid less than comparable male jobs). In other words, improvements in job evaluation would be nice, but even the current, unimproved plans are likely to have some beneficial effect.

The Steinberg and Haignere paper focuses on developing criteria for achieving comparable worth through job evaluation. Its discussion of the need for the consistent and bias-free application of job evaluation and its critique of the many features of existing plans that tend to incorporate and perpetuate discrimination are comprehensive and practical. Their list of often overlooked job factors is extremely useful: coordinating meetings, cleaning up after others, training others, stress from sitting and limited movement, skills and stress related to humans relations tasks, producing under time pressure, and record-keeping in human service jobs. The examples of specific problems taken from their work in New York and their discussion of race as well as sex bias are also important contributions.

Some of the approaches taken to specific problems in New York may prove useful to others; some, however, will be less useful. One useful approach is the way the New York study dealt with the job classification problem. A common problem in conducting job evaluation for comparable worth purposes is that the jobs that have the same official title and rank are not in fact similar when real job descriptions are developed and compared. It is difficult to evaluate the job secretary, for example, when secretary can mean vastly different things depending on where in the organization the secretarial job is located. Some studies of state civil service systems have first evaluated the accuracy of job descriptions, job titles, and their current classification before proceeding further. The first step often takes considerable time (though, as Acker reports, it can be done expeditiously as it was in Oregon, with the aid of 32,000 questionnaires completed by workers). To obviate that step, the New York study accepted the titles as given and evaluated them no matter how disparate they were across actual jobs. Note was made however of the dispersion across the various questionnaires for the same job title.

The particular policy-capturing approach used in New York may prove less useful to others, unless it is packaged in a way that imitates plans with more standard methods. Their method uses the worker-provided descriptions of job content, gathered by questionnaire, statistically massaged (via factor analysis), to derive the weights of the various factors (via regression against the wage rates New York currently pays). The use of the current wages to derive the weights is the policy-capturing aspect of this approach; with this method the analyst can determine what the employer currently values in its wage structure—among the "job factors" that are commonly identified are sex and race discrimination. That is, the analyses that have been conducted so far generally find that employers currently reward maleness and whiteness. The unique aspect of the New York study is its use of statistical methods, applied directly to the questionnaire results, to identify the compensable factors. This is not the only way policy-capturing can be carried out. Their method skips the phase of using an expert or a committee to identify factors and to evaluate and rate job descriptions using human judgment. As they note, such human intervention generally enters the process before the wage regression equations that determine the weights are calculated. For the New York research to be useful to others, a packaged job evaluation plan that could be readily installed elsewhere should be developed. If such a plan used the more traditional rating of jobs by humans according to criteria for various factor levels, more descriptive information about the factors, along with rating guidelines, would need to be provided.

In discussing how the project developed items for the questionnaire (and therefore the resulting factors), Steinberg and Haignere state that they looked for factors that are highly identified with female jobs and correlated with low pay. The use of a system developed in this way would almost certainly work to raise the pay of women's jobs. Of course, other developers of job evaluation plans—in the past—may have looked for factors that would justify high pay for male jobs. For example, in the system Acker discusses, one task force member argues that human relations skills are counted twice for managers but not for other workers, or in the New York case Steinberg and Haignere discuss how "male jobs" appear to receive credit twice, once for ability to carry out a task and once for willingness to do so. That these motivations can influence the design of job evaluation plans makes job evaluation a highly controversial technique in comparable worth implementation. What the authors of both these chapters seek to do is to *reveal* the motivations that seem to have entered these systems in the past, perhaps intentionally—perhaps unintentionally—and to replace them with chosen goals.

Although this procedure, substituting one set of goals for another, has led to claims that job evaluation is not scientific (*e.g.:* if there is not one right answer, then how can it be used to compare jobs objectively?), it actually is a traditional and logically necessary feature of job evaluation as it has been practiced for decades. As Steinberg and Haignere point out, job evaluation measures the content of jobs according to a set of value criteria; the value criteria must be provided, either by the consultant or the employer. Objectivity for the value judgments inherent in comparable worth is rarely claimed by advocates; objectivity of measurement, once values are determined, is claimed, however. Moreover, a political consensus that supports comparable worth—a social commitment to justice and fairness—is sometimes claimed by advocates. The value that a job evaluation plan be bias-free, that it not discriminate by sex or race, is widely-shared and may, under some interpretations of Title VII of the Civil Rights Act, already be the law of the land. Nevertheless, the issue of values is a basic issue that anyone seeking to improve job evaluation by removing its current biases, and anyone seeking to implement comparable worth, must confront. One can certainly envision future law suits from white male workers alleging reverse discrimination if a job evaluation plan is seen as unfairly biased in favor of women's jobs. While one might have wished for more discussion of political issues such as this one, the Steinberg and Haignere paper makes a major contribution to developing the technical tools that advance the value of bias-free job evaluation plans.

Joan Acker's chapter, in discussing one example of bias in some detail, provides political as well as technical analysis. In her view, male managers who subscribe to basic tenets of male power are the instruments by which beliefs of male dominance enter the wage structure. I believe the power of male workers must also be added to this equation, specifically their gender interest as well as their class interest (Hartmann, 1976). As Phillips and Taylor (1980) argue, male workers can have input into the labelling of women's work as skilled or unskilled. Although Acker notes the potential for conflict between female and male workers, she does not pursue the topic using the Oregon case materials. Acker's study does however provide a useful discussion of what actually happens when *a priori* plans are implemented. As she describes, the consulting company, when it was in the process of seeking the contract from the State of Oregon, had agreed that its plan could be modified to take into account the concerns of the Comparable Worth Advisory Committee. The consultants modified their plan to add Work Demands as a factor as well as another level on the factor designed to measure Human Relations skills (in order to distinguish the level of Human Relations skills required in the average female job from the lower level required in many jobs that have minimal contact with people). In actual practice, however, these new factors were rarely used. The consulting company remained in control of the process because they taught the local committee how to evaluate the jobs. With their training, in essence, even the new plan added up to the same old thing. Here Acker notes that the same old thing, uniformly applied across the board, would nevertheless have the effect of raising wages, especially for women in the lowest paid jobs. With improved recognition of women's skills in higher level jobs, such as executive secretaries, women might do substantially better all across the board.

After considerable discussion, the task force voted to include Work Demands under the Working Conditions factor in the job evaluation plan. Time Demands, Role Overload, and Emotional Demands were to be evaluated for such jobs suggested by the task force as a secretary working for several bosses or under time pressure or a human services worker working with severely ill patients or experiencing conflict between enforcing state rules and helping clients. In practice, however, the criteria and training provided by the consultants resulted in only 20 of the 346 evaluated jobs receiving points for Work Demands.

The treatment of Human Relations skills was another important issue in the Oregon case. The consultants explicitly stated that they did not want to recognize that the same types of skills could occur in nonmanagement jobs as occur in management jobs. To do so would reduce the wage differential between managerial and other jobs. Yet we know that many secretaries do much of the same kind of work as their bosses do, and help to train their bosses' replacements, too. Moreover, many additional Human Relations skills (dealing with irate customers) are distinct from managerial Human Relations skills. The United States, relative to other industrialized nations such as Japan and the countries of Western Europe, probably has more wage spread between managers and others. In my view, and Acker agrees, closing that wage gap is an important goal itself, even abstracting from its effect on the male/female wage gap. The relative underpayment of the "underlings" in this country leads to a less professional work relationship. Administrative support staff rather than being seen as part of a working team each with a different role but contributing to the overall goal of the organization, are often used for personal favors and experience arbitrary treatment. Perhaps other noncash rewards can be found for managers that would give them the status it is thought is required to induce them to be managers.

As Acker notes, comparable worth as it is proceeding might act to reduce this managerial/nonmanagerial wage gap somewhat as many women's jobs might be paid more. Women's status relative to their supervisors would be higher. In this way, of course, comparable worth is not only a gender strategy but also a class strategy. It raises wages going to the working class, especially its female members. Many have pointed out that comparable worth has something in common with the Swedish *solidarity* policy of bringing up the bottom workers. This reduces wage spread and brings a similar standard of living within reach of all workers.

I have argued elsewhere (1986) that comparable worth is more revolutionary as a gender strategy than as a class strategy, however, and that, in fact, the economic-based resistance to comparable worth is really a cover for gender-based resistance. That is, many who argue against comparable worth do so on the grounds that it will disrupt the economy and throw people out of work. In my view, however, the policy is not revolutionary for the economy. The economy can adjust to the kinds of increases in wage costs that are typically occurring—5 to 10 percent of the total wage bill, often phased in over a number of years. Can this modest cost be revolutionary in any way? Why is it so modest, if revolutionary?

The modest cost makes sense when we consider what is known about wage differentials. The gross gap between women and men across the entire economy is about 40 percent; women earn about 60 percent of what men earn. Studies (see, for example, Treiman and Hartmann, 1981) indicate that about half of this difference can be regarded as due to differences in the attributes that women and men bring to the job, their education, training, and experience and are generally not regarded as being due to discrimination in the employment arena (although these differences too may be the result of discrimination somewhere in the process). Since comparable worth can be understood as attempting to remedy the results of discrimination, then, at most half the gap could be closed. If fully half the gap were closed, and if women made up half of an employer's labor force (a slight overestimate economy-wide, since women are now 43, percent of the labor force) the increase in the wage bill would be 12.5 percent. But that is a maximum estimate for the effects of comparable worth, because comparable worth can only get at that part of the wage gap that occurs within firms (not between firms). Research shows that much of the wage gap is due to the fact that women and men work for different kinds of employers as well as in different kinds of jobs; in general men work for employers who pay higher wages. Hence, we would expect it to cost less than 12.5 percent of the wage bill. Moreover, comparable worth would not change the basic nature of the labor market—a labor market in which there is still wage hierarchy, generally job scarcity and some unemployment, and functions in a capitalist economy.

But, I would argue comparable worth nevertheless has revolutionary implications for gender relations. Women whose wages are raised would receive increases in the neighborhood of 10 to 30 percent. Such increases would enhance their ability to be self-supporting or to contribute equally with their husbands to family income. Men would cease to have a monopoly on having sufficient income to support a family, and perhaps for the first time in human history, women would have free choice (at least not economically coerced choice) about whether to marry and live with men. Economic survival would not require it. If widely implemented, comparable worth is a reform with truly revolutionary implications in gender relations.

Comparable worth potentially has other progressive results as well: as a strategy it encourages collective struggle and unionization, and it encourages openness about the bases for remunerating work. Indeed the central reason comparable worth has emerged first in the public sector is that only in the public sector is information about wages and job requirements generally available. And as Acker points out, raising the compensation for features found in many women's jobs will have a tendency to reduce the gap between the high and the low paid and between managerial and non-managerial work.

In concluding, I would like to echo the statements others have made elsewhere in this volume. Comparable worth, to become a fully successful strategy for advancing women's economic position, must be coupled with other policies aimed at and beyond the labor market. Although we do not know the likely size of the effect, there is some danger that comparable worth, paying more for women's jobs, could lead to decreased employment in women's jobs (as price rises, demand falls). In the absence of a full employment policy or strenuous affirmative action efforts that open up all jobs in the economy to women, women are likely to bear the brunt of any unemployment that might result. This is why it is crucial that comparable worth be coupled with strong affirmative action policies and political pressure for full employment.

Moreover, comparable worth is but one plank in an overall agenda that would insure economic independence for women. Such an agenda would include adequate income support programs for those between jobs or unable to be employed as well as programs that entail recognition that child rearing and the well-being of children are responsibilities that must be publicly, as well as privately, supported. We must think about what women need in the broadest terms, understanding their class as well as their gender position and understanding as well their traditionally greater responsibilities for the care of other human beings.

CHAPTER 16

In Praise of Useable Research
for an Action Agenda

Cynthia H. Chertos

Ten years ago (1975) Martha Blaxall and Barbara Reagan organized a conference on women's employment entitled "The Implications of Occupational Segregation." Many of the papers presented were not unlike those presented at this conference on "Ingredients for Women's Employment Policy." Scholars documented women's employment status from a variety of disciplinary vantage points and made research and policy recommendations.

A contemporary review of that volume of papers is instructive, providing a sense of our progress in the last decade. Would our conference in 1985 just be a chance to get together and say it all again? Or would we have advanced our knowledge in the ten year period? I must report that as I reread those papers, I felt encouraged.

Ten years ago, the existence of occupational segregation had been well documented. Moreover, we not only knew where and how it existed, we had generated sound hypotheses as to why it existed; we also knew many of the consequences of it. Surprisingly, we had even made some good policy recommendations to reduce it, if we could not eliminate it altogether.

Yet, with all of that knowledge based on scholarly research completed over a decade ago, we still had a lot to learn. In both the universities and in the real world—the applied setting where the subjects of social science research live, we continued to have problems. We had implemented some Affirmative Action programs to integrate occupations, but we did not know how to make them successful. We had little or no understanding of the issue of pay equity either in a scholarly or an applied sense—it was not yet even a part of our vernacular. We had hypotheses about the effects of tipping—women increasingly entering formerly male occupations until they make up the majority—but we had little more than anecdotal evidence concerning that phenomenon. Our base of knowledge was insufficient to fully inform our policy decisions relating to these problems. Many of the research findings presented here are important pieces of the new informational core on which sound change programs and future research will be based.

I would like my comments to help move the discussion of research on women's employment issues away from research and intellectual pursuit for its own sake because we are interested in *knowing*, to a fuller discussion of the use of this knowledge, because we also are interested in *doing*.

As I reviewed Blaxall and Reagan's book, I found Kenneth Boulding's comments at that conference exceptionally helpful. They provide the context for my major point of discussion.[1] Boulding drew the distinction between positive science and normative science. As all social scientists know, positive science studies "what is," it "divides the possible from the impossible" to use Boulding's phrase. Normative science, on the other hand, studies what "should be." It is interesting to note that Boulding felt compelled to remind us that normative science is also a legitimate part of social science. When we do research on women's employment, many of us are involved in normative science: we are involved in conducting research so as to influence what we think should be.

A major problem for us is that positive science, by definition, constrains normative science. For, as Boulding pointed out, "what should be cannot be what cannot be" (p.76) according to positive science. That would almost stop those of us who want to use normative science to conduct analyses which will help us determine how to make the world a better place in which to live. Except, and I quote Boulding here one last time, "normative science can force us to widen the boundaries of the possible, for if something which is now not possible should be, we have an incentive to figure out how to make it possible" (p.76). For those of us who actively use social science research to make change, this is the real challenge. Concerning women's employment, the challenge is: how do we make access, opportunity, equality, and equity possible? How do we make those things happen?

Many of the papers presented at this conference raise explicit points about the status of women in our society. They describe contrasts between "what is" in a positivist sense and "what should be" in a normative sense. Virtually all of the authors assume that women should have access to the full range of employment opportunities. Many of the authors also assume that women should have pay equity—to be paid fairly for their work in traditionally lower paid female-dominated occupations. Although some research reported here is quite locally focused, other research is more global in scope. The methods used are very different, some reflect years of highly quantitative primary and secondary analyses, others utilize smaller qualitative intensive interviews. However, regardless of the scope and method selected, the normative conclusions of the papers most often are complementary.

What interests me greatly as an applied social scientist, straddling the fence between the scholarly and real worlds, is that very few authors ended their papers with a litany of ideas for future research projects which will tell us more about the status of women. Concluding with a list of further research needs is the traditional model for social science and it is surely useful in directing the scholarly agenda for the future. But all too often that is the only direction that is offered. Rather, most of the papers presented here lead us to a discussion of policy implications. From these papers we can build an agenda of interventions, of things to do to create employment equity for women.

I suggest that sociologists and other social scientists who know more about how our society and institutions operate than those in any other profession, write more reports, write more articles, and deliver more papers which not only present findings, or even make *broad* policy recommendations (for instance, that we integrate occupations), but which continue in this tradition to lead the way in explaining how to make things happen, how to change our social reality, how to make the society more equitable.

The papers presented at this conference do this. They direct us as to what we can *DO*. They are based on theory. They give us data, presented as findings, and they interpret their findings so that both scholars and practitioners will find them meaningful. They tell us what we still need to know in terms of future research. Then, most importantly, they tell us how their findings can be used now to improve the employment condition of women.

When social science does all of that, it rises to meet its full potential contribution to a society.

NOTES

1. See Martha Blaxall and Barbara Reagan (eds.), *Women and the Workplace,* The University of Chicago Press, Chicago, 1976. Especially of interest is Kenneth Boulding's "Comments I", pp 75-77.

References

Acker, Joan, 1985. "Societal Stratification: A Theoretical Analysis by Jonathan Turner," pp. 97–98. *Contemporary Sociology,* Vol. 14, No. 1, January.

_____, 1983. "Gender and the Construction of Class." Working paper. Eugene, Oregon: Center for the Study of Women in Society, University of Oregon.

_____, 1978. "Issues in the Sociological Study of Women's Work," In *Women Working: Theories and Facts in Perspective,* edited by Ann H. Stromberg and Shirley Harkess, pp. 134–161, Palo Alto: Mayfield Publishing.

Aldridge, Delores, 1975. "Black Women in the Economic Marketplace: A Battle Unfinished." *Journal of Social & Behavioral Scientists* 21 (Winter): 48–61.

Almquist, Elizabeth McTaggart, 1979. *Minorities, Gender and Work.* Lexington: D.C. Heath.

Almquist, Elizabeth M. and Shirley S. Angrist, 1970. "Career Salience and Atypicality of Occupational Choice Among College Women." *Journal of Marriage and the Family* 32:242–249.

American Federation of Labor-Congress of Industrial Organizations, 1985. *The Changing Situation of Workers and Their Unions.* Washington, D.C.:AFL-CIO News Release February 21.

Aneshensel, Carol S. and Bernard C. Rosen, 1980. "Domestic Roles and Sex Differences in Occupational Expectations." *Journal of Marriage and the Family* 42:121–131.

Angrist, Shirley, 1972. "Variations in Women's Adult Aspirations During College." *Journal of Marriage and the Family* 34:465–468.

Anyon, Jean, 1983. "Work, Labor and Economic History, and Textbook Content," In *Ideology and Practice in Schooling,* edited by Michael W. Apple and Lois Weis, pp. 37–61, Philadelphia: Temple University Press.

Ashmore, Richard D. and Frances K. Del Boca, 1986. "Gender Stereotypes." In *The Social Psychology of Female-Male Relations,* edited by R.D. Ashmore and F.K. Del Boca. Orlando, FL: Academic.

263

————, 1979. "Sex Stereotypes and Implicit Personality Theory: Toward a Cognitive-Social Psychological Conceptualization." *Sex Roles* 5:219–248.

Asian Studies Program, University of California-Los Angeles, 1979. "Asian Women as Leaders," In *Asian Women*, pp. 102–103, Los Angeles: Asian Studies Program, University of California, Los Angeles.

Barbanel, Josh, 1980. "Many New Lawyers Find Practice is Limited to Looking for Work." *New York Times*, November 4:B1.

Baron, James N. and William T. Bielby, 1985. "Organizational Barriers to Gender Equality: Sex Segregation of Jobs and Opportunities." pp. 233–252. In *Gender and the Life Course*, edited by A.S. Rossi, New York: Aldine.

————, forthcoming. "The Proliferation of Job Titles in Organizations," *Administrative Science Quarterly*.

Baron, James N., Alison Davis-Blake and William T. Bielby, 1986. "The Structure of Opportunity: How Promotion Ladders Vary Within and Among Organizations," *Administrative Science Quarterly*, June.

Baron, James N., Brian S. Mittman and Andrew S. Newman, 1985. "The Dynamics of Gender Inequality: Organizational and Environmental Influences on Sex Segregation in the California Civil Service, 1979–1985." Paper presented at the 45th Annual Meeting of the Academy of Management, San Diego, CA.

Barrera, Mario, 1979. *Race and Class in the Southwest*. Notre Dame: University of Notre Dame Press.

Bass, Bernard M., 1981. *Stodgill's Handbook of Leadership: A Survey of Theory and Research*. New York: The Free Press.

Batstone, Erik, Ian Boraston and Stephen Frankel, 1977. *Shop Stewards in Action*. Oxford: Basil Blackwell.

Beardsley, Richard K., John W. Hall and Robert E. Ward, 1959. *Village Japan*. Chicago, IL: The University of Chicago Press.

Beatty, Richard W. and James R. Beatty, 1984. "Some Problems with Contemporary Job Evaluation Systems," In *Comparable Worth and Wage Discrimination*, edited by Helen Remick, pp. 59–78, Philadelphia: Temple University Press.

Bellak, Alvin, 1982. "The Hay Guide-Chart—Profile Method of Job Evaluation," In *Handbook of Wage and Salary Administration*, 2nd edition, edited by Milton L. Rock, pp. 1511–16, New York: McGraw-Hill.

Beller, Andrea, 1984. "Trends in Occupational Segregation by Sex and Race, 1960–1981," In *Sex Segregation in the Workplace*, edited by Barbara Reskin, pp. 11–26, Washington D.C.: National Academy Press.

————, 1982. "Trends in Occupational Segregation by Sex, 1960–1981." Paper commissioned by the Committee on Women's Employment, National Research Council/National Academy of Sciences.

Bergquist, Virginia A., 1974. "Women's Participation in Labor Organizations," *Monthly Labor Review*, 97(10) October: 3–9.

Bertaux, Daniel, 1981. "From the Life-History Approach to the Transformation of Sociological Practice," In *Biography and Society: The Life History Approach in the Social Sciences*, edited by Daniel Bertaux, pp. 29–46, Beverly Hills, Ca: Sage Publications.

Bianchi, Suzanne and Nancy Rytina, 1984. "Occupational Change, 1970-1980." Paper presented at the Annual Meetings of the Population Association of America, Minneapolis, May.

Bielby, William T. and James N. Baron, 1986. "Men and Women at Work: Sex Segregation and Statistical Discrimination." *American Journal of Sociology* 91:759-799.

_____, 1984. "A Woman's Place is with Other Women: Sex Segregation within Organizations." In *Sex Segregation in the Workplace: Trends, Explanations, Remedies*, edited by Barbara F. Reskin, pp. 27-55, Washington, D.C.: National Academy Press.

Blakemore, Arthur E. and Stuart A. Low, 1984. "Sex Differences in Occupational Selection: The Case of College Majors." *Review of Economics and Statistics* 66(1):157-163.

Blau, Francine D., 1977. *Equal Pay in the Office*. Lexington, Mass: Heath.

Blau, Francine D. and Marianne A. Ferber, 1986. *The Economics of Women, Men and Work*. Englewood Cliffs, NJ: Prentice-Hall.

Blau, Francine D. and Andrea H. Beller, 1984. "Trends in Earnings Differentials by Sex and Race: 1971-1981." Paper presented at the American Economic Association Meetings, Dallas.

Blau, Francine D. and Wallace E. Hendricks, 1979. "Occupational Segregation by Sex: Trends and Prospects." *Journal of Human Resources* 14:197-210.

Blitz, Rudolph C., 1974. "Women in the Professions, 1870-1970." *Monthly Labor Review* (May)34-39.

Bluestone, Barry and Bennet Harrison, 1982. *The Deindustrialization of America: Plant Closings, Community Abandonment, and the Dismantling of Basic Industries*. New York: Basic Books.

Bock, E. Wilkin, 1971. "Farmer's Daughter Effect: The Case of the Negro Female Professionals." In *The Professional Woman*, edited by Athena Theodore, pp. 119-131, Cambridge, MA: Schenkman.

Bonacich, Edna and Lucie Cheng, 1984. "Introduction: A Theoretical Orientation to International Labor Migration." In *Labor Immigration Under Capitalism: Asian Workers in the United States Before World War II*, edited by Lucie Cheng and Edna Bonacich, pp. 1-56, Berkeley, CA: University of California Press.

Boraston, I., H.A. Clegg and M. Rimmer, 1975. *Workplace and Union*. London: Heinemann.

Bott, Elizabeth, 1957. *Family and Social Network: Roles, Norms, and External Relations in Ordinary Urban Families*. London: Tavistock.

Braden, Richard T., 1979. "Computerized Processing of Group Health Insurance Claims." *Bests Review, Life/Health* 79:92-96.

Braverman, Harry, 1974. *Labor and Monopoly Capital*. New York: Monthly Review Press.

Bridges, William, 1980. "Industry Marginality and Female Employment: A New Appraisal." *American Sociological Review* 45:58-75.

Brown, William, Robert Ebsworth and Michael Terry, 1978. "Factors Shaping Shop Stewards' Organization in Britain." *British Journal of Industrial Relations* 16:139-159.

Browning, Harley L. and Joachim Singlemann, 1978. "The Transformation of the U.S. Labor Force: The Interaction of Industry and Occupation." *Politics and Society* 3-4:481-509.

————, 1975. "The Emergence of a Service Society: Demographic and Sociological Aspects of the Sectoral Transformation of the Labor Force in the U.S.A." Springfield, VA: National Technical Information Service.

Bullock, Henry Allen, 1967. *A History of Negro Education in the South*. New York: Praeger Publishers.

Bumpass, Larry and Ronald R. Rindfuss, 1979. "Children's Experience of Marital Disruption." *American Journal of Sociology* 85(1):49-65.

Burke, Mary Jean, 1983. "The Change in the Proportion of Female Bus Drivers: 1960-1980." Graduate Seminar Paper, Indiana University.

Burris, Val and Amy Wharton, 1982. "Sex Segregation in the U.S. Labor Force." *Review of Radical Political Economics* 14 (Fall):43-56.

Burstein, Paul, 1985. *Discrimination, Jobs, and Politics*. Chicago: University of Chicago Press.

Burtless, Gary, 1983. "Why is Insured Unemployment So Low?" *Brookings Papers on Economic Activity I.*

Business Week, 1982. "The Instant Offshore Office." March 5, pp. 136-37.

Cain, Pamela Stone, 1985. "Prospects for Pay Equity in a Changing Economy." In *Comparable Worth: New Directions for Research,* edited by Heidi I. Hartmann, pp. 137-166. Washington, D.C.: National Academy Press.

Carter, Michael J. and Susan Boslego Carter, 1981. "Women's Recent Progress in the Professions or, Women Get a Ticket to Ride after the Gravy Train Has Left the Station." *Feminist Studies* 7(Fall):476-504.

Center for Budget and Policy Priorities, 1984. "An Analysis of the Impact of Reagan Policies on Female Headed Households." Washington, D.C.

Cerullo, Margaret with Roslyn Feldberg, 1984. "Introduction: Women Workers, Feminism and the Unions." *Radical America* 18(5) September-October:2-5.

Collins, Eliza G.C., 1983. "Managers and Lovers." *Harvard Business Review* 61(5):142-149.

Collins, Sharon, 1983. "The Making of the Black Middle Class." *Social Problems* 30 (April):369-382.

Cook, Alice H., 1984. "Introduction," In *Women and Trade Unions in Eleven Industrialized Countries,* edited by Alice H. Cook, Val R. Lorwin, and Arlene Kaplan Daniels, pp. 3-36, Philadelphia: Temple University Press.

————, 1983. *Comparable Worth: The Problem and States' Approaches to Wage Equity*. University of Hawaii at Manoa: Industrial Relations Center.

————, 1962. "Dual Government in Unions, A Tool for Analysis," *Industrial and Labor Relations Review* 15 (April):323-349.

Cooper, Joel and Russel H. Fazio, 1979. "The Formation and Persistence of Attributes that Support Intergroup Conflict." In *The Social Psychology of Intergroup Relations,* edited by William Austin and Stephen Worchel, pp. 149-159, Monterey, CA: Brooks/Cole Publishing.

Corcoran, Mary and George J. Duncan, 1979. "Work History, Labor Force Attachment, and Earnings Differences Between the Races and Sexes." *Journal of Human Resources* 1(Winter):3-20.

Corcoran, Mary, Greg J. Duncan, and Michael Ponza, 1984. "Work Experience, Job Segregation, and Wages." In *Sex Segregation in the Workplace: Trends, Explanations, Remedies*, edited by Barbara F. Reskin, pp. 171–191. Washington, D.C.: National Academy Press.

Cornfield, Daniel B., Polly A. Phipps, Diane P. Bates, Deborah K. Carter, Trudie W. Coker, Kathleen E. Kitzmiller, and Peter B. Wood, 1986. "Clerical Workers, Office Automation and Labor Relations in the Insurance Industry." Forthcoming in *Workers, Managers and Technological Change, Emerging Patterns of Labor Relations*, edited by Daniel B. Cornfield. New York: Plenum.

Council of Economic Advisors, 1973. *Economic Report of the President, 1973*. Washington, D.C.: Government Printing Office.

Dahm, Margaret and Phyllis Fineshriber, 1980. "Disqualifications for Quits to Meet Family Obligations," In *Unemployment Compensation: Studies and Research*. Washington, D.C.: National Commission on Unemployment Compensation.

D'Amico, Ronald J., R. Jean Haurin and Frank L. Mott, 1983. "The Effects of Mothers' Employment on Adolescent and Early Adult Outcomes of Young Men and Women." In *Children of Working Parents: Experiences and Outcomes*, edited by Cheryl D. Hayes and Sheila B. Kamerman, pp. 130–219. Washington, D.C.: National Academy Press.

Darley, J.M. and R.H. Fazio, 1980. "Expectancy Confirmation Sequences." *American Psychologist* 35:867–881.

Davies, Margery, 1982. *Woman's Place Is at the Typewriter*. Philadelphia: Temple University Press.

Deaux, Kay, 1985. "Sex and Gender." *Annual Review of Psychology* 36:49–81.

Deckard, Barbara, 1979. *The Women's Movement*. New York: Harper and Row.

Devens, Richard M. Jr., Carol E. Leon, and Debbie L. Springle, 1985. "Employment and Unemployment in 1984." *Monthly Labor Review* 108 (2) February:3–15.

Dill, Bonnie Thornton, 1983. " 'On the Hem of Life': Race, Class, and the Prospects for Sisterhood." In *Class, Race, and Sex: The Dynamics of Control*, edited by Amy Swerdlow and Hanna Lessinger, pp. 173–188. Boston: G.K. Hall.

Doeringer, Peter B. and Michael J. Piore, 1971. *Internal Labor Markets and Manpower Analysis*. Lexington, MA: D.C. Heath.

Donato, Katharine M., 1985. "Women in Systems Analysis." Unpublished preliminary case study. State University of New York, Stony Brook.

Donato, Katherine and Patricia Roos, 1985. "Gender and Earnings Inequality among Computer Specialists." Paper presented at American Sociological Association annual meeting, Washington, D.C., August.

Drake, St. Clair and Horace R. Cayton, 1970. *Black Metropolis*. New York: Harper Torchbook.

Dubnoff, Steven, 1979. "Beyond Sex Typing: Capitalism, Patriarchy and the Growth of Female Employment, 1940–1970." Paper presented at Eastern Sociological Society, New York, March.

Dumas, Rhetaugh Graves, 1980. "Dilemmas of Black Females in Leadership." In *The Black Woman*, edited by La Frances Rodgers-Rose, pp. 203–215. Beverly Hills, CA: Sage.

Duncan, Greg J., et al., 1984. *Years of Poverty, Years of Plenty*. Ann Arbor, Michigan: Institute for Social Research.

Embree, John F., 1939. *Suye Mura: A Japanese Village*. Chicago: The University of Chicago Press.

England, Paula, 1982. "The Failure of Human Capital Theory to Explain Occupational Sex Segregation." *Journal of Human Resources* 17 (3):358-70.

———, 1981. "Assessing Trends in Occupational Sex Segregation, 1900-1976." In *Sociological Perspectives on Labor Markets*, edited by Ivar Berg, pp. 273-295, New York: Academic Press.

England, Paula and Steven D. McLaughlin, 1979. "Sex Segregation of Jobs and Male-Female Income Differentials." In *Discrimination in Organizations*, edited by Rodolfo Alvarez et al., pp. 189-213, San Francisco: Jossey-Bass.

Epstein, Cynthia Fuchs, 1983. *Women in Law*. Garden City: Doubleday & Anchor.

———, 1973. "The Positive Effects of the Multiple Negative: Explaining the Success of Black Professional Women." *American Journal of Sociology* 78 (January): 912-35.

Etaugh, C., 1974. "Effects of Maternal Employment on Children: A Review of Recent Research." *Merrill-Palmer Quarterly* 20(2):71-98.

Etzioni, Amitai, ed., 1969. *The Semi-Professions and their Organization*. New York: Free Press.

Farnquist, Robert L., David R. Armstrong and Russel P. Strausbaugh, 1983. "Pandora's Worth: The San Jose Experience." *Public Personnel Management* 12(4):358-68.

Feldberg, Roslyn and Evelyn Nakano Glenn, 1977. "Degraded and Deskilled: The Proletarianization of Clerical Work." *Social Problems* 25 (July):52-64.

Ferree, Myra Marx, 1983. "German Feminist Approaches to Working Class Women and Work." University of Connecticut, stencil.

Fishman, Pamela M., 1982. "Interaction: The Work Women Do." In *Women and Work*, edited by Rachel Kahn-Hut, Arlene Kaplan Daniels, and Richard Colvad, pp. 170-180. New York: Oxford University Press.

Ford, W. Scott, 1984. "Interracial Public Housing in a Border City: Another Look at the Contact Hypothesis." *American Journal of Sociology* 78:1426-47.

Fox, Mary Frank and Sharlene Hesse-Biber, 1984. *Women at Work*. Palo Alto: Mayfield.

Freeman, Richard B. and James L. Medoff, 1984. "What Unionism Does to Nonorganized Labor." In *What Do Unions Do?*, edited by R. Freeman and J. Medoff, pp. 150-161, New York: Basic Books.

Friedland, Roger, 1983. *Power and Crisis in the City: Corporations, Unions and Urban Policy*. New York: Schocken Books.

Frye, V.H. and S.C. Dietz, 1973. "Attitudes of High School Students Toward Traditional View of Women Workers." *Journal of Student Personnel Association or Teacher Education* 11:102-108.

Gallup, George Jr., 1985. "Public Fears Poverty Spreading, Wants Redistribution of Wealth." *San Jose Mercury*, February 10: 8H.

Gettys, Linda D. and Arnie Cann, 1981. "Children's Perceptions of Occupational Sex Stereotypes." *Sex Roles* 7(3):301–308.

Glenn, Evelyn Nakano and Roslyn L. Feldberg, 1979. "Women as Mediators in the Labor Process." Paper presented at the 74th Annual Meeting of the American Sociological Association, Boston.

Goldberg, Roberta, 1983. *Organizing Women Office Workers: Dissatisfaction, Consciousness, and Action.* New York: Praeger Publishers.

Goodman, Leo A., 1976. "The Relationship Between Modified and Usual Multiple-Regression Approaches to the Analysis of Dichotomous Variables." In *Sociological Methodology,* edited by D. Heise, pp. 83–110, San Francisco: Jossey-Bass.

Goode, William C., 1982. "Why Men Resist." In *Rethinking the Family,* edited by Barrie Thorne with Marilyn Yalom, pp. 121–50, New York: Longman.

———, 1971. "Force and Violence in the Family." *Journal of Marriage and the Family* 33:624–36.

Goodman, J.F.B. and T.G. Whittingham, 1969. *Shop Stewards in British Industry.* London: McGraw-Hill.

Granovetter, Mark, 1981. "Toward a Sociological Theory of Income Differences." In *Sociological Perspectives on Labor Markets,* edited by Ivar Berg, pp. 11–47, New York: Academic Press.

Great Britain, Royal Commission on Trade Unions and Employers' Associations, 1968. *Report Presented to Parliament (The Donovan Report),* London: HMSO.

Greenbaum, Joan, 1976. "Division of Labor in the Computer Field." *Monthly Review* 28:19–39.

Greer, William R., 1986. "Women Now the Majority in Professions." *New York Times.* March 19:C1, C10.

Gregory, R.G., P. McMahon, and B. Whittingham, 1985. "Women in the Australian Labor Force: Trends, Causes, and Consequences." *Journal of Labor Economics* 3 (Supplement):S293–S310.

Gross, Edward, 1968. "Plus Ca Change . . . ? The Sexual Structure of Occupations over Time." *Social Problems* 16:198–208.

Hacker, Sally, 1979. "Sex Stratification, Technology and Organizational Change: A Longitudinal Analysis." *Social Problems* 26:539–57.

Hallock, Margaret, 1984. "Oregon's Comparable Worth Project." Paper prepared for Oregon Public Employees Union, SEIU Local 503, AFL-CIO, Salem, Oregon.

Hamilton, David L., 1981. *Cognitive Processes in Stereotyping and Intergroup Behavior.* Hillsdale, NJ: Erlbaum.

Hannan, Michael T. and John Freeman, 1984. "Structural Inertia and Organizational Change." *American Sociological Review* 49:149–64.

Hanushek, Eric A. and John E. Jackson, 1977. *Statistical Methods For Social Scientists.* A volume of *Quantitative Studies in Social Relations.* New York: Academic Press.

Hare, Nathan and Julie Hare, 1970. "Black Women, 1970." *Transaction* 8 (December):65–68, 90.

Harlan, Anne and Carol Weiss, 1981. "Moving Up: Women in Managerial Careers." Working Paper No. 86. Center for Research on Women, Wellesley College, Wellesley, MA.

Harrington, Michael, 1984. "Solidarity." *Democratic Left,* January-February.

Hartmann, Heidi I., 1986. "Pay Equity for Women: Wage Discrimination and the Comparable Worth Controversy." In *The Moral Foundations of Civil Rights,* edited by Robert K. Fullwinder and Claudia Mills, Totowa, NJ: Rowman and Littlefield.

————, 1985. *Comparable Worth: New Directions for Research.* Washington, D.C.: National Academy Press.

————, 1984. "Research Needs in Comparable Worth." Paper presented at the Annual Meeting of the Industrial Relations Research Association, ASSA, December 29, Dallas, Texas.

————, 1976. "Capitalism, Patriarchy and Job Segregation by Sex." In *Women and the Workplace: The Implications of Occupational Segregation,* edited by Martha Blaxall and Barbara Reagan, pp. 137–69, Chicago: University of Chicago Press.

Hartmann, Heidi I. and Donald J. Treiman, 1983. "Notes on the NAS Study of Equal Pay for Jobs of Equal Value." *Public Personnel Management* 12 (Winter):404–417.

Hartmann, Heidi I., Patricia A. Roos, and Donald J. Treiman, 1985. "An Agenda for Basic Research on Comparable Worth." In *Comparable Worth: New Directions for Research,* edited by Heidi I. Hartmann, pp. 3–36, Washington, D.C.: National Academy Press.

Hechter, Michael, 1978. "Group Formation and the Cultural Division of Labor." *American Journal of Sociology* 84:293–318.

Henley, Nancy and Jo Freeman, 1984. "The Sexual Politics of Interpersonal Behavior." In *Women: A Feminist Perspective,* edited by Jo Freeman, 2nd edition, pp. 391–401, Palo Alto: Mayfield.

Herbers, John, 1983. "Census Shows Gains in Jobs by Women and Blacks in '70's." *New York Times,* April 24:1, 38.

Hernandez, Aileen, 1981. "Dialogue with Elizabeth Almquist, Barbara Christian, Sharon Marley, Aileen Hernandez, Julianne Malveaux, Harriette McAdoo." In *Black Working Women.* Proceedings of a Conference on Black Working Women in the U.S., University of California, Berkeley.

Herzog, A. Regula, 1982. "High School Seniors' Occupational Plans and Values: Trends in Sex Differences 1976 Through 1980." *Sociology of Education* 55:1–13.

Hewitt, L.S., 1975. "Age and Sex Differences in the Vocational Aspirations of Elementary School Children." *Journal of Social Psychology* 96:173–77.

Higginbotham, Elizabeth, 1985. "Race and Class Barriers to Black Women's College Attendance." *Journal of Ethnic Studies* 13 (Spring):89–107.

Hills, Stephen M., forthcoming. "The Attitudes of Union and Nonunion Male Workers Toward Union Representation." *Industrial and Labor Relations Review.*

Hirata, Lucie Cheng, 1979. "Free, Indentured and Enslaved: Chinese Prostitutes in Nineteenth Century America." *Signs* 3:3–29.

Hoffman, Lois W., 1974. "Effects on Child." In *Working Mothers,* edited by Lois W. Hoffman and F. Ivan Nye, pp. 126–66, San Francisco: Jossey-Bass.

Howe, Louise Kapp, 1977. *Pink Collar Workers: Inside the World of Women's Work*. New York: Avon Books.

Hughes, Diane, 1984. "Earrings as Signs in the Italian Renaissance City." *The Committee for Gender Research*. No. 4, University of Michigan, Fall.

Hull, Gloria T., Patricia Bell Scott, and Barbara Smith, 1982. *But Some of Us Are Brave*. Old Westbury, NY: Feminist Press.

Ibraham, Barbara, 1980. "Social Change and the Industrial Experience: Women As Productive Workers in Urban Egypt." Unpublished doctoral dissertation, Indiana University.

Ichihashi, Yamato, 1932. *Japanese in the United States*. Stanford, CA: Stanford University Press.

Izraeli, Dafna N., 1982. "Avenue into Leadership for Women: The Case of Union Officers in Israel." *Economic and Industrial Democracy* 3:515-29.

Jackman, Mary R. and Marie Crane, 1985. " 'Some of My Best Friends Are Black...': Interracial Friendships and Whites' Racial Attitudes." Unpublished Manuscript.

Jackman, Mary R. and Michael J. Muha, 1984. "Education and Intergroup Attitudes." *American Sociological Review* 49:751-69.

Jacobs, Jerry, n.d. "Historical and Demographic Trends in Occupational Segregation by Sex." Unpublished manuscript, University of Pennsylvania.

Jarboe, Chris, 1985. "JTPA and Women Workers." May, Unpublished memo: Available from the author.

Joe, Tom, 1982. "Profile of Families in Poverty in FY 1982." Center for the Study of Social Policy, Washington, D.C.

Johnson, Charles S., 1969. *The Negro College Graduate*. College Park, MD: McGrath.

Johnson, Beverly L. and Elizabeth Waldman, 1983. "Most Women Who Maintain Families Receive Poor Labor Market Returns." *Monthly Labor Review* 106(12):30-34.

Jones, Jacqueline, 1985. *Labor of Love, Labor of Sorrow*. New York: Basic Books.

Kahn, Lawrence, 1978. "The Effect of Unions on the Earnings of Nonunion Workers." *Industrial and Labor Relations Review* 31 (2) January: 205-216.

Kahn, Si, 1982. "Leaders." In *Organizing: A Guide for Grassroots Leaders*, edited by S. Kahn, pp. 21-54, New York: McGraw-Hill.

Kalleberg, Arne, Michael Wallace, Karyn A. Loscocco, Kevin T. Leicht, and Hans-Melnut Ehm, 1986. "The Eclipse of Craft: The Changing Face of Labor in the Newspaper Industry." Forthcoming in *Workers, Managers, and Technological Change: Emerging Patterns of Labor Relations*, edited by Daniel B. Cornfield, New York: Plenum Press.

Kanter, Rosabeth Moss, 1977. *Men and Women of the Corporation*. New York: Basic Books.

Kaplan, David L. and M. Claire Casey, 1958. *Occupational Trends in the U.S. 1900 to 1950*. Working Paper No. 5. Washington, D.C.: Bureau of the Census.

Kaufman, Debra, 1984. "Professional Women: How Real Are the Recent Gains?" In *Women: A Feminist Perspective*, edited by Jo Freeman, 2nd edition, pp. 353-69, Palo Alto: Mayfield.

Katzman, David M., 1978. *Seven Days A Week*. New York: Oxford University Press.

Keniston, Kenneth, 1964. *The Uncommitted*. New York: Random House.

Kessler-Harris, Alice, 1982. *Out to Work*. New York: Oxford University Press.

Killingsworth, Mark R., 1985. "The Economics of Comparable Worth: Analytical, Empirical, and Political Questions." In *Comparable Worth: New Directions for Research*, edited by Heidi I. Hartmann, pp. 71–85. Washington, D.C.: National Academy Press.

Kilson, Marion, 1977. "Black Women in the Professions." *Monthly Labor Review* 100 (May):38–41.

Kitano, Harry H.L., 1976. *Japanese American: The Evolution of a Subculture*. 2nd edition, Englewood Cliffs, NJ: Prentice-Hall.

Klein, Sarah P., 1983. "Trends in Employment and Unemployment in Families." *Monthly Labor Review* 106 (December):21–25.

Kochan, Thomas A., 1979. "How American Workers View Labor Unions." *Monthly Labor Review* 102 (4) April:23–31.

Koziara, Karen S. and Patrice J. Insley, 1982. "Organizations of Working Women Can Pave the Way for Unions." *Monthly Labor Review* 105 (6) June: 53–54.

Koziara, Karen S. and David A. Pierson, 1980. "Barriers to Women Becoming Union Leaders." *Industrial Relations Research Association Proceedings*, Thirty-third Annual Meeting, Denver: 48–54.

Koziara, Karen S., Mary I. Bradley, and David A. Pierson, 1982. "Becoming a Union Leader: The Path to Local Office." *Monthly Labor Review* 105 (2) February:44–46.

Kraft, Philip, 1984. "Computers and the Automation of Work." Paper presented to the Conference on Technology and the Transformation of White Collar Work, Bell Communications Research, June 14–15, New Brunswick, NJ.

———, 1979. "The Industrialization of Computer Programming: From Programming to 'Software Production.' " In *Case Studies on the Labor Process*, edited by Andrew Zimbalist, pp. 1–17, New York: Monthly Review Press.

Kraft, Philip and Steven Dubnoff, 1983. "Software Workers Survey." *Computerworld*, November 14.

Kritt, Barbara, 1984. "Women in Baking." Unpublished preliminary case study, University of Michigan, Ann Arbor, MI.

Kuhn, Thomas S., 1970. *The Structure of Scientific Revolutions*. 2nd edition. Chicago: Chicago University Press.

Kusmer, Kenneth, 1978. *A Ghetto Takes Shape*. Urbana, IL: University of Illinois Press.

Larson, Magali Safatti, 1977. *The Rise of Professionalism: A Sociological Analysis*. Berkeley: University of California.

Law, Sylvia, 1983. "Women, Work, Welfare and the Preservation of Patriarchy." *University of Pennsylvania Law Review* 131 (6) May: 1249–339.

Lawler, Edward E. III, 1981. *Pay and Organizational Development*. Reading, MA: Addison-Wesley.

LeGrande, Linda H., 1978. "Women in Labor Organizations: Their Rankings are Increasing." *Monthly Labor Review* 101 (8) August:8–14.

Leon, Carol Boyd, 1982. "Occupation Winners and Losers: Who They Were During 1972-1980." *Monthly Labor Review* 105 (June):18–28.

Levin, Henry M. and Russell W. Rumberger, 1983. "The Educational Implications of High Technology." Project Report No. 83-A4, Institute for Research on Educational Finance and Governance, School of Education, Stanford University, February.

Lieberson, Stanley, 1980. *A Piece of the Pie*. Berkeley: University of California Press.

Lueptow, Lloyd B., 1981. "Sex-Typing and Change in the Occupational Choices of High School Seniors: 1964-1975." *Sociology of Education* 54:16-24.

Maccoby, E.E. and C.N. Jacklin, 1974. *The Psychology of Sex Differences*. Stanford, CA: Stanford University Press.

Macke, Anne Statham and William E. Morgan, 1978. "Maternal Employment, Race, and Work Orientation of High School Girls." *Social Forces* 57(1):187-204.

Major, Brenda, Dean B. McFarlin, and Diana Gagnon, 1984. "Overworked and Underpaid: On the Nature of Gender Differences In Personal Entitlement." *Journal of Personality and Social Psychology* 47:1399-1412.

Malveaux, Julianne, 1984. "The Status of Women of Color in the Economy: The Legacy of Being Other." Paper presented at the National Conference on Women; The Economy and Public Policy, June 19-20.

————, 1981. "Shifts in the Occupational and Employment Status of Black Women; Current Trends and Future Implications." In *Black Working Women*, Proceedings of a Conference on Black Working Women in the U.S., University of California, Berkeley.

Marini, Margaret Mooney and Mary C. Brinton, 1984. "Sex Typing and Occupational Socialization." In *Sex Segregation in the Workplace: Trends, Explanations, Remedies*, edited by Barbara F. Reskin, pp. 192-232. Washington, D.C.: National Academy Press.

Marsh, Arthur, 1973. *Managers and Shop Stewards Shop Floor Revolution*, London: Institute of Personnel Management.

Marshall, Ray and Beth Paulin, 1984. "The Employment and Earnings of Women: The Comparable Worth Debate." In *Comparable Worth: Issue for the '80's*, Vol. 1, pp. 196-214, Washington, D.C.: U.S. Commission on Civil Rights.

Mason, Karen O., J.L. Czajka, and S. Arber, 1973. "Change in U.S. Women's Sex Role Attitudes, 1964-1974." *American Sociological Review* 41:573-96.

Matney, Williams, 1983. "America's Black Population." Washington, D.C.: U.S. Bureau of the Census (PIO/POP-83-1).

McAdams, Kenneth G., 1974. "Job Evaluation and Classification." *Journal of American Water Works Association* 66 (7):405-409.

McArthur, Leslie Zebrowitz, 1985. "Social Judgement Biases in Comparable Worth Analysis." In *Comparable Worth: New Directions for Research*, edited by Heidi I. Hartmann, pp. 53-70. Washington, D.C.: National Academy Press.

McCarthy, W.E.J., 1966. *The Role of Shop Stewards in British Industrial Relations*. London: Royal Commission on Trade Unions And Employers' Associations.

McCarthy, W.E.J. and S.R. Parker, 1968. *Shop Stewards and Workshop Relations*. Royal Commission on Trade Unions and Employers' Associations, Research Paper No. 10, London: HMSO.

McCormick, Ernest J., P.R. Jenneret, and Robert C. Mecham, 1969. *Position Analysis Questionnaire*. West Lafayette, Indiana: Purdue University.

McPherson, J. Miller and Lynne Smith-Lovin, 1986. "Sex Segregation in Voluntary Associations." *American Sociological Review* 51:61–79.

Mercury News Wire Services, 1984. "Court Helps Ailing Firms Break Union Contracts." *San Jose Mercury,* February 23:1A.

Michl, Thomas, 1985. "The Crisis of U.S. Trade Unions." *Monthly Review* 36 (10) March: 60–64.

Milkman, Ruth, 1980. "Organizing the Sexual Division of Labor: Historical Perspectives on 'Women's Work' and the American Labor Movement." *Socialist Review* 49:95–150.

Milkovich, George T., 1980. "The Emerging Debate." In *Comparable Worth: Issues and Alternatives,* edited by E. Robert Livernash, pp. 23–48, Washington, D.C.: Equal Employment Advisory Council.

Miller, Delbert C. and William H. Form, 1951. *Industrial Sociology*. New York: Harper.

Miller, S.M. and Donald Tomaskovic-Devey, 1983. *Recapitalizing America: Alternatives to the Corporate Distortion of National Policy*. Boston: Routledge and Kegan Paul.

Millis, H.A., 1915. *The Japanese Problem in the United States*. New York: MacMillan.

Mills, C. Wright, 1948. *The New Men of Power: America's Labor Leaders*. New York: Harcourt, Brace and Company.

Mincer, Jacob and Solomon Polachek, 1978. "Women's Earnings Reexamined." *Journal of Human Resources* 13 (Winter):118–34.

———, 1974. "Family Investments in Human Capital: Earnings of Women." *Journal of Political Economy* 82 (2) March/April: S76–S108.

Mortimer, Delores M. and Roy S. Bryce-Laporte, 1981. *Female Immigrants to the United States: Caribbean, Latin American and African Experiences*. Occasional Paper No. 2, Research Institute on Immigration and Ethnic Studies, Washington, D.C.: Smithsonian Institution.

Moskowitz, Daniel B., 1985. "A New Drive to 'Reaganize' Equal Opportunity." *Business Week* 2885:42.

Myrdal, Gunnar, 1962. *An American Dilemma*. New York: Harper and Row.

Nakane, Chie, 1967. *Kinship and Economic Organization in Rural Japan*. London School of Economics Monograph on Social Anthropology No. 32, London: The Atholone Press.

Nash, Al, 1983. *The Union Steward: Duties, Rights and Status*. Ithaca, NY: ILR Press.

National Longitudinal Study of Youth Labor Market Behavior, Ohio State University, Columbus, Ohio.

Nelson, Anne, 1984. "Women in High-Level Union Offices." A Paper presented to the Third Women and Organizations Conference, Boston, MA, August.

Newman, Dorothy K., Nancy Amider, Barbara Carter, Daron Day, William Kruvant, and Jack Russell, 1978. *Protest, Politics and Prosperity*. New York: Pantheon Books.

New York Times, 1984. "Unions Battle Against Jobs in the Home." Bill Keller, May 20: 1, 35.

Nicholson, Nigel, 1978. "The Role of the Shop Steward: An Empirical Case Study." *Industrial Relations Journal* 9:32–41.

Nicholson, Nigel, Gill Ursell, and Paul Blyton, 1981. *The Dynamics of White Collar Unionism: A Study of Local Union Participation*. London: Academic Press.

Noble, Kenneth B., 1985. "Fading Labor Power Means Fewer Strikes." *San Jose Mercury*, March 26:2F.

Norwood, Janet, 1982. "The Female-Male Earnings Gap: A Review of Employment and Earnings Issues." *Bureau of Labor Statistics Report* 673:2, Washington, D.C.

Nussbaum, Karen, 1982. Personal Communication, (Nine to Five) Local of Service Employees International Union, Cleveland, OH.

Nyden, Philip W., 1984. *Steelworkers Rank-and-File: The Political Economy of a Union Reform Movement*. New York: Praeger Publishers.

O'Connor, James, 1984. *Accumulation Crisis*. New York: Basil Blackwell.

O'Farrell, Brigid and Sharon L. Harlan, 1984. "Job Integration Strategies: Today's Programs and Tomorrow's Needs." In *Sex Segregation in the Workplace: Trends, Explanations, Remedies*, edited by Barbara F. Reskin, pp. 267–91, Washington, D.C.: National Academy Press.

O'Neill, June, 1984. "An Argument Against Comparable Worth." In *Comparable Worth: Issue for the '80's*, vol.1, pp. 177–86, Washington, D.C.: U.S. Commission on Civil Rights.

Oppenheimer, Valerie, 1970. *The Female Labor Force in the United States*. Berkeley, CA: University of California Press.

_____, 1968. "The Sex-labeling of Jobs." *Industrial Relations* 7 (May):219–34.

Oregon Task Force on State Compensation and Classification Minutes, November 1983-July 1985. Salem, Oregon: Archives of the State of Oregon.

Osofsky, Gilbert, 1971. *Harlem: The Making of a Ghetto*. New York: Harper and Row.

Osterman, Paul, 1984. "Introduction: The Nature and Importance of Internal Labor Markets." In *Internal Labor Markets*, edited by Paul Osterman, pp. 1–22, Cambridge: MIT Press.

Patterson, Michelle and Laurie Engleberg, 1978. "Women in Male-Dominated Professions." In *Working Women*, edited by Ann Stromberg and Shirley Harkess, pp. 266–92, Palo Alto: Mayfield.

Pavetti, Donna, 1985. "Low-Income Women Workers and Comparable Worth." Unpublished paper, available from the author, January.

Pearce, Diana, 1985. "Toil and Trouble: Women Workers and Unemployment Compensation." *Signs* 10 (3) Spring:439–59.

Peck, Sidney M., 1963. *The Rank-and-File Leader*. New Haven, CT: College and University Press.

Pedler, M., 1973. "Shop Stewards as Leaders." *Industrial Relations Journal* 4:43–60.

Peterson, Iver, 1983. "Women Far Surpass Men in Gains in Employment over the Recession." *New York Times*, September 3:9.

Pettigrew, Thomas R., 1969. "Racially Separate or Together?" *Journal of Social Issues* 25:43–69.

Phillips, Anne and Barbara Taylor, 1980. "Sex and Skill: Notes Towards a Feminist Economics." *Feminist Review* 6:79–88.

Phipps, Polly A., 1985a. "Preliminary Case Study of Pharmacists." University of Michigan, Ann Arbor.

————, 1985b. "Occupational Resegregation: A Case Study of Insurance Adjusters, Examiners and Investigators." To be presented at the 1986 Meetings of the American Sociological Association, New York City.

Phizacklea, Annie. 1983. *One Way Ticket*. London: Routledge, Kegan Paul.

Piore, Michael J., 1979. *Birds of Passage*. Cambridge: Cambridge University Press.

Piven, Frances Fox and Richard A. Cloward, 1982. *The New Class War: Reagan's Attack on the Welfare State and Its Consequences*. New York: Pantheon Books.

Pleck, Elizabeth H., 1979. "A Mother's Wages: Income Earning Among Married Italian and Black Women, 1896-1911." In *A Heritage of Her Own: Toward A New Social History of American Women*, edited by Nancy F. Cott and Elizabeth Pleck, pp. 367-98, New York: Simon and Schuster.

Polachek, Solomon W., 1984. "Women in the Economy: Perspectives on Gender Inequality." In *Comparable Worth: Issues for the '80's*, pp. 34-53, U.S. Commission on Civil Rights. Washington, D.C.: Government Printing Office.

————, 1979. "Occupational Segregation Among Women: Theory, Evidence, and A Prognosis." In *Women in the Labor Market*, edited by Cynthia B. Lloyd, Emily S. Andrews, and Curtis L. Gilroy, pp. 137-57, New York: Columbia University Press.

————, 1975. "Discontinuous Labor Force Participation and Its Effect on Women's Market Earnings." In *Sex, Discrimination, and the Division of Labor*, edited by Cynthia B. Lloyd, pp. 90-122, New York: Columbia University Press.

Portman, Lisa, Joy Ann Grune, and Eva Johnson, 1984. "The Role of Labor." In *Comparable Worth and Wage Discrimination*, edited by Helen Remick, pp. 219-37, Philadelphia: Temple University Press.

Power, Marilyn, 1984. "Falling Through the 'Safety Net': Women, Economic Crisis, and Reaganomics." *Feminist Studies* 10 (1) Spring:31-58.

Prial, Frank J., 1982. "More Women Work at Traditional Male Jobs." *New York Times*, November 15:A1, C20.

Priebe, John, 1980. "Occupational Classification in the 1980's." Paper presented at the Southern Sociological Society.

Raphael, Edna E., 1974. "Working Women and Their Membership in Labor Unions." *Monthly Labor Review* 97 (5) May:27-33.

Reinhold, Robert, 1980. "Government Takes Steps to Avert Glut of Doctors." *New York Times*, September 2: C1, C2.

Remick, Helen, 1984a. *Comparable Worth and Wage Discrimination: Technical Possibilities and Political Realities*. Philadelphia: Temple University Press.

————, 1984b. "Dilemmas of Implementation: The Case of Nursing." In *Comparable Worth and Wage Discrimination*, edited by Helen Remick, pp. 90-98, Philadelphia: Temple University Press.

————, 1984c. "Major Issues in *a priori* Applications." In *Comparable Worth and Wage Discrimination*, edited by Helen Remick, pp. 99-117, Philadelphia: Temple University Press.

————, 1980. "Beyond Equal Pay for Equal Work: Comparable Worth in the State of Washington." In *Equal Employment Policy for Women*, edited by Ronnie Steinberg-Ratner, pp. 405-19, Philadelphia: Temple University Press.

————, 1979. "Strategies for Creating Sound Bias-Free Job Evaluation Systems."

In *Job Evaluation and EEO: The Emerging Issues*, pp. 85-112, New York: Industrial Relations Counselors, Inc.

Remick, Helen and Ronnie Steinberg, 1984. "Technical Possibilities and Political Realities." In *Comparable Worth and Wage Discrimination*, edited by Helen Remick, pp. 285-302, Philadelphia: Temple University Press.

Reskin, Barbara F. and Patricia A. Roos, 1985. "Collaborative Research on the Determinants of Changes in Occupations' Sex Composition between 1970 and 1980." National Science Foundation Grant No. 85-NSF-SES-85-12452, March.

Reskin, Barbara F. and Heidi Hartmann, 1985. *Women's Work, Men's Work: Segregation on the Job*. Washington, D.C.: National Academy Press.

Rich, Adrienne, 1980. "Compulsory Heterosexuality and Lesbian Existence." *Signs* 5(4):631-60.

Riche, Richard W., *et al.*, 1983. "High Technology Today and Tomorrow: Small Slice of Employment." *Monthly Labor Review* 106 (November):50-58.

Robertson, Don and Tom Schuller, 1982. *Stewards, Members and Trade Union Training*. Glasgow: Center for Research in Industrial Democracy and Participation, Glasgow University.

Roos, Patricia A., 1983. "Marriage and Women's Occupational Attainment in Cross-Cultural Perspective." *American Sociological Review* 48:852-64.

———, 1981. "Sex Stratification in the Workplace: Male-Female Differences in Economic Returns to Occupation." *Social Science Research* 10:195-224.

Roos, Patricia A. and Barbara F. Reskin, 1984. "Institutional Factors Contributing to Sex Segregation in the Workplace." In *Sex Segregation in the Workplace: Trends, Explanations, Remedies*, edited by Barbara F. Reskin, pp. 235-60. Washington, D.C.: National Academy Press.

Rosen, Bernard C. and Carol S. Aneshensel, 1978. "Sex Differences in the Educational-Occupational Expectation Process." *Social Forces* 57(1):164-86.

Rosen, Sumner M., 1982. "Labor—A Movement at Risk?" In *What Reagan Is Doing To Us*, edited by Alan Gartner, Colin Greer, and Frank Riessman, pp. 206-29, New York: Harper and Row.

Rosenbaum, James E., 1985. "Jobs, Job Status, and Women's Gains from Affirmative Action: Implications for Comparable Worth." In *Comparable Worth: New Directions for Research*, edited by Heidi I. Hartmann, pp. 116-36, Washington, D.C.: National Academy Press.

Rosenfeld, Rachel, 1983. "Sex Segregation and Sectors: An Analysis of Gender Differences in Returns from Employer Changes." *American Sociological Review* 48:637-55.

Rosenthal, Jack, 1972. "For Women, A Decade of Widening Horizons." *New York Times*, April 10:1.

Rotella, Elyce J. and Robert A. Margo, 1981. "Sex Differences in the Market for School Personnel: Houston, Texas, 1892-1923." Department of Economics, Wellesley College Working Paper No. 45.

Rule, Sheila, 1982. "Blacks Believe White Women Lead in Job Gains." *New York Times*, March 25:B14.

Rumberger, Russell and Henry Levin, 1983. "The Educational Implications of High Technology." Project Report #83-84. Institute for Research in Educational Finance and Governance, Stanford University.

Rytina, Nancy F. and Suzanne M. Bianchi, 1984. "Occupational Reclassification and Changes in Distribution in Gender." *Monthly Labor Review* 107 (March):11–17.

Salancik, Gerald R., 1977. "Commitment and the Control of Organizational Behavior and Belief." In *New Directions in Organizational Behavior*, edited by Barry Staw and Gerald Salancik, pp. 1–54, Chicago: St. Clair.

San Jose Mercury, Editors, 1985. "New Union Goals." *San Jose Mercury*, March 13:8B.

Sargent, Jon, 1982. "The Job Outlook for College Graduates During the 1980's." *Occupational Outlook Quarterly* (Summer):1–5.

Sarri, Rosemary, 1984. "The Impact of Federal Policy Change on AFDC Recipients and their Families." Center for Policy Studies, Institute for Social Research, University of Michigan, Ann Arbor, Michigan.

Saxton, Alexander, 1971. *The Indispensable Enemy: Labor and the Anti-Chinese Movement in California*. Berkeley, CA: University of California Press.

Sayles, Leonard R. and George Strauss, 1953. *The Local Union: Its Place in the Industrial Plant*. New York: Harper and Row.

Schafran, Lynne Hecht, 1981. *Removing Financial Support from Private Clubs that Discriminate against Women*. New York: Women and Foundations Corporate Philanthropy.

Schuller, Tom and Don Robertson, 1983a. "Union Representatives and Their Members: Learning and Communication." *New Zealand Journal of Industrial Relations* 8:179–92.

———, 1983b. "How Representatives Allocate Their Time: Shop Steward Activity and Membership Contact." *British Journal of Industrial Relations* 21 (3):330–42.

Schwab, Donald P., 1980. "Job Evaluation and Pay Setting: Concepts and Practices." In *Comparable Worth: Issues and Alternatives*, edited by E. Robert Livernash, pp. 49–78, Washington, D.C.: Equal Employment Advisory.

Sen, Gita, 1980. "The Sexual Division of Labor and the Working Class Family: Towards a Conceptual Synthesis of Class Relations and the Subordination of Women." *The Review of Radical Political Economy* 12 (2) Summer:76–86.

Service Employees International Union, 1984. "Report to the Clerical Division." Dearborn, Michigan: 18th International Convention, May.

Sewell, William H. and Robert M. Hauser, 1975. *Education, Occupation and Earnings: Achievements in the Early Career*. New York: Academic Press.

Shack-Marquez, Janice, 1984. "Earnings Differences Between Men and Women: An Introductory Note." *Monthly Labor Review* 107 (June):15–16.

Shea, John R., *et al.*, 1970. *Dual Careers: A Longitudinal Study of Labor Market Experience of Women*. Vol. I, Columbus, Ohio: Center for Human Resource Research.

Shaeffer, Ruth G. and Edith F. Lynton, 1979. *Corporate Experiences in Improving Women's Job Opportunities*. Report No. 755, New York: The Conference Board.

Shepela, Sharon Toffey and Ann T. Viviano, 1984. "Some Psychological Factors Affecting Job Segregation and Wages." In *Comparable Worth and Wage Discrimination*, edited by Helen Remick, pp. 47–58, Philadelphia: Temple University Press.

Silvestri, George, *et al.*, 1983. "Occupational Employment Projections through 1995." *Monthly Labor Review* 106 (November):37–49.

Singleman, Joachim and Harley L. Browning, 1980. "Industrial Transformation and Occupational Change in the U.S., 1960–70." *Social Forces* 59 (September):246–64.

Singleman, Joachim and Marta Tienda, 1985. "The Process of Occupational Change in a Service Society: The Case of the United States, 1960–80." In *New Approaches to Economic Life: Economic Restructuring, Unemployment and the Social Division of Labor*, edited by Bryan Roberts, Ruth Finnegan, and Duncan Gallie, pp. 48–67, Manchester, England: University of Manchester Press.

Smith, Dorothy E., 1979. "A Sociology for Women." In *The Prism of Sex: Essays in the Sociology of Knowledge*, edited by Julia A. Sherman and Evelyn Torton Beck, pp. 135–87, Madison: University of Wisconsin Press.

_____, 1977. *Feminism and Marxism: A Place to Begin, A Way to Go*. Vancouver, Canada: New Star Books.

Smith, James P. and Michael P. Ward, 1984. *Women's Wages and Work in the Twentieth Century*. The Rand Corporation, R-3119-NICHD.

Smith, James P. and Finis Welch, 1984. "Affirmative Action and Labor Markets." *Journal of Labor Economics* 2:269–301.

Smith, Peter B., 1973. *Groups Within Organizations*. London: Harper and Row.

Smith, Robert J. and Ella Lury Wiswell, 1982. *The Women of Suye Mura*. Chicago: The University of Chicago Press.

Smith, Shelley A. and Marta Tienda, forthcoming. "The Doubly Disadvantaged: Women of Color in the U.S. Labor Force." In *Women Working*, edited by Ann Stromberg and Shirley Harkess, 2nd edition, Mayfield Publishing Company.

Sokoloff, Natalie J., 1986. "A Review of Sex and Race Segregation in the Occupational Literature: A Profile of the General Labor Force and the Professions." Paper presented at the American Sociological Association Meetings, New York.

_____, 1980. *Between Money and Love: The Dialectics of Women's Home and Market Work*. New York: Praeger Publishers.

Spear, Allan, 1967. *Black Chicago: The Making of a Ghetto*. Chicago: University of Chicago Press.

Steinberg, Ronnie, 1984. "A Want of Harmony: Perspective on Wage Discrimination and Comparable Worth." In *Comparable Worth and Wage Discrimination*, edited by Helen Remick, pp. 3–27, Philadelphia: Temple University Press.

Steinberg, Ronnie, Carol Possin, and Donald Treiman, 1984. *Job Content Questionnaire*. Albany, NY: Center for Women in Government.

Stevenson, Mary, 1975. "Women's Wages and Job Segregation." In *Labor Market Segmentation*, edited by Richard Edwards, Michael Reich, and David Gordon, pp. 243–55, Lexington, MA: D.C. Heath.

Stinchcombe, Arthur L., 1965. "Social Structure and Organizations." In *Handbook of Organizations*, edited by James G. March, pp. 142–93, Chicago: Rand McNally.

Stolzenberg, Ross M., 1982. "Industrial Profits and the Propensity to Employ Women Workers." Paper presented at the Workshop on Job Segregation by Sex, Committee on Women's Employment, National Research Council, Washington, D.C.: May.

Strober, Myra H. and Carolyn Arnold, 1984a. "The Dynamics of Occupational Segregation by Gender: Bank Tellers." Paper presented at the Conference on Gender in the Workplace, Washington, D.C.

———, 1984b. "Integrated Circuits/Segregated Labor: Women in 3 Computer Related Occupations." Project Report No. 84-A27, Institute for Research on Educational Finance and Governance, Stanford University, Stanford, CA.

Strober, Myra H. and Laura Best, 1979. "The Female/Male Salary Differential in Public Schools: Some Lessons from San Francisco, 1879." *Economic Inquiry* 17:218–36.

Sweezy, Paul M., 1984. "What's Wrong With the American Economy?" *Monthly Review* 36 (1) May:1–10.

Szymanski, Albert, 1974. "Race, Sex, and the U.S. Working Class." *Social Problems* 21 (June):706–25.

Tentler, Leslie Woodcock, 1979. *Wage-Earning Women*. New York: Oxford University Press.

Terry, Michael, 1982. "Organizing a Fragmented Workforce: Shop Stewards in Local Government." *British Journal of Industrial Relations* 20 (1) March:1–19.

Terry, Sylvia, 1983. "Work Experience, Earnings, and Family Income in 1981." *Monthly Labor Review* 106 (April):13–20.

Theodore, Athena, 1971. "The Professional Woman: Trends and Prospects." In *The Professional Woman*, edited by Athena Theodore, pp. 1–35, Cambridge: Schenkman.

———, 1971. *The Professional Woman*. Cambridge: Schenkman.

Thompson, E.P., 1978. *The Poverty of Theory and Other Essays*. New York: Monthly Review Press.

———, 1963. *The Making of the English Working Class*. New York: Random House.

Tienda, Marta, Leif I. Jensen, and Robert L. Bach, 1984. "Immigration, Gender, and the Process of Occupational Change." *International Migration Review* 18 (4):1021–44.

Tienda, Marta and Jennifer Glass, 1985. "Household Structure and Labor Force Participation of Black, Hispanic and White Mothers." *Demography* 22 (3):381–94.

Tienda, Marta, Vilma Ortiz, and Shelley A. Smith, 1985. "Industrial Restructuring and Earnings: A Comparison of Men and Women." Unpublished manuscript, University of Wisconsin-Madison.

Tilly, Louise A. and Joan W. Scott, 1978. *Women, Work and Family*. New York: Holt, Rinehart and Winston.

Touhey, John C., 1974. "Effects of Additional Women Professionals on Ratings of Occupational Prestige and Desirability." *Journal of Personality and Social Psychology* 29:86–89.

Treiman, Donald J., 1984. "Effect of Choice of Factors and Factor Weights in Job Evaluation." In *Comparable Worth and Wage Discrimination*, edited by Helen Remick, pp. 79–89, Philadelphia: Temple University Press.

_____, 1979. *Job Evaluation: An Analytic Review*. Washington, D.C.: National Academy of Sciences.

Treiman, Donald J. and Heidi I. Hartmann, 1981. *Women, Work and Wages: Equal Pay for Jobs of Equal Value*. Washington, D.C.: National Academy Press.

Treiman, Donald J. and Kermit Terrell, 1975. "Women, Work, and Wages: Trends in the Female Occupational Structure since 1940." In *Social Indicator Models*, edited by Kenneth C. Land and Seymour Spilerman, pp. 157–200, New York: Russell Sage Foundation.

Treiman, Donald J., Heidi I. Hartmann, and Patricia A. Roos, 1984. "Assessing Pay Discrimination Using National Data." In *Comparable Worth and Wage Discrimination*, edited by Helen Remick, pp. 137–54, Philadelphia: Temple University Press.

Tyack, David B., 1974. *The One Best System: A History of American Urban Education*. Cambridge: Harvard University Press.

Tyack, David B. and Myra H. Strober, 1981. "Jobs and Gender: A History of the Structuring of Educational Employment by Sex." In *Educational Policy and Management*, edited by Patricia Schmuck and W.W. Carters, pp. 131–52, New York: Academic Press.

U.S. Bureau of the Census, 1985. *Money Income and Poverty Status of Families and Persons in the United States, 1984*. Current Population Reports, Series P-60, No. 149, Washington, D.C.: U.S. Government Printing Office.

_____, 1984. *Detailed Occupations of the Experienced Civilian Labor Force by Sex for the United States and Regions: 1980 and 1970*. Supplementary Report PC80-S-15, Washington, D.C., U.S. Department of Commerce.

_____, 1983a. *Detailed Occupations and Years of School Completed by Age, for the Civilian Labor Force by Sex, Race, and Spanish Origin: 1980*. Supplementary Report PC80-S1-8, Washington, D.C., U.S. Department of Commerce.

_____, 1983b. *Census of Population and Housing 1980: Public Use Microdata Samples, Technical Documentation*. Washington, D.C.: U.S. Government Printing Office.

_____, 1983c. *Characteristics of the Population: General Social and Economic Characteristics*. PC 80-1-C1. Washington, D.C.: Government Printing Office.

_____, 1982. *Statistical Abstract of the United States, 1982–83* (103d edition). Washington, D.C.: U.S. Government Printing Office.

_____, 1972. *Public Use Samples of Basic Records from the 1970 Census: Description and Technical Documentation*. Washington, D.C.: U.S. Government Printing Office.

_____, 1943. *Statistical Abstracts of the United States, 1942*. Washington, D.C.: Government Printing Office.

U.S. Department of Labor, Bureau of Labor Statistics, 1986a. *Employment and Earnings*. Washington, D.C.: Government Printing Office. January.

———, 1986b. *Employment and Earnings*. Washington, D.C.: Government Printing Office, February.

———, 1985. *Employment and Earnings*. Vol. 32, No. 8, (July) Washington, D.C.: U.S. Government Printing Office.

———, 1984. *Employment and Earnings*. Vol. 31, No. 12 Table A-23. Washington, D.C.: Government Printing Office.

———, 1983. *Employment and Earnings*. Washington, D.C.: Government Printing Office.

———, 1981. *Employment and Unemployment: A Report on 1980*. Special Labor Force Report 244, Washington, D.C.: Government Printing Office.

———, 1980. *Perspectives on Working Women: A Databook*. Bulletin 2080, Washington, D.C.

———, 1979. "Earnings and Other Characteristics of Organized Workers, May 1977." Report No. 556, Washington, D.C.: Government Printing Office.

U.S. Women's Bureau, Department of Labor, 1975. *1975 Handbook on Women Workers*, Bulletin 297.

Ursell, G.D.M., T.D. Clegg, C.W. Lubbock, P.R. Blyton, and Nigel Nicholson, 1979. "Shop Stewards' Attitudes to Industrial Democracy." *Industrial Relations Journal* 10:22-30.

van den Berghe, Pierre, 1960. "Distance Mechanisms of Stratification." *Sociology and Social Research* 44:155-64.

Walshok, Mary Lindenstein, 1981. *Blue Collar Women: Pioneers on the Male Frontier*. New York: Anchor Books.

Wallace, Phyllis A., 1980. *Black Women in the Labor Force*. Cambridge: MIT Press.

Watanabe, Theresa M., 1977. *A Report from the Japanese American Community Study*. Seattle, WA: Department of Anthropology, University of Washington.

Welter, Barbara, 1966. "The Cult of True Womanhood: 1820-1860." *American Quarterly* 43:151-74.

Wertheimer, Barbara Mayer, 1984. "The United States of America." In *Women and Trade Unions in Eleven Industrialized Countries*, edited by Alice H. Cook, Val R. Lorwin, and Arlene Kaplan Daniels, pp. 286-311, Philadelphia: Temple University Press.

Wertheimer, Barbara M. and Anne H. Nelson, 1975. *Trade Union Women: A Study of Their Participation in New York City Locals*. New York: Praeger Publishers.

Westcott, Diane Nilsen, 1982. "Blacks in the 1970s: Did They Scale the Job Ladder?" *Monthly Labor Review* 105 (June):29-38.

Williams, Gregory, 1979. "The Changing U.S. Labor Force and Occupational Differentiation by Sex." *Demography* 16:73-88.

———, 1975. "A Research Note on Trends in Occupational Differences by Sex." *Social Problems* 22 (April):543-47.

Wilson, William J., 1978. *The Declining Significance of Race*. Chicago: University of Chicago Press.

Witt, Mary and Patricia K. Naherny, 1975. *Women's Work—Up from 878: Report on the DOT Research Project*. Madison, Wisconsin: Women's Education Resources, University of Wisconsin-Extension.

Wrenn, Rob, 1985. "The Decline of American Labor." *Socialist Review* 82-83 (July-October):89-117.

Wright, Erik Olin, Cynthia Costello, David Hachen and Joey Sprague, 1982. "The American Class Structure." *American Sociological Review* 47(8) December:709-26.

Young, Anne McDougall, 1977. "Median Earnings in 1977 Reported for Year-round, Full-time Workers." *Monthly Labor Review* 102 (June):35-39.

Contributors

CHRISTINE BOSE is Associate Professor of Sociology at the State University of New York at Albany, where she also served as director of the Women's Studies Program from 1978 through 1981. She holds a joint appointment in the Department of Latin American and Caribbean Studies. Dr. Bose has published in the areas of occupational prestige, gender and status attainment, women's home and paid employment at the turn of the century, and the social impact of household technology. She is the author of *Jobs and Gender: A Study of Occupational Prestige* (Praeger, 1985) and her articles have appeared in *American Sociological Review, Social Science Research, American Journal of Sociology, Women's Studies International Quarterly,* and *Technology and Culture.* She is currently engaged in a research project on Hispanic women's employment in the contemporary urban United States and is coediting a book with Natalie Sokoloff, Roslyn Feldberg and the Women and Work Research Group entitled *Hidden Aspects of Women's Work* (Praeger, 1987).

GLENNA SPITZE is Associate Professor at the State University of New York at Albany. She holds an adjunct appointment in the Women's Studies Program. Her major research has centered around the relations between women's employment and family, particularly the division of household labor, family migration, and divorce. She coauthored (with Joan Huber) *Sex Stratification: Children, Housework and Jobs* (Academic Press, 1983), and coedited (with Gwen Moore) *Women and Politics: Activism, At-*

titudes, and Office-holding (Jai Press, 1986). Her articles have appeared in *American Sociological Review, American Journal of Sociology, Social Forces, Journal of Marriage and the Family,* and other journals and edited volumes. Her current research involves the linkages between family structure and adult intergenerational relations.

JOAN ACKER is Professor of Sociology and former Director of the Center for the Study of Women in Society at the University of Oregon. She has written on class and gender, feminist theory and methodology, women and trade unions in Sweden, women and work in sociology, and middle aged women in transition. She was a member of the State of Oregon Task Force on Compensation and Classification Equity from 1983 to 1985. The material for her paper was gathered during her work on this task force. She is currently writing a case study of the Oregon project titled "Class, Gender, and Comparable Worth."

JAMES N. BARON is Associate Professor of Organizational Behavior in the Graduate School of Business (and, by courtesy, in the Department of Sociology) at Stanford University. He is currently studying organizational and environmental factors affecting desegregation trends by race and sex in the California Civil Service, as well as analyzing the economic and psychological consequences of job segregation for workers. Baron is also examining contemporary changes in the employment relationship, including the recent growth of "flexible" employment arrangements, such as temporary work, subcontracting, employee leasing, and homework.

SUE E. BERRYMAN (Ph.D., Johns Hopkins University, 1972) directs the Institute on Education and the Economy and the National Center on Education and Employment at Teachers College, Columbia University. Her publications of the last year include: *Status, Change, and Causes of Minority Shares of Management Degrees and Jobs,* published by the Graduate Management Admission Council; *The Adjustments of Youth and Educational Institutions to Technologically-Generated Changes in Skill Requirements,* published by the National Commission for Employment Policy; and *Women in Nontraditional Occupations: Choice and Turnover,* published by the Rand Corporation. Her current research interest is understanding what individuals' movements among occupations reveal about the human capital requirements of jobs and the ways in which individuals acquire the skills they need.

WILLIAM T. BIELBY is Professor of Sociology at the University of California, Santa Barbara. His recent research with Denise D. Bielby has examined gender and commitment to work and family, sex differences in the allocation of effort, and structural barriers to employment of women and minority writers in the entertainment industry. Other recent research of his examines decision making in organizations and methodological issues in covariance structure models. "Men and Women at Work: Sex Segregation and Statistical Discrimination" (with James N. Baron) appeared in the January 1986 issue of the *American Journal of Sociology*.

FRANCINE D. BLAU is Professor of Economics and Labor and Industrial Relations, University of Illinois at Urbana-Champaign. Her research has centered on women's economic status and discrimination against women and minorities. She has also studied a variety of issues related to immigration, job search and turnover, union impact, and racial differences in wealth. She is the author of *Equal Pay in the Office* and, with Marianne Ferber, of *The Economics of Women, Men, and Work.* She has contributed extensively to professional journals and collections of essays. She currently serves on National Academy of Sciences Panels on Technology and Women's Employment and on Pay Equity Research. She has served as an expert witness in employment discrimination cases and testified in Congress on issues relating to women's employment.

CYNTHIA H. CHERTOS is the Director of Research and Implementation at the Center for Women in Government, a unit of the Institute for Government and Policy Studies at the State University of New York at Albany. Her research has included such topics as the implementation of Affirmative Action, the implications of organizational career ladder structure, the processes of organizational promotion, the impact of personnel policies and practices, and the question of pay equity. Her current research interests include the various mechanisms of institutional and organizational discrimination in employment and the implementation of organizational change. Dr. Chertos has an M.A. and Ph.D in Sociology from the University of Michigan.

ROSLYN L. FELDBERG is Associate Director of Labor Relations at the Massachusetts Nurses Association. She has previously taught sociology at Boston University and the University of Aberdeen (Scotland) and recently completed a Radcliffe Research Scholarship. Her background includes scholarly and advocacy work in a wide variety of settings. She has contributed to public policy debates on women clerical workers and office automation, comparable worth, and women and labor unions. Among other commitments, she has served as an advisor at the National Academy of Sciences, the Office of Technology Assessment, and 9 to 5. She holds a B.A. from the University of Illinois and an M.A. and Ph.D. from the University of Michigan, all in sociology.

EVELYN NAKANO GLENN is an Associate Professor of Sociology at the State University of New York at Binghamton. Her research, writing and teaching interests center on issues of women and work, the political economy of the family, and the intersection of race and gender stratification. She has published articles on these topics in *Social Problems, Feminist Studies, Journal of Marriage and the Family, Review of Radical Political Economics,* and in various edited collections. She has recently completed a book on Japanese American women domestic workers (Temple University Press). Current projects include a collaborative manuscript on women clerical workers in large scale enterprises and a sociohistorical study of the effects of racial oppression of black, latina, and Asian American women with members of the Inter-University Group Researching the Intersection of Race and Gender.

LOIS HAIGNERE is Senior Research Associate at the Center for Women in Government, a unit of the Institute of Government and Policy Studies in the Graduate School of Public Affairs, State University of New York at Albany. She is Director of the Washington State Comparable Worth Study and the Comparable Worth in Small Jurisdictions Project. She was Assistant Director of the now completed New York State Comparable Worth Study. In addition, Dr. Haignere is the senior member of the Center's Comparable Worth Technical Consulting Team. Among other projects, this team has assessed the Massachusetts Classification Study under a contract with the Massachusetts Special Legislative Committee on Comparable Worth and for National AFSCME completed the Iowa Comparable Worth Study. She is coauthor with Ronnie Steinberg of several published papers and reports on pay equity. Prior to joining the Center, Dr. Haignere received her Ph.D. in 1981 from the University of Connecticut where she was a fellow in the Community Medicine Social Sciences program. Her work included research examining the admission of women and minorities to medical school in 1980.

HEIDI I. HARTMANN is Study Director of both the Committee on Women's Employment and Related Social Issues and the Panel on Technology and Women's Employment at the National Research Council. She previously served as associate executive director of the Commission on Behavioral and Social Sciences and Education and as research associate to the Committee on Occupational Classification and Analysis. In that capacity she coedited (with Donald J. Treiman) the committee's final report on comparable worth. Her research has concentrated on employment issues related to women and minorities, particularly discrimination and internal labor markets, and on political economy and feminist theory. She is the author of several articles on women's economic status; she lectures frequently on that and other topics and has testified in congressional hearings on comparable worth. She has a B.A. from Swarthmore College and M.Ph. and Ph.D. degrees from Yale University, all in economics.

ELIZABETH HIGGINBOTHAM is Assistant Professor of Sociology and Social Work and a Research Associate at the Center for Research on Women at Memphis State University. Her publications have included "Race and Class Barriers to Black Women's College Attendance," in the *Journal of Ethnic Studies,* "We Were Never on a Pedestal: Women of Color Continue to Struggle with Poverty, Racism, and Sexism," in *For Crying Out Loud,* edited by Witborn and Lefkowitz, and she is a coauthor of "The Costs of Exclusionary Practices in Women's Studies," in *Signs.* She is currently completing a manuscript entitled, "Too Much to Ask: The Cost of Black Female Success in a Racist Society," which is an exploration of class differences in the mobility strategies of educated Black women. Recently, Dr. Higginbotham has been involved in curriculum integration and a new research project on Black and White professional and managerial women in the Memphis area.

VILMA ORTIZ is currently a Research Scientist at the Educational Testing Service. Her past publications focus on the social conditions faced by Hispanics in the United States, particularly in the areas of female labor force participation, educational attainment and high school completion, ethnic identification, adolescent childbearing, mental health status, and Puerto Rican migration. Her current research interests are on reading proficiency and literacy among Hispanic youth and on minority access to graduate education.

DIANA M. PEARCE coined the phrase "the feminization of poverty" (which is the title of a 1978 article), and has written widely on the subject of women and poverty, the social welfare system, and unemployment. She coauthored, with Harriette McAdoo, *Women and Children: Alone and in Poverty.* Her Ph.D. is from the University of Michigan, and is in Sociology and Social Work. Her dissertation on housing discrimination has been followed by studies, reports and expert witness testimony on school segregation/desegregation, particularly its impact on housing patterns. Dr. Pearce taught for five years at the University of Illinois at Chicago (then Chicago Circle), and was Director of Research for the Center for National Policy Review (a civil rights research and advocacy organization) at Catholic University Law School for five years. She is presently Director of the Women and Poverty Project.

BARBARA F. RESKIN is Professor of Sociology at the University of Illinois. Most of her research focuses on sex inequality, including sex differences in scientists' careers and statistical methods for assessing discrimination and legal evidence of discrimination. Results of her study of the determinants of juror's verdicts in sexual assault cases have appeared in *Social Problems* and *Law and Society Review.* The findings of her National

Academy of Sciences study on sex segregation were published in *Sex Segregation in the Workplace: Trends, Explanations and Remedies* and *Women's Work, Men's Work: Segregation on the Job* (with Heidi Hartmann). She and Patricia Roos are investigating the causes and consequences of women's entry into several traditionally male-dominated occupations.

PAMELA ROBY is Professor of Sociology at the University of California-Santa Cruz. She has coauthored *Women in the Workplace*, coauthored *The Future of Inequality* with S.M. Miller, and edited *The Poverty Establishment* and *Child Care—Who Cares? Foreign and Domestic Infant and Early Childhood Development Policies* as well as having published on the subjects of education, prostitution, and income policies. A past-president of Sociologists for Women in Society and past-chair of the American Sociological Association's Section on Sex and Gender, Dr. Roby is currently conducting a study of the similarities and differences in the goals, leadership perspectives, and leadership experiences of female and male trade union stewards in northern California locals of the nine major international unions.

PATRICIA A. ROOS is Assistant Professor of Sociology at the State University of New York at Stony Brook. With Barbara Reskin, she is currently funded by the National Science Foundation and the Rockefeller Foundation to study the determinants of change in the sex composition of occupations between 1970 and 1980. She has also conducted research on institutional factors contributing to sex segregation in the workplace, cross-cultural research on sex differences in occupational and earnings attainment, and analyses of ethnic differences in occupational and earnings attainment. She has a B.A. from the University of California, Davis, and a Ph.D. from the University of California at Los Angeles, both in sociology. Recent publications include *Gender and Work: A Comparative Analysis of Industrial Societies* (SUNY Press), "Institutional Factors Contributing to Sex Segregation in the Workplace" (with Barbara Reskin, in *Sex Segregation in the Workplace*), and articles in *American Sociological Review, American Journal of Sociology,* and *Social Science Research.*

JOAN SMITH is Professor of Sociology at the State University of New York at Binghamton where she served as Director of Women's Studies for seven years. She has written on the issue of women and work and the connection between women's paid and unpaid labor. She is currently completing a National Endowment for the Humanities sponsored research project on households and labor force formation.

NATALIE J. SOKOLOFF is Associate Professor of Sociology at the John Jay College of Criminal Justice-City University of New York, where she teaches in the Department of Sociology and Thematic Studies as well as the graduate program in criminal justice. She holds a bachelor's degree from the University of Michigan, a master's degree from Brown University, and a doctorate from the City University of New York, Graduate Center. Professor Sokoloff is the author of *Between Money and Love: The Dialectics of Women's Home and Market Work* (Praeger, 1980) and is coeditor of *The Criminal Justice System and Women: Women Offenders, Victims and Workers* (Clark Boardman, 1982). She is in the process of coediting *The Hidden Aspects of Women's Work* (Praeger, 1987), a collection of essays by the Women and Work Research Group of which she is a founding member.

RONNIE STEINBERG is Assistant Professor of Sociology at Temple University. As Director of Research and Implementation at the Center for Women in Government, SUNY Albany, she developed a program on comparable worth. She has directed five comparable worth studies, including the New York State study, the largest yet undertaken. Dr. Steinberg is author of *Wages and Hours: Labor and Reform in Twentieth Century America* and editor of *Equal Employment Policy for Women*. She is also editor of a series of books on Women in the Political Economy for Temple University Press.

MARTA TIENDA, Professor of Rural Sociology at the University of Wisconsin, has had extensive experience analyzing the labor market position of Hispanic-origin workers, has recently published *Hispanics in the U.S. Economy* with George Borjas, and completed a census monograph on the Hispanic population of the United States with Frank D. Bean. She has also investigated the effects of structural economic changes on employment in the United States from 1960–1980. Professor Tienda is a member of the Panel on Technology and Employment of the National Academy of Science and a member of the National Council on Employment.

LINDA J. WAITE is Senior Sociologist in the Behavioral Sciences Department at the Rand Corporation. She has long-standing research interests in women's employment choices, especially as these relate to family roles. Thus, she has examined changes over time in the determinants of women's employment, the relationship between employment and fertility and how this changes with age (with Ross M. Stolzenberg), the development and consequences of young women's attitudes toward work (with Glenna Spitze), and the effects of child care cost and availability on the relationship between presence of children and women's employment. She recently completed a series of papers (with Gus Haggstrom and David Kanouse) on the consequences of parenthood for the employment, job characteristics, and marital stability of young adults. With Arleen Leibowitz she is examining the causal relationships between women's employment, fertility, and child care arrangements.

Index

293